THIRD EDITION

Consultation, Collaboration, and Teamwork for Students with Special Needs

Peggy Dettmer

Kansas State University

Norma Dyck

Kansas State University

Linda P. Thurston

Kansas State University

Allyn and Bacon

Boston ■ London ■ Toronto ■ Sydney ■ Tokyo ■ Singapore

Vice President, Editor in Chief, Education: *Sean W. Wakely*
Editorial Assistant: *Karin Huang*
Marketing Managers: *Ellen Dolberg and Brad Parkins*
Editorial Production Service: *Chestnut Hill Enterprises, Inc.*
Manufacturing Buyer: *Megan Cochran*
Cover Administrator: *Jennifer Hart*

Internet: www.abacon.com

Between the time Website information is gathered and published,
some sites may have closed. Also, the transcription of URLs can result
in typographical errors. The publisher would appreciate notification
where these occur so that they may be corrected.

Library of Congress Cataloging-in-Publication Data
Dettmer, Peggy
    Consultation, collaboration, and teamwork for students with
special needs / Peggy Dettmer, Norma Dyck, Linda P. Thurston. — 3rd.
ed.
        p. cm.
    Includes bibliographical references and index.
    ISBN: 0–205–29065–5
    1. Special education—United States.   2. Collaborative consultants–
United States.   3. Teaching teams—United States.   I. Dyck, Norma.
II.   Thurston, Linda P.   III.   Title.
LC4031.D47   1998
371.9'0973—dc21   98-30852
                                                                              CIP

Printed in the United States of America
10 9 8 7 6 5 4 3 2 1   03 02 01 00 99 98

CONTENTS

PART II: Process

5   Problem-Solving Strategies   123

P A R T I I I : Content

PREFACE

The time for consultation, collaboration, and teamwork in schools is now, more than ever before. Society's problems are immense and complex. Well-educated, well-prepared men and women are vital for the survival of our planet and the civilization upon it. The public is demanding that school graduates enter the work world as capable, competent citizens, and it holds professional educators accountable for ensuring that they are.

To meet these demands, sweeping educational reforms have been proposed, attempted, discarded, rethought, and reinstated in the past several decades of the final century in a waning millennium. These reform movements generated complex goals. Innovative plans were ripped from administrative and legislative drawing boards to be put to use before the pages were dry, much less well researched. Meanwhile, as test scores declined and school structures crumbled, teachers continued to cope hour by hour and day by day with their formidable assignment—that of preparing today's students to be knowledgeable, caring, and ethical citizens in tomorrow's world.

In the midst of all the criticism and directives flung at school systems and the teaching profession, the sage words of Henry David Thoreau to "Simplify, simplify" are appealing. As we close out one remarkable millennium in civilization's history and move into the next, can it be that we have overlooked very simple, fundamental concepts that could do much to improve the education of our children and youth? Do we not need to think, process, plan, and practice the basic elements deemed necessary for the well-being and development of all?

Consultation, collaboration, and teamwork are processes that, when put into practice by professional educators with parents as their partners, can be key elements in effective education environments for the twenty-first century. These processes may appear obvious, but they are not easy to install. Indeed, they are challenging to manage, and they do stir up changes that can be unsettling for some. But they do not require costly bureaucratic overlays and they carry enormous, ongoing potential for positive ripple effects. The content of collaborative school consultation can guide educators into meaningful and productive interactions as teaching and learning teams with students, their families, other professionals, interagency groups, and the public.

This book is designed to serve as a bridge between theory and practice. It contains both background information and field-tested recommendations to help teachers, parents, administrators, and support personnel become more proficient in working together as collaborators and in teams within their existing school contexts. Each chapter contains applications and activities that encourage single readers or groups of readers to delve into the subtleties and intricacies of these powerful interactive processes.

The book is organized into three sections to focus in turn on context, processes, and content as they relate to school consultation, collaboration, and teamwork such as co-teaching. Part One is the *Context* section. Chapter 1 presents collaborative school consultation and describes key elements in planning, implementing, evaluating, and preparing for consultation and collaboration roles. Chapter 2 includes a brief history, theoretical bases, research bases, and models of school consultation. Chapter 3 focuses on the constructive use of individual differences among adults, which is one of the most powerful but too-often-neglected factors in school consultation, collaboration, and teamwork. In addition, diversity issues are addressed that can have significant impact on the ability of people to work together. Chapter 4 features home-school collaboration with family members as partners in their children's education.

In Part Two, the *Process* section, Chapters 5 through 8 introduce process skills and problem-solving tools needed for effective consultation and collaboration. Chapter 5 presents a ten-step problem-solving process. Chapter 6 addresses verbal and nonverbal communication, and suggests techniques for dealing with resistance and conflicts among educators. In Chapter 7, time management, data organization, record keeping practices, and technology are addressed. Several procedures and tools for the evaluation of consultation and collaboration outcomes are offered in Chapter 8.

Part Three, the *Content* section, includes chapters 9 through 12. Chapter 9 stresses co-planning as the key component of successful co-teaching. Chapter 10 provides an overview of related and support personnel, interagency collaboration, and other sources for assistance and funds to address students' special needs. Chapter 11 promotes professional development as an integral part of consulting, collaborating, and co-teaching. Finally, Chapter 12 emphasizes the importance of developing support systems and advocacy techniques to encourage collaboration and teamwork for our changing world's educational and social needs. Collaborative consultation trends are examined, and benefits are proposed that can result from collaborative school consultation and teaming in educational settings. This concluding chapter predicts that the ideal outcome from school consultation, collaboration, and teamwork will be a transformation of school learning environments into settings where education is special for all students, and educators are successful in their complex, demanding roles.

ACKNOWLEDGMENTS

The first edition of this book in 1993 was dedicated to our graduate students whose education roles required that they develop and use effective consultation and collaboration skills. As we explained at that time, our students both hindered and helped us with the writing. When we needed to write, they hindered because they were always there—taking classes, seeking information, requesting in-service, engaging in collaborative consultation with us for assistance with their own demanding roles. On the other hand, they helped us greatly with our writing by allowing us to "discover what we knew," and they verified that it was indeed important knowledge for bringing about better teaching and learning. Many of them contributed the seed of an idea, a key phrase, a caution, a necessary filter of skepticism, or, blessedly, a vote of confidence for our work. We sensed that we were on the right track.

Three years later, as we prepared the 1996 second edition, concepts of collaboration and consultation were filtering into many areas of contemporary life. School consultation was being promoted as a key component in the success of educational reform movements. The word *collaboration* appeared more and more often in the educational literature even as it was becoming a major element for progress in other professions, in business, and in government and international affairs. The concept of teamwork, employed so effectively in fields such as sports and music, was being applied increasingly to professional endeavors from industry to medicine to education. In the second edition we acknowledged practicing educators–teachers, administrators, support personnel, and parents—who work hard each day to make education appropriate and attainable for every student.

For all our former students in teacher-preparation programs, and our current colleagues who encouraged us with their purpose and perseverance as educators, we have been very grateful. We continue to applaud the dedication and commitment they bring to their demanding roles. Their energy, enthusiasm, and expertise have been, and continue to be, truly inspirational. Consultation, collaboration, and teamwork in a variety of professional fields now are recognized as essential parts of preparation programs for educators. We were pleased that our personnel preparation grants, graduate degree programs, school-district staff development, and the first edition of the book had a part in that development.

Now, in the preparation of the third edition, we want to thank our reviewers—Susan Miller, Northern Arizona University; Mark B. Goor, George Mason University; and Andrea Zetlin, California State University, Los Angeles—for their astute observations and suggestions. The field of education is so complex and changes in the past decade have been so extensive that material for use by educators benefits immensely with consultative input from many sources. The reviewers have provided that helpful consultation.

When possible, we have credited individuals along the way for their contributions to our thinking and writing. However, within a collegial, collaborative process it is not easy to tell just where the contribution of one person occurs, another interfaces, and then yet another takes over from there. As we addressed this dilemma, we realized once again the complexity and the beauty of collaborative consultation. We know that the perceptions and suggestions of our students and educational colleagues have been shared unselfishly without need for recognition or praise, in the spirit of professionalism and progress. That is what collaborative consultation is all about. Any oversights, omissions, or errors in the book are ours, of course, but the essence of our philosophy has come from many educators, community leaders, and ultimately from the children and youth, and the schools and homes, they represent.

Now, at the close of this exciting decade, century, and millennium, we look to the future. In doing so, we dedicate the 1999 edition to all educators to come. It is our fervent hope that many more bright, energetic, competent, caring women and men will rise to the challenge of becoming teachers and leaders in education. We trust that the material in this book will serve as a guide for the consultation, collaboration, and teamwork that can help educators meet the very special needs of every student in our schools.

1 Working Together in Schools

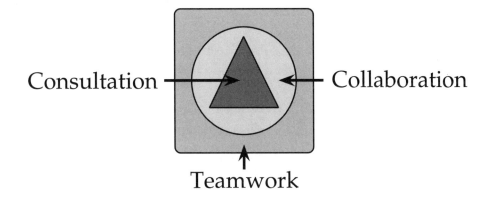

Consultation ← → Collaboration

Teamwork

Life presents many situations for which we do not have all the information and expertise we need to meet the challenges. In today's increasingly interdependent and specialized world, it is unlikely that any one person possesses enough knowledge and ability for every circumstance. So it is reasonable and prudent that we consult, collaborate, and team up with others to attain our goals.

Consultation services are escalating in fields as varied as business, medicine, law, industry, fashion, construction, decorating, and finance. Sometimes consultants even have their own consultants! *Collaboration* is emphasized more and more in a wide range of work arenas, from professions to trades to government to community affairs. *Teamwork* is promoted as an efficient and productive way of achieving goals. However, until recently these three concepts—consultation, collaboration, and teamwork—had been overlooked or ignored as key elements in structuring and maintaining a strong educational system.

Parameters for these new, interactive roles in school settings have been unclear to this point. Allocation of the time needed, and construction of a practical framework for collaborative, consultative, or team interaction among educators, have not been forthcoming. Preparation for the complex process of working together in the school environment is sporadic or nonexistent in the conventional teacher-preparation program. However, the increasing complexity of teaching and learning, and various movements for educational reform, restructuring, and accountability, are catalyzing the processes and content needed for working collaboratively in school contexts.

Focusing Questions

1. What definitions of consultation, collaboration, and teamwork are appropriate for the educational setting?
2. What is collaborative school consultation and what is it not?
3. What are key elements in collaborative school consultation?
4. How can collaborative school consultation and team effort produce multiplier effects throughout the school context?
5. What collaborative process and content skills are needed within diverse school contexts?
6. How is collaborative school consultation synergistic?

Key Terms

autonomy	consulting teacher	role clarification
caseload	cooperation	role delineation
client	coordination	role parity
collaboration	co-teaching	school context
communication	multiplier effects	synergy
consultant	onedownsmanship	teamwork
consultation	preservice teachers	
consultee	professional development	

Educators' Responsibilities in Schools

> Here is Edward Bear, coming downstairs now, bump, bump, bump, on the back of his head, behind Christopher Robin. It is, as far as he knows, the only way of coming downstairs, but sometimes he feels that there really is another way, if only he could stop bumping for a moment and think of it.
>
> (*Winnie the Pooh,* p. 3, by A. A. Milne)

Teaching is a multidimensional responsibility. This complex, demanding role has never been easy and it is becoming more challenging each year. School personnel are bombarded with significant changes in the ways they are to function. These changes are comprehensive and school-wide. Cosmetic alteration of existing programs and policies simply will not be sufficient to address the multitudinous issues and concerns.

In the past, teachers tended to function autonomously in their classrooms (Goodlad, 1984). After they completed attendance forms, lunch counts, and other daily procedures,

Scenario 1.A

The setting is the faculty room of a typical high school where three faculty members are sharing school news and airing their concerns.

ENGLISH TEACHER: I'm getting another special education student next week—severe learning disabilities, the cumulative folder says. I guess this is more fallout from Public Law 94-142 or IDEA or inclusion, or whatever it's called now—along with the behavior-disordered student I've been coping with all semester.

MATH TEACHER: (grinning) Must be because you're doing such a great job with that one. (serious tone) But I know what you mean. Our special education teachers aren't taking these kids out of our classes as much as they did when I started teaching, before we'd ever heard the word inclusion.

ENGLISH TEACHER: They say somebody called a "consulting teacher" is coming to our next departmental meeting to talk about helping the students with special needs. And we're going to be asked to collaborate—whatever that will mean—along with all the other things we do, of course.

PHYSICAL EDUCATION TEACHER/COACH: Say, don't those two words cancel each other out? "Consult" and "collaborate," that is. I believe you English teachers call that an oxymoron. Now, I'd be inclined to *consult* a tax accountant for some expert advice, but isn't *collaboration* where everyone works together to accomplish goals? And as for *teamwork,* I can tell you what a difficult process that is when you have a group of independent thinkers and free spirits who like to do things their own way and be a star!

ENGLISH TEACHER: Frankly, I'm not interested in word games or coaching problems right now. I'm more concerned about finding out where the time is going to come from to do one more thing. And I want to know who will have bottom-line responsibility for which students, and when, and where. And how!

MATH TEACHER: Right. I've had some concerns about mainstreaming all along. Now I think we'll need some help with inclusion, and I hope we get it.

COACH: Sounds like quite a challenge for us all.

---

they closed the classroom door and taught their specialized content. They tried to handle each school situation with minimal assistance. After all, hadn't the teacher of eight grades in a one-room schoolhouse gotten along without special help? To ask for assistance would have been tantamount to proclaiming incompetency.

Teacher Autonomy and Collegiality

Teachers are autonomous within a context of isolation (Goodlad, 1984). Because they seldom have the privilege of rich professional dialogue with colleagues, they are isolated from sources of ideas beyond their own background of experiences. The chunking of a typical school day is insulating. Teachers often go through an entire school day without speaking to other adults in a reflective, planful way (Eisner, 1988). Few structured arrangements exist to assist teachers. This is particularly problematic at the high-school level where teachers might teach five classes, prepare two or more lessons, and face as many as 150 students during a school day that is sliced into 50-minute periods (Cuban, 1986). So, although in a certain sense schools are very social places and multidimensional centers of activity, the individual teacher may feel stranded on a crowded island devoid of adult inter-action and professional stimulation.

In a poll of over 1,000 teachers conducted by *Learning* magazine and reported by the Education Commission of the United States a decade ago, 78 percent of the respondents said that isolation from their colleagues is a major or moderate problem (Turner, 1987). On the other hand, teachers may wish for more small-group meetings on mutual interests, reg-ular grade-level meetings, frequent chances to observe other teachers, and richer opportu-nities for in-service training, but many are not comfortable engaging in collaborative efforts. Some state candidly that they did not choose a teaching career to work all that much with adults. Others feel that calling on a colleague or requesting services from a school consultant will be perceived as a sign of professional weakness.

In addition, teachers have few incentives for getting together to collaborate or co-teach. They rarely have an opportunity to observe educators in other school settings to obtain new ideas and revitalize their enthusiasm. When they do have the time and opportu-nity to interact with colleagues, it is likely to be during in-service or staff-development ses-sions. Unfortunately, these activities often are too highly structured, inappropriately designed, or poorly managed to allow meaningful interaction. Many are scheduled at the end of a hectic day, when teachers are tired and want to turn their attention toward home or community activities.

Now and then teachers are visited in their classrooms by supervisors, administrators, student teachers, and sometimes parents. However, these occasions tend to create more feelings of anxiety and defensiveness than support and collegiality. Some schools encour-age co-teaching as a way of allowing teachers to support each other and broaden their teach-ing repertoires. But well-intentioned efforts to co-teach too often result in turn-teaching—"You teach this part of the lesson and then take a break while I handle the next part."

Wildman and Niles (1987) stress that professionals cannot be coerced into being col-legial. Teachers who are accustomed to being in charge and making virtually all the day-to-day decisions in their classrooms cannot be ordered to just go out and collaborate with each other or co-teach to any meaningful degree. They need structure, training, practice, and feedback about their effectiveness in order to perform these sophisticated, demanding functions well. Unfortunately, the typical teacher-preparation program provides little or no instruction and practice in collaborating with professional peers.

Meanwhile, a growing body of school reform literature and research forecasts wider use of consultation service and greater interest in collaboration and co-teaching in the future. Current books, periodicals, conferences, staff-development sessions, and media messages are convincing educators that by consulting, collaborating, and working together as teams, school personnel and parents can combine the best that they have to help all stu-dents learn and achieve. Educational reform movements of the past three decades have strengthened these convictions. Effective teaching and learning will not likely occur in the future without extensive interaction among educators, parents, and resource personnel in the home, in school, and in community settings.

What Collaborative School Consultation Is

In recent years no education legislation has been passed by Congress, or has been considered, for that matter, that does not foster collaboration (Lewis, 1992). Now that reform movements have fueled the interest of educators and parents in the concepts of consultation, collaboration, and working together as teams, it is imperative that schools follow through to implement plans of action. Just what *is* school consultation? How can collaboration be a meaningful part of consultation? In what ways can school consultation and collaboration promote teamwork and effective partnerships among educators and parents for the special needs of students?

Many of the major issues in education recently have centered around serving students with special needs. Educational leaders are proposing that unless changes occur in the field of special education, the field is destined to become more a problem and less a solution in providing for exceptional students (Reynolds, Wang, & Walberg, 1987). An integral element for ensuring school success in the wake of school reform efforts is the ability of the school staff to collaborate (Friend & Cook, 1990). Yet despite the increasing interest in collaborative formats, implementation of such formats has been sporadic. A collaboration ethic is needed, with general and special educators as co-consultants pooling interdisciplinary content, processes, and expertise (Phillips & McCullough, 1990).

Defining Consultation, Collaboration, and Teamwork

Definitions of consultation, collaboration, and co-teaching for school settings must be general enough to apply to a wide range of school structures and circumstances, yet flexible enough for useful adaptation to each context of local school needs. *Webster's Third New International Dictionary, unabridged* (1976), and *Webster's New Collegiate Dictionary, 8th edition* (1981), provide a wealth of synonyms for these terms and many other related words such as communication, cooperation, and coordination. These words complement each other to form a foundation for consultation, collaboration, and teamwork in schools. Examples are:

> *consult:* Advise, confer, confab, huddle, parley, counsel, deliberate, consider, examine, refer to, group, communicate, review, apply for information, take counsel, discuss, seek the opinion of, and/or have prudent regard to.
>
> *consultation:* Advisement, care, counsel, conference, or formal deliberation.
>
> *consulting:* Deliberating together, asking advice or opinion of, or conferring.
>
> *consultant:* One who gives professional advice or services in a field of special knowledge and training, or simply one who consults another.
>
> *consultee:* As described in social science literature, the mediator between consultant and client (Tharp, 1975).
>
> *client:* Individual, group, agency, department, community, or sometimes even a nation, that benefits from the services of a consultant. (*Target* is sometimes used as a synonym.)

collaborate: Labor together or work jointly, especially in an intellectual endeavor, assist, associate, unite, pool.

teamwork, teaming: Joining forces or efforts, with each individual contributing a clearly defined portion of the effort, but also subordinating personal prominence to the efficiency of the whole.

communication: The act of transmitting, giving, or exchanging information, or the art of expressing ideas.

cooperation: The act of uniting, banding, combining, concurring, agreeing, consenting, or conjoining.

coordination: Bringing elements into a common action, movement, or condition, synchronizing, attuning, adjusting.

co-teaching: Two or more teachers planning and implementing instruction, usually in an inclusive classroom setting.

Descriptions of Collaborative School Consultation and Co-teaching

In order to fit a variety of school contexts and student needs, consultation and collaboration for schools are interwoven and defined in this book as follows:

> **Collaborative school consultation is interaction in which school personnel and families confer, consult, and collaborate as a team to identify learning and behavioral needs, and to plan, implement, evaluate, and revise as needed the educational programs for serving those needs.**

The collaborative consultant in schools is defined here as follows:

> **A collaborative school consultant is a facilitator of effective communication, cooperation, and coordination who confers, consults, and collaborates with other school personnel and families as one of a team for addressing special learning and behavioral needs of students.**

The role of the consultant in collaborative school consultation is to contribute specialized information toward an educational need. The consultee uses the information and expertise of consultants and other collaborators to provide direct service to the client. All who are involved—consultant(s), consultee, and client—are collaborators working together in a combined effort to address a particular need. For example, in the scenario at the beginning of this chapter, the client is a new student who has a learning disability. The learning-disabilities consultant will serve the student indirectly, for the most part, by collaborating with the classroom teacher who will be the consultee and provider of direct service to the student. Some direct service might be provided by the learning-disabilities consultant to the student, but for the most part the direct service will be given by the classroom teacher.

Consultation involves sharing of expertise. Those in the consultant role do not hold claim to all the expertise. Competent consultants also listen and learn. They sometimes help consultees discover what they already know. They help others recognize their own talents and trust their own skills.

To collaborate is to labor together. Collaborators do not compromise so much as they confer and contribute. Compromise can imply giving up some part or conceding something; however, collaboration means adding to and making more. In collaboration the differentiated tasks can be allocated among individuals with various skills to contribute. Sometimes collaboration means recognizing differences and finding ways to accommodate those differences. The collaborative process is enhanced by diversity among the collaborators—diversity of experience, values, abilities, and interests.

Individual differences of adults who consult and collaborate are rich ingredients for successful collaborations. The great need to recognize and maximize adult differences and use them constructively in group work will be the focus of Chapter 3. Antonyms for collaborating include "struggling" and "resisting." Indeed, resistance from professional colleagues or parents is one of the major obstacles to effective collaborative interactions in the school setting. Communication, cooperation, and coordination are crucial aspects of effective collaboration. This discussion will be continued in Chapter 6.

The concept of co-teaching as teams in school settings is receiving increased attention among school professionals. Teamwork is working for the good of the whole—where individual preferences are subdued or set aside for the larger cause. Many heads and hearts are better than one, and the pooled experience, talent, knowledge, and ideas of a group are better even than the sum of the individual parts. As part of a team, each co-teacher contributes a clearly defined portion of the effort that comes together in creating a complete plan of action. Thus consultation with collaboration and team effort is not an oxymoron, but a *synergy*—"a behavior of whole systems unpredicted by the behavior of their parts taken separately" (Fuller, 1975, p. 3). Teams of educators and family members working together for children can energize and inform each other in dozens of ways.

How Consultation, Collaboration, and Co-teaching Differ

All three processes—consultation, collaboration, and co-teaching—as they occur in the school context involve interaction among school personnel, families, and students working together to achieve common goals. However, subtle distinctions among the three do exist.

In school consultation, the consultant contributes specialized expertise toward an educational problem, and the consultee delivers direct service utilizing that expertise. Consultants and consultees collaborate by assuming equal ownership of the problem and solutions. Collaboration is a way of working in which both power struggles *and* ineffectual politeness are regarded as detrimental to team goals. Friend and Cook (1990) distinguish between consultation and collaboration by describing collaborations as styles or approaches to interactions that occur during the consultation process. They propose that a collaborative approach can be used at some stages of consultation and not others, and with some consultees but not others. In their view collaborative consultation must be voluntary, with one professional assisting another to address a problem concerning a third party. They emphasize that successful consultants use different styles of interaction under different circumstances and within different situations.

APPLICATION **1.1**
Collaborating as a School Team

Think of many things you could do in team settings, using collaborative processes, that are virtually impossible to do in traditional, relatively autonomous roles in school or business settings. What positive effects might this teamwork have both in and beyond that situation?

Teamwork such as co-teaching typically creates leader and follower roles. An individual working with a team feels less alone and vulnerable. This is particularly helpful in circumstances involving change or innovation. Teamwork fuels group spirit, develops process skills that help teachers interact in more productive ways, and fosters a more intellectual atmosphere (Maeroff, 1993). One of the best examples of teamwork is in musical ensembles. Whether one is accompanying, performing with a small group, or playing with an orchestra, band, or choir, it is the united effort that creates the musical experience. In similar fashion, co-teachers work in concert to create an effective learning experience for all students in the class. Consultation, collaboration, and co-teaching provide consultants, consultees, and teaching partners the opportunity to engage in a "strengths" type of interaction, with each person using and building on the strengths of the others. Several examples of problem-solving within a school context will demonstrate similarities and differences among consultation, collaboration, and teamwork.

Problem-Solving with Consultation.   A preschool teacher is concerned about a child in the group who is not fluent in speech. So the teacher asks the speech pathologist to help determine whether or not this is a matter of concern, and if so, what to do about it. The speech pathologist consults with the teacher, getting more information about the observed behavior, and makes additional observations. The consultant then uses expertise in speech pathology to address the teacher's questions.

In another instance, a speech pathologist provides individual therapy for a preschool child who has articulation errors or fluency disorders and dysfluent speech. The speech pathologist wants to know how these speech patterns are affecting the child's social development as well as performance in pre-academic skills such as letter-naming and sound discrimination. The speech pathologist asks the teacher to serve as a consultant regarding this issue, and the preschool teacher provides the information requested.

Problem-Solving with Collaboration.   The preschool teacher and the speech pathologist are both concerned about a child's generalization of speech skills learned in speech-therapy sessions. The two teachers meet to discuss their mutual concern. Both parties discuss their observations and engage in problem-solving activities to identify the problem clearly and select possible solutions. Both parties agree to make some changes in their respective settings to solve the problem. If the solutions do not work, both are committed to try other possibilities.

In another situation, a teacher of students with behavioral disorders, along with the school counselor, three classroom teachers, and a student's parents, meet to discuss the behavior of that student. The individuals involved in the meeting engage in problem-solving to formulate a plan for addressing the problem. Each individual has a role to play in implementing the plan.

Problem-Solving with Teamwork.   A special education teacher and a general classroom teacher engage in co-teaching, a form of teamwork unique to classroom settings. The teachers meet weekly to engage in co-planning. During the co-planning they decide when, where, and how to share responsibilities for meeting the instructional needs of all students in the classroom during a specified class period each day. Each teacher uses his or her areas of expertise and strength whenever feasible. The co-teachers come to consensus on evaluation systems and assign grades for all students by mutual agreement. They no longer speak of "my students" or "your students" and instead they speak of, plan for, and teach "our students."

A team of professionals provides services for severely and profoundly disabled infants and toddlers, each having an area of expertise and responsibility. The social worker has the leadership role because she is responsible for most family contacts and often goes into homes to provide additional assistance for families. The nurse takes responsibility for monitoring the physical well-being of each child and keeps in close contact with other medical personnel and families. The speech pathologist works with the children to develop speech and language skills. The occupational therapist is responsible for teaching the children self-help skills. The physical therapist follows through with the medical doctor's prescribed physical therapy. Special education teachers provide language stimulation and modeling, coordinate schedules, and facilitate communication among the team, which meets twice weekly to discuss individual cases.

When Educators Consult, Collaborate, and Co-teach

Educators—including special education teachers, classroom teachers, school administrators, related services and support personnel—as well as parents consult, collaborate and work as team members when they take part in one or more of these:

- Discuss students' needs.
- Listen to colleagues' concerns about the teaching situation.
- Help identify and define educational problems.
- Facilitate problem-solving in the school setting.
- Promote classroom alternatives as first interventions for students with special learning and behavior needs.
- Serve as a medium for student referrals.
- Demonstrate instructional techniques.
- Provide direct assistance to classroom teachers who have students with special learning and behavior needs.
- Lead or participate in professional-development activities.

- Assist teachers in designing and implementing behavior-change programs.
- Share resources, materials, and ideas with colleagues.
- Participate in co-teaching or demonstration teaching.
- Engage in assessment and evaluation activities.
- Serve on curriculum committees, textbook committees, and school advisory councils.
- Follow up on educational issues and concerns with colleagues.
- Ease colleagues' loads in matters involving students' special needs.
- Network with other professionals and outside agencies.

What Collaborative School Consultation Is Not

School consultation is not therapy, nor is it counseling for the consultee (Brown, Wyne, Blackburn, & Powell, 1979). The focus must be upon educational issues relevant to the needs of the client, not the personal concerns of the consultee. West and Idol (1987) and Morsink, Thomas, and Correa (1991) differentiate between counseling and consultation by describing counseling as focused on individuals, and consultation as focused on issues.

Collaboration among professional colleagues is not talk or discussion for its own sake. It does not involve taking on the authority of school administrators, and it should not be a substitute for the individual teacher's accountability (Smith, 1987).

The consulting teacher is not the equivalent of a resource teacher who just spends more time with the regular classroom teacher (Huefner, 1988). Furthermore, the consultant role is not always the responsibility of the educational specialist.

Collaborative school consultation also should *not* be regarded primarily as a money-saving approach for schools. In the award-winning movie *Educating Peter,* the array of related services and support personnel needed for management of that school situation was not featured, and the high cost of Peter's inclusion in a regular third-grade classroom was not apparent to the casual viewer.

Role Responsibilities for Collaborative School Consultation

When facing new responsibilities in collaborative settings, educators voice concerns that are reflected in questions such as:

- Who am I in this role?
- How do I carry out responsibilities of the role?
- How do I know whether or not I am succeeding?
- How do I prepare for the role?

First, central administrators and policy-makers must authenticate the need for consultant and consultee roles. Then building-level administrators must stress the significance of the consultant role and ensure consultant parity among their staff. A key variable is allocation of time for the interactions to take place. Teachers must support consulting teachers with their cooperation and not impede consultation and collaboration through apathy or resistance. Related services personnel and support personnel should be integrated into the

Scenario 1.B

Now consider another scenario. This one takes place in a school-district conference room, where three special education teachers are talking before their special education director arrives for a planning meeting.

LEARNING DISABILITIES TEACHER: I understand we're here to decide how we're going to inform staff and parents about the consultation and collaboration practices that we'll be implementing soon. But I think we'd better figure out first just what it is we *will* be doing.

BEHAVIORAL DISORDERS TEACHER: Definitely. I have a really basic question. What do I do the first day, and the first week, as a consulting teacher? I know you had some training in collaboration and consulting for your former job in another state, but this is new to the rest of us.

GIFTED EDUCATION TEACHER: Good question. And I've been thinking about all those personalities and teaching styles and subject areas we will be interacting with. They won't all like or want the same things.

LEARNING DISABILITIES TEACHER: I doubt this is something we can pick up and put into place overnight or by next week. From what little I've had a chance to read about the term "collaborative school consultation," the secret for success with it lies in using good process skills.

GIFTED EDUCATION TEACHER: Yes, but at the same time we have to take into consideration the content that each student needs to learn. So I'm a bit apprehensive about this new role, but I'm looking forward to trying it, too.

BEHAVIORAL DISORDERS TEACHER: Yes, I've suspected for some time now that our present methods of dealing with learning and behavior problems are not as effective and efficient as they should be. I agree that we must be optimistic about the benefits both students *and* teachers could receive from this.

---

school-consultation context. Families need to receive information about the service and have assurance that this type of service is appropriate for their child's needs. Students should have opportunity to be consultants and consultees, also, not just clients. Ultimately, community members must be aware of the long-range purposes and probable benefits of these indirect services before they can be expected to support and pay for them.

Initiating School Consultation, Collaboration, and Teamwork

Educational reforms, social concerns, and economic issues may convince educators that consultation, collaboration, and teamwork are promising practices for helping students with special needs, but the conversion of paper plans and philosophies to real-world roles and responsibilities is not simple. The questions that were put forth in the school-district conference-room scenario reflect real-world concerns that must be addressed thoughtfully:

- Where do I begin as a school consultant?
- What do I do the first day on the job?

- Let me see a sample schedule for the first week.
- Where am I to be headed by the end of the year?

Other questions and concerns which are likely to surface include:

- Will I have the opportunity to work with students at all? That is why I chose teaching as a career.
- Where's my room? Will I get office space and supplies?
- Can I fit at least a small group of students into that space for some group work?
- I think I will need special training for consultation, so where do I get it?
- How will I be evaluated in this position, and by whom?
- If consulting prepares consultees for direct delivery of services for special needs, am I really working myself out of a job?

Those who will be engaging in consultation services primarily as consultees may be thinking:

- Will this process make me look and feel incompetent?
- How much of my ever-dwindling time with all my students will be eroded by this method of service?
- When in the world will I find time to interact with other folks?

Participants in consultation and collaboration must be able to voice their concerns, confusions, and feelings of inadequacy such as those above while they sort out the requirements of their new roles. School administrators have a responsibility to initiate open expression of these concerns and to encourage intensive discussion of questions and issues among those embarking upon any significantly different service-delivery approaches.

Interchangeable Roles

Consultants become consultees when they seek expertise and information from a classroom teacher, school psychologist, administrator, parent, or resource person in the community. On some occasions a general classroom teacher is consultant for a special education teacher in order to contribute information about a student's problems within a social context not available to the special education teacher. In another instance, a parent might act as consultant for a situation in which the principal functions as consultee to help a teacher as client in a classroom situation.

A student could be consultant to a teacher consultee in a situation where the family is the client because the family situation is accentuating the student's school problems. The student might contribute to problem identification and interventions, with the teacher providing direct service to parents.

The client of consultation is typically an individual; however, clients also can be a group or team of individuals, such as a family or a within-class group of students. On occasion the client might even be an entire staff, school system, or community.

An individual who serves as consultant (specialist), consultee (mediator), or client (target) in one consultative situation may exchange roles under different circumstances.

For example, a special education teacher might be a consultant for one situation and consultee in another. The student is typically the client, or target, for the direct and indirect services of consultee and consultant, but in some cases the student could be a consultee or consultant. Consultation may be initiated by a special education teacher, school administrator, supervisor, or support-service professional who has determined that a student's learning or behavior need requires attention from a collaborative team. It also might be initiated by a teacher, parent, or student acting in a consultee role. In either case, both parties—consultant and consultee—share responsibility for working out a plan to help the client (Heron & Harris, 1982).

Although roles and responsibilities may vary among individuals from situation to situation, with appropriate role delineation a collaborative spirit can prevail. Collaboration to achieve a common goal generally produces more beneficial results than isolated efforts by an individual. The whole of the combined efforts then is greater than the sum of its parts (Slavin, 1988). It is the basic idea that two heads are better than one, and several heads are better yet. The consultation process channels each individual's strengths and talents toward serving the client's needs. (See Figure 1.1, mixing and matching roles among the three columns to fit your school contexts.)

Key Elements in Consulting and Collaborating

Four areas of analysis for the roles and responsibilities generated by collaborative school consultation processes are pictured in Figure 1.2:

- Preparation
- Framework
- Evaluation
- Role delineation

Within the four categories, twelve key elements need to be addressed. The sequence of these twelve elements is very important. Note the starting point. In many school contexts, educators begin "too late in the day," metaphorically speaking, to implement consultation, collaboration, and teamwork. Involvement and acceptance—the "four p.m. and five p.m." positions in the clock-like figure—should not be starting points. If they are, failure of school consultation is all but assured. Instead, educators in all educational contexts—administrators, teacher educators, teachers, support staff—must begin "very early in the morning," at approximately the "six a.m." position, to prepare for collaborative school consultation roles and teaming. The preparation should take place at preservice, graduate, and in-service levels.

Each of these twelve facets of the four-part figure will be addressed, and some will be discussed in more detail in subsequent chapters. A "tool box" of practical suggestions for role delineation appears in this chapter as Application 1.2. Additional "toolboxes" of suggestions for framework, evaluation, and preparation applications will appear in Chapters 7, 8, and 11, respectively. Also, the Tips for Consulting and Collaborating sections at ends of the chapters provide additional recommendations and reminders.

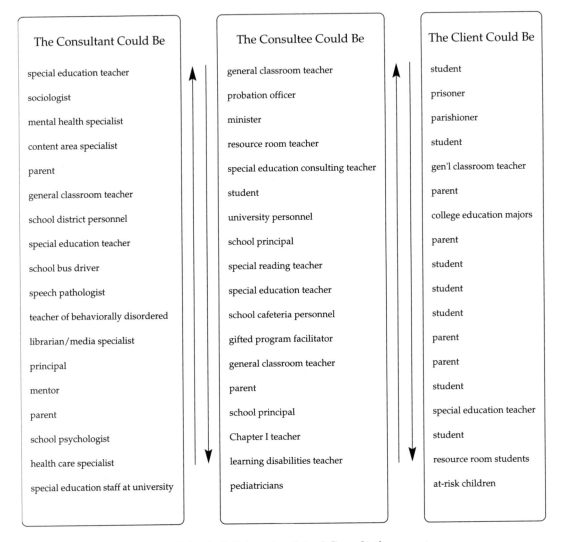

The Consultant Could Be	The Consultee Could Be	The Client Could Be
special education teacher	general classroom teacher	student
sociologist	probation officer	prisoner
mental health specialist	minister	parishioner
content area specialist	resource room teacher	student
parent	special education consulting teacher	gen'l classroom teacher
general classroom teacher	student	parent
school district personnel	university personnel	college education majors
special education teacher	school principal	parent
school bus driver	special reading teacher	student
speech pathologist	special education teacher	student
teacher of behaviorally disordered	school cafeteria personnel	student
librarian/media specialist	gifted program facilitator	parent
principal	general classroom teacher	parent
mentor	parent	student
parent	school principal	special education teacher
school psychologist	Chapter I teacher	student
health care specialist	learning disabilities teacher	resource room students
special education staff at university	pediatricians	at-risk children

FIGURE 1.1   Interchangeable Roles in Collaborative School Consultation

Role Delineation in Collaborative School Consultation

As noted in Figure 1.2, the starting point for school personnel in school consultation, collaboration, and teamwork is careful *preparation* for those roles. However, role delineation will be discussed first here in order to put the purpose of the preparation into perspective.

Having a specific school role such as counselor, general classroom teacher, specialist in learning disabilities, speech pathologist, or facilitator for the gifted program does not delineate a consultation role. The consultation role is created by a circumstance that targets

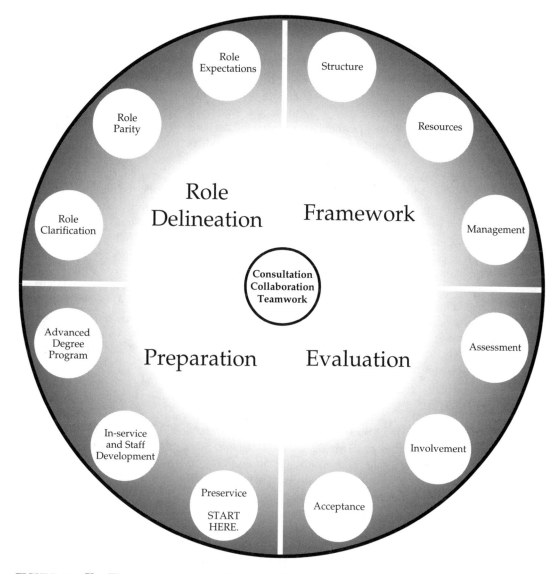

FIGURE 1.2 Key Elements for Working Together Effectively

the need. The consultant, consultee, or client role might be assumed by a parent who provides information to the school administrator, or a learning disabilities teacher who helps the coach assess a student athlete's learning problem, or a mentor who provides gifted program facilitator material for class use by a gifted student.

A consultee teams up with and collaborates with the consultant to provide direct service for helping students succeed in school. The client role is delineated by the identified need or problem. This concept reflects the contemporary approach to special services where student needs, not student labels, determine the service and delivery method, and services are made available to address those needs.

Role Clarification. The most important element in role delineation is clarification of roles. Until educators become familiar with the concepts of consultation and collaboration and ways they can participate as partners and team members, doubt and confusion about roles may exist. School personnel sometimes are not sure why they have consulting teachers or what these people are supposed to be doing. For example, a facilitator for gifted programs who was in a consultative role in a large urban high school for several years kept hearing variations on the same concern—"Just how do you spend your day with only 30 students assigned to you? After all, they *are* fast learners." So the facilitator developed a job matrix to categorize the planning, implementation, and evaluation aspects and expectations of the role, and shared it with teaching colleagues and administrators (Hay, 1984).

Classroom teachers may blame their heavy caseloads of students on the seemingly lighter caseloads of consulting teachers. One high-school English teacher told a newly appointed consulting teacher, "If you were back in your classroom teaching English instead of 'facilitating' for a few high-ability students, my own student load wouldn't be so big." Paradoxically, consulting teachers often have excessively high caseloads when travel time among schools, and preparing or locating special materials, are taken into account. If the caseload is too great, the effectiveness of consulting service will be diminished severely, for there will be little time for the coordination and communication so critical to consultation success.

Achieving coherent instructional plans for students' learning and behavioral needs requires extensive knowledge of role responsibilities among all involved (Allington & Broikou, 1988). A classroom teacher and a reading specialist may have information to share in addressing a struggling reader's strengths and deficits, yet may know relatively little about each other's curriculum, educational priorities, or expectations for the student. They must coordinate their efforts, or those efforts may be counterproductive. In one unfortunate case, a reading specialist was instructing a fifth-grader with reading problems to slow down and read more deliberately, while the learning disabilities specialist was encouraging him to read much more rapidly and wanted to refer him for gifted program services. The student, a pleasant and cooperative child, was trying valiantly to please both teachers simultaneously.

Although there has been minimal study of general education teachers' roles as collaborators with special educators, some research does suggest a gap between teacher perceptions of actual and ideal performance in collaborative roles. Harris and Zetlin (1993) emphasize that collaborative consultation requires people to relinquish their traditional roles in order to exchange skills and to rotate their assignments in ways that expand educational experiences for both students and the adults involved.

Consultees may question a consultant's ability to address their unique classroom situation, especially if the consultant is young and inexperienced. As one classroom teacher put it when asked about involving the special education consulting teacher, "I'd never ask for *her* help. What does she know about a full classroom of students? She's never had more than five or six at a time, and she never has taught in a regular classroom." Keller (1981) describes with irony some of the more common perceptions of resource teacher roles: the "invisible woman" who seldom ventures out of her room; the "fifth wheel" who is not taken seriously; the "new fellow on the block" who is perceived as an expensive extra providing no visible help to others; the "sweet young thing" just out of graduate school with limited classroom experience; and "Mr. or Ms. Wizard" who is supposed to work magic and fix children. While not all resource or consulting teachers suffer from such characterizations, the possibilities are there.

Role Parity.   Along with role ambiguity and misunderstanding, special education consulting teachers may feel an absence of role parity. They may feel as if they do not belong to any one school or faculty. They may feel minimally important to students and the educational system, or cut off and isolated from general classroom teachers because of differing responsibilities, and from special education colleagues because of distance and schedules.

Substitutes may not be provided for consulting teachers when they are absent. In fact, these teachers may be pulled out of their own roles on occasion to substitute for absent classroom teachers, or to perform other tasks that come up suddenly. Consulting teachers have been asked to guide visitors on a school tour, drive the school bus, and perform secretarial tasks. Meanwhile, classroom teachers are not going to wait with open arms for consulting personnel to come and save them. Inevitably, school bells ring, classroom doors open, and the school day commences. Life, and school, will go on every day for students and their teachers with or without support from others. All of this conveys a message of diminished parity for the consulting role and a subtle or not-so-subtle impression of non-importance.

Stress and burnout can result from an absence of role clarity and role parity. Teachers who feel as if they are "second-class" colleagues, not accepted or appreciated as a vital part of the staff, may develop defenses that erode their effectiveness. Some who travel extensively among schools in their cars have been dubbed "windshield" personnel. These problems are accentuated by the misconception that consultants have no ownership in student welfare and development. Ongoing recognition and reinforcement of consulting teacher contributions toward student success are important for the credibility of the role and professional morale, but students served indirectly by the consultant tend not to be viewed as "belonging" to the consultant.

Role Expectations.   Sometimes colleagues have unreasonable expectations for the consultant role, rather like the Mr./Ms. Wizard situation mentioned earlier, and expect instant success and miraculous student progress in a very short while. When results with students are slower than the consultees have hoped, or do not happen at all, their attitudes may range from guarded skepticism to open disapproval of the consultation approach. A school consultant cannot be a panacea for every student's difficulties. Acknowledging this reality helps avoid another barrier—the ill-conceived notion that consulting teachers are going to threaten teacher job security.

Educators may expect too much, or too little, from the consulting role. They may wish to see results too soon, or neglect to monitor results and then let ineffective service drag on too long. Consultees may exploit consulting service by expecting the consultant to "fix" the student, and if this does not happen, then downplay consultation as a failure and collaboration as a flop. Consulting teachers may expect to work, and wish to work, with students only and not with adults. "I was trained to work with kids, and that's what I enjoy," confided one consultant whose assigned role was providing indirect service only. Unrealistic and unreasonable expectations must be set aside in the early planning stages of school consultation methods. Consultants should set reasonable goals for themselves and not try to do too much.

The team approach may be awkward for an educator at first, not only for a consultant, but for the consultee as well. Sometimes the most difficult part of a support role is backing out once the consultee experiences success in meeting the client's needs (Stainback & Stainback, 1988). It is highly improbable that effective consultation will mean elimination of the position, as some consulting teachers fear. The more successful consultation services are, the more the teachers and administrators seem to value them for both their immediate contribution and their long-range positive ripple effects.

The involvement of as many school personnel as possible, through needs assessments, interviews, staff development, and both formal and informal communications, will minimize unwarranted expectations for consulting roles. Building successful collaborations with more receptive and cooperative colleagues at first will generate confidence in the consultant and respect for the approach.

Educators sometimes avoid collaborating because they feel the need to remain separate and to be independently visible. In too many instances jobs and professional identities depend on separate systems (Shepard, 1987). This fosters role separatism. Unless school personnel are prepared for consultation and involved in implementation of the plan, they may maximize the concern about potential problems and underestimate the power this educational service can generate when conducted appropriately.

Framework for School Consultation, Collaboration, and Teamwork

The framework for school consultation, collaboration, and teamwork calls for structures that provide time and facilities in which to meet, as well as management of the details so consultation is as convenient and non-intrusive as possible. Structure will be addressed in more detail in Chapter 2, and time and resource management in Chapters 7 and 10.

Structure.   Consultants need a structure within which to carry out their roles and responsibilities. It is one thing to design a hypothetical method of consultation, quite another to design multiple methods for different situations, and an even greater challenge to select and put into motion the right method for each situation. This is easier if preceded by role clarification and assurance of role parity and appropriate role expectations.

The consultant will want to formulate several methods for consultation and collaboration in a variety of grade levels, subject areas, special-needs categories, and school, community, and family contexts. The consultation structure should attend to the context of the system (such as school, neighborhood, family, athletic, or business arena). It also should include perspectives such as models, which will be discussed in Chapter 2. Consultants

APPLICATION **1.2**

How to Begin

1. Read, study, think, interview others, and complete coursework if possible, to gain information and skills for the role.
2. Formulate your own personal philosophy of school consultation, collaboration, and teamwork.
3. Meet with central administrators of your school(s) to listen to their perceptions of this role, if this possibility is open to you within the "chain of command" in that school context.
4. If an advisory council is available, engage the members in discussion about consultation and collaboration roles. The council should include general and special education teachers, support personnel, administrators, parents, and other community leaders.
5. Meet with each building administrator to whom you are assigned, to practice responsive listening (see Chapter 6 for techniques) and learn their viewpoints. This is a *very important* step.
6. After meeting with all principals, reorganize your own thoughts and ideas, and gather more information if necessary.
7. Develop a tentative role description and goals based on central and building administrators' views as well as your own perspective.
8. Return to central administration if appropriate to do that in your district, trying out your role description and goals with them, and revise if necessary.
9. Return to building administrators to share the revised package and obtain their approval and support. Again, this is *very* important.
10. After honing your document to a concise format, put it up for discussion, explaining it to teaching staff and non-teaching staff and refining it even further, based on their comments.
11. Meet with parent groups to inform them about school consultation service and solicit their opinions.
12. Keep stressing the opportunities and benefits inherent in collaboration and teamwork enterprises to all who will listen.
13. Work out a master schedule for your role, and distribute it to administrators whose attendance centers will be affected.
14. Have an open house in your work area, with refreshments if possible, and distribute handouts that outline your goals and schedule.
15. Post your schedule for access by administrators, teachers, support staff, and especially secretaries.
16. Conduct needs-sensing and needs-assessment surveys to find out what school personnel and parents want to have happen. If appropriate, ask students, too. (See Chapter 11 for more information about needs surveys.)
17. Ask for time during in-service or staff-development meetings to discuss the program.
18. Begin to work first with receptive, enthusiastic teachers as consultees.
19. Begin right away to log consultations and related activities, for accountability and evaluation purposes.
20. Solicit and welcome input from all, continually refining and reclarifying the role.
21. Get involved in each building where you are scheduled by accepting lunch, bus, playground duty. Offer to help during book fairs, school carnivals, ball games, as much as time and energy will allow. (One elementary teacher said to a consulting teacher who showed up for an open house event at her school, "What are *you* doing here? You surely don't come to these in all your buildings!" But she did.)

(continued)

22. Don't be seen around the building doing nothing, or *seeming* to be doing nothing. Spending time in the library to locate resources for a consultee or student may be misperceived by others as recreational reading. The purpose of such an activity should be clear to those who might like to minify or challenge the role.

23. Invite colleagues and family members to your room. Have student work displayed, and occasionally serve refreshments. One resource-room teacher for behavioral disorders was disappointed that no teachers ever came to her room. So she began a 4:00 P.M. exercise class there for 15 minutes daily. Her room soon became the hub of after-school activity, and colleagues became much more knowledgeable about her students' work in the resource room and their special needs in the classroom.

24. Avoid hierarchical relationships by practicing the communicative art of *onedownsmanship* (Conoley & Conoley, 1982). This is the opposite of a oneupmanship demeanor of being the expert in a superior role.

25. If you have any choice in the matter, locate your work space in the mainstream of the school. Of course, consultee and client rights to privacy and confidentiality must be protected, but when consulting teachers are located at the far ends of hallways they are easily isolated and ignored. One consulting teacher expressed his frustration in feeling cut off from the life of the school. His room was in a most out-of-the-way location. "I am viewed as that teacher over there they occasionally send kids to," he said, "so I have tried to make myself visible and available before and after school."

26. Promote the value of consultation in education just as it is valued in the medical and legal professions. The "second opinion" is sought widely in these service areas, but teachers often are expected to handle problems by relying solely on their own resources.

27. Eat lunch with other staff members, and interact just enough, but not too much, in the teacher workroom. (See Chapter 11 for more about the "teachers' lounge.")

28. Ask teachers for their advice on educational issues and encourage them to demonstrate some of their favorite techniques. However, do not share their own favorites with others unless you receive their permission to do so.

29. Dress for the school and the occasion. Variables such as high/low status, titles, and clothes have a significant impact on consultation effectiveness (Kratochwill & Van Someren, 1985). One consulting teacher confided that she was having trouble being accepted by one particular school's staff. She approached the problem straight on and asked what she was doing wrong. The reply surprised her. "You don't come here to *work* like the rest of us. You come in a suit and heels, all dressed up, to observe and supervise." She quickly altered her style of dress and was rewarded with changed attitudes at that school. In sharing her story with another consultant, the second replied, "Yes, I learned to do that. I have two schools, and luckily for me, the ones who like to dress up are in my morning school. At noon I whip off the earrings and accessories, and slip on tennis shoes. Then I fit in at both places. It paid off for me."

30. The golden question to ask of any colleague is this: "What can I do for you and your students *that you don't have the time and materials to do?*" Compare that question with any comment which might imply, "What can I do that you don't have the expertise to do?" After asking what you can do to help the busy, overworked, classroom-bound teacher, then suggest that you both talk about the need and how you can help. This is the starting point for collaboration and team effort.

31. Provide colleagues with information that helps them see the fallacy of the "quick fix" for complex learning and behavior problems. Practical information written in realistic terms for practitioners will be most effective.

32. Promote an exchange-of-roles day in which consultants teach the class, and teachers observe, plan modifications, and consult with others.

33. Review goals with consultees, revise the objectives, and document successes, no matter now small they might seem.

34. Discourage any tendency of colleagues to regard the consultants as supervisors, evaluators, or therapists. Pugach and Johnson (1989b) identify a major problem in achieving parity within collaborative models as the tendency among specialists to take on the expert role and disregard experienced classroom teachers as resources for students' special needs. They report that one candid specialist said in reference to classroom teachers, "Why doesn't anyone ask about all the things I have learned from *them*?"

35. Refrain from making any recommendations that conflict with administrative policy or teacher values.

36. When a consultee wishes only to have a student removed from the classroom, *right now,* just pretend not to hear, and instead suggest something that the consultee, or you and the consultee together, might try.

37. Know content areas well for the students about whom you consult. Also, be knowledgeable about regulations and recommendations governing special education, education for students at risk of failure, and school reform movements.

38. Develop a newsletter for school personnel and parents to inform readers, without breach of privacy or confidentiality, about program activities, educational issues, materials, and home/school partnerships, taking care not to identify individuals.

39. Seek out and provide resources for teachers and parents.

40. Continue to read, study, attend conferences, and take courses in consultation and related professional development.

41. Teach students in or out of classrooms where feasible.

42. Demonstration-teach for teachers who request. (Make the offer if no initial requests are forthcoming.)

43. Observe in classrooms, always following up with the teacher very soon. (See Chapter 7 for observation techniques.)

44. Maintain contact with parents.

45. Observe students outside the classroom (playground, lunch, extracurricular events) to get a different perspective.

46. Make attractive bulletin boards that complement the goals of consultation and collaboration, stressing teamwork and partnerships.

47. With a colleague or two or three, brainstorm periodically for ways to improve services and enhance collaborative efforts among educators.

48. Reach out to more reluctant colleagues, asking for their views, and offering materials, information, and assistance as it fits into their plans.

49. Encourage collaborative staff-development activities and partnerships such as "Teachers Helping Teachers."

50. Find texts and basals that work best in collaborative efforts.

51. Design curriculum materials and modifications to meet collaborator and student needs.

52. Reassess your plans, time allocation, resources, and program results, and revise them if necessary.

53. Engage in research efforts for new knowledge about consultation and collaboration practices.

54. Carry out advocacy and public relations efforts for excellent education.

should design their own consultation method through trial and error in order to fit that model to school needs. Polling teachers to find out how they would use a consultant for their students is a good way to begin. Studying and observing structures from other school systems also is helpful.

Resources.   One of the most overwhelming and frustrating obstacles to school consultation is lack of time for consultation to occur. Scarcity of time is a major deterrent to success of the collaborative consultation process (Johnson, Pugach, & Hammittee, 1988; Idol-Maestas & Ritter, 1985; Speece & Mandell, 1980; McLoughlin & Kelly, 1982). Idol (1986) recommends that resource teachers have at least one-third of their school time available for consultations. In an earlier study by Neel (1981), 48 percent of the special education teachers queried reported that they have no time scheduled for consultation and are expected to provide consultation services beyond regularly scheduled teaching hours. Most often they must use their own planning time for consultation, which is not an ideal way to instill positive attitudes toward the consultation approach.

Many special education teachers and classroom teachers report that their school day is simply not designed to accommodate collaboration (Stainback & Stainback, 1988; Idol-Maestas, 1983). Even if the consultant can arrange and coordinate a schedule for meeting with consultees and following up on outcomes, it can be next to impossible to arrange significant blocks of consultee time to participate in the collaboration. Working out such a plan is one of the most formidable tasks facing a consultant, particularly one who also has direct teaching responsibilities at specific times.

Administrators must assume responsibility for allocating time needed by consultants and consultees to collaborate and co-teach. If they lend their authority to this endeavor, school personnel will be more willing to brainstorm ways of getting together. Schenkat (1988) points out that if working conditions in schools were restructured to allow greater flexibility in scheduling, teachers could find the time to collaborate with colleagues. This would help build bridges between special education and general education, while expanding services to all students who have special needs.

When consulting teachers first initiate consultation and collaboration, it is very likely that these activities will have to come out of their own time—before school, after school, during lunch hours, perhaps even on weekends. Even so, this temporary accommodation should be replaced as soon as possible with more appropriate times during the school work day. This is not only for their well-being, but also to emphasize that consultation and collaboration are not simply add-on services that will be supplied as an extreme role overload by a zealous, dedicated few.

When time *is* arranged for a consultation, facilities must be available in which to conduct the consultation. The area should be pleasant, quiet, and relatively private for free exchange of confidences. Such a place is at a premium in a bustling school community.

Management.   There is a risk of letting fiscal issues, rather than student needs, dictate the service delivery method. The caseload issue must be addressed carefully. Assigning large caseloads to consulting teachers may save money in the short run, but could cost more eventually if student performance does not improve or if teachers burn out as a result (Huefner, 1988). Problems related to caseload are complex. For example, the average time needed to complete one Individual Education Program (IEP) has been assessed as 6.5 hours (Heron & Kimball, 1988; Price & Goodman, 1980). A consulting teacher with an overwhelming caseload of students and time-consuming responsibilities such as development of IEPs will have no time to consult and collaborate. Although direct service can be a strategy for easing into indirect service, the load must be manageable. If a consulting teacher's caseload is too great, direct service is inadequate, possibilities for indirect services are minimal, and the program is self-defeating.

In the Resource/Consulting Teacher model (to be discussed more fully in Chapter 2), Idol-Maestas (1983) recommends that teachers spend 20 to 40 percent of their school day in consultation-related activities, such as discussing educational problems, presenting ideas for use in regular classrooms, in-service, observation, performing curriculum-based assessment, demonstrating instructional techniques (Wiederholt, Hammill, & Brown, 1983), and coordinating the program.

A consultant must be very organized and efficient. Greenburg (1987) notes a number of studies indicating that although resource teachers may be committed to direct contact as their major activity, considerable portions of their time are required for recordkeeping, paperwork, and teacher-consultant responsibilities (McGlothlin, 1981; Miller & Sabatino, 1978; Evans, 1980). Consulting teachers manage and monitor consultee use of materials as varied as books, tests, kits, tapes, films, and media equipment. They help teachers develop systems of observation, monitoring, and assessment, along with performing these activities themselves. Their paperwork, scheduling, and communication systems must be efficient and effective. Techniques for managing these activities will be presented in Chapter 7.

Recommended caseload numbers vary depending on school context, travel time required, grade level, exceptionalities and special needs served, and structure of the consulting method. The numbers must be kept manageable to fulfill the intent and promise of consultation and collaboration. The key lies in documenting carefully all consultation activities *and* making note also of those which should have happened but were precluded by time constraints. Consultants can negotiate with their administrators for reasonable caseload assignments and blocks of time in which to consult, collaborate, and co-teach.

Evaluation and Support of Consultation and Collaboration

The third of four key elements in school consultation features evaluation and support. Educators will need to document the effectiveness of consultation and collaboration in order to ensure continuing support for this kind of educational service. School personnel are understandably skeptical of indirect service if it does not demonstrate its usefulness. They may be involved initially because they are told to, or because they have been talked into giving it a try, but their interest will wane if positive results are not forthcoming. There will be out-and-out resistance if they sense that it is detrimental to children specifically and to the educational process in general.

Assessment.   Assessment of consultation is a requisite for continuing to obtain consultation time and facilities. Involvement and acceptance by school personnel will increase when effectiveness of consulting as a professional practice in education is assessed. In keeping with the philosophy of collaboration, evaluation of the consultation should be designed cooperatively by personnel from varying roles.

Only two kinds of evaluation measures are readily available in the published research on education-based consultation (Tindal & Taylor-Pendergast, 1989): (1) rating scales of judgments that represent a variety of skills and activities, and (2) estimates of engaged time that note the activities required or demanded. Administrators, advisory-council members, and policy-makers will need to study carefully the few procedures that are available for assessment, and beyond that, use their skills to design more helpful and practical assessment techniques that fit their school context and consultant role responsibilities.

The context of the school setting must be assessed as well. For example, a consultant may have excellent communication skills and a wealth of content with which to consult and collaborate, but if no time is provided for interaction, there will be few positive results. Consultants will want to evaluate every stage of the process to keep heading in the right direction. (See Chapter 8 on formative evaluation.) Evaluation should include a variety of data-collection methods to provide the kinds of information needed by target groups. When assessment is completed, consultation and collaboration practices must not be judged inadequate for the wrong reasons or under erroneous assumptions. If time has not been allocated for the interactions, if staff have not had preparation and encouragement, and if administrator support is lacking, those elements should be targeted for improvement before consultation is disparaged or discouraged.

Involvement.   As mentioned earlier, Friend and Cook (1990) emphasize that collaborative programs must address "voluntariness" before detailed planning can occur. Others have stressed that participation in collaboration must be voluntary on the part of the consultee. However, for some school personnel that desirable condition may never appear. In these instances administrator influence and appealing tactics by the consultant may help. Sometimes a bandwagon effect can exert power in getting everyone on for the ride. Broadcasting the successes and promoting the benefits of consultations and collaborations that have occurred may get the bandwagon rolling and the reluctants on board. Most important, however, is involving people right from the start in needs assessments, planning efforts, evaluations, staff-development presentations, and personal contacts to instill ownership and even arouse a little curiosity. Techniques and incentives for promotion of consultation, collaboration, and teamwork through staff development will be discussed in Chapter 11.

Acceptance.   Consultation signals change. Collaboration requires practice. Co-teaching means giving up part of the ownership. These realities make acceptance of school consultation more difficult and enthusiastic involvement by all school personnel more challenging for its advocates. Consultation in the minds of many general educators is associated with special education. If teachers resent having more responsibility for special education students, they may blame school consultation and consultants for this condition. Consultees and support personnel need a precedence for accepting and adapting to this model. Most of all, they need administrator support and encouragement. Consultants must seize every opportunity to cultivate these conditions.

Preparation for School Consultation and Collaboration

Preparation programs for mastering the skills of school consultation and collaboration are a necessity. Opportunities and incentives must be provided for three populations:

- Preservice students should prepare to be consultees and potential consultants.
- Graduate students in degree programs should develop skills in consulting and in preparing others to be consultants and consultees.
- In-service teachers should prepare for roles as consultees and advocates for integrating consultation and collaboration into their school contexts.

Skills of the consultant and consultee are enhanced through training activities, coaching, and feedback in process and content skill areas.

Preservice Preparation.   Teacher-preparation programs do not often include consulting process skills such as communication and conflict resolution in teaching methods. Not so many years ago, studies revealed that collaborative consultation training for preservice teachers in college and university programs was very much the exception rather than the rule (Lilly & Givens-Ogle, 1981). Some progress has been made since that time in teacher-preparation programs, but much more is needed (West & Brown, 1987). Another much-neglected area in preservice teacher preparation is family issues. Education students should have opportunities to interact with families and regard them as valuable team members while they are still formulating their ideas and strategies (Kerns, 1992).

Phillips, Allred, Brulle, and Shank (1990) suggest that collaboration and consultation skills can be cultivated by teacher educators at the preservice level. They recommend that teacher-preparation programs provide introductory education courses in which general and special education preservice teachers participate jointly in practicum experiences that serve a diverse range of children's needs. However, this approach requires concerted effort by college and university personnel, for many of them have not been prepared themselves to perform collaboration and consultation functions, let alone facilitate development of these behaviors in their students.

Some veteran educators will be nervous about having "novice teachers" address consultation practices before they have experienced student teaching and real-world teaching. Nevertheless, the seeds of awareness can and should be planted early, because they will bear fruit later in important ways. After all, for most new teachers there is not much time or experience gained between that last day of teacher education and the first day of being an autonomous professional and virtually alone in the classroom with students.

Graduate Certification and Degree Programs.   Formal training in consultation lags behind the increasing demands for service (Curtis & Zins, 1988). White and Pryzwansky (1982) assert that resource teachers in schools are not prepared to deliver consultation and are keenly aware of their insufficiencies in that regard. If teachers are not trained in consultation, they will tend to shy away from pertinent feedback and provide only broad generalizations or retreat into paperwork associated with the role (Gersten, Darch, Davis, & George, 1991). Kauffman (1994) contends that training of special educators is often so superficial and general that that they have no real expertise as instructional specialists and no in-depth understanding of disabling conditions and their instructional demands. He stresses that special education teachers who are being prepared to consult and collaborate with general educators must have special instructional and behavior-management expertise or their input will have little meaning beyond that of the general educators.

The number of preparation programs is increasing (Dickens & Jones, 1990; Gersten, Darch, Davis, & George, 1991; Thurston & Kimsey, 1989), but universities have far to go to meet the needs. Some states require development of consultation skills for teacher certification. Inclusion of this training in standards for accreditation of teacher-education programs would be one way to encourage more emphasis on collaborative school consultation and collaboration at the graduate and preservice levels. School administrators should recruit prospective consultants who welcome the opportunity for working with adults as well as students in school settings. Each training program will be unique; however, a basic program for collaboration should include:

- Delineating their roles
- Creating a framework that allows them to fulfill their roles
- Evaluating their effectiveness
- Helping prepare colleagues for collaborative consultation even as they expand their own proficiencies

Preparation programs must provide experiences well beyond the "mentioning" mode of professional training that offers only superficial exposure to a large amount of information and minimal or no practice with complex ideas and behaviors. Course syllabi should include not only the conventional learning strategies of lecture, reading, and discussion, but a strong focus on experiential content. Small-group activities, simulations and role-plays, interviewing, videotaped consultation practice, reaction and reflection papers, resource searches, and practice with the tools and strategies of technology will help practicing educators be more comfortable and capable in interactive school roles.

In-service and Staff Development.   In 1987 West and Idol reported that staff development for school collaboration had received little attention (West & Idol, 1987). Friend and Cook (1990) assert that teachers are being set up to fail when they enter the profession with content expertise and method but without skills for working effectively with colleagues. The lack of preparation for consultation is compounded by a dearth of empirical studies that might provide evidence for or against various components of consultation training. However, movements such as school reform, restructuring, and mainstreaming have stimulated some efforts such as those reported by Rule, Fodor-Davis, Morgan, Salzberg, and Chen (1990). In their study, Rule and colleagues identified the need for administrative support, technical assistance, and follow-up assistance, as well as the in-service training.

At the in-service and staff-development level, consultation and collaboration programs can be tailored to each school context. Staff development should be looked upon by consultants as a golden opportunity for promoting consultation, collaboration, and team-work. It can help teachers become more successful in their very complex roles.

Multiplier Effects of Collaborative School Consultation

The use of specialized intervention techniques for many more students than those identi-fied, categorized, and remediated in special education programs is a positive outcome that can be expected from collaborative school consultation. Multiple benefits, often described as positive ripple effects, often extend well beyond the immediate classroom because con-sulting teachers are in a unique position to facilitate interaction among many target groups. These effects that ripple out from mutual planning and problem-solving across grade lev-els, subject areas, and schools are powerful instruments for initiating positive changes in the educational system.

Multiplier effects provide compelling arguments for consultation, collaboration, and teaming. They create benefits beyond the immediate situation involving one student and that student's teachers. For example, through collaboration school personnel are modeling this powerful social tool for their students who are quite likely to experience collaborative climates in their future workplaces.

Consulting teachers who might suspect that their positions will be eliminated if classroom teachers are given full responsibility for special learning needs need not be con-cerned. As teachers become more proficient in collaborating with consulting teachers, they tend to find those services more indispensable to their goals of serving all students' educa-tional needs effectively.

Problem Areas to Avoid

Educators with experience as consultants describe several problems that can surface:

- Losing touch with the students
- Uncertainty about what and how to communicate with resistant consultees
- Being treated as a teacher's aide, "go-fer," or quick-fix expert
- Having consultation regarded as a tutorial for students
- Territoriality of school personnel
- Rigid curriculum and assessment procedures
- Unrealistic expectations toward the role
- Not having enough information or appropriate materials to share
- Being perceived as a show-off, or a bossy expert
- Professional politeness, but not acceptance
- Difficulty managing time and resources
- Lack of training for the role
- An excessive caseload that short-circuits effectiveness
- Too many "hats" to wear in the role
- Most of all, a reluctance of colleagues to change

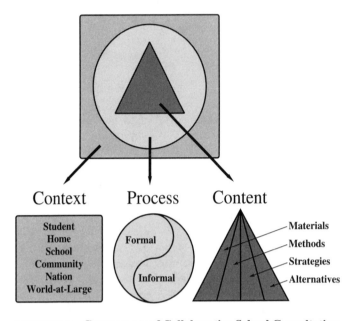

FIGURE 1.3   Components of Collaborative School Consultation

Knowing potential problems can help educators offset them by ensuring role delineation, consultation framework, evaluation of the process, and preparation to develop the necessary skills. Some of the mystique surrounding special education is reduced when classroom teachers become familiar with special education techniques and come to appreciate and understand special education roles.

Process and Content in the School Context

School consultation combines process skills and content knowledge within the school context of each educational setting. (See Figure 1.3.) Schools have characteristics of hierarchy, subsystems, and rules (Hansen, Himes, & Meier, 1990). The school context is composed of many ecological factors that greatly affect consultation practices, such as community and political structures, cultural and ethnic diversity, the financial climate, personality structures of personnel, and student characteristics. These systems continuously exert pressures on the schools (Gallessich, 1973), and are not always within the control of school personnel, particularly teachers. Lack of organizational sensitivity to school contexts can be disastrous.

The context of the school setting can be categorized into several descriptive areas: Student, Home, School, Community, Nation, and World-at-Large. (See Figure 1.4.)

Each of these areas affects the ease and efficiency with which consultation can occur. Everyone involved in consultation brings unique experiences and understanding to each

FIGURE 1.4 Examples of Collaborative School Consultation Components

CONTEXT

Student	Needs, styles, accomplishments, handicaps, interests, achievement levels, social skills, talents, peer status, gender, age, physical development, ability level...
Home	Family constellations, siblings, socio-economic status, cultural identity, family stability, parent involvement, cooperation, support...
School	School philosophy, climate, setting, staff, morale, instructional leadership, staff development, follow-up, modeling and coaching, facilities, support...
Community	Economic level, stability, resources, media, awareness levels partnerships, law and order, neighborhood unity, educational level...
Nation	Public support, citizenship, democracy, educational standards...
World	Peace, diversity, self-sufficiency, models, political conditions, equity, resources...

PROCESS

Formal	Meetings, structured problem-solving sessions, training activities, scheduled communications, planned innovations...
Informal	Conversations, shared responsibilities, compensations for personality differences, idea swapping, spontaneous innovation...

CONTENT

Materials	Books, worksheets, programmed instruction, kits, study aids, computer-based applications, tests, media, learning machines, laboratory equipment, instruments, artifacts...
Methods	Cooperative learning, peer tutoring, grouping arrangements, direct instruction, independent study, computer-assisted instruction, self-directed learning...
Strategies	Test taking practice, behavior managements, sensory augmentation, reinforcement schedules, flexible pacing, curriculum compacting...
Alternatives	Course options, testing alternatives, test-out and dual credit or half credit, revisions of requirements, modification of materials

collaborative situation (Henning-Stout, 1994). Critical contexts of the educational system in regard to consultation and collaboration include public attitudes, geographic features of the school environment, staff support, financial structure, parent involvement, political action, and legal issues. Characteristics of each school's context must be assessed objectively, understood, and appreciated by the school consultant.

Process skills include but are not limited to communication, coordination, and cooperation. They can occur in formal or informal settings. (Refer again to Figure 1.3.) With these skills the consultant and consultee listen to each other and interact, seek to identify the problem, share information and ideas, resolve conflicts, conduct observations, develop courses of action, coordinate activities, follow through on results, and assess the outcomes for further planning and implementation. Process skills are described by Idol (1990) as the artful base of consultation.

Content skills include selection of materials and resources, proficiency with a variety of teaching methods and strategies, and awareness of learning options and alternatives. (Refer again to Figure 1.3.) It is too often the unfortunate case that consultees jump ahead to content, "buying" a quick remedy for the immediate situation rather than identifying the problem and collaborating on viable plans to resolve the problem. The content or knowledge base a consultant brings to the consulting process is described by Idol (1990) as the scientific base of consultation. Scientific bases and artful bases must be merged to produce school consultants and consulting teachers who can practice the scientific art of classroom consultation (Idol, 1990).

Synergy of Context, Process, and Content

Effective school consultation results from the interaction of process skills and content methodology within the immediate school context. Contexts of a school setting are a "given" in the assessment of the educational scene. Schools without content would be unnecessary. Processes are the most malleable and promising of the parameters that delineate school consultation, but processes such as communication, problem-solving, conflict resolution, time and resource management, and constructive use of adult differences tend to be either neglected or poorly carried out in too many school situations.

Can there be content-free processes for consultation? No, because process is composed of content (Tharp, 1975). This is one of the greatest strengths of consultation. Process incorporates content to provide services for students in each school context. Collaboration that occurs in conjunction with consultation requires harmonious, efficient teamwork. Consultants and consultees meet to assess the student's situation, develop courses of action to help the student, carry out the actions, and follow through on the results. Each party contributes points of view, information, and suggestions for resolution of the situation.

So, as described earlier in this chapter, consultation with collaboration is not an oxymoron, but a *synergy* of whole systems unpredicted by the behavior of their parts taken separately. When teamwork is effective, there is synergy. Each member contributes expertise both directly and indirectly, without superior–inferior connotations, in order to develop educational plans within a climate of equality.

Process skills and content methodology are ineffectual unless grounded in the specifics of each particular school context. For example, a process-based educational approach that is exclusively process-specific will be perceived as "talk, talk, talk—never mind about what" (Britt, 1985) without firm roots in the consultees' content skills. But a synergistic combination of process skills, content methodology, and school context considerations can set the stage for effective consultation, collaboration, and teamwork to help students with special needs succeed in school.

Tips for Working Together in Schools

1. Value consultation and collaboration as tools for improving long-range planning and coordination among educators.
2. Do not wait to be approached for consultation and collaboration.
3. Try not to press for one's own solutions to school needs, educators' needs, or student needs. Strive instead for collaborative efforts to problem-solve together.
4. Refrain from assuming that colleagues are waiting around to be "saved."
5. Call on building administrators when you are in the building, leaving brief notes that you stopped by, if they are unavailable.
6. Do not share problems or concerns with classroom teachers unless they can have significant input or you have a suggestion for them that might help.
7. Carry your share of the load in contributing to social funds, work schedules, and other professional obligations and courtesies.
8. Attend extracurricular functions of assigned schools as much as possible, and offer to help if feasible.
9. Have lunch, workroom breaks, and informal visits with building staff often.
10. Attend monthly grade-level/departmental meetings to interact with colleagues and to learn of their needs and concerns.
11. Ask for help when you have a problem, because it has a humanizing, rapport-building effect.
12. Find ways to inform, support, and interact with principals, promoting the idea that each is a "prince-and-a-pal" or "princess-and-a-pal."
13. Leave the door open, both figuratively and literally, for future partnerships and collaborations.
14. Know when to stay in the consultation, and when it is time to get out.
15. "Dress for success" in each setting, matching your level of dress with the context in order to establish parity.
16. Visit every teacher in the building regularly.
17. Don't be seen around your building(s) doing nothing.
18. Be available—and available—and available.

CHAPTER REVIEW

1. Consultation, collaboration, and co-teaching involve sharing expertise and concerns, laboring together, and planning and working together as a team to identify students' special needs and implement programs to facilitate learning and achievement.

2. Collaborative consultation in schools can be described as interaction in which school personnel and parents confer and collaborate as a team within the school context to identify learning and behavioral needs, and to plan, implement, and evaluate educational programs for serving those needs. The school consultant is a facilitator of effective communication, cooperation, and coordination who confers and collaborates with other school personnel and parents as a team to serve the special learning and behavioral needs of students.

3. Key elements in school consultation and collaboration are role delineation, a framework for these activities, evaluation and support of the efforts, and preparation for consultation and collaboration. A consultant, consultee (or mediator), and client (or target) in one school-related situation may function in any of the other capacities under different circumstances. Several questions reflect the immediate concerns of consultants and consulting teachers: What do I do? How do I begin? What is my schedule for a week? How do I know I am succeeding? How do I prepare for this kind of role?

4. When preparation is provided, roles are understood, a framework is created, and interactive processes are evaluated, collaborative school consultation can produce beneficial multiplier effects throughout the total school context.

5. The most effective strategy for school consultation and collaboration will be a synthesis of context, process, and content in which communication, problem-solving, coordination, time and resource management, constructive use of adult differences, and family partnerships are blended to create situation-specific methods for serving students' special learning needs.

TO DO AND THINK ABOUT

1. Using material in this chapter, a dictionary, interviews, recollections from teaching experiences, discussion with colleagues or classmates, and any other pertinent references, formulate a description and philosophy about collaborative school consultation which reflects your viewpoint at this time.

2. List all the responsibilities you can think of that a teacher typically performs during the course of a school year. Use your recollections of student days, college coursework, student teaching, and any teaching experience that you have had. You will probably develop a lengthy list of a wide range of duties and activities, and it most likely will include opportunities with potential for using consultation and collaboration tools.

    If you team up with other teachers in various grade levels, content areas, and specialized roles to do this exercise, the combined lists could become a colorful and impressive mosaic of teaching responsibilities. The process itself will be an example of teamwork, with each person adding information from his or her own perspectives and experiences. And so—collaborative consultation!

3. Using your list generated in activity 2, sort the list into kinds of responsibilities such as, for example, instructional, curricular, managerial, logistical, evaluative, and supportive. Then look for teacher responsibilities in those categories in which consultation and collaboration efforts might take place appropriately and helpfully for students with special needs. For example, under the managerial responsibility of ordering books and supplies, teams of teachers might collaborate to pool library money and plan orders of materials that address special needs of students for remediation and enrichment. In this way shared decision-making in selecting resources could lead to shared planning and implementation of programs that use the resources collaboratively.

4. Interview three school professionals (elementary, middle school, and high-school levels, if possible) and two parents to find out their views of school consultation and collaboration, and the consulting teacher role. You can approach this in one of two ways—by giving interviewees definitions if they ask "What do you mean?" by the terms, or by encouraging them

to share their own perceptions of the terms to define them in their own way. Compare the interview results, and make inferences. Note any indication of willingness to collaborate or glimmer of awakening interest in consultation, and determine how these positive signs might be followed up productively. For example, one interviewer was rewarded with this experience: "This secondary school teacher saw a special education consultant as a 'prescriptive and purchase' person to a great extent. After talking a little longer, however, he was making statements like, 'Maybe they could show me how to make adjustments with my homework or class assignments so the students could be successful.' I see a possibility here for long-term effects and transfer....").

5. Think of scenarios from your own school context that could be described, with anonymity and confidentiality, of course. Using Figure 1.1 in this chapter, mix and match roles among the three columns to discuss briefly or act out those scenarios. You may want to identify consultants with red tags, consultees with green, and clients with blue (Knackendoffel, personal communication, September 22, 1997). If you think of other personnel who would be pertinent to include, add them to any of the three lists. (A copy might be made of the figure, and the three cut strips inserted into slits in a cardboard frame, creating a three-part sliding scale for a mix-and-match activity to facilitate discussion.)

6. What questions or concerns about consultation and collaboration are uppermost in your mind at the end of this chapter?

FOR FURTHER READING

Brown, D., Pryzwansky, W. B., & Schulte, A. C. (1991). *Psychological consultation: Introduction to theory and practice.* Boston: Allyn & Bacon. Chapters 6 and 7, on roles of consultants and consultees.

Conoley, J. C., & Conoley, C. W. (1982). *School consultation: A guide to practice and training.* New York: Pergamon Press.

Educational leadership. (December 1994/January 1995). *52*(4). Entire periodical, a topical issue on the inclusive school.

Hansen, J. C., Himes, B. S., & Meier, S. (1990). *Consultation: Concepts and practices.* Englewood Cliffs, NJ: Prentice-Hall.

Hay, C. (1984). One more time: What do I do all day? *Gifted Child Quarterly, 28*(1), 17–20.

Henning-Stout, M. (1994). Consultation and connected knowing: What we know is determined by the questions we ask. *Journal of Educational and Psychological Consultation, 5,*(1), 5–21.

Heron, T. E., & Harris, K. C. (1987). *The educational consultant: Helping professionals, parents, and mainstreamed students.* Austin, TX: PRO-ED. Chapter 2 on the consultant role.

Hoy, W. K. (1990). Organizational climate and culture: A conceptual analysis of the school work place. *Journal of Educational and Psychological Consultation, 1*(2), 149–168.

Idol, L., Paolucci Whitcomb, P., & Nevin, A. (1986). *Collaborative consultation.* Austin, TX: PRO-ED.

Journal of Educational and Psychological Consultation, 4(4). (1993). Topical issue on Culture and Consultation.

Maeroff, G. I. (1993). Building teams to rebuild schools. *Phi Delta Kappan, 74* (7), 512–519.

Morsink, C. V., Thomas, C. C., & Correa, V. I. (1991). *Interactive teaming: Consultation and collaboration in school programs.* New York: Macmillan. Chapter 4 on understanding roles and perspectives of team members.

Reynolds, M. C., & Birch, J. W. (1988). *Adaptive mainstreaming: A primer for teachers and principals* (3rd ed.). New York: Longman.

Stainback, S., Stainback, W., & Forest, M. (1989). *Educating all students in the mainstream of regular education.* Baltimore, MD: Brookes.

2 Background, Theory, Research, and Structure

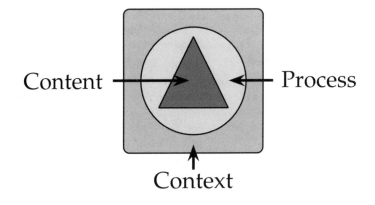

Consultation, collaboration, and teamwork probably began around cave fires ages ago. As men and women listened to the ideas of others in the group and voiced their own opinions, they honed skills of communication and collaboration. As they planned hunting and food-gathering forays, they developed strategies for teamwork. Then they undoubtedly assessed the outcomes in order to achieve greater success the next time.

Such skills have become more and more essential for survival and progress in an increasingly complex, interconnected world. All members of every society must interact effectively and work together cooperatively if the world is to progress. Educators who do this are modeling for young people the interpersonal skills they will need for survival in the world they will inherit.

Focusing Questions

1. How do educational reform and restructuring movements signal the need for collaborative school consultation?
2. What is the concept of the inclusionary school?
3. What is the history of school consultation?

4. Is there a theoretical base for school consultation?
5. What research is needed to determine best practices in collaborative school consultation?
6. What structural elements are components for developing appropriate consultation methods to fit school contexts and student needs?
7. What models of consultation, collaboration, and teamwork have evolved in education?
8. How might educators incorporate existing models and other structural elements into useful school consultation methods?

Key Terms

approach	mode	Stephens/systems model
collaborative consultation model	model	system
	perspective	thought problem
Goals 2000	prototype	transition from preschool to
IDEA (Public Law 101-476)	Resource/Consulting Teacher	school and school to work
inclusion/full inclusion	Program model (R/CT)	triadic model
least restrictive environment	School Consultation	Vermont Consulting Teacher
mainstreaming	Committee model	Program model
method	semantics	

School Reform Movements

During the 1970s, 1980s, and into the 1990s educators witnessed an explosion of reports, proposals, and legislative mandates calling for educational reform. The first wave of formal educational reform sought to strengthen the rigor of American public education (Michaels, 1988). The issues focused on accountability, lengthening of school days and years, and increased investments of time, money, and effort in education. The second wave of reform featured the individual school as the unit of decision-making. It promoted the development of collegial, participatory environments among students and staff, with particular emphasis on personalizing school environments and designing curriculum for deeper understanding (Michaels, 1988). One component of this second wave of reform was school restructuring. Many states initiated some form of school restructuring; however, few schools truly were restructured. Where restructuring efforts occurred, they tended to be idiosyncratic in that they were carried out by a small group of teachers, creating only marginal, easily eroded changes (Timar, 1989).

In the 1980s a position paper was issued by Madeline Will, former director of the U.S. Office of Special Education and Rehabilitative Services, stating that too many children were inappropriately identified and served in learning disabilities programs. She called for collaboration between special education and general education personnel in providing services within the general classroom. Two distinct groups emerged to support her call, the high-incidence group speaking for learning disabilities, behavioral disorders, and mild/moderate mental retardation, and the low-incidence group speaking for students with severe intellectual disabilities. A few in the latter group spoke out for the elimination of

Scenario 2

The setting is a school administration office where the superintendent, the principal, and the special education director are having an early-morning conference.

SPECIAL EDUCATION DIRECTOR: I've assigned five people on our special education staff to begin serving as consulting teachers in the schools we targeted at our last meeting.

PRINCIPAL: I understand the high school is to be one of those schools. I'm all for trying a new approach, but at this point I'm not sure my staff understands how this method of service is going to affect them.

SUPERINTENDENT: Are you saying we need to spend a little more time at the drawing board and get the kinks out of our plan before flinging it at the teachers?

PRINCIPAL: Yes, and I think the parents also will want to know what will be happening.

SPECIAL EDUCATION DIRECTOR: I've been compiling a file of theoretical background, research studies, program descriptions, even cartoons and satire, involving consultation and collaboration approaches. Let me get copies of the most helpful material to you and the principals of the other targeted schools. Perhaps we should plan in-service sessions for teachers and awareness sessions for parents before we proceed.

SUPERINTENDENT: That sounds good. Draft an outline and we'll discuss it at next week's meeting. I'll get the word out to the other principals to be here.

---

special education altogether (Fuchs and Fuchs, 1994). Both groups shared the following three goals:

- To merge special and general education into one inclusive system;
- To increase dramatically the number of children with disabilities in mainstream classrooms; and
- To strengthen the academic achievement of students with mild and moderate disabilities, as well as that of underachievers without disabilities.

To achieve these goals it was necessary to become involved in the total restructuring of schools. "Increasingly, special education reform is symbolized by the term 'inclusive schools'" (Fuchs & Fuchs, 1994, p. 299).

Reports such as *A Nation at Risk,* submitted by the National Commission on Excellence in Education in 1983, and as many as thirty other major reform reports in the 1980s directed the nation's attention to the status and conditions of its schools. The *America 2000* report presented in 1991 by President Bush and Secretary of Education Lamar Alexander and the 1994 federal school reform package known as *Goals 2000* signed into law by President Clinton identified goals to be met in the nation's schools by the year 2000. The latter report in particular stipulated that home and school partnerships are essential for student success. After these reports were publicized, public pressure to improve schools escalated.

Effective restructuring calls for rethinking. Futrell (1989) asserts that schools truly can be restructured only through cooperation, collaboration, and teamwork among many factions. The emerging interest in collaboration and co-teaching adds a new dimension that could be the impetus for realizing major changes through school reform efforts.

The Regular Education Initiative (REI) in Retrospect

A significant ripple that helped create waves of educational reform was the Regular Education Initiative (REI), which called for a merger of general education and special education efforts. Demands for cost containment and growing concerns over labeling of students fueled interest in a merger of general education and special education. The primary impetus for the merger was the mainstreaming movement brought about in the 1970s by passage of Public Law 94-142. At the heart of this legislation was the concept of least-restrictive environment (LRE). Educators could no longer arbitrarily place individuals with disabilities in a special school or self-contained classroom. A continuum of service options was to be available and the type of service or placement was to be as close to the normal environment as possible, with classroom teachers responsible for the success of those students. In order to meet this new responsibility, teachers were to receive help from special education personnel.

Thus the Regular Education Initiative, referred to by some educators as the General Education Initiative (GEI), precipitated major changes in the way education is delivered. All students, with the exception of the severely handicapped, were from that time to be served primarily in a regular education setting. The rationale for the REI was that:

> The changes will serve many students not currently eligible for special education services;

> The stigma of placement in special education programs separate from age peers will be eliminated;

> Early intervention and prevention will be provided before more serious learning deficiencies occur; and

> Cooperative school-parent relationships will be enhanced (Will, 1986).

Public Law 94-142 was amended in 1990 by Public Law 101-476, the Individuals with Disabilities Education Act (IDEA), with key elements being:

> All references to "handicapped" children were changed to children with disabilities;

> New categories of autism and traumatic brain injury (TBI) were added, to be served with increased collaboration among all special education teachers, classroom teachers, and related services personnel;

> More emphasis was placed on requirements to provide transition services for students 16 years of age and older.

Also in 1990, the Americans with Disabilities Act (ADA) was passed, prohibiting discrimination against persons of all ages with disabilities in transportation, public access, local government, and telecommunications.

In 1997 reauthorization and amendments of IDEA, or P.L. 105–17, was approved by Congress and signed into law by President Clinton. Among other elements, this legislation contains:

- Provisions for improved parent/professional partnerships;
- Requirement for states to provide mediation for parents and schools in resolving differences;
- Increased cost-sharing among agencies with reduced financial burdens for special education locally;
- Accountability of education for students with disabilities by way of participation in district, state, and nationwide assessments;
- Assurance that children with disabilities will not be deprived of educational services as a result of dangerous behavior, while enabling educators to more easily remove them from current educational placement if needed;
- Disclosure requirements are tightened, with families having greater access to their children's records, and more information available in the IEPs.
- Revamped ways school districts receive federal funding, with elimination of the child-count formula and gradual reliance on census data with more accountability for poverty.

Somewhat disappointing to special educators in the reauthorization is the added paperwork, particularly in regard to IEPs, and the failure to authorize specific funding levels for IDEA support programs such as research and development, technology, and personnel preparation. There also is no language detailing public involvement and accountability for the comprehensive plan for the support programs. Another area of particular concern is omission of the appropriate inclusion of general education teachers on IEP teams.

Inclusive or Unified School Systems

The concept of inclusion did not suddenly emerge out of a vacuum. Indeed, it appears to be the latest in a long line of special education program changes that have grown out of concern for more appropriate education. Early efforts to address special needs began in special schools or residential institutions where specialized therapy and care could be provided by a well-trained staff. When educators began to provide special services in schools, special classes were formed. A belief was prevalent that those with disabilities were not successful in the regular classroom because that setting could not provide for their needs. This assumption was not challenged until the 1960s when advocates for individuals with mental retardation argued for normalization. These advocates asserted that individuals with mental retardation should have opportunities for patterns and conditions of everyday life as close as possible to norms of mainstream society. This logic influenced the deinstitutionalization movement.

The courts have upheld the right of individuals to refuse treatment and supported the civil rights belief that segregated education is inherently unequal and a violation of children's rights. Inclusive schools will *include* students with special needs in the total school experience, rather than "exclude" them by placing them in special schools or classrooms.

The movement toward inclusion in the 1990s was built on this early foundation. (See Figure 2.1.)

The inclusionary movement began rather quietly but quickly snowballed into a popular position in which special education and regular education would merge into a unified school system structured to meet the needs of all students. Proponents of this position assert that all students are unique individuals with special needs requiring differentiated individual attention; therefore, practices that are effective for exceptional students should be used with all students (Stainback & Stainback, 1984).

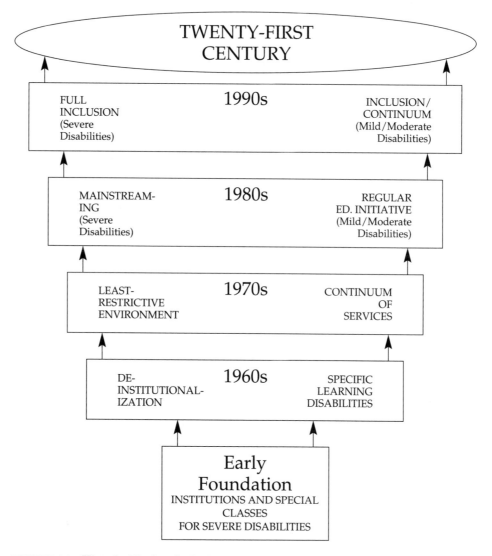

FIGURE 2.1   Historical Path to Inclusion

Essential Elements for Success of Inclusion.   The term *inclusion* is erroneously viewed by many professionals as a synonym for least-restrictive environment (LRE) as mandated by federal legislation. However, legislation does not define inclusion or the unified educational system, just as it did not include the term *mainstreaming*. Instead, inclusion is one of several alternatives within a continuum. Formal definitions that do exist will differ based on the interest group fostering the definition.

While mainstreaming placed students with disabilities in general education settings only when they could meet traditional academic expectations there with minor adaptations (Beakley, 1997), inclusive schools integrate students with special needs into their home schools with grade peers whether or not they can meet traditional standards. Special services are brought to the students instead of having students removed, or "pulled out," to go to the special services.

Selected definitions from the literature appear below:

> *Inclusion: The commitment to educate each child to the maximum extent appropriate in the school and classroom he or she would otherwise attend* (Rogers, 1993). The current focus for inclusion is on location of instruction and grouping of students; it is arbitrary across states and across districts within a state, and ideally it involves a regular teacher and a special education teacher co-teaching in one classroom (Beakley, 1997).

> *Full (or Total) Inclusion: The belief that instructional practices and technological supports are presently available to accommodate all students in the schools and classrooms they would otherwise attend if not disabled* (Rogers, 1993).

> *Inclusive Schools: Schools where all members accept their fair share of responsibility for all children, including those with disabilities.* Aids and resources are utilized where needed regardless of official classifications of disability (Fuchs and Fuchs, 1994).

Characteristics of Inclusive Schools.   The National Center on Educational Restructuring and Inclusion (NCERI) conducted a study in 1994 to determine the current status of the inclusion movement. Although most students with disabilities continued to be educated in separate settings, inclusion programs were being implemented in many states across the country. The NCERI researchers determined that the following six factors are necessary for inclusion to succeed (Lipsky, 1994):

> *Visionary Leadership.* School leaders must have a positive view about the value of education for students with disabilities, and an optimistic view of teachers who can change and schools that can accommodate the needs of students with special needs. An overriding attitude that all children can benefit from inclusion is important.

> *Collaboration.* Successful inclusion presumes that "no one teacher can or ought to be expected to have all the expertise required to meet the educational needs of all students in the classroom" (Lipsky, 1994, p. 5). The processes of consultation, collaboration, and co-teaching are recognized as essential for effective inclusion programs.

Refocused Use of Assessment. Inclusive schools tend to use more authentic assessment measures, such as those that will be discussed in Chapter 8. Assessment focuses on monitoring student progress.

Supports for Staff and Students. Two essential support factors reported in the study are systematic staff development and flexible planning time for special education personnel and general educators to meet and work together. Families are involved in the planning processes. Other useful supports include assignment of school aides, curriculum adaptation, therapy services integrated into the regular school program, peer supports, computer technology, and other assistive devices.

Funding. Funding formulas in many states need to be changed in order for inclusion to be implemented successfully.

Effective Parental Involvement. Inclusive programs place emphasis on substantive parent involvement through family-support services and the development of educational programs that engage parents as co-learners with their children.

The survey also highlighted classroom practices of co-planning and co-teaching. These will be discussed more fully in Chapter 9.

Effective Inclusionary Schools.   Inclusive schools emphasize learning for all students, with teachers and staff who work together to support a learning climate in which all students can succeed. All educators share responsibility for student achievement and behavior. Para-educators provide continuity and support for students, teachers, and families. They participate actively on the team and help with planning and delivery of appropriate services. Teachers refer to "our kids," rather than "your kids" and "my kids." Every inclusive school looks different, but is characterized by a sense of community, high standards, collaboration and cooperation, changing roles and an array of services, partnership with families, flexible learning environments, strategies based on research, new forms of accountability, and continuing professional development (Working Forum on Inclusive Schools, 1994).

Inclusion's Shortcomings.   Inclusion is not perceived positively by all educators. Some believe students are affected adversely when teachers with insufficient support are responsible for several students with disabilities. Critics point to situations where teachers receive little to no assistance and sometimes are not even informed about their students' disabilities. Others contend that special education teachers also have difficulties managing educational programs of their students when they are dispersed among several classrooms.

Van Tassel-Baska (1998) notes that studies in gifted and talented education within inclusionary settings are limited, but reveal some troubling trends. Research shows that students with high ability and remarkable talents do not receive instruction that is appropriately intensive enough for their needs in the inclusionary classroom. Only with positive working relationships in ongoing collaborative teaching tasks does teacher follow-through on use of strategies and intervention plans approach 40 percent. Inclusion reduces placement options to only one, and this could have a limiting effect on optimal development of talents.

Problems in inclusionary settings develop when children with disabilities are "dumped wholesale" into classrooms, with budget cuts and no planning and collaboration. In addition, a backlash is surfacing among parents of nondisabled who feel their children's education is being compromised. And, finally, skeptics of full inclusion insist that reported successes are not true achievement, but simply acceptance that the students do not disrupt and their teachers do cope with the situation ("Inclusion Gains Ground," December 1995).

The Council for Exceptional Children expressed concerns about the award-winning Home Box Office film *Educating Peter* because the well-trained, many-member team that helped create Peter's success was not shown or explained. For example, the situation involved: A one-to-one aide with Peter at all times, trained teachers and inclusion specialists, careful selection of a classroom with only 19 students and peer-mentor training for them, no other students with special needs in the classroom, a cadre of IEP and transition team members, and supportive administration.

So cautious educators applaud the intent and the gains from inclusionary settings for all students, and all teachers, and all families, but do not want them regarded as a panacea for teaching all special education students in general classrooms using all regular education curricula. Narrow definitions, myopic practices, and most of all, failure to prepare school personnel in collaborative and co-teaching strategies will short-circuit this promising school approach.

Transition from Preschool to School and from School to Work

Concern for preschoolers from poverty-level environments and other conditions of disadvantage gained momentum in the 1960s. Transition from the preschool settings to kindergarten-school programs requires strong, continuous efforts in collaborative school consultation. The passage of P.L. 99-457 in 1986 expanded attention to preschoolers, with public schools required to provide special services for children ages 3 and above who have disabilities. This law reaches beyond classrooms to include family, social workers, speech and language pathologists, medical personnel, and other professionals. Collaboration, consultation, and team efforts are at the heart of these programs.

At the opposite end of the continuum from early childhood needs are the needs of students leaving school to enter the world of work and adult living. Heightened awareness of this important transition period for young people with disabilities grew in the 1980s, with the program goal of assisting students with disabilities in obtaining education services that will enable them to lead meaningful and productive lives. One of the realities was that no one parent, teacher, or counselor can adequately provide the necessary assistance. It will require a team effort provided by all parties involved in the interest of the students.

In the 1990s educational and social reform movements escalated attention to this age-group population of students who have special needs (Halpern, 1992). Schools now are responsible for generating Individual Transition Plans (ITPs) to assess students' career interests and help them focus on career possibilities. Community support is given through vocational transition liaisons, job coaching, work-awareness classes, and school employment.

Without concerted team effort, students with disabilities do not make successful transition to adult life. More than 50 percent remain unemployed or under-employed. Students, parents, teachers, guidance counselors, and other support personnel need to contribute to development of the ITP. In order for the transition process to be successful, all parties and agencies are required to work together systematically to plan for it (Clark & Knowlton, 1988; Rusch & Menchetti, 1988). Collaborative consultation has been helpful in providing this support (Sileo, Rude, & Luckner, 1988). This topic will appear again in Chapter 10 on linking with external agencies.

Summary of School Reform Movements

By sharing their responsibilities for students with special learning needs, all educators can contribute not only to remediation of problems, but to prevention of problems as well. Special educators are contributing members of the general education community, and should work for integration of special education and general education (Lilly, 1987). In the meantime, however, people are not waiting for special educators to come and save them (Conoley, 1985). School doors open each morning, bells ring, students congregate, and classes begin. In those classes many students have special learning and behavior needs. Up to one-third of all school-age children can be described as experiencing difficulty in school, and when the significant learning needs of gifted students are included, this figure increases substantially. As many as 10 percent of the students enrolled in public schools are eligible for special education services, while another 10 to 20 percent have mild to moderate learning problems that interfere with their school progress (Idol, West, & Lloyd, 1988; Will, 1986).

A Brief History of School Consultation

School consultation probably originated in mental health and management fields (Reynolds & Birch, 1988). Friend (1988) cites the work of Caplan (1970) in training staff members to counsel troubled adolescents in Israel at the close of World War II. Building upon Caplan's work, mental health services escalated and moved into school settings, where consultation services of school psychologists generated promising results. Gallessich (1974) and Pryzwansky (1974) discuss the role of consultation in school psychology as it was broadened to encourage collaborative relationships. Such relationships were nurtured to help teachers, administrators, and parents deal with future problems as well as immediate situations.

School Consultation before 1970

Gallessich (1973) notes that a professional dialogue emerged during the 1950s which stimulated the development of strategies for implementing consultative services in schools. By the mid-1960s the term *school consultation* was listed in *Psychological Abstracts* (Friend, 1988). School counselors began to promote the concept of proactive service, so that by the early 1970s consultation was being recommended as an integral part of contemporary counseling service. This interest in collaborative relationships on the part of counselors and psychologists reflected a desire to influence those individuals, groups, and systems that most profoundly affect students (Brown, Wyne, Blackburn, & Powell, 1979).

Examples of consulting in the areas of speech and language therapy, and in hearing-impaired and visually-impaired programs, date from the late 1950s. Emphasis on teacher consultation for learning disabled and behavior-disordered students surfaces in the literature as early as the mid-1960s. At that time consultants for the most part were not special educators, but clinical psychologists and psychiatric social workers.

The behavioral movement, which was gaining momentum in the late 1960s and early 1970s, fueled interest in alternative models for intervention, and efficient use of time and other resources. This interest sparked development of a text by Tharp and Wetzel (1969) in which they presented a triadic consultation model using behavioral principles in school settings. This triadic model is the basic pattern upon which many subsequent models and methods for consultation were constructed.

By 1970 the special education literature contained references to a method of training consulting teachers to serve handicapped students at the elementary level (McKenzie, Egner, Knight, Perelman, Schneider, and Garvin, 1970). The Vermont Consulting Teacher Model, using a consulting teacher to serve students with mental handicaps, was put into place in 1970 (Haight, 1984).

School Consultation after 1970

The decade of the 1970s was a very busy time in the field of special education. Intensive special education advocacy, federal policy-making for exceptional students, and technological advancements affected special education practices for handicapped students (Nazzaro, 1977). By the mid-1970s consultation was being regarded as a significant factor in serving students with special needs. Special education became a major catalyst for promoting consultation and collaboration in schools (Friend, 1988).

Haight (1984) cites several sources for learning more about special education teacher consultation as it has occurred since 1970: Chandler (1980); Coleman, Eggleston, Collins, Holloway, & Rider (1975); Evans (1980); Knight, Meyers, Paolucci-Whitcomb, Hasazi, & Nevin (1981); McKenzie et al. (1970); McLoughlin & Kass (1978); Miller & Sabatino (1978); Neel (1981); and Nelson & Stevens (1981). Much of this literature on consultation focuses upon indirect service to students by consultants who worked with consultees, direct service by resource consulting teachers, and various combinations of direct and indirect service.

By the mid-1980s consultation was becoming one of the most significant educational trends for serving students with special needs. To investigate this trend, a questionnaire was sent by West and Brown (1987) to directors of special education in the fifty states. Thirty-five state directors responded. Twenty-six of the respondents stated that service-delivery models in their states include consultation as an expected role of the special educator. These states reported a total of ten different professional titles for consultation as a job responsibility of special educators. About three-fourths of the respondents acknowledged the need for service-delivery models that include consultation. However, only seven stated that specific consultation competency requirements are included in their policies.

As interest in school consultation escalated in the 1980s, the National Task Force on Collaborative School Consultation, sponsored by the Teacher Education Division of the Council for Exceptional Children, sent a publication to state departments of education with recommendations for teacher consultation services in a special education services continuum (Heron & Kimball, 1988). Guidelines were presented for: Development of consultative assistance options; definition of a consulting teacher role with pupil–teacher ratio recommended; and in personnel development requirements in preservice, in-service, and certification preparation programs. The report included a list of education professionals skilled in school consultation and a list of publications featuring school consultation.

By 1990 a new journal focusing on school consultation, *Journal of Educational and Psychological Consultation,* appeared in the literature. A preconvention workshop sponsored by the Teacher Education Division (TED) of the Council for Exceptional Children (CEC) on school consultation and collaboration programs and practices was a featured event at the 1990 annual CEC conference in Toronto.

Discussion of consultation practices in the field of education for gifted students has been minimal, although this promises to be one of the most viable fields for extensive use of collaborative consultation. Dettmer (1989), Dettmer and Lane (1989), and Idol-Maestas and Celentano (1986) recommend consultation practices to assist with learning needs of gifted and talented students. Dyck and Dettmer (1989) suggest methods for facilitating learning programs of gifted/ learning disabled students within a consulting teacher plan.

All in all, social movements and schools reforms of the 1980s and early 1990s fueled the interest in school consultation, collaboration, and teamwork that had begun in the 1960s and 1970s. The result has been an increasing number of journals, periodicals, studies, pilot programs, federal and state grants, training projects, as well as a number of teacher-preparation programs, for the application of consultation and collaboration practices in schools.

Theoretical Bases of School Consultation

Is school consultation a theory-based practice or an atheoretical practice related to a problem-solving knowledge base? Differing points of view exist in regard to this issue. A decade ago West and Idol (1987) proposed that school consultation can be regarded as theory-based if it is identified across more than one literature source focusing upon the relationship between consultant and consultee. On the other hand, if the topic is identified by problem-solving methods, then it should be regarded as knowledge-based in the area of problem-solving. They suggested ten models of consultation exist, of which six have clearly identifiable theory or theories. The six include mental health, behavioral, process, advocacy, and two types of organizational consultation. West and Idol further noted that a seventh model, the collaborative consultation model, has the essential elements for building theory because it contains a set of generic principles required for building collaborative relationships between consultants and consultees.

Research Bases of School Consultation

During the 1980s many analyses and discussions of school consultation were forthcoming. By the time of the 1987 Austin Symposium on school consultation, Heron and Kimball

(1988) noted that the emerging research base in school consultation addressed several areas:

Theory and models (West & Idol, 1987);

Methodology (Gresham & Kendell, 1987);

Training and practice (Friend, 1984; Idol & West, 1987);

Professional preferences for consultation service (Babcock & Pryzwansky, 1983; Medway & Forman, 1980);

Guidelines (Salend & Salend, 1984);

Competencies for consultations (West & Cannon, 1988).

Gresham and Kendell (1987) described most consultation research as descriptive, which is useful for identifying key variables in consultation processes and outcomes, but not for determining interactions between variables or directions of influence upon the outcomes of consultation. They stressed that consultation research must assess the integrity of consultation plans, since many plans are not being implemented by consultees as designed (Witt & Elliott, 1985). Fuchs, Fuchs, Dulan, Roberts, and Fernstrom (1992) shared the views of Pryzwansky (1986) that many studies on consultation are poorly conceptualized and executed. Conducting the research well requires careful planning, attention to detail, interpersonal skills, flexibility, positive relationships with school personnel, and research skills (Fuchs et al.)

West and Idol (1987) pointed out that efforts to conduct research in the complex, multidimensional field of school consultation are impeded by lack of psychometrically reliable and valid instrumentation and controls. Requirements for control during research studies violate the need for flexible responses during the delivery of consultation services. In addition, research should be designed to move beyond studies for simply justifying consultation roles, and focus upon determining the efficacy of consultation and collaboration in practice.

Gresham and Kendell (1987) found little empirical evidence to show that what people are calling consultation actually *is* consultation. They urged researchers to define the research variables more explicitly, control them more carefully, and measure them more accurately. Pryzwansky and Noblit (1990) recommended qualitative research using a case-study approach to maximize the observations and experiences of the consultant. Witt (1990) purported that research on collaboration is a dead end unless it can be shown that collaboration is related to important student outcomes.

One more recent and promising format for effective research studies is collaborative action research (Calhoun, 1993). Participants build collegiality and learn to manage the group process. The process has the potential to improve the organization as a problem-solving entity. Not only teachers and students, but parents and the general community become involved in collecting and interpreting data and selecting options for action (*School Team Innovator,* April 1994). Clearly, collaborative school consultation will be more widely utilized when solid research substantiates its benefits to students and positive ripple effects for education.

Structure for School Consultation

Overlapping philosophies of consultation have evolved out of a blending of consultation knowledge and practices from several fields. This overlap creates a tangle of philosophy and terminology which is problematic for educators endeavoring to develop viable school consultation structure. It is time to sort out and refine the myriad consultation terms, theories, research findings, and practices into structures that are useful and well received in the school setting.

Semantics

When focusing upon complex educational issues and school concepts, it is tempting for educators to slip into "educationese" (convoluted and redundant phrases), "jargon" (in-house expressions that approximate educational slang), and "alphabet soup" (acronyms that seem like uncracked codes to lay people). In order for theories and applications for school consultation to become an accepted, integral part of school programs, it is advantageous to draw upon semantics, the study of meanings, as a way of crystallizing concepts.

Semantics is a helpful tool with which to begin simplifying and sorting out the tangle of concepts. Meanings of words vary from user to user and from context to context. This semantic principle is obvious in regard to abstract words such as education, and democracy, and society, but more elusive when deciding on the meaning of a word as simple as *chair* (Sondel, 1958). For example, chair to a dentist might mean an appliance that is used at work. To a college professor it might mean a coveted position, while to a convicted murder it might portend death (Sondel, 1958).

> Words make the trip through the nervous system of a human being before they can be referred outward to the real thing—chair, or whatever it is. Don't assume that everyone responds to your words in precisely the same way you do. Make the context in which you use the words clear, and do this through the use of words that refer to specific things (Sondel, 1958, p. 55).

We will use the tool of semantics to organize the existing maze of philosophy and terminology about consultation in a number of fields into six basic elements for structuring viable methods of school consultation.

Structural Elements

Consultation terms and procedures involve components of six elements—system, perspective, approach, prototype, mode, and model. (See Figure 2.2.) These six elements are defined in this book as:

> *System*—the unity of many parts serving common purpose
> *Perspective*—a particular viewpoint
> *Approach*—a preliminary step toward a purpose
> *Prototype*—a pattern

Mode—a form or manner of doing

Model—an example

Characteristics of these six elements can be drawn to create a workable school consultation method for each local context and learning situation.

For brevity and graphic clarity, we designate the six elements by the uppercase form of their first letters—for example, System = S. (When two elements begin with identical letters, another prominent letter in the word is used.) Thus the six categories are designated as S (system), P (perspective), A (approach), R (prototype), E (mode), and M (model). A good method of school consultation attends to elements from each of the six categories, but is designed specifically for the school context in which it will be implemented.

Systems

The first structural element to be discussed is system. The word *system* (S) is a powerhouse of semantic utility. System means a complex unity composed of many diverse parts which serve a common purpose. The most natural system within which to conduct school consultation and collaboration is, obviously, the school. However, educators are involved not only in the academic or cognitive aspect of student development, but also in physical, emotional, social, and life-orientation aspects. Educators include not only teachers, but parents, related services and support personnel, other caregivers, and the community in general.

Systems (S) in which educators function to serve special needs of students include: Home and family, community, medical and dental professions, mental health, social work,

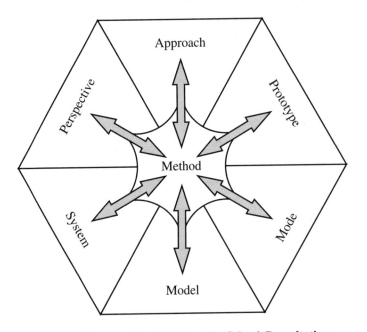

FIGURE 2.2   Structure for Collaborative School Consultation

counseling, extracurricular, and advocacy and support groups. Other systems with which consultants and collaborators might be involved from time to time in addressing very specialized needs are: Therapy, industry, technology, mass communications, cultural enrichment, and special interest areas such as talent development.

Perspectives

A *perspective* (P) is an aspect or object of thought from a particular viewpoint. Consultation perspectives that have evolved in education and related fields include:

> Purchase
> Doctor-patient
> Process

These categories have sometimes been referred to as approaches, and at other times as models. However, in order to organize the terminology, we will differentiate them here as perspectives.

Purchase.   A *purchase* perspective is one in which the consumer shops for a needed or wanted item. The consumer, in this case the consultee, "buys" services that will help that consultee serve the client's need. For example, the teacher of a developmentally delayed student might ask personnel at the instructional media center for a list of low-vocabulary, high-interest reading material with which to help the student have immediate success in reading. The purchase perspective makes several assumptions (Neel, 1981): (1) That the consultee describes the need precisely; (2) the consultant is in the right "store" to get something for that need; (3) the consultant has enough "inventory" (strategies and resources) to fill the request; and (4) the consultee can assume the costs of time, energy, or modification of classroom procedures.

As a consumer the consultee is free to accept or reject the strategy or resource, using it enthusiastically, putting off trying it, or ignoring it as a "bad buy." Even if the strategy is effective for that case, the consultee may need to go again to the consultant for similar needs of other clients. Many things have to go right in order for this perspective to work, so the consultee must think through the consequences of the purchase technique (Schein, 1969). Little change can be expected in consultee skill as a result of such consumer-type interaction. Thus the overall costs are high, and the benefits are limited to specific situations.

Doctor-Patient.   This perspective casts the consultant in the role of diagnostician and prescriptor. The consultee knows there is a problem, but is not in a position to correct it. Consultees are responsible for revealing helpful information to the consultant. Again, this perspective makes several assumptions: (1) The consultee describes the problem to the consultant accurately and completely; (2) the consultant can explain the diagnosis clearly and convince the consultee of its worth; (3) the diagnosis is not premature; and (4) the prescribed remedy is not *iatrogenic* (a term from the medical profession that describes professionals' actions which turn out to be more debilitating than the illness they were designed to treat). An iatrogenic effect from educational services would create more problems for student, educators, or school context than the initial condition did. For example, an iatrogenic effect created by teachers who have gifted students leave classrooms to attend gifted program activities could be resentment and antagonism felt toward them by their peers and perhaps even by adults.

A classroom teacher might use a doctor-patient perspective by calling on a special education teacher and describing the student's learning or behavior problem. The consultant's role would be to observe, review existing data, perhaps talk to other specialists, and make diagnostic and prescriptive decisions. As in the medical field, there is generally little follow-up activity on the consultant's part with the doctor-patient perspective, and the consultee does not always follow through with conscientious attention to the consultant's recommendations.

Process.   In a *process* perspective, the consultant helps the client perceive, understand, and act upon the problem (Neel, 1981; Schein, 1969). Consultative service does not replace the consultee's direct service to the client. In contrast to the purchase and doctor-patient perspectives, the consultant neither diagnoses nor prescribes a solution. As Neel puts it, the consultee becomes the consultant's client for that particular problem.

Schein (1978) sorts process consultation into two types—a catalyst type in which the consultant does not know a solution but is skilled toward helping the consultee figure out one, and the facilitator type where the consultant contributes ideas toward the solution. In both catalyst and facilitator types of process consultation, the consultant helps the consultee clarify the problem and develop solutions. Skills and resources used to solve the immediate problem might be used later for other problems. Assumptions are: (1) The consultee can diagnose the problem; (2) the consultant is able to develop a helping relationship; (3) the consultant can provide new and challenging alternatives for the consultee (who is the consultant's immediate client) to consider; and (4) decision-making about the alternatives will remain the responsibility and privilege of the consultee. In the process perspective for consultation, the consultee who needs help with a student or school situation collaborates with a consultant to identify the problem, explore possible alternatives, and develop a plan of action. The consultee then implements the plan.

All three of these perspectives—purchase, doctor-patient, and process—have strengths; therefore, each is likely to be employed at one time or another in schools (Vasa, 1982). One factor influencing the adoption of a particular perspective is the nature of the problem (West, 1985). For example, in a non-crisis situation the consultee may value the collaborative approach. However, all three have limitations as well. In crisis situations the consultee may need a quick solution, even if temporary, for the problem. In such cases the purchase or doctor-patient perspectives would be preferred. Situations that immediately affect the physical and psychological well-being of students and school personnel require immediate attention and cannot wait for process consultation. However, when process consultation is employed regularly, many of the skills and resources that are developed for solving a particular problem can be used again and again in situations involving similar problems. This makes process consultation both time-efficient and cost-effective for schools.

Approaches

An *approach* (A) is a preliminary step toward a purpose. School consultation approaches may be formal or informal. Formal consultations occur in planned meetings such as staffings, conferences for developing Individual Education Plans (IEPs), arranged meetings between school personnel, and organized staff development activities. They also include scheduled conferences with parents, related services personnel, and community resource personnel.

In contrast, informal consultations often occur "on the run." These interactions have been called "vertical consultations" because people tend to engage in them while standing on playgrounds, in parking lots, at ball games, even in grocery stores. They are dubbed "one-legged consultations" when they occur in hallways with a leg propped against the wall (McDonald, 1989; Hall & Hord, 1987). Conversations also take place frequently in the teacher workroom. This aspect will be addressed more fully in Chapter 11 as a form of informal staff development. It is very important to designate these informal interactions as consultations because they do require expenditures of time and energy on the part of both consultant(s) and consultee(s). Highlighting them as consultations will help establish the concept of school consultation and promote efforts toward constructing a suitable framework for the support of consultation and collaboration. Informal consultations should be encouraged because they can initiate more planful, productive consultation and collaboration. They often become catalysts for meaningful in-service and staff-development activities. In some cases they may cultivate team efforts that would have been overlooked or neglected in the daily hustle and bustle of school life.

Prototypes

A *prototype* (R) is a pattern. Consulting prototypes include mental health consultation, behavioral consultation, advocacy consultation, and process consultation.

Mental Health.   This prototype has a long history (Conoley & Conoley, 1988). The concept originated in the 1960s with the work of psychiatrist Gerald Caplan. Caplan conceived of consultation as a relationship between two professional people in which responsibility for the client rests on the consultee (Hansen, Himes, & Meier, 1990). Caplan (1970) proposed that consultee difficulties in dealing with a client's problems usually are caused by any one, or all, of four interfering themes categorized as "lack-ofs":

> Lack of knowledge about the problem and its conditions;
> Lack of skill to address the problem in appropriate ways;
> Lack of self-confidence in dealing with the problem;
> Lack of professional objectivity in approaching the problem.

The consultant not only helps resolve the problem at hand, but enhances the consultee's ability to handle future situations more effectively. Caplan's most important intervention goal is to reduce the consultee's loss of professional objectivity whereby the consultee identifies subjectively with the client, or tries to fit the client into a category and assume an inevitable outcome (Conoley & Conoley, 1982). When the mental health prototype is used for consultation, consultee change may very well precede client change. Therefore, assessment of success should focus on consultee attitudes and behaviors more than on client changes

(Conoley & Conoley, 1988). School-based mental health consultation is characterized by consultant attention to teacher feelings and the meaning the teacher attaches to the student's behavior (Slesser, Fine, & Tracy, 1990).

Behavioral Consultation.   This problem-solving procedure is also intended to improve the performance of both consultee and client. Behavioral consultation is characterized by clear, explicit problem-solving procedures (Slesser, Fine, & Tracy, 1990). It is based on social learning theory, so skills and knowledge contribute more to consultee success than unconscious themes such as objectivity or self-confidence (Bergan, 1977). Behavioral consultation probably is more familiar to educators and thus is more easily introduced into the school context than is mental health consultation. The consultant is required to define the problem, isolate environmental variables that support that problem, and plan interventions to reduce the problem. Conoley and Conoley (1988) regard behavioral consultation as the easiest prototype to evaluate, since problem delineation and specific goal-setting occur within the process. Evaluation results can be used to modify plans and to promote consultation services among other potential consultees. Cipani (1985) notes that behavioral consultation can fail to bring results if it focuses on problematic social behavior, such as aggression or being off-task, when that behavior emanates from poor or inadequate academic skills.

Advocacy Consultation.   Here the client is the community, not the established organization (Gallessich, 1974), with the consultant serving the "client" directly as trainer and catalyst, and indirectly as advocate (Raymond, McIntosh, & Moore, 1986). This concept is considered by some as highly political, with one group trying to overcome another for a greater share of the finite resources. Advocacy consultants stress that power, influence, and politics are the motivating influences behind human behavior (Conoley & Conoley, 1982). At some place in the consulting relationship, these consultants face the realization that facilitation of the school context goals is contrary to their values. Advocacy consultants need specific consulting skills for organizing people and publicizing events to serve special needs appropriately.

Process Consultation.   This is sometimes included as a fourth prototype, along with mental health, behavioral, and advocacy consultation. However, in this book it is treated as a perspective, not a prototype.

Modes

A *mode* (E) is a particular form or manner of doing something. Modes for school consultation can be regarded as direct consultation for the delivery of service to clients, or indirect consultation for delivery of service to consultees.

Direct.   Here the consultant works directly with a special-needs student. For example, a learning disabilities consulting teacher or a speech pathologist specialist might use a technique with the student, while a parent or classroom teacher consultee observes and assists with the technique. Direct service to students usually is carried out for students subsequent to a referral (Bergan, 1977). The consultant may conduct observations and discuss the learning or behavioral need directly with the student (Bergan, 1977; Heron & Harris, 1987). The consultant becomes an advocate, and the student has an opportunity to participate in decisions made pertinent to that need. Another example of direct service is teaching coping skills to students for their use at home or at school (Graubard, Rosenberg, & Miller, 1971; Heron & Harris, 1987).

Indirect.   This service delivery mode calls for "back-stage" involvement among consultants and consultees to serve client needs. The consultant and consultee interact and problem-solve together. In doing so the consultant provides direct service to the consultee, who then provides related direct service to the client. School consultation typically is regarded as indirect service to students through direct work with their teachers or parents (Lilly & Givens-Ogle, 1981); however, variants of service delivery are possible in particular circumstances. It is in this arena that some of the most significant changes have occurred since the enactment of Public Law 94-142, and, more recently, "the movement."

Models

Models are patterns, examples for imitation, representations in miniature, descriptions, analogies, or displays. A model is not the real thing, but an approximation of it. It functions as an example through which to study, mimic, replicate, approximate, or manipulate intricate things. Models are most useful for examining things or ideas that are too big (such as a model of the solar system) or too small (a DNA molecule) to copy. They help to understand things that cannot be replicated because they are too costly (a supersonic jet plane), too complex (the United Nations system), or too time-intensive (travel to outer space). These qualities make the model a useful structure on which to pattern complex human processes such as school consultation and collaborative interactions.

Some of the more well-known models adopted or modified for school consultation over the past 25 years are:

> The triadic model
> The Stephens/systems model
> The Resource/Consulting Teacher Program model
> The School Consultation Committee model
> The Vermont Consulting Teacher Program model
> The collaborative consultation model

Triadic Model.   The triadic model, developed by Tharp and Wetzel (1969), is a classic consultation model from which many school consultation models have evolved. It includes three roles—consultant, consultee (or mediator), and client (or target). In this most basic of the existing consultation models, services are not offered directly, but through an intermediary (Tharp, 1975). The service flows from the consultant to the target through the mediator. The consultant role is typically, although not always, performed by an educational specialist such as a learning disabilities teacher or a school psychologist. The consultee is typically, but not always, the classroom teacher. The client or target is usually the student with the learning or behavioral need. An educational need may be a disability or a talent requiring special services in order for the student to approach his or her learning potential.

When studying the triadic model, or any other consultation model, it is important to recall the discussion in Chapter 1 about school consultation roles. Roles are interchangeable among individuals, depending upon the school context and the educational need. For example, on occasion a learning disabilities consulting teacher might be a consultee who seeks information and expertise from a general classroom teacher consultant. At another time a student might be the consultant for a resource room teacher as consultee, and parents as the clients, or targets for intervention that is intended to help their child. Tharp gives the following example:

> Ms. Jones, the second-grade teacher, may serve as mediator between Brown, the psychologist, and John, the problem child. At the same time, she may be the target of her principal's training program and the consultant to her aide-mediator in the service of Susie's reading problem. The triadic model, then, describes relative position in the chain of social influence (Tharp, 1975, p. 128).

In later years Tharp elaborated upon the linear aspect of the triadic model to include influences of others on consultant, mediator, and target, and the interactions that those influences facilitate (Tharp, 1975).

Tharp identifies several advantages of the triadic model (Tharp, 1975), including the clarity it provides in delineating social roles and responsibilities, and the availability of evaluation data from two sources—mediator behavior and target behavior. However, it may not be the most effective model for every school context and each content area with the process skills and resources that are available. Advantages and concerns in using a triadic model of school consultation are included in Figure 2.3.

Stephens/systems Model.   The systems model constructed by Stephens (1977) is an extension of his directive teaching approach (Heron & Harris, 1982). It includes five phases:

> Assessment, observation, data collection;
> Specification of objectives, problem-identification;
> Planning, finding ways of resolving the problem;
> Implementation of the plan, measurement of progress;
> Evaluation, data analysis.

Baseline data are collected on target behaviors. Then interventions are planned, and additional data are collected in order to compare intervention effects. If the plan of treatment is not effective, further assessment is conducted. The consultant helps the consultee devise criterion-referenced assessments or coding devices (Heron & Harris, 1987). This helps consultees become an integral part of the program and acquire skills to use after the consultant leaves. If interventions for one behavior or learning need are effective, then other target behaviors can be selected for modification, beginning with the first step in the

FIGURE 2.3

Triadic Types of Models

Advantages	*Possible Concerns*
A way to get started with consultee	Little/no carry-over to other situations and problems
Quick and direct	Needed again for same or similar situations
Informal and simple, keeps problems in perspective	Only one other point of view expressed
Objectivity on the part of the consultant	Expert consultation skills needed by consultant
Student anonymity if needed	May not have necessary data available
Appropriate in crisis situations	Little or no follow-up
Time-efficient	Tendency to blame lack of progress on consultant
May be all that is needed	
Can lead to more intensive consultation/ collaboration	

Stephens/systems Types of Models

Advantages	*Possible Concerns*
Each step in concrete terms	Extensive paperwork
Follows familiar IEP development system	Assumes spirit of cooperation exists
Collaborative	Time-consuming
Changes easily made	Might become process-for-process sake
Formative and developmental	May seem "much ado about little"
Strong record-keeping	Assumes training in data-keeping and observation
Avoids the "expert" role	Multiple steps overwhelming to busy teachers
Has an evaluation component	Delayed results
Much accountability	
Provides whole picture of need, plan,and results	

Resource/Consulting Teaching Types of Models

Advantages	*Possible Concerns*
Provides direct and indirect service	Energy-draining
Parent involvement	Time often not available
"In-House" approach to problems	Scheduling difficult
Opportunity for student involvement	High caseloads for consulting teacher
Compatible with non-categorical/interrelated methods	Indirect service not weighted as heavily as direct
Ownership by many roles in problem-solving	Training needed in effective interaction
More closely approximates classroom setting	Delayed, or no, reinforcement for consultant
Spreads the responsibility around	Administrator support and cooperation essential
Opportunity to belong as a teacher/consultant	
Opportunity for regular contact between consultant/consultee	

(continued)

FIGURE 2.3 (Continued)

School Consultation Committee Types of Models

Advantages	*Possible Concerns*
Administrator involved	Only one day of training for special assignment
Multiple sources of input	Time-consuming
Skill gains from other teachers	Possible resentment toward specialized expertise
Familiar to those using preassessment/building team	Potential for too much power from some committee members
Time provided for professional interaction	Solution might be postponed
Many points of view	Confidentiality harder to ensure
Good for major problem-solving	Indirect, not direct service to student
Focuses on situations of the school context	Could diffuse responsibility so no one feels responsible
Involves a number of general education staff	
Can minimize problems before they get too serious	

Vermont Consulting Teacher Types of Models

Advantages	*Possible Concerns*
Active participation by parents and teachers	Time, travel, scheduling
Teachers learning from the training	Possible chain-of-command problems
New, even experimental, procedures possible	Teachers may resent "imported expert"
Student performance, not label, determining placement	Job security dependent on number of students identified
Supports mainstreaming and parent involvement requirements	Time needed for task analysis for participating role
Collaborative efforts with major institutions	Time required for personnel to reach general consensus
Different professional perspectives	Perhaps not feasible in larger states
Ongoing program evaluation	Requires specification of minimum achievement levels in certain time frame

Collaborative Types of Models

Advantages	*Possible Concerns*
Fits current reform movements	Little or no training in collaboration
Professional growth for all through shared expertise	Lack of time to interact
Many ideas generated	Working with adults not preference of some educators
Maximizes opportunity for constructive use of individual differences among adults	Requires solid administrator support
Allows administrator to assume facilitative role	Takes time to see results
Parent satisfaction	

model. Other advantages of using the systems model, as well as possible concerns to be considered, are included in Figure 2.3.

Resource/Consulting Teacher Program Model.   The Resource/Consulting Teacher Program model (R/CT) has been implemented at the University of Illinois and in both rural and large urban areas (Idol, Paolucci-Whitcomb, & Nevin, 1986). It is based on the triadic model, with numerous opportunities for interaction among teachers, students, and parents. The resource/consulting teacher offers direct service to students through tutorials or small-group instruction and indirect service to students through consultation with classroom teachers for a portion of the school day. Students who are not staffed into special education programs can be served along with exceptional students mainstreamed into general classrooms. Parents are sometimes included in the consultation.

In the R/CT model, emphasis is placed on training students in the curricula used within each mainstreamed student's general classroom (Idol-Maestas, 1983). Close cooperation and collaboration between the R/CT and the classroom teacher are required so that teacher expectations and reinforcement are the same for both resource room and regular class setting (Idol-Maestas, 1981). Advantages and concerns regarding the R/CT model are included in Figure 2.3.

School Consultation Committee Model.   McGlothlin (1981) provides an alternative approach for school consultation in the form of a School Consultation Committee model. The committee typically includes a special education teacher, a primary classroom teacher, an upper-grade classroom teacher, the building principal, and persons involved in ancillary and consultant roles. After a one-day training session conducted by an outside consultant, the committee meets as frequently as needed in order to screen referrals, assess problems and develop plans, and evaluate the results of those plans. The consultant remains available to help the committee as needed (McGlothlin, 1981).

The School Consultation Committee is a familiar approach for school personnel who have had experience on preassessment or prereferral teams. It is a meeting of the minds, where responsibilities are shared in a group effort to produce desired outcomes. Such an approach addresses learning and behavior problems in the general classroom before considering special education eligibility. Advantages and concerns for using this model are given in Figure 2.3.

Vermont Consulting Teacher Program Model.   The Vermont Consulting Teacher Program model is a collaborative effort of local school districts, the Vermont State Department of Education, and University of Vermont personnel for providing consultative services statewide to teachers who have children with disabilities in their classrooms (Heron & Harris, 1987). This model, another adaptation of the triadic model, includes four phases after student referral:

> Entry level data-collection and diagnosis;
> Specification of instructional objectives;
> Development and implementation of a plan; and
> Evaluation and follow-through.

There are three forms of instruction within the model: (1) University coursework for teachers, (2) specialized workshops as an alternative to the coursework format, and (3) consultation through working partnerships between consulting teacher and classroom teacher (Knight, Meyers, Paolucci-Whitcomb, Hasazi, & Nevin, 1981). Through the coursework teachers learn principles of measurement, behavior analysis, and instructional design. These principles then are applied to the teaching and learning processes in the classroom. A key feature is that the consulting teacher must individualize the program to meet the specific needs of the classroom teacher (Heron & Harris, 1987). Parent involvement is an integral component of the model. Advantages and concerns related to the model are listed in Figure 2.3.

Collaborative Consultation Model.   The collaborative consultation concept is a model in which the consultant and consultee are equal partners in consultation—identifying problems, planning intervention strategies, and implementing recommendations through collaboration (Idol, Paolucci-Whitcomb, & Nevin, 1986; Raymond, McIntosh, & Moore, 1986). Pryzwansky (1974) provided the basic structure of the collaborative approach by emphasizing the need for mutual consent on the part of both consultant and consultee, mutual commitment to the objectives, and shared responsibility for implementation and evaluation of the plan. The consultant, mediator, and target have reciprocally reinforcing effects on one another, which encourages more collaborative consultation at a later date (Idol-Maestas, 1983). Each collaborator, as part of the team, contributes a clearly defined portion of the effort so that all comes together to create a complete plan or solution.

Collaborative consultation can be blended with other approaches for particular contexts. One teacher in a small school with as many as six different lesson preparations and coaching a different sport each season finds a combination of the collaborative and triadic models as very time efficient. It can be conducted informally, utilizes both consultant and consultee knowledge efficiently, and has the aspect of confidentiality that is so important in a small, rural school. Again, see Figure 2.3 for advantages and concerns of this model.

Variations of Collaborative Consultation.   These include:

1. *The Adaptive Learning Environments Model (ALEM)* (Wang, 1986). This is one of the earliest of the more recent models. The goal of ALEM is to eliminate the need for pull-out programs by providing classroom alternatives that will address the learning needs of all students. Extensive collaboration between parents, teachers, administrators, and other professionals is critical for the success of ALEM.

2. *Class-within-a-Class (CWC)* (Reynaud, Pfannenstiel, & Hudson, 1987). This is an innovative delivery model that strives to reduce pull-out programs by serving learning disabled students full-time in general classes. Special education teachers go into the classrooms during instruction to collaborate and consult with the teacher and provide additional support to learning disabled students in the class.

3. *Success-for-All (SFA)* (Madden, Slavin, Karweit, & Livermon, 1989). It is a comprehensive program aimed at preschool and primary levels. Its main purpose is to prevent failure by assuring reading success during the early school years. Individual tutoring, cross-age grouping, and extensive collaboration are important features of this program.

4. *Mainstream Training Project (MTP)* (Tindal, Shinn, Waltz, & Germann, 1987). This uses in-service training for preparing classroom teachers at the secondary level to serve students who have learning difficulties. When classroom teachers have been trained in using effective teaching methods for students with learning and behavior problems, special education consultants work closely with them to monitor student progress and assist in implementation of newly learned teaching techniques.

5. *Schoolwide Enrichment Model (SEM)* (Renzulli & Reis, 1985). It is designed to provide more challenging learning experiences for gifted and talented students in the regular classroom. Classroom teachers are supported by consultation services from facilitators for gifted programs. Teachers and facilitators collaborate in providing gifted and talented students with curriculum options and alternatives such as flexible pacing, enrichment, personalized instruction, and challenging group experiences.

Synthesizing Structural Elements into Methods of Collaborative Consultation

Any plan for collaborative school consultation should take into account the school's needs by including facets from all the components that have been introduced:

S. System (school systems, other social systems)

P. Perspective (purchase, doctor-patient, process)

A. Approach (formal, informal)

R. pRototype (mental health, behavioral, advocacy)

E. modE (direct, indirect)

M. Model (triadic, Stephens/systems, Resource/Consulting Teacher Program, School Consultation Committee, Vermont Consulting Teacher Program, collaborative consultation and variant models)

The most relevant factors of these six key components can be synthesized into an appropriate method for serving special needs of student or educator as they occur. Once again, refer to Figure 2.2. Note that the Method area in the middle draws from each of the six descriptive elements to provide components for developing consultations for special needs.

Educators will recognize the need for having all six elements—systems, perspectives, approaches, prototypes, modes, and models—understood and available for potential combination into appropriate methods for serving special needs of students within every school context. *Locally developed methods* for addressing *special learning needs* are the most effective practices that educators can employ.

APPLICATION **2.1**

Reflecting on Structures

A helpful activity for thinking about complex functions is the thought problem. Thought problems, practiced by eminent scientists such as Einstein, take place in the mind, not in the laboratory or classroom. The idea is to manipulate variables and concepts mentally, "seeing" them from all angles and deferring judgment until all conceivable avenues have been explored. A thought problem is an opportunity to reflect upon something intently before presenting it for discussion and critique by others. Much of the time this type of activity precedes intricate processes such as collaborative consultation.

The following thought problem has several parts, one for each of the models described earlier. This exercise encourages you to be *very* "Einsteinian" as you reflect on school consultation, and manipulate and embellish your images of the models.

1. First, study again the brief descriptions of the models. Then select one and manipulate its components mentally to create a graphic way of illustrating a consultation method that could be useful in your school context. Einstein used trains, clocks, kites, rushing streams, and even swirling tea leaves to reflect upon phenomena and conceptualize his ideas. You may find it helpful to use computer graphics, illustrations, building blocks, toy people, or other special effects as you manipulate the elements of your ideas. Here are examples for starters:

   1. How might you picture the interactions intended for the triadic model? One enterprising consultant drew a bow, with arrow poised for flight toward a target. The bow represents the consultant, the arrow is consultee, and the bull's-eye is the problem or need. Another created a restaurant scene, with the consultant as behind-the-scenes cook, the consultee as the cook-and-server, and the client as the diner. A third person devised the heads graphic in Figure 2.4. How do you visualize an interactive graphic for a triadic type of consultation?
   2. Try visualizing the possibilities for interaction provided by the Resource/Consulting Teacher Program model. What benefits can an itinerant version of the model provide for students with special needs? (See Figure 2.5.)
   3. An illustrator might select a more linear design for illustrating components of the School Consultation Committee model. One possible interpretation is a mobile design (see Figure 2.6), and another could be a computer-type flow chart.

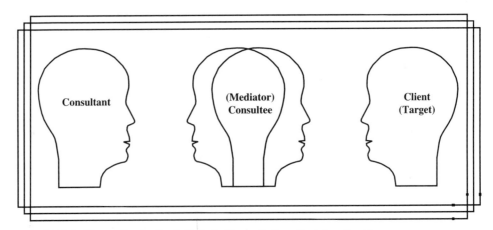

FIGURE 2.4   Example of a Basic Triadic Consultation (By Arlene Haack)

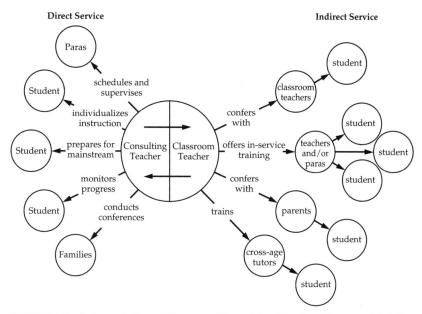

FIGURE 2.5   Interpretation of Resource/Consulting Teacher Program Model

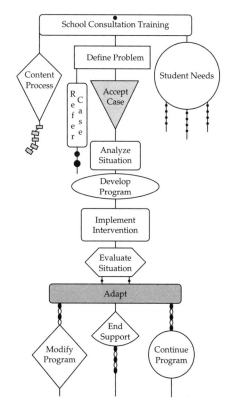

**FIGURE 2.6   Interpretation of School
Consultation Committee Interaction**

(continued)

4. Note the development of a triadic school consultation interpretation (see Figure 2.7) into a more collaborative method for consultation (see Figure 2.8). How might it look to you in your educational context?

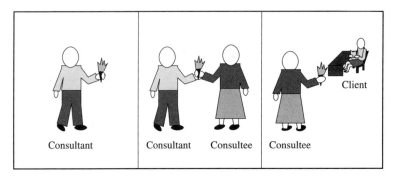

FIGURE 2.7   Interpretation of a Triadic Foundation for School Consultation (By Sharon Arnold)

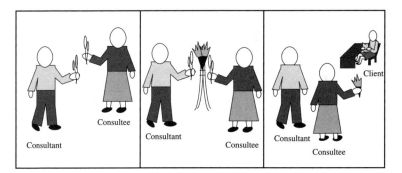

FIGURE 2.8   Interpretation of a Triadic Foundation for Collaborative School Consultation (By S. Arnold and P. Dettmer)

APPLICATION **2.2**

Formulating an Outline for a Collaborative Consultation Model

Now, after creating your model graphics, try explaining their key steps with words, either in outline or paragraph form. Then re-read the advantages and concerns section (Figure 2.3), and test your graphics to see if they point out the most important benefits and avoid the potential shortcomings of each type.

APPLICATION **2.3**

Selecting an Appropriate Method for Specific Situations

Seven potential situations for school consultation, collaboration, and/or teamwork are presented below. There are no right or wrong configurations for structuring methods to address the needs presented within these seven situations. Each should be approached by considering several points:

1. Is this a situation in which consultation and collaboration will be beneficial for the person(s) in need? (If the answer is yes, proceed to next points.)
2. Who best fits the consultant, consultee, and client roles in each?
3. How might interaction among roles be structured? What should happen first? Who will do what? When will the interaction conclude? (Do not dwell on the specific consultation process at this time. That will be addressed in Chapter 5.)
4. Consider the structural elements that will be included in the method you develop for addressing each of the situations:

   4.1 In what *system* (school, home, medical) will the consultation be conducted?
   4.2 Will the most helpful *perspective* be a purchase, a doctor-patient, or a process relationship?
   4.3 Should the *approach* be formal or informal?
   4.4 Is the most descriptive *prototype* the mental health, behavioral, process, or advocacy pattern?
   4.5 Will the consultation be provided in a direct or an indirect service delivery *mode*?
   4.6 Which *model* seems to fit the need and the other five consultation components best?

   One person doing this exercise may decide that the best way to address the identified problem is with the triadic model, using indirect service from the consultant to the client, in an informal behavioral interaction within the school system. Another person's problem may have been served most appropriately within a School Consultation Committee model, similar to preassessment teams or building teams used in some schools. To carry out this task, recall that *methods* of consultation should be designed by using facets of the six structural elements which will best meet each student's special needs.

5. What may be major obstacles in carrying out the collaborative consultation process? Major benefits? (Remember the all-important multiplier effects—those positive ripple effects that allow educators to serve a wider area of need than the immediate client.)

Situations to Use in This Application

Situation 1: A fourth-grade boy has been in the educable mentally handicapped (EMH) program since first grade. He was first diagnosed as learning disabled, but later staffed into the EMH program. The mother presented a birth history that supported the decision and seems to have accepted it. However, two older brothers living away from home insist that there is nothing wrong with their little brother. Each time the mother visits with them she becomes confused, intimidated, and frustrated. The child is becoming more resistant and passive, and is gaining weight rapidly. How should the EMH teacher address the problem?

Situation 2: The speech pathologist has been asked by the gifted program facilitator to consult with her regarding a highly gifted child who has minor speech problems, but is being pressured by parents and kindergarten teacher to "stop the baby talk." The child is becoming very nervous and at times withdraws from conversation and play. How can the speech pathologist structure consultation and collaboration?

(continued)

APPLICATION **2.3** **Continued**

Situation 3: A school psychologist is conferring with a teacher about a high-school student she has just evaluated. The student is often a behavior problem, and the psychologist is discussing methods for setting up behavior limits with appropriate contingencies and rewards. The teacher makes numerous references to the principal as a person who likes teachers to be self-sufficient and not "make waves." How should the school psychologist handle this?

Situation 4: A fifth-grade student with learning disabilities (LD) is not having success in social studies. The student has a serious reading problem, but is a good listener and stays on task. The LD resource teacher suspects that the classroom teacher is not willing to modify materials and expectations for the child. The teacher has not discussed this situation with the LD teacher, but the student has. Parent-teacher conferences are next week. What should happen here, and who will make it happen?

Situation 5: In a third-grade class a student is an average learner but is often seen in the halls walking near the wall with one hand touching the wall. He appears sad, lonely, and unsure of himself. The special education teacher of a self-contained classroom for students with behavioral disorders has heard of this child getting into fights on the bus and the playground. Today the third-grade teacher stops the special education teacher during the lunch break and says the student was crying at recess and resisting communication. He is not doing any work, but just sitting and eyeing his classmates with a look of frustration and anger. What should the special education teacher do?

Situation 6: A high-school learning disabilities consultant is visiting with a principal at the principal's request. The principal expresses concern about the quality of teaching of two faculty members and asks the consultant to observe them and then provide feedback. How should the consultant handle this situation?

Situation 7: A local pediatrician contacts the director of special education and asks her to meet with local doctors to discuss characteristics and needs of children with disabilities. How should this opportunity be structured for maximum benefit to all?

Tips for Structuring Collaborative School Consultation

1. Be knowledgeable about the history and outcomes of school reform movements.
2. Keep up to date on educational issues and concerns.
3. Be aware of education legislation and litigation.
4. Be on the alert for new methods, or revisions of existing methods through which consultation and collaboration can occur in your school context.
5. Create specific ways that teachers can get your help.
6. Read current research on school consultation and collaboration, and highlight references to these processes in other professional material you read.
7. Visit programs where models different from those in your school(s) are being used.
8. Find conference sessions that feature different models and methods, and attend them to broaden your knowledge about educational systems.

CHAPTER REVIEW

1. School reform movements which highlight the need for consultation and collaboration include the Regular Education Initiative and restructuring efforts, curriculum modifications for students with special needs, transition from preschool into school, and transition from school into the adult world.

2. An increasing number of professional educators and parents contend that students with disabilities should not be excluded from their neighborhood school programs and student peer groups. This movement, called inclusion, is another effort to define and operationalize the concept of least-restrictive environment. It is tied to broader school reform movements that have evolved over the last two decades.

3. School consultation evolved from practices in the mental health and medical services fields. The earliest uses of school consultation were in areas of speech and language therapy, and services for visually-impaired and hearing-impaired students.

4. Differing points of view exist concerning the existence of a theoretical base of school consultation. Some researchers consider school consultation theory-based if the relationship between consultant and consultee can be identified across more than one literature source.

5. Research in school consultation and collaboration has been conducted to assess situational variables, outcome variables, and organizational change. There is a need for more reliable and valid instrumentation, more specific definition of variables, and more careful control of variables during the research.

6. Structural elements to develop effective methods of school consultation can be categorized as: Systems (institutions and contexts); Perspectives (purchase, doctor-patient, problem-solving); Approaches (formal, informal); Prototypes (mental health, behavioral, advocacy); Modes (direct, indirect); and Models (see (7) below).

7. Several collaborative consultation models are: Triadic, Stephens/systems, Resource/Consulting Teacher Program, School Consultation Committee, Vermont Consulting Teacher Program, and the collaborative consultation model. Variants of the collaboration consultation model include the Adaptive Learning Environments Model (ALEM), Class-within-a-Class (CWC), Success-for-All (SFA), Mainstream Training Project (MTP), and School-wide Enrichment Model (SEM).

8. Educators should introduce into their school context a structure combining consultation, collaboration, and co-teaching that is tailored in the fashion of the system, perspective, approach, prototype, mode, and model of that specific setting.

TO DO AND THINK ABOUT

1. Using material in this chapter and Chapter 1, a dictionary, interviews, recollections from teaching experiences, discussion with colleagues or classmates, and any other pertinent references, formulate a description and philosophy about inclusive schools systems which reflects your viewpoint at this time.

2. Pinpoint several changes that have occurred in special education during the past twenty years, and suggest implications for school consultation methods.

3. Locate articles focusing on consultation, collaboration and teamwork, summarize highlights, and prepare a "fact sheet" for other school staff, including administrators.

4. Have the entire article you shared in activity 3 available for any who might ask to read the entire work.

5. Using other references and sources, make a timeline of key educational policies and reform which helped initiate interest in school consultation, collaboration, and teamwork. (An old window shade is a good material on which to make and display this kind of product.)

6. Make a list of the positive aspects, and another list of the negative aspects, in regard to the concept of inclusion. You may want to specify whether your list is indicative of inclusion for those with mild disabilities only, or full (total) inclusion for all special-needs students in regular classrooms.

7. Brainstorm with a group to list current issues and major problems in education. (See Chapter 5 for a discussion of brainstorming if you are not familiar with the technique.) After generating as many ideas as possible, mark those that seem most amenable to solutions afforded by consultation, collaboration, and teamwork. You might want to asterisk those that in the past have "belonged" to special education, and discuss what part general education plays in dealing with those issues now.

8. Using your list generated in activity 7, look for areas of teacher responsibility in which consultation and collaboration efforts might take place appropriately and helpfully for students with special needs. For example, under the managerial responsibility of ordering books and supplies, teams of teachers might collaborate to pool library money and plan orders of materials that address special needs of students for remediation and enrichment. In this way shared decision-making in selecting resources could lead to shared planning and implementation of programs that use the resources collaboratively.

9. Make sketches or three-dimensional representations of the models you visualized in the applications exercise above. Does your graphic capture the intent of the model? Does it permit analysis of the model in order to determine its advantages and cautions in a variety of school settings?

10. Visit schools where consultation and collaboration play an integral role in serving students' special needs. Using the information related to Figure 2.2, analyze the consultation systems, perspectives, approaches, prototypes, modes, and models that seem to be in use in those schools. Then summarize the results into brief, innovative descriptions of the methods that seem to have evolved from the synthesis of these components.

11. Make a bulletin board for the teacher workroom depicting models you created with the material in this chapter.

FOR FURTHER READING

(Note: The reader is advised to focus upon the key points of these recommended readings without getting tangled in the maze of philosophies and terms which, as explained in this chapter, often are not consistent across authors and consultation structures.)

Bassett, D. S., Jackson, L., Ferrell, K. A., Luckner, J., Hagerty, P. J., Bunsen, T. D., & MacIsaac, D. (1996). Multiple perspectives on inclusive education: Reflections of a university faculty. *Teacher Education and Special Education, 19*(4), 355–386.

Brown, D., Pryzwansky, W. B., & Schulte, A. C. (1991). *Psychological consultation: Introduction to theory and practice.* Boston: Allyn & Bacon. Chapters 1, 2, and 3 in particular.

Conoley, J. C., & Conoley, C. W. (1982). *School consultation: A guide to practice and training.* New York: Pergamon Press, Inc.

Educational leadership. (December 1994/January 1995), *52*(4). Topical issue on the inclusive school.

Journal of Educational and Psychological Consultation. All issues, and in particular Volume 1, Number 4, 1990, and Volume 3, Number 2, 1993.

Morsink, C. V., Thomas, C. C., & Correa, V. I. (1991). *Interactive teaming: Consultation and collaboration in special programs.* New York: Merrill. Chapter 2 in particular.

Remedial and Special Education journal. Issues focusing on school consultation and collaboration.

Scruggs, T. E., & Mastropieri, M. A. (1996). Teacher perceptions of mainstreaming/inclusion, 1958–1995: A research synthesis. *Exceptional Children, 63*(1), 59–74.

Van Tassel-Baska, Joyce. (1998). *Excellence in educating gifted and talented learners* (3rd ed.). Denver, CO: Love.

3 Diversity in Collaborative School Environments

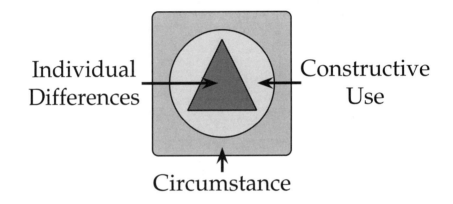

Individual Differences → ← Constructive Use

↑ Circumstance

Constructive use of individual differences is extremely important in a collaborative school environment. However, even educators who are well attuned to recognizing individual differences of students and planning for their learning needs in a variety of ways too often fail to consider the individual differences among *adults* with whom they work.

Recognizing and respecting the panoply of individual differences among adults are vital preparations for engaging in productive professional interactions. Tolerance for diverse perspectives on school-related problems and issues is one of an educator's most important assets for collaboration and team teaching. It is easy in the busy and public but relatively autonomous school setting to overlook the impact that differing professional values, teaching styles, and personal interests of colleagues have upon professional collaboration and teamwork. Unfortunately, the study of adult differences and emphasis on constructive use of those differences is, for the most part, neglected in too many teacher-preparation programs.

Focusing Questions

1. What are major differences among educators' styles and preferences that influence interactions in the school context?

2. How do these differences affect collaborative school consultation and teamwork?
3. How can educators benefit from self-study of their own preferred functions and styles?
4. What elements of diversity influence school consultation, collaboration, and teamwork?
5. In what ways might adult differences be used constructively to better serve culturally diverse groups, rural and isolated schools, and students who move often, including military dependent children?

Key Terms

chronemics	microculture	personality
cultural diversity	military dependent students	preferences
ethnic group	multiculturalism	proxemics
haptics	nonverbal behaviors	"psychopest"
kinesics	oculesics	rural
macroculture	paralanguage	

Valuing Individual Differences

A school is like a patchwork quilt, with pieces of varying color, texture, and design. If every piece were identical, the quilt would seem drab and dull. Interesting, lively patchworks are those in which each different piece contributes its brightness and uniqueness to the overall collage of colors and textures. Even if a few of the colors or textures clash individually, when aggregated into the overall patchwork design, the result is a vibrant, colorful structure that brightens its setting.

Scenario 3

(Comments overheard at various times of the school day in the teachers' workroom):

"I was eager to try that teaching strategy in our school. Why don't other people on the faculty want to give it a shot? It's been working so well with the faculty across town…"

"Here we go again. Another newfangled idea to spin us around for our latest ride on the school-reform merry-go-round…"

"Why are some people so negative toward new ideas before they even try them or give them a chance?…"

"We just never see eye-to-eye on anything in our department. It's really frustrating…"

"Seems like we do the same old thing, with people falling to line like sheep to stay together and never try new ground. I say, let's take some risks and do something different for a change…"

"I just can't figure out where that parent is coming from…"

"*Another* meeting? They drag on and on, and we have nothing to show for all the time wasted…"

"What a frantic mess that meeting was! Not enough time even to figure out what the problem is, much less arrive at some sensible solutions…"

"Wasn't that a great meeting? We're off to a good start. Now our next step should be…"

In much the same way schools are patchworks of attitudes, personalities, values, preferences, and interests. Each individual in the school setting is different, with every one contributing her or his uniqueness to invigorate the whole. Sometimes people differ markedly and even take serious issue with each other, but if the individualities of students *or* adults are ignored or repressed, the school atmosphere is lackluster and devoid of life and energy.

Adult Differences in the School Context

Much of the seemingly random variation in human behavior is actually quite orderly and consistent, because it is based on the way people prefer to use their perception and judgment (Lawrence, 1982; Keirsey & Bates, 1978). If one person views the world and reacts to it in ways unlike another, it is because that person processes information differently. Different viewpoints contribute diverse insights which help broaden understanding of problems and generate promising alternatives for problem solutions.

It is easy and convenient, but myopic, to endorse only one way of doing something—one's own—while wondering why everyone else is not clever enough and agreeable enough to concur and fall into step. However, a situation perceived one way by one educator might be looked upon quite differently by another.

APPLICATION **3.1**

Putting the Pieces Together

The leader prepares several puzzles ahead of time. Pictures of adults interacting, schoolroom pictures, or pictures of children working or playing, are effective. There should be one puzzle for each five or six people, and the size should be 8½ × 11 inches or larger. A 1-inch "frame" around each picture should be left intact, and the rest of each picture cut into a few large pieces so every participant can have two or three pieces. After dividing into groups of five or six people, one person in each group takes the frame. Every participant (including the frame-holder) takes two or three pieces of the disassembled puzzle. (The puzzle pieces should be large enough that several words can be written on them with a dark felt pen.) The group then discusses their similar and different characteristics and preferences. The person with the frame writes around that frame several characteristics *everyone* in that group shares—for example, "We are all female," or "We all *don't* have a cat." Next, each person writes on each of his or her pieces a personal characteristic that belongs to no one else in the group—for example, "Born in a taxicab en route to the hospital," or "Brussels sprouts are my favorite vegetable." Then the group assembles the puzzle and shares the information with all groups. When displayed with an interaction-focused title, the assembled and glued puzzles make effective bulletin-board displays or discussion tools. (Occasionally puzzles may be provided that are missing a piece or two. This metaphorically illustrates the "missing element" that might decrease the effectiveness of a group that has a task to complete.)

A variation of the activity is to distribute a background page and a flower center to each group for recording their things in common, and then give two or three cut-out "petals" to each person for listing his or her unique characteristics. Affix individual petals to the flower center, creating a beautiful flower garden of differences and similarities.

In order to serve students best, educators do not need to think alike—they need to think together. Thinking together divergently is not oxymoronic—it can be very productive. Understanding and valuing the uniquenesses of adults in their orientations toward the world, and their styles and preferences for processing information, are key factors in the success of collegial relationships.

Educators who make conscientious efforts to respect the individualism and independence of their students need to respect and protect these rights for their colleagues and the parents of their students as well. Madeline Hunter advised teachers to move toward dialectical thinking. This does not mean to abandon one's own position, but to build correction into one's own viewpoints by taking the opposing view momentarily. Hunter urged that all should "come out of armed camps...where we're not collaborating, so that 'I understand why you think it's right for your students to line up while I think it's better for them to come in casually'" (Hunter, 1985, p. 3). She stressed that when educators show respect for others' points of view, they model the cooperation students need for the future.

Today's students will be leaders of a shrinking global community. It is vital that educators prepare them to function successfully in diverse, multicultural societies. The most effective way of preparing students is to model such skills every day in the school setting with their colleagues. The collaborative consultation and co-teaching roles are natural and appropriate vehicles for facilitating the constructive use of individual differences among people of all ages, and collaborative school consultation can drive that vehicle. One of the most overlooked but crucial factors in teacher preparation is the ability to relate constructively to others, including colleagues, by responding to them and their preferences and needs with emotional maturity (Jersild, 1955).

Assessing Individual Preferences

During the 1970s and 1980s numerous methodologies and instruments were developed to help people understand human behavior and improve human relationships. A number of the instruments have been used in such diverse social service areas as education, counseling (for marriage and family, personal, and career needs), religion, business and industry, and others. Personality theory, cognitive style theory, and aptitude-treatment interaction (ATI) were precursors to a mushrooming interest in learning-styles paradigms (Keefe and Ferrell, 1990).

Learning styles became an everyday concept in the educational vocabulary of the 1970s and 1980s, although it has had its detractors in the 1990s. In his synthesis of learning style research, Lawrence (1984) suggests that although the term "learning styles" is loosely and variously defined, it generally includes:

- Cognitive style, in the sense of preferred or habitual patterns of mental functioning, information processing, and formation of ideas and judgment.
- Patterns of attitudes and interests which influence what a person attends to in potential learning situations.
- Disposition to seek out learning environments compatible with one's cognitive style, attitude and interest, and to avoid those that are not.
- Disposition to use certain learning tools and avoid others.

Assessment of individual differences can take place with one or more instruments among a wide range of existing tools and techniques, including Gregorc's instrument for profiling learning style (Gregorc & Ward, 1977), aptitude-treatment interaction theories relating individual differences to instructional method, Kolb cognitive-style concepts (Kolb, 1976), the McCarthy (1990) 4MAT system, the Dunn and Dunn learning-style assessment (Dunn & Dunn, 1978), and the Myers Briggs Type Indicator (Myers, 1962), to name only a few of the more prominent examples. Each of these systems has been used in a variety of contexts to increase awareness and understanding of human preferences that influence behavior. To balance the zeal of those who support each system, there are others who caution against overgeneralizing and oversimplifying complex human attributes through techniques such as self-report assessment and dichotomous interpretations—for example, concrete/abstract, morning/evening, extrovert/introvert, or impulsive/reflective comparisons. Nevertheless, Carl Jung, eminent Swiss psychologist, professed in convincing fashion that people differ in fundamental ways even though all have the same instincts driving them from within (Jung, 1923).

Personality distinguishes an individual and characterizes him or her in relationships with others. It results from inner forces acting upon and being acted upon by outer forces (Hall & Lindzey, 1978). Any one of a person's individual instincts is not more important than any one of another person's instincts. What *is* important is the person's own *preferences* for personal functioning. These individual preferences provide the "patchwork quilt" of human interaction that can be so constructive and facilitative for teamwork and group problem-solving. For example, a person who looks for action and variety, shares experiences readily, prefers to work with others, and tends to get impatient with slow, tedious jobs, is indicating preferences that are quite different from one who prefers working alone, laboring long and hard on one thing, and seeking abundant quiet time for reflection. An individual who is interested in facts, works steadily and patiently, and enjoys being realistic and practical contrasts with one who prefers to generate multiple possibilities, attends to the whole aspect of a situation, and anticipates what will be said or done.

A person who needs logical reasons, holds firmly to convictions, and contributes intellectually while trying to be fair and impartial has different type preferences from one who relates freely to most people, likes to agree with others, and cultivates enthusiasm within the group. An individual who likes to have things decided and settled, functions purposefully, and seeks to make conditions as they "should be," does not have the same type preferences as one who has a more live-and-let-live attitude, leaving things open and flexible with attitudes of adaptability and tolerance.

Every person is equipped with all the attributes and can use them as needed, but typically *prefers* to focus intensively upon one or the other at a time. Murphy (1987) explains this point by using the example of color. Just as red cannot be blue, one cannot *prefer* both polarities simultaneously. If a person prefers to apply experiences to problems, that person cannot also prefer to apply imagination to those problems. But he or she can use imagination if need be, and may benefit from practicing such skills in order to use that approach more productively.

Jung (1923) proposed that each individual has everything needed to function completely. One's least-preferred functions as well as most-preferred functions can contribute to productivity and self-satisfaction. The less-preferred functions provide balance and completeness. They are also the well-springs of enthusiasm and energy. Being an individual's most childlike and primitive functions, they can be quite constructive by creating a certain awkwardness and unrest that cultivates innovation. But people generally call upon their preferred functions when ease, comfort, and efficiency are most important.

Self-Study of Preferred Styles and Functions

Until individuals engage in self-study, they are likely to see others through the biases and distortion of their own unrecognized needs, fears, desires, anxieties, and sometimes hostile impulses (Jersild, 1955). School consultants should analyze their own values and preferences before attempting to work intensively with other people and *theirs* (Brown, Wyne, Blackburn, & Powell, 1979).

When educators do reflect, they often make comments such as these:

"I have lots of skills, but I don't seem to get them put together to do what I want."

"I am fed up with these reports that have to be done on such short notice. If data are turned in hastily and carelessly, what is their value?"

"I worked really hard on that project, and then everybody else seemed to forget that the ideas were mine when it came time to give out recognition."

"Should I state my views, or wait and see what everyone else thinks and then fall in line?"

"It seems like all I do with this faculty is put out fires."

"If I didn't show up tomorrow, I'm not sure any of my colleagues would notice or care, so long as there is a substitute teacher here to corral the kids."

Self-study can be undertaken through a variety of methods and settings, including group work, role playing, reading, conferences, and workshops. Personality, temperament, and learning-style tools such as those named earlier in this chapter are useful when discussed in in-service and staff-development sessions or in department meetings with small-group activities to highlight the rich variety inherent in human nature. Of course, no single journal article, book, conference, or training package will provide sufficient material to fully understand the sophistication and complexity of individual differences. As stated earlier, oversimplification and overgeneralization of complex constructs such as personality must be avoided. Conclusions should not become labels. Rigid interpretations must give way to open mindedness and respect. With these cautions, teachers *can* begin to deal with their colleagues more effectively and serve their students more successfully (Dettmer, 1981). As an additional incentive, it usually is lots of fun!

It is not necessary to use a formal personality assessment to explore the constructive use of individual differences. Meaningful discussions about human variability, in which care is taken to refrain from overgeneralizing and stereotyping, can allow some very general subgrouping for getting a perspective on the value of human variability in problem-solving situations. There is inherent value in keeping this process informal and non-definitive. The goals are to increase self-understanding by exploring possible differences, and broaden one's ability to respect and truly value differences in others.

The importance of self-understanding is substantiated by these comments from an educator during coursework to prepare her for the consulting-teacher role in special education:

> Having now taken the [personality instrument] two times, I have a better understanding of myself. More important, however, is that I have an increased understanding of type theory. Being a bit wary of type-casting, I was surprised to find that my type profile did not change from one administration to the next. Of course, caution must be exercised in using any instrument. With little or no understanding of the theories behind it, one easily could dismiss the instrument or misinterpret it. Even more detrimental would be using results to stereotype or place blame or make excuses. Without further study, I doubt I could determine anyone else's type. Yet being aware of different preferences is enough to foster my long-held belief that a teacher must approach the curriculum in a myriad of ways. By being sure there is "something for everyone," a teacher can make the best attempt at reaching all the students.

Self-study helps educators become more aware of their own attributes and weave their own best qualities into new combinations for helping students with diverse interests and learning needs (Dettmer, 1981). Too few teacher-preparation programs provide opportunities for this important self-exploration. Conoley (1987) was an early advocate in promoting the awareness that individual differences of collaborating adults was the key to a theory and practice of school consultation. More recently, S. Safran (1991) criticized the shortsightedness of researchers who omit factors such as personality, interpersonal affect, and "domineeringness," for example, from their research designs that focus on consultation and collaboration. Also, Salzberg and Morgan (1995) contend that an important but noticeably absent topic in their research on preparing teachers to work with paraeducators is personality variables.

Constructive Use of Adult Differences
for School Consultation

Understanding differing preferences and types is particularly helpful when one person communicates with another, or lives with another, or makes decisions that affect another's life (Myers, 1980a). Problems in human relationships are minimized when the basis of the misunderstanding is realized. In his material on *The 7 Habits of Highly Effective People,* Covey (1989) stresses that individuals must seek first to understand—*to understand and then be understood.* He advocates building skills of empathic listening that will inspire openness and trust.

Six graduate students in a university class for developing collaborative consultation skills wrote about their experience with a personality-preference indicator:

■ *Lori:* "When we split into groups in class, it was really interesting to discuss things because [with the way in which we were grouped] everybody was on the same wave length. It would be nice and comfortable if, when we collaborate, we could work with people in the same type category; however, that would make work and life dull and uninteresting. As I was skimming through descriptions of other types from mine, I noticed that there are some types I would tend to go head-to-head with—the people who have to have everything organized, or those who think their opinion is the only opinion."

■ *Donna:* "In reviewing descriptions provided by the personality instrument, I can visualize people I know and work with. This information can be valuable to me planning consultant groups. I usually gravitate toward those who are most like me. I've always thought we worked more quickly and efficiently together. I see now the importance of a diverse group of professionals in preparing the most suitable guidelines and educational plans for exceptional children."

■ *Tonya:* "A fact I found interesting is that the most effective groups are those that have a span of different preferences. The responses and outcomes of a widely spanned group are more diverse, global in perspective, and possibly even more open-minded...A teacher must be a facilitator to all students and therefore has an obligation to be flexible and ingenious with teaching methods."

■ *Janet:* "Since I have taken the personality assessment I have been more aware of different types, especially at meetings I have attended. I like to observe and study human behavior and the information I obtained is helping me to have a better insight as to why people react the way they do in different situations. It has also helped me to understand that I need to have patience and understanding for those who do not think the same way I do."

■ *May, a graduate student from Taiwan:* "The most valuable benefit I earned from this self-report inventory is that I became more understanding of myself and more aware of the difference among people. I have been thinking what kind of person I really am for a long time. Now, I discover the answers. Because of its results, I know my work habits, communication types, preferred teaching situation and interaction. More important, however, is that I have become more respectful of the differences among other people. Each person's individual preferences and values are indispensable for effective teamwork. For being a consulting teacher, to understand the team members' different preferences has become more important."

■ *Elizabeth:* "I can easily state what I gained most from the activity. It was an opening of my mind. Being human I have had a tendency to think my personality type is the best or most conducive for teaching. I have learned this session that there is not a best type for teaching. Rather, opposite types each have strengths which need to be recognized even though they are different from mine...I have always preferred to work with others whom I felt comfortable with, probably because they had a similar personality type to mine. This, I have discovered, is not necessarily the best scenario for being productive. As a whole, then, I would say what I learned was to openly accept and work with opposite types without criticism and with a realization that much success can be garnered from opposing types working together."

Data from a variety of occupational and academic groups have been used to study vocational preferences, aesthetic preferences, aptitudes, work habits, family and marriage relationships, creativity, and values. Isabel Briggs Myers (1975) liked to help married couples reconcile their different points of view by pointing out three alternatives:

You can consider that it is wrong of your partner to be different from you, and you can be indignant. That diminishes your partner and gets you nowhere. Or you can consider that it is wrong of you to be different from your partner and be depressed. That diminishes you and gets you nowhere. The proper solution is to consider that the two of you are justifiably and interestingly different, and be amused (Myers, keynote address October 16, 1975).

Differences among people in interaction styles, preferred situational outcomes, work habits, and communication styles are important for school consultants to acknowledge when they are facilitating consultations and collaborations. J. Safran (1991) contends that educators are missing an important variable in not addressing the effects of personality on consultation and collaboration, and S. Safran (1991) criticizes omission of such factors as personality, interpersonal affect, and domineeringness in professional analyses of verbal-interaction processes.

Differing Teacher Styles

Teachers often differ dramatically in their preferences. A consultant may work with one teacher who pays close attention to detail, examining every test score and asking questions about particular assignments, and another who scarcely looks at the test scores, preferring instead to solicit verbal, generalized assessment of the student's capabilities from other professionals. A study by Lawrence and DeNovellis (1974) revealed that teachers with different preferences tend to behave differently in the classroom.

Later, Carlyn (1977) studied the relationship between personality characteristics and teaching preferences of prospective teachers. Some are more interested in administrative functions, and others have a strong need for independence and creativity. Some prefer planning school programs, while others enjoy working with small groups of students. Some people like action and variety more than quiet and reflection. Some like to work with others in groups, whereas others prefer to work alone or with one person. Some people get impatient with slow jobs and complicated procedures. Others can work on one thing for a long time, and they resent interruptions. Carlyn concluded in her study that teachers of different personality-type preferences also preferred different kinds of teaching situations. These kinds of preferences and values help explain why some teachers will experiment with modifications and materials a consultant suggests, while others resist or just never seem to get around to doing it.

When educators with different type preferences collaborate, they have the opportunity to contribute a variety of strengths within the interaction. Those who like to bring up new possibilities and suggest ingenious ways of approaching problems will benefit from having other people supply pertinent facts and keep track of essential details. When some are finding flaws and holding to an existing policy, others contribute by selling the idea, conciliating, and arousing enthusiasm (Myers, 1980b).

Opposite types may or may not attract, but they definitely need to be available for greatest team productivity. Such differences can be useful, but managing them elegantly is a tremendous challenge for a consultant or consulting teacher. As stated earlier, the primary goal in consulting, collaborating, and working as a team is not to think alike, but to think together. Each person's individual preferences and values are important to the effec-

APPLICATION **3.2**
Sharing a Professional Experience

In a small group of five or six people who share your general type preferences, describe an experience from your teaching or schooling in which you put forth significant effort but ended up feeling unappreciated, unreinforced, and perhaps a bit of a failure in that instance. After all in the group have shared a personal example (with each having the privilege of passing up the opportunity if they prefer not to share), discuss ways in which members of the group reacted to each other's experience.

tiveness of interaction. Differences in schools and classrooms are not just disagreements between adult and child, or teacher and student, or administrator and teacher, or paraeducator and consulting teacher. They reflect differing orientations to the world, individual learning styles, personal values, and individual work habits. These differences, when understood and appreciated, can be constructive for serving student needs.

Using Adult Differences to Facilitate Productive Team Interaction

Good teamwork calls for the recognition and use of certain valuable differences among all members of the team (Myers, 1974; Kummerow & McAllister, 1988). The most effective teams do not agree all the time, but they use individual differences constructively (Kummerow & McAllister, 1988; Truesdell, 1983). Individuals have far more potential than they use at any one time, and the power of this potential in team settings is exponential.

Some researchers and practitioners focus on the need for collaborators to view problems from mutual perspectives and shared frames of reference using a common language (Lopez, Dalal, & Yoshida, 1993; Friend & Cook, 1990). These mindsets are without doubt important for rapport-building and initiating exploration of a problem or need. However, greatest team success will come from division of labor and efforts toward mutual respect of members' differences, from openness to the contributions of others no matter how they differ, and from facilitative communication that respects and accommodates a variety of verbal and nonverbal styles.

Needing to view matters through a shared lens, yet doing so with different eye structures, may be a conundrum but nevertheless a sensible one. As Lopez et. al (1993) note, consultants and consultees must understand how divergent points of view may predispose them to see problems in conflicting ways. This divergency is an asset in problem-solving, not a liability, when utilized by skilled collaborators. Educators can learn a great deal from talking with colleagues with whom they differ both theoretically and methodologically (Gallesich, 1973). With a common vocabulary and a framework of respect for individuality, teamwork can be much more productive.

APPLICATION   **3.3**

Adult Preferences in Using Individual Differences Constructively

Choose a favorite lesson or subject area and imagine that you and a consultee will be team-teaching this material. How would you go about this? Although it would be important to know something about your co-teacher's style and preferences, are there things you should study about *yourself* first before embarking on this collaborative endeavor? How can you share that information with your colleague, and learn comparable information about that person, in order to team co-plan and co-teach more effectively?

Adult Differences in Communication

Many communication problems among team members are due to individual differences. A statement that seems clear and reasonable to one person may sound meaningless or preposterous to another (Myers, 1974). One may want an explicit statement of the problem before considering possible solutions. Another member of the team might want at least the prospect of an interesting possibility before buckling down to facts. Yet another may demand a beginning, a logically arranged sequence of points, and an end (*especially* an end, Myers cautioned). And still another will really listen only if the discussion starts with a concern for people and the direct effects of the issue on people. Myers stressed, "It is human nature not to listen attentively if one has the impression that what is being said is going to be irrelevant or unimportant" (Myers, 1974, p. 4). Communication is such a critical part of successful consultation and collaboration that it will be the focus of concern in Chapter 6.

Adult Differences in Problem-Solving Styles

Individual differences play a significant role in the efficiency of problem-solving (Campbell & Kain, 1990). Some individuals are more accurate in problem identification, while others need less time to come up with possible solutions. One person may focus more on the problem and the facts, while another focuses on process and the meaning behind the facts. If an individual needs to solve a problem alone, he or she must manage multiple perspectives, but problem-solving by a well-mixed team of individuals enables most perspectives to be represented efficiently. The adage "Many heads are better than one" applies here. With pooled experiences, interests, and abilities, synergy results.

No specific preference is predictive of success in communication or problem-solving within the group, and research shows that teams with a complete representation of types outperform virtually any single-type or similar-type team (Blaylock, 1983). The likelihood of having such team versatility is better than might be expected, for a single group of several individuals will contain many, if not most, of the preferences.

APPLICATION **3.4**

Preferred Recognition and Reward

In Application 3.2 you shared an experience with colleagues who have similar styles and preferences. This time, form groups of five or six who have differing styles. Discuss ways in which you would like to be recognized, and perhaps rewarded, reinforced, or even praised, for something you did that required effort and skill. Then talk over with the group the variations in outcomes that different individuals prefer. How might this affect a work context such as the school and the teaching profession? How could you provide reinforcement to people who have different preferences from yours?

Using Knowledge of Adult Differences Wisely

The phrase "A little knowledge is a dangerous thing" should be heeded when addressing the issue of knowledge about individual differences. Just as teachers have learned to be discriminating in applying learning-styles methodology to the classroom, so should consultants apply principles of type theory judiciously.

The following points summarize cautions along with possibilities for using knowledge about adult *or* student differences constructively:

1. Consultants can work from a knowledge of personality-assessment or learning-style concepts without knowing the formal profiles of individuals in that group; in fact, they probably *should* do so. This premise will be more fully developed by the next several points.

2. It is not always possible, necessary, or even desirable to ascertain people's preferences with a standardized instrument. The most important need is to develop the attitude that human differences are not behaviors intended to irritate and alienate each other. Rather, they are systematic, orderly, consistent, often unavoidable differences in the way people prefer to use their perception and judgment.

3. Each set of preferences is valuable, and at times indispensable, in every field.

4. Well-researched personality or temperament theory does not promulgate the labeling of individuals. Learning-styles theory and right-left brain function research have fallen victim on occasion to unwarranted use of labels—"He's so right-brained, that he can't..." and "She's a concrete sequential, so she won't..." The world probably does not need any more labels for individuals, and this is particularly cogent in the field of special education. Such labels often contain hierarchical connotations (IQ tests, entrance exams); negative connotations ("stuck up" or "flaky"); derogatory overtones ("operates in the fast lane"); and trendy associations ("horoscope reader") (*The Type Reporter, No. 37,* pp. 1–2). Consultants must take care to avoid such connotations, as well as phrases containing absolutes ("always…never…") and stereotyping through humor, anecdotes, excuses, and job division based on type (Lawrence, 1988).

5. Problems in human relationship caused by the conflict between opposite types can be lessened when the basis of the conflict is understood.

6. As the saying goes, "The map is not the territory." Type preferences never tell all there is to know about the rich and abundant variety of individuals that make up the human population of the world.

7. Any individual can reserve the right to change, experiment, or surprise another by being "out of character." Some of the most adamant resistance to type theory has come from those who regard type descriptions as stereotyping. Most people do not want to be regarded as completely predictable and unoriginal (*The Type Reporter No. 37*, p. 2). People resent the "psychopest" who professes to know all about them and gives unsolicited interpretations (Luft, 1984).

8. Even among people with the same type preference, no two will function the same. It is like a garment of apparel—no two people look the same in it (*The Type Reporter No. 37*). It is inappropriate and unjust to assume too much from analysis of individual differences. No generalization should be applied to a single case, for any case could be an anomaly. As an example, Hammer (1985) stresses that a book (*Moby Dick,* for example) can be read in different ways by different people. One reader may have an eye toward the narrative as a thrilling sea adventure, while another may appreciate the symbolism of the whale's whiteness. The danger is in *assuming* what pleases others and how it pleases, to the point of denying opportunities for other experiences. Teachers who assume that "her type does not like to read," may stop offering her books. A teacher who believes that a student will not enjoy a particular kind of learning experience may be denying the student necessary opportunities to develop (Hammer, 1985). These lessons were learned "the hard way" in uses and misuses of learning-styles theory by others before us and should not have to be relearned.

9. Preferences should not be used to make decisions during hiring, voting, or similar selection processes. The appropriate use is to explain a job or a role requirement to an applicant in terms of what it entails, and allow the applicant to determine whether or not he or she feels it is a goodness-of-fit (*The Type Reporter, No. 37*).

10. All good teaching methods have value for some students at certain times and in particular places. By the same token, each method will be received differently by each student (Murphy, 1987a). (Recall the analogy of the garment mentioned above.)

11. Valuing individual differences will require more than merely tolerating them. It means accepting the fact that people *are* different and that the world is the better for the diversity (Murphy, 1987a).

12. Teacher-preparation programs must be more enterprising and effective in preparing graduates to have a superlative ability for understanding individual differences among educator-colleagues as well as students.

13. Much more research is needed on the constructive use of individual differences, especially in the area of school consultation, collaboration, and working in professional teams.

APPLICATION **3.5**

Using Educator Differences in the School Context

Discuss, and if possible, try out these suggestions for making the most of adult differences among school personnel.

1. Visit other teachers' classrooms, labs, shops, or fields to observe methods of presentation, physical arrangements, and management techniques.
2. Have an in-service to make teachers aware of individual differences. Use one of the more popular learning styles/preferences instruments.
3. While working on curriculum-revision or textbook-analysis teams, take time to discuss individual differences that affect individual recommendations and team decisions.
4. Before team-teaching, discuss similarities and differences in styles and preferences with the teaching partner.
5. Make a collage of school staff and faculty depicting favorite pastimes, or most fun vacations, or pets, or most-liked foods, or any other interesting attribute. Display it in a prominent place so all—including students and family members—can enjoy and learn about the constructive differences among adults within the school.

Educators with Disabilities

The teaching ranks undoubtedly include individuals with disabilities—physical, learning, perhaps behavioral—but this is not a well-researched area. Adults with a physical disability, such as missing limb, hearing or visual impairment, or disfigurement, occasionally prepare for a career in the teaching profession. Children can be quite blunt (as seventh graders queried a former war veteran, now teacher, who has a prosthesis for the right arm, "Where'd you get that thing?") and also remarkably accepting as they receive their paper with the prosthesis or shake "hands" with their teacher.

Teachers who have learning problems with memory, spelling, or comprehension can model tenacity toward achievement and share learning strategies that have helped them be successful. They can inspire children with anecdotes about how hard it was to succeed in college, but with goals and good habits to push them forward, they succeeded in obtaining degrees and a teacher license. Adults who have overcome eating disorders, obsessive-compulsive disorders, or who have completed drug- and alcohol-abuse programs also have much to offer children and youth as they model coping, resilience, and a conquering spirit.

According to an article printed in 1997 in *The New York Times,* six to nine million adults have ADHD, or attention deficit with hyperactivity disorder (*Manhattan Mercury,* 1997, September 2), and some of these millions surely are in the education profession. Meanwhile teachers despair over helping their own ADHD students succeed in school. However, many adults with ADHD tend to excel in crises and have learned adaptive strategies for dealing with paperwork and details. One former salesman said he could not keep an accurate count of his merchandise, so he left that job and found fulfillment working in a restaurant and teaching reading "to the disabled."

The incidence of disability among school personnel, analysis of their abilities to handle the conditions, and impact this has on schools and students are topics about which much more information is needed. School collaboration is an arena in which these topics may be openly discussed, or they may linger below the surface, adversely affecting the quality of communication and problem-solving. The latter effect would be an example of an interfering theme (Caplan, 1970), identified in Chapter 2 as a lack of objectivity, in which there might be theme interference in helping students with their special needs.

Effects of Diversity on School Consultation and Collaboration

After generations of being hailed as a cultural melting pot, the United States began to be regarded more descriptively as a "salad bowl." In a salad bowl each component has its own flavor and piquancy which contributes significantly to the whole. More recently a mosaic metaphor has emerged for describing the United States in the 1990s. Each socioeconomic, racial, ethnic, religious, age, and gender group contributes a facet to society, while shared values and institutions of the whole provide the frame and glue. The mosaic concept taken a bit further would be a tapestry. Threads of all texture, hue, and length are woven into a colorful, interesting fabric; one with knots, occasional raveling and fraying, but every thread having its purpose and significance in the design.

Melting pot, salad bowl, mosaic, and tapestry metaphors for cultures underscore key ideas that have enhanced multicultural sensitivity in this country over the past two hundred years or so. (Developing illustrative metaphors for such topics in education will be addressed in Chapter 12.)

As Hallahan and Kauffman propose (1991):

- Cultural diversity is to be valued just as the varied colors, sizes, textures contribute to the whole.
- Common cultural values hold our society together as the framework synergizes pieces into a connected, meaningful whole.

So, what is culture then? Webster's Dictionary (1976) puts it this way:

Culture is the body of customary beliefs, social forms, and material traits constituting a distinct complex of tradition of a racial, religious, or social group.

It is helpful to think of culture as made up of six major elements (Banks, 1988; Hallahan & Kauffman, 1991):

1. Values and behavioral styles
2. Languages and dialects
3. Nonverbal communication
4. Awareness of one's cultural distinctiveness
5. Frames of reference, or normative world views and perspectives
6. Identification, or feeling a part of the cultural group

These six elements comprise a nation's culture (the macroculture), while smaller cultures (the microcultures) provide unique variations of them (Banks & Banks, 1989; Hallahan & Kauffman, 1991). It is constructive to define culture broadly, because demographic variables (age, gender, residence), status variables (social, educational, economic), and affiliations (formal, informal) all contribute.

Demographers project that by the year 2056, over 50 percent of the U.S. population will be persons of color (Howey & Zimpher, 1991). The number of students from diverse cultures is expected to grow to 24 million, or 37 percent, of the school-age population by the year 2010 ("Making Assessments of Diverse Students Meaningful," 1997, October). It is essential for educators to become acquainted with cultures of families and students with whom they work. Unfortunately many gain only minimal knowledge, primarily through exposure to multicultural materials that "offer a smattering of stereotypical elements of cultures" (Correa & Tulbert, 1993, p. 255.) As one example, Correa and Weismantel (1991) point out that typical Hispanic families find the process of collaborative partnership to be unfamiliar and uncomfortable. Thus the responsibility for constructing and maintaining the partnership falls on school personnel.

The teaching force does not symbolize cultural diversity. About 16 percent of students in the United States are African American, but only 10 percent of teachers are, and that figure is declining. About 9 percent of students are Hispanic, but fewer than 2 percent of teachers are. In urban populations, one in three youth are persons of color and poor, with multiple learning disabilities. Only one in three teacher-education graduates will serve in those schools. Attrition among the least-experienced teachers is increasing alarmingly, particularly those of color. Profiles of prospective teachers continue to be primarily white females from small towns or suburban communities who go to colleges or universities not far from home and intend to return to places similar to home for their teaching career. They reflect middle-class backgrounds and values and have limited travel experience in which to become acquainted with diverse cultures. Fewer than 3 percent can teach in a language other than English.

Different regions of the country are becoming more unlike in very important ways, and a policy or practice which benefits one region may be questionable, objectionable, or unworkable in another (Hodgkinson, 1985). Educational systems will be called upon more and more during the next several decades to serve new pluralities, and to do so effectively. The old concepts about cultural affiliations no longer suffice.

Assessing Multicultural Awareness of Educators for Special Needs Students

Multiculturalism in the 1990s resonates throughout all areas of society. In education the mandates of multiculturalism are to:

> Increase knowledge about cultural diversity;
>
> Foster positive attitudes toward cultural pluralism; and
>
> Cultivate skills in arranging multiple learning environments that enable individuals from every culture to develop their potential.

Hallahan and Kauffman (1991) stress that educators must become comfortable with their own microcultural identification. Only after they have assessed their own attitudes and values toward cultural diversity, will they be able to promote understanding and appreciation of diverse cultural groups. They must examine their attitudes about cultures different from their own, taking care to ferret out any narrow viewpoints or shallow thinking. As just one example of a teacher's shrunken perspective, an elementary-school student of American Indian heritage brought a printed program home from school with an illustration of "The Pilgrims' First Thanksgiving." The child's father wryly noted the caption under the illustration "informing" readers that the Pilgrims had served pumpkin, turkey, corn, and squash to the Indians, a feast the likes of which the Indians had never seen before (Dorris, 1979).

Sample items for assessing one's multicultural awareness are provided in Figure 3.1. The items can be used for personal reflection and self-study. Discussion and expansion of

FIGURE 3.1   Examples of Multicultural Assessment Items

A = Always; U = Usually; S = Sometimes; R = Rarely; N = Never

Personal Sensitivity

_____ 1. I realize that any individual in a group may not have the same values as others in the group.

_____ 2. I avoid words, statements, expressions, and actions that members of other culture groups could find offensive.

_____ 3. I read books and articles to increase my understanding and sensitivity about the hopes, strengths, and concerns of people from other cultures.

_____ 4. I counteract prejudicial, stereotypical thinking and talking whenever and wherever I can.

School Context Efforts

_____ 5. I include contributions of people of color as an integral part of the school curriculum.

_____ 6. I strive to nurture skills and develop values in students and colleagues that will help members of minority groups thrive in the dominant culture.

_____ 7. I know where to obtain bias-free, multicultural materials for use in my school.

_____ 8. I have evaluated the school resource materials to determine whether or not they contain fair and appropriate presentation of people of color.

Parent/Community Relations

_____ 9. I invite parents and community members from various cultural backgrounds to be classroom resources, speakers, visiting experts, or assistants.

_____ 10. I value having a school staff composed of people from different cultural backgrounds.

_____ 11. I exhibit displays showing culturally diverse people working and socializing together.

_____ 12. I advocate for schools in which all classes, including special education classes, reflect and respect diversity.

the list would provide a powerful staff development experience. This list also could be administered as part of a study module for a teacher-preparation course on consultation and collaboration, or a professional development in-service activity. Several appropriate objectives would be:

1. Acquire a knowledge of the philosophy, theory, and application of multicultural education.
2. Increase awareness of the value of cultural diversity.
3. Expand knowledge of current issues in multicultural education.
4. Acquire information about contemporary and historical cultural experiences of various ethnic groups, including their contributions to American society.
5. Recognize potential cultural biases in school functions such as student assessment, parental involvement, staff development, and consultation.
6. Increase ability to interact successfully in cross-cultural settings.
7. Accept differences in patterns of child development within and between cultures in order to form realistic student goals and objectives.
8. Demonstrate familiarity with appropriate multicultural resources, which will include people, places, and things.

Efforts to raise cultural awareness and improve the skills of educators for working with students and families of color have not caught up with the large cultural gap in many schools and communities (Preston, Greenwood, Hughes, Yuen, Thibadeau, Critchlow, & Harris, 1984). Furthermore, problems in assuring truly multicultural education are compounded by lack of people of color as special education professionals.

Responding to Cultural Diversity
in Collaborative Settings

Multicultural education as it relates to students with special needs must ensure that ethnicity is not mistaken for exceptionality (Hallahan & Kauffman, 1991). As one important example, the word "disadvantaged" should not be paired with *cultural*. A person is not disadvantaged by having an affiliation with any culture. The appropriate term is *cultural diversity*. Neither should ethnic standards for a group be held up as measures for standards of another group, an ethnic group being described by Banks (1988) as one that shares a common ancestry, culture, history, tradition, and sense of peoplehood in becoming a political- and economic-interest group. Multicultural awareness means that people can disagree without the need to regard one side as right and the other as wrong. Tyler (1979) stresses that "right ways" of conducting particular social activities in various ethnic groups can be diametrically opposed.

Cross-cultural variations have important effects on collaborative problem-solving. In their recommendations for doing fieldwork in another culture, Bogdan and Biklen (1998) provide insight that is helpful for collaborative school consultants as well. They remind us that all cultures do not share middle-class American definitions of terms. Carrying this concept further, in different cultures there are different rules about human communications and relationships. One such instance is that it is not acceptable in some cultures to share beliefs and opinions with people outside the group. Another is being quiet in the presence of authority figures. This can be disconcerting to school personnel who are trying to solicit active parent input during conferences and staffings.

Some examples of ethnically based values and behaviors that can affect group interaction are preferences regarding (Sue & Sue, 1990; Adler, 1993):

Proxemics (personal space, such as physical distance between communicants and arrangement of furniture for seating)

Kinesics (or body movement), such as body orientation, gestures, facial expression)

Chronemics (time orientation)

Oculesics (eye movement and position)

Haptics (touch)

Paralanguage (vocal cues beyond words, such as loudness, hesitations, inflections, and speed, and both verbal and nonverbal messages)

In some cultures, responding to a question in a way that shows finesse means to skirt the subject and arrive at it indirectly, while in a different culture being direct and forthright are admirable. As another example, in certain cultures public congratulation is offensive because group accomplishment is valued more than individual achievement, while in other cultures public congratulation would be an incentive to continue excelling. Variations of actions involving handshakes, head nods, eye-brow raising, and finger-pointing have widely different meanings in diverse groups.

Labeling issues may become more pronounced during multicultural collaboration. This may be caused by real or perceived feelings of superiority, prejudice, stereotyping, and unreasonable expectations (Adler, 1993). For example, the statistics showing overrepresentation of children of color in programs for mentally retarded and underrepresentation in gifted and talented programs are well known by special education personnel. A more subtle concern, however, is the lowered expectation level that educators too often have for students in minority cultures.

The socioeconomic variable that includes class, status, position, and prestige has many ramifications for teaching and learning, and may be even more pronounced in collaborative endeavors. Gender and age also affect interactions, particularly when they intersect with characteristics of some culture groups. Collaborators must monitor their own behavior for use of fair and balanced gender-specific language. For example:

- Use persons or women and men, not men or mankind.
- Use the term homemaker, not housewife.
- Avoid saying *female* doctor, *male* nurse; say simply doctor or nurse.
- Instead of saying "He adds the balances," say "The accountant adds the balances."
- Avoid man and wife, replacing it with the couple or husband and wife.
- Refrain from using terms such as the fair sex, woman's work, man-size job.

- Say "Susan is a successful executive," not "Susan is a successful lady."
- Identify someone as a supervisor rather than a foreman.

Sue and Sue (1990) provide helpful tables of generic cultural characteristics of counseling in the majority culture of the United States, and in Asian, African American, Hispanic, and American Indian cultures. For example, in the Asian culture one-way communication from the authority figure to a person is expected. Silence signifies respect, and there are well-defined, concrete patterns of interaction. The Hispanic culture offers a different time perspective, focus on the extended family, and typically a bilingual background. The African American culture is action oriented with a sense of peoplehood and importance placed on nonverbal behavior. The American Indian culture includes cooperation, not competitive individualism, and values creative and intuitive approaches, with immediate, short-range goals. Hispanic, Asian, and American Indian cultures all promote respect for elders and authority figures and not speaking until spoken to. Therefore, a consulting teacher hoping to engage the family in collaborative problem-solving may be met with silence or short phrases as a sign of respect, and may erroneously interpret this response as being negativity.

Bogdan and Biklen (1998) propose that being able-bodied and working with individuals having disability(ies) can create tension and misunderstanding. They are careful to point out that differences do not always impinge on the staff member's effectiveness, but need to be taken into account and planned for so that potential difficulties can be avoided. Some cultures throughout the world have very different perceptions of disability from those of Anglo-Americans ("CFC Today," 1997, September). In such cultures those with "disabilities" are accepted as having a place in the community, with no stigma or shame but rather a talent and uniqueness to contribute. This is challenging for educators who feel strongly about providing special services for their different needs.

Consultants will want to avoid negative words, using language instead that indicates a desire to help students expand their abilities, not to help them "get better." What is perceived as mild criticism or simply suggestion in one culture may bring about severe punishment to the child or disillusionment about the student's ability from a family of another culture.

Idioms should not be used that might be misunderstood in another language—for example, "He will work his way out of this," or "Let's put this on the back burner for now," or "We need to get her to up to speed in that," or "Students need to toe the line in her classroom," or "That's a Catch-22." Consultants should listen carefully to family members to learn more about the student and capitalize on the strengths, which is good strategy for any situation involving any student, for that matter.

Awareness of these differences, and respect for different customs within diverse cultures, can become major factors in interaction within school settings and in collaborative efforts by school personnel. Consulting teachers and collaborators must model respect for diversity and assist other school personnel in cultivating ethnic identities of students through classroom activities that range from traditional through atraditional styles. This will reduce stereotyping and accommodate diversity, much to the advantage of multicultural students with special needs (Heron & Harris, 1987). One powerful and constructive way educators can model respect is to convey intentions of learning *from* another culture, and not just learning *about* it.

A Chinese student studying special education in the United States was enrolled in a university course on school consultation and collaboration. This student wrote:

> Since I came to the United States, I have been involved in a totally different circumstance I have never confronted before…. I really observe and analyze a life with different implications and features. I was puzzled at the scene in which American students rushed in and out of the classroom each day, while in China we may have more leisure time chatting or discussing among students. Classmates in China usually stand for [sic] close friends, who take years to study, work, play, and live together. Here in America, only a few faces are familiar to me as one semester passed…I sometimes feel myself retiring, quietly friendly, sensitive, modest about my abilities. This in fact reflects some aspect of culture in our society. I was nurtured to become a "good boy"—courteous and modest. Thus I, like many other Chinese students, shun disagreements, do not force my opinions or values on others.

Involvement of Culturally Diverse Families

Professional educators will want to encourage parents of students from culturally diverse groups to become involved in their child's education to the greatest extent possible. However, Heron and Harris (1987) caution that parent-training programs must convey respect for parents' language, culture, knowledge, and any environmental constraints.

Barriers to active parent participation include work responsibilities, time conflicts, transportation problems, and child-care needs. These findings (Lynch & Stein, 1990) have been supported across all ethnic and income groups. Educators should not apply stereotypical

---

APPLICATION **3.6**

Multicultural Autographs

Find a person who fits each item below and have that person autograph your paper. Try to use a different name for each item. You may enter your own autograph once if you qualify for that item.

1. Someone who speaks Spanish.
2. Someone who has been in more countries than you have.
3. A person who owns a world atlas.
4. Someone who has eaten sushi.
5. A person who has driven on the left side of the road.
6. A person who has seen a movie in a foreign language.
7. Someone who knows the time in England right now.
8. A person who has studied French.
9. Someone who has a pen pal in another country.
10. Someone with a friend or a relative from another culture.

When you have completed your autograph page, sit down and interact with those around you, sharing descriptions of multicultural experiences you have had, and discussing places you would like to travel to and cultures about which you would like to learn more.

characteristics to all individuals from a given cultural group (Heron & Harris, 1987; Sue & Sue, 1990). Students are individuals, and different generations of families have different perspectives. Consulting teachers should seek information about culturally diverse populations from primary and contemporary sources. This includes direct information from people as well as recent publications about community values which differentiate the traditional from those that are more integrated with the context in which they occur. More will be presented about families of students with disabilities and the influence of cultural diversity in Chapter 4.

Language Needs of Students from Culturally Diverse Groups

Linguistics plays a major role in the ways parents and school personnel communicate about students (Lynch & Stein, 1990). Non-English speaking students in the schools present major new challenges in education. Consultants should consider language and culture as means to appropriate programs and not as ends (Baca & Cervantes, 1984; Heron & Harris, 1987). The cultural background of many minorities dictates different patterns of communication (Sue & Sue, 1990). School personnel will need to articulate student needs carefully so that suitable programs are designed for students from culturally diverse populations who have special needs.

There has been much emphasis in recent years on programs for bilingual education and English as a second, or perhaps even a third, language. Bilingual education is an unresolved issue, with educators not in agreement about the most effective processes. However, it does seem that bilingual programs using both English and non-English languages for instruction are more beneficial than those emphasizing only one language (Heron & Harris, 1987). English as a second language (ESL) is a program which can be offered independently or incorporated into bilingual programs.

Needs in Rural and Isolated Schools

What is *rural?* Some definitions are based on population density, others on miles from major services, and still others on the attitude of people living in the area. Perhaps more than anything else, rural is a state of mind—an "I can do it" philosophy growing out of the necessity of functioning independently without the built-in support system that is more available in urban settings (Teagarden, 1988). Rural schools in remote areas are characterized by geographic isolation, cultural isolation, too few students for some kinds of grouping, too few staff members covering too many curricular and special program areas, resistance of students to being singled out, limited resources, and most of all, distance that necessitates great amounts of personnel time spent in travel. Some special education resource personnel spend up to half of their work day on the road (Meyen & Skrtic, 1988). The consulting teacher has become a mainstay of school districts in which miles and more miles separate students who have special learning and behavior needs.

Communication is more likely to be person-to-person in rural areas, whereas it may be written or phoned in urban settings. In the rural setting teachers are highly visible and therefore more vulnerable to community pressure and criticism. Rural educators are left much to themselves to solve problems and acquire skills for their roles (Thurston & Kimsey, 1989). These qualities of rural school life create advantages for consulting teacher approaches, yet certain disadvantages for indirect service delivery. Few rural schools are fully prepared and able to meet the needs of special needs students without consultation and other indirect services. Therefore, it is necessary for consulting teachers to become intensively involved in providing learning options and alternatives for students. Consulting teachers can coordinate collaborative effort among teachers, administrators, parents, and other community members so that few resources seem like more.

In a comparative study of consultant roles and responsibilities in rural and urban areas, Thurston and Kimsey (1989) found that rural and urban teachers conduct similar consulting activities, but rural teachers have less formal recognition of their consulting roles. They seem less confident in their consulting skills than their urban counterparts. Major obstacles include:

- Too many other responsibilities
- No time
- Lack of administrative support
- Too much paperwork
- Minimal professional interaction due to sparse population (electronic communication helpful here)
- Long distances to travel and often poor roads and weather conditions for driving
- More lesson preparations and extracurricular duties
- Differentness more noticeable in small populations

In contrast, obstacles reported by consulting teachers in urban areas include too many other responsibilities, too much paperwork, and disinterested parents.

Rural-area students tend to be resourceful, open to a wide range of experiences, somewhat independent, and capable of self-direction. These pluses can be used to advantage by consultants in designing collaborative arrangements for special needs. Since students in rural areas often dislike being singled out, it is important to involve them in planning learning programs in which they are comfortable and interested.

Rural teachers do have advantages in carrying out their consulting roles. Many tend to be creative and innovative problem-solvers (perhaps paralleling the farmer/rancher who can fix most anything with improvisation and what is on hand.) In no other setting is the multiplier effect more useful than in rural areas having limited access and resources. These multiplier benefits can be maximized by playing upon the strengths of the rural community, including smaller class sizes, more frequent interaction between students and staff, greater involvement of parents in the school and its activities, and students who participate in most phases of school life.

Needs of Students Who Move Frequently

With up to one-fifth of the population in the United States on the move each year, many school-age children's educational programs are disrupted. Moving and the events leading up to and following a major move can be traumatic for anyone, and for the student with disabilities it may be particularly troublesome. Records must be forwarded, new teachers and texts and classmates assimilated, and even home conditions of sleep, meals, and schedules may be disjointed while the child is getting settled in. Walling (1990) describes several characteristics and some major effects on the family that moves. Frequently moving families tend to be younger with young, school-age children, and they are more apt to rent than own a home. However, more professional people with high incomes, and more unemployed people move than do working-class/middle-class families. Neighborhood ties are disrupted and parents are adjusting to new jobs in many cases. Single-parent families have a particularly difficult time because there is no other adult with whom to share responsibilities and repercussions of the move.

Students with special needs should be assisted by the collaborative team in handling their stress and disorientation as soon as they appear in school. Children may feel they cannot measure up to expectations in the new school. One with a disability that was accepted by peers in the former school has to begin all over again to win friends and influence adults. Belonging to a minority group (for example, a black student in a white majority classroom, or a white student in a primarily black classroom) is another factor in feeling welcome and being accepted. Limited ability with English will add yet another dimension to acclamation and academic success. Some plans that have proven successful are (Walling, 1990):

- Peer-support groups, particularly helpful when there is seasonal influx such as migrant worker employment
- Mentors (best if adult) to serve as the new student's advocate and confidant
- Parent-support groups
- Periodic orientation programs at various times of the year
- In-service programs for school personnel to focus on the needs of transient students, particularly those with disabilities, in their adjustment to the new school and neighborhood

Needs of Military Dependent Students

Military dependent children and youth, as a group whose families often move frequently, are largely overlooked as a population having special needs and who can benefit significantly from consultation services. When families move from site to site, they frequently become frustrated with the tangled web of records, referrals, screenings, and conferences. They need accurate, clear records to ease their transition from school to school. Consultants can become a lifeline by assisting busy classroom teachers with coordination and synchronization of student records, and coordination of orientation activities and conferences.

Consultants also can facilitate the integration of students into activities with their new peers. Much more could be done in the way of making military dependent and transitory students feel welcome in new environments. They could be assigned to buddies who help with orientation to the school and integration into peer groups. Selected classmates could interview the "new kid on the block," focusing on things they like to do. Teachers can plan activities in which all students participate in making a class album or collage mural, highlighting unique qualities of everyone in the class. Ethnicity could be addressed by reminding students that everyone has a cultural heritage (German, Finnish, Korean, Samoan, Irish, Nigerian, and so on). Each could research his or her own heritage, and a variety of project extensions are possible.

Curricular units and learning centers that highlight a student's travels and former experiences will be constructive for other students even as they make the military family's child feel more welcome. Their strengths can be used to remediate gaps they may have incurred from dissimilar educational programs and frequent adjustments to new situations. Furthermore, students who have traveled widely can be valuable resources for their classmates and teachers, and they should be encouraged to do so.

Practices for Promoting Multicultural Education

Educators will want to design activities that not only reduce prejudice and stereotypes, but also promote the contributions from culturally diverse groups representing minority populations in particular. Multicultural education is not an activity for the last 30 minutes of school on Friday. The principles of multicultural awareness and acceptance should be infused throughout the entire school program. Consultants can be particularly facilitative and supportive in this endeavor as they assist in assessing the instructional environment and designing effective instruction for culturally diverse groups.

The hidden curriculum is a critical area for multicultural awareness and acceptance. Informal discussions, bulletin-board displays, selections read to the class, and speakers brought into the classroom are all helpful if planned carefully. Selected teaching activities can promote an acceptance of and even a fascination with differences, as well as allowance for different opinions and points of view, and increased understanding of how people sometimes are limited by their cultural assumptions. Consulting and collaborating teachers can designate a permanent bulletin-board area for multicultural news and displays. They can work with the library/media center to provide and publicize special displays and materials. Feature stories in the school newspaper and parent newsletter, along with radio spots and inserts into the daily announcements at school, can highlight diversity and multicultural events. In and of itself, the school curriculum is an ideal vehicle for developing multicultural awareness and nurturing cultural sensitivity. Consultants must work to ensure that curriculum builds, and does not destroy, positive attitudes and understanding.

Collaborative consultants also are in a position to encourage fuller use of resources within the entire community. They might bring in successful citizens who represent culturally diverse groups to tell about their heritage, their interests, and their roles in society. They might pair these resource people with students having special needs, particularly if they have the same cultural background as the student. Since studies show that parents from some culturally diverse populations tend to be less knowledgeable about and involved in their children's education than other parents (Ramirez, 1990; Lynch & Stein, 1990), consultants will be challenged to find ways of collaborating with them to inform and involve them. (See Figure 3.2). Awareness, appreciation, and sensitivity toward individual differences and cultural diversity are vital attributes for consultants as they communicate, cooperate, and coordinate with a wide range of resource and support personnel, teachers, parents, and the students themselves.

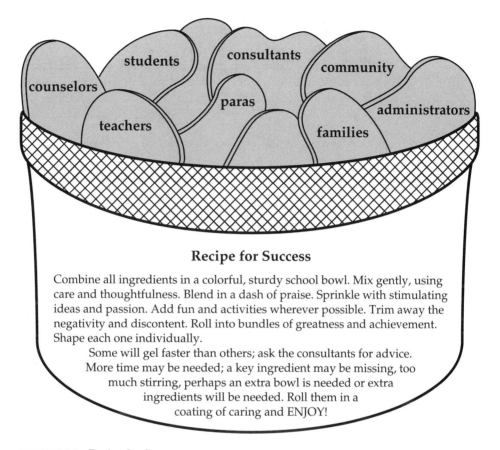

counselors

students

consultants

community

teachers

paras

administrators

families

Recipe for Success

Combine all ingredients in a colorful, sturdy school bowl. Mix gently, using care and thoughtfulness. Blend in a dash of praise. Sprinkle with stimulating ideas and passion. Add fun and activities wherever possible. Trim away the negativity and discontent. Roll into bundles of greatness and achievement. Shape each one individually.

Some will gel faster than others; ask the consultants for advice. More time may be needed; a key ingredient may be missing, too much stirring, perhaps an extra bowl is needed or extra ingredients will be needed. Roll them in a coating of caring and ENJOY!

FIGURE 3.2   Recipe for Success
—by Robin Bauer

Tips for Using Diversity in School Settings

1. Listen to the other person's point of view. Seek to understand the content of the person's ideas and the meaning it has for that person.
2. Encourage each member of a collaborative group to share knowledge and perceptions about an issue, in order to establish a solid framework in which to discuss the issue.
3. Take the time to assess preferences of consultees before deciding upon a consultation method.
4. Encourage input from as many sources as possible when deliberating upon a difficult problem, in order to take advantage of many styles, preferences, and cultural perspectives.

5. Appreciate perceptions and preferences different from one's own by engaging in a dialectical conversation. Do not feel that it is necessary to change your position, or to convert the other person to your position.

6. When students with special needs are mainstreamed, share with receiving teachers any helpful information about the students' learning styles and preferences; but, take care not to stereotype students or alter teacher expectations inappropriately.

7. Everyone is not an expert at everything. Find ways to acknowledge and use suggestions from others.

8. Respect the rights of others to hold different beliefs. While one may not agree with others, one must assume they are acting in ways they believe appropriate.

9. Really care about another person's feelings and ideas, and show it through actions.

10. Reasons exist for things that people do or say, so try to discover them.

CHAPTER REVIEW

1. Most educators are attuned to the need for responding to individual differences of their students; however, little attention has been given to individual differences among school personnel and ways in which those differences affect the school context and professional interactions.

2. Adult differences affect professional interactions in communicating, identifying problems, generating solutions to problems, evaluating performance.

3. Before educators attempt to understand the uniqueness and individuality of their colleagues, they should analyze their own preferences and individuality.

4. Problems caused by disharmony between opposite types can be lessened when the basis of the disagreement is understood. Adult differences can be used to advantage in teamwork and problem-solving. When all preference types are available through contribution of varying preferences among team members, all facets of a problem can be studied and a wide range of options generated.

5. School consultants and consulting teachers are in ideal positions to infuse multicultural education into the school context. They can facilitate greater parent involvement from culturally diverse populations, coordinate bilingual and English as second language programs, and develop awareness and sensitivity toward needs of culturally diverse groups. Their services are particularly valuable with students in rural areas, as well as with military dependent children and others who move frequently.

TO DO AND THINK ABOUT

1. Discuss ways provocative issues related to individual preferences and styles might be explored without endangering professional collegiality and school spirit.

2. Design a bulletin board that celebrates individual differences among adults. Where might you display it?

3. Interview teachers from schools having multicultural populations, asking them to suggest ways in which consultation and collaboration might help meet students' special needs. What steps should be taken to carry out these ideas?

4. Visit with colleagues or classmates about open-ended topics such as:

- What do I think is good and what is not good about being a teacher?
- What changes do I hope will take place in education in the next 10 years, and how will I need to change if they do happen?
- What are my best attributes as a teacher?
- What teaching strengths do I value in others?
- (If group members know each other well enough) What teaching strengths do I value within this group?

FOR FURTHER READING AND LISTENING

Adler, S. (1993). *Multicultural communication skills in the classroom.* Boston: Allyn & Bacon.

Bennett, C. (1999). *Comprehensive multicultural education: Theory and practice* (4th ed.). Boston: Allyn & Bacon.

Brownwood, A. W. (1987). *It takes all types!* San Anselmo, CA: Baytree.

Bruner, J. S. (1960). *The process of education.* Cambridge, MA: Harvard University Press.

Corey, M. S., & Corey, G. (1992). *Group processes and practice.* Pacific Grove, CA: Brooks/Cole.

Covey, S. R. (1989). *The 7 habits of highly effective people.* New York: Simon & Schuster, Inc. (Book or tape format)

Cushner, K., McClelland, A., & Safford, P. (1992). *Human diversity in education: An integrative approach.* New York: McGraw Hill.

Jersild, A. T. (1955). *When teachers face themselves.* New York: Teachers College Press, Columbia University.

Journal of Educational and Psychological Consultation, 4(3), several articles on consultation, collaboration, conflict resolution.

Journal of Psychological Type (formerly named *Research in Psychological Type*). All issues.

Jung, C. G. (1923). *Psychological types.* New York: Harcourt Brace.

Keirsey, D., & Bates, M. (1984). *Please understand me.* Del Mar, CA: Gnosology.

Kummerow, J. M., & McAllister, L. W. (1988). Team building with the Myers Briggs type indicator: Case studies. *Journal of Psychological Type, 15,* 26–32.

LaTorre, E. (1995). Appreciation of cultural diversity through awareness of personality types. *Delta Kappa Gamma Bulletin, 61*(2), 13–17.

Lawrence, G. (1982). *People types and tiger stripes: A practical guide to learning styles* (2nd ed.). Gainesville, FL: Center for Applications of Psychological Type, Inc.

Morsink, C. V., Thomas, C. C., & Correa, V. I. (1991). *Interactive teaming: Consultation and collaboration in special programs.* Columbus, OH: Merrill. Chapter 6 on considering cultural diversity in the interactive process; Chapter 10 on implementation with culturally diverse students.

Myers, I. B. (1980). *Gifts differing.* Palo Alto, CA: Consulting Psychologists Press.

Schmuck, R. A., & Schmuck, P. A. (1979). *Group processes in the classroom* (3rd ed.). Dubuque, IA: Wm. C. Brown.

Sue, D. W., & Sue, D. (1990). *Counseling the culturally different: Theory and practice* (2nd ed.). New York: John Wiley.

Townsend, B. L., Thomas, D. D., Witty, J. P., & Lee, R. S. (1996). Diversity and school restructuring: Creating partnerships in a world of difference. 19(2), 102–118.

Tyler, V. L. (1979). *Intercultural interacting.* Provo, UT: BYU, David M. Kennedy Center.

Walling, D. R. (1990). *Meeting the needs of transient students,* Fastback #304. Bloomington, IN: Phi Delta Kappa Educational Foundation.

4 Family-Focused Home-School Collaboration

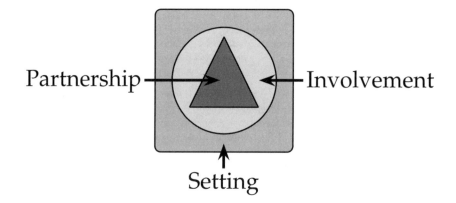

Interacting with families of students who have special needs can be one of the most rewarding aspects of an educator's work. It can also be frustrating and discouraging at times. Whether families are supportive and cooperative, or antagonistic and uncooperative, educators must include them in planning, implementing, and evaluating the student's individual educational program.

Family involvement is mandated by federal law and state policy. However, the necessity for family involvement and support is much more than just meeting a mandate. Family members are the child's first and most influential educators. Up to 87 percent of a child's waking hours from birth to age 18 are spent under the control of the home environment, leaving only 13 percent of the time to be under supervision of schools (Bevevino, 1988). The family setting is critical to a student's performance in school.

Although much of the responsibility for a child's learning has been turned over to schools in recent years, it is now time to cultivate home-school collaboration that will allow both school educators and home educators to fulfill their commitments to develop each child's potential. Home-school partnerships provide students the best opportunity for overcoming risks and handicaps and becoming all they can be in a complex, challenging world.

Focusing Questions

1. How does involvement by families in partnerships and collaboration with school personnel benefit students and their families?
2. What does family-focused collaboration require?
3. What are barriers to home-school collaboration?
4. How can educators examine their values and attitudes toward families?
5. How can educators build collaborative relationships with families?
6. How should educators initiate home-school interactions?
7. How should educators individualize parent involvement?
8. How can home-school collaboration be evaluated?

Key Terms

cultural competency	equal partnership model	home-school partnerships
efficacy	family-focused collaboration	Individual Family Service Plan (IFSP)
empowerment	home-school collaboration	parent involvement

Mandates for Family Involvement

The Education for All Handicapped Children Act of 1975 (P.L. 94-142) prescribed several rights for families of children with disabilities. Succeeding amendments have extended those rights and responsibilities. The congressional intent was clearly to assure the educational partnership of home and school, not just to provide a rubber stamp of school decisions. Legislation mandating family involvement is part of P.L. 94-142, the Handicapped Children's Protection Act, Early Intervention for Infants and Toddlers (Part H of P.L. 99-457), and the Individuals with Disabilities Education Act (IDEA, P.L. 101-476).

The passage of P.L. 94-142 in 1975 guaranteed families the right to due process, prior notice and consent, access to records, and participation in decision-making. To these basic rights the 1986 Handicapped Children's Protection Act added collection of attorney's fees for parents who prevail in due process hearings or court suits. The Early Intervention Amendment was part of the reauthorized and amended P.L. 94-142. Passed in 1986, it makes important provisions for children from birth through five years and their families. Part H addresses infants and toddlers with disabilities or who are at risk for developmental delays. Procedural safeguards for families are continued and the additional right of participation in the Individualized Family Service Plan (IFSP) is added. The IFSP is developed by a multidisciplinary team with family members as active participants. Part B, Section 691, mandates service to all children with disabilities ages three to five, and permits noncategorical services. Children may be served according to the needs of their families, permitting a wide range of services including parent training. The legislation speaks of

Scenario 4

The setting is a junior high school. The learning disabilities itinerant teacher has just arrived at the building, hoping to make some contacts with classroom teachers before classes begin, when the principal walks out of her office briskly, with a harried look.

PRINCIPAL: Oh, I'm glad you're here. I believe Barry is part of your caseload this year, right? His mother is in my office. She's crying, and says that everybody's picking on her son.

LD CONSULTANT: What happened?

PRINCIPAL: He got into an argument with his English teacher yesterday, and she sent him to me. After he cooled down and we had a talk, it was time for classes to change, so I sent him on to his next class. But he skipped out. The secretary called and left word with the babysitter to inform the mother about his absence. He must have really unloaded on her, because she's here, quite upset, and saying that the teachers do not care about her son and his problems. Could you join us for a talk?

LD CONSULTANT: O.K., sure. (Enters the principal's office and greets Barry's mother.)

MOTHER: I am just about at my wit's end. It's not been a good week at home, but we've made an effort to keep track of Barry's work. Now this problem with his English teacher has him refusing to come to school. Sometimes I feel that we're at cross purposes—us at home and you at school.

LD CONSULTANT: We certainly don't want this to happen. I'd like to hear more about your concerns, and the problems Barry and his teachers are having. Is this a good time, or may we arrange for one that is more convenient for you?

MOTHER: The sooner, the better. I don't want Barry missing school, but with the attitude he has right now, it wouldn't do him any good to be here.

LD CONSULTANT: Let's discuss some strategies we can work on. We are all concerned about Barry, and we need for him to know that.

---

families in a broad sense, not just the mother-father pair as the family unit. Families' choices are considered in all decisions.

The 1990 amendments under P.L. 101-476 increase participation in the community by children and adults with disabilities and their families. An example is the formation of community transition councils with the active participation of parents in the groups. Subsequent court decisions and statutory amendments have clarified and strengthened parent rights (Martin, 1991).

The Individuals with Disabilities Education Act (IDEA) Amendments of 1997 were signed into law in June of 1997 after two years of analysis, hearings, and discussion. This reauthorization of IDEA, as Public Law 105-17, brings many changes to P.L. 94-142. Parent participation in eligibility and placement decisions and voluntary mediation as a means of resolving parent-school controversies are two critically important areas of change. P.L. 105-17 strengthens the involvement of parents in all decision-making involving their children (National Information Center for Children and Youth with Disabilities,

1997). This legislation adds to the impetus of *Goals 2000: Educate America Act,* which has parent involvement and participation in promoting the social, emotional, and academic growth of children as one of its eight goals.

Educational Rationale for Family Involvement

A student's school, family, and community provide overlapping spheres of influence on child behavior, development, and achievement. These spheres should all be included in the collaborative team that operates with the student as the center of the model for partnerships.

Strong home-school relationships support student development and learning (Epstein, 1995; Hansen, Himes, & Meier, 1990; Reynolds & Birch, 1988). Extensive research about the effects of family involvement demonstrates that involvement with the school by a student's family members enhances the student's chances for success in school and significantly improves student achievement. Students improve in terms of both academic behavior and social behavior, with higher attendance rates and lower suspension rates. They have higher test scores, more positive attitudes toward school, and higher completion rates for homework (Christenson & Cleary, 1990).

Children are not the only beneficiaries of family involvement. Family members benefit from improved feelings of self-worth and self-satisfaction, and increased incentive to enhance the educational environment of the home (Hoover-Dempsey & Sandler, 1997; Murphy, 1981). They have the opportunity to learn skills that help with their child's needs, such as behavior management techniques and communication strategies. As parents and teachers work together, they have the opportunity to express their own wisdom. When home and school educators recognize their shared interests and responsibilities for children to work together, better programs and opportunities for students are developed.

Teachers also benefit from family involvement by learning more about their students' backgrounds. They receive support from family members who are valuable sources of information about their children's interests and needs.

School systems benefit from home-school collaboration through improved attitudes toward schools and advocacy for school programs. A positive home-school relationship helps others in the schools and the community. Family involvement increases positive communication among all who are involved on the education team and enhances school and community accountability for serving special needs (Turnbull, Turnbull, & Wheat, 1982). These points all provide strong evidence that "reaching the family is as important as reaching the child" (Rich, 1987, p. 64).

Family Empowerment

Special education laws and changes in laws require significantly new and different ways of working with families. Empowerment is the goal (Royster & McLaughlin, 1996; Turnbull & Turnbull, 1997). Staples suggests this definition of empowerment:

> An ongoing capacity of individuals and groups to act on their own behalf to achieve a greater measure of control over their lives and destinies (Staples, 1990, p. 30).

In their research with families of children in early intervention services, Thompson et al. (1997) looked at "pathways to family empowerment":

- Family-level empowerment, in management of day-to-day situations
- Service-level empowerment, in families working with the systems of professionals and agencies
- Community/political-level empowerment, in parent advocacy for improved services to all children with special needs

To maximize all levels of empowerment of families with children with special needs, educators will want to hold timely meetings with appropriate interagency attendance, help families identify and build their social-support systems, and provide models and mentors for parents to learn and adopt skills in each of the three levels.

The Research and Training Center on Family Support and Children's Mental Health uses a similar three-fold approach to empowering families of children with emotional disorders, namely empowerment of individuals with respect to their own circumstances, with respect to others, and of groups in relationship to the larger society (Koren & DeChillo, 1995).

Moving from Parent Involvement to Family-Focused Collaboration

Educational consultants and their colleagues must recognize the realities of today's families. Challenges today in working with families are very different from those faced a decade or two ago. Significant changes have taken place in society. New legislation and new demands for accountability for student outcomes coincide with the emergence of the new American family configurations. In the last decade, there has been an increase in poverty, births to unwed adolescent parents, and rise of non-biological parents as primary caretakers (foster care, grandmothers, extended family, adoptive parents). In addition, there are increasing numbers of families of cultural minority background. Families can include single parents, parents with disabilities, gay and lesbian parents, families in poverty, and extended families.

Many families are overwhelmed by family crises and life events; many face multiple and prolonged stressors such as long work hours, illness and disability, and multiple responsibilities. Many are discouraged and burned out. Multiple cultures and languages, differences in perceptions of the role and value of education, multiple stressors, and economic and educational barriers will make collaboration a challenge for many consultants and many families. Educational legislation and social reality call for recognition of all types of families in school-home collaboration for positive educational outcomes for children. This inclusiveness gives educators the opportunity and flexibility to work collaboratively with persons who may be helpful and supportive of the child's success in school.

Broadened Conceptualization of Family

Changing times and changing families require new ideas, new languages, and new models. The first step in these changes is to think in terms of *family* rather than parent. Many children do not live with both parents, or with either biological parent. Part H and Section 619 of IDEA refer to *families* rather than parents. A broad, inclusive definition of family should be used by consultants who are collaborating with adults responsible for the development and well-being of children with special needs. A new, inclusive definition of the family was suggested to the Office of Special Education and Rehabilitation Services (OSERS) by the Second Family Leadership Conference:

> A family is a group of people who are important to each other and offer each other love and support, especially in times of crisis. In order to be sensitive to the wide range of life styles, living arrangements, and cultural variations that exist today, family…can no longer be limited to just parent/child relationships. Family involvement…must reach out to include mothers, fathers, grandparents, sisters, brothers, neighbors, and other persons who have important roles in the lives of people with disabilities *(Family and Integration Resources,* 1991, page 37).

Beyond Involvement to Collaboration

It is possible for families to be involved in educational activities without being collaborative. Although the two terms—collaboration and involvement—have been used interchangeably in the literature, collaboration goes beyond involvement. Educators too often regard involvement as giving parents information, conducting parenting classes, and developing advocacy committees. However, this kind of involvement does not assure that family needs and interests are being heard and understood. It does not signify that educators are setting program goals based on family member concerns and input. It might involve parents in a narrow sense but not in *working together* to form a home-school partnership.

It is important to distinguish between parent involvement and family collaboration in this way:

- Parent involvement is parent participation in activities that are part of their children's education—for example, conferences, meetings, newsletters, tutoring, and volunteer services.
- Collaboration is the development and maintenance of positive, respectful, egalitarian relationships. It includes mutual problem-solving and shared decision-making.

James Comer (1989), at the Yale Child Study Center, reports a decline in student failure after families and community members from diverse areas of expertise contribute in the schools, and collaborate with school personnel. Comer also documents improvement in the educational achievement of parents as well as their children (Morsink, Thomas, & Correa, 1991). Family involvement *can* create possibilities for collaboration and development of relationships essential to student achievement (Christenson & Cleary, 1990).

Values for Home-School Collaboration

Collaboration with families adds a dimension to home-school relationships. Not only should family members be involved with schools, educators must be involved with families. Metaphorically speaking, a one-way street becomes a two-way boulevard to provide an easier road to "Success City" for students. Family-focused home-school collaboration is based on these principles:

- Families are a constant in children's lives and must be equal partners in all decisions affecting the child's educational program.
- Family involvement includes a wide range of family structures.
- Diversity and individual differences among people are to be valued and respected.
- All families have strengths and coping skills that can be identified and enhanced.
- Families are sources of wisdom and knowledge about their children.

Barriers to Collaboration with Families

Just about all families care about their children and want them to succeed, and are eager to obtain better information from schools. In that same vein, just about all teachers and administrators would like to involve families (Epstein, 1995). A study by Bennett, DeLuca, and Bruns (1997) reported positive teacher attitudes toward family involvement, although the young teachers in their sample were more positive than the experienced teachers. In reviewing research about family involvement, Bennett, DeLuca, and Bruns (1997) conclude that although family involvement is endorsed by educational professional organizations and is considered the best practice, it is more theory than actual practice. Epstein (1995) calls this the "rhetoric rut."

Why is home-school involvement more an ideal than a reality? Barriers to effective collaboration can be programmatic, school and consultant related, or family related. Finders and Lewis (1994) suggest that family-involvement practices too often use the deficit-approach model, that is, programs are based on the assumption that educators are the experts and family involvement is for the purpose of remediating parents and family members.

School consultants who are aware of potential barriers to home-school collaboration will be better prepared to use strategies that bridge the gap between home and school. Barriers include teacher factors, lack of organizational and cultural competence, and family historical, attitudinal, or perceptual factors. Figure 4.1 lists some possible reasons family members may not be involved with home-school collaboration.

FIGURE 4.1   Possible Reasons for Non-involvement in Home-School Collaboration

is ill	differs in linguistic/cultural practices
works and cannot leave job	lives in rural area
has little education	lives in inner city
is poor	is depressed
feels inadequate	does not trust teachers
has no transportation	does not understand disability
cannot read or write	does not have a phone
does not think school is important	is from a very young family
is not assertive	is too busy
is a single parent	fears being blamed
is burned out	comes from a different culture
has economic constraints	had own bad school experiences

Adapted from PEATC, 1991b

Cultural Competence of Educators

Culture is a key concept in family-centered services. It is critical to understand the belief systems that inform the parenting, nurturance, discipline, and other practices of families. Knowledge in cultural factors is essential to effective collaboration with the parents of students with special needs. Cross (1996) suggests that professionals learn about cultures they serve by observing healthy and strong members of the different groups. Other recommendations include spending time with people of that culture, identifying a cultural guide, reading the literature (professional as well as fiction) by and for people of the culture, attending cultural events, and asking questions in sensitive ways.

Traditional approaches to reaching out to families are not always appropriate for families from minority groups. Research has demonstrated cultural differences in the utilization of services and the stated needs of families having children with disabilities or other risk factors (Arcia, Keys, Gallagher, & Herrick, 1992; Sontag & Schacht, 1994). Educators must develop cultural competence (Cross, 1996; Lynch & Hansen, 1992; Mason, 1994; Anderson & Goldberg, 1991). Cultural competence means accepting, honoring, and respecting cultural diversity and differences. Individualizing programs for students must be done in a manner that respects a family's culture. It is important to learn from family members how their beliefs and practices will affect programs for children with special needs. Because disability is a culturally and socially constructed phenomenon, the families of culturally and linguistically diverse families may understand and perceive the differences labeled as disabilities in a different way than the school's definition. Some families may have culturally based or religiously based views of causes and treatment of disability. As noted in Chapter 3, a situation that custom considers a disability or problem in one culture may not be regarded as a disability or problem in others.

Educational consultants who work with families must be aware of the family's perceptions of disability. Linan-Thompson and Jean (1997) suggest taking time to learn about family perceptions of special needs, carefully and thoroughly explaining the whole special education process, using informal assessments in addition to formal assessment tools (which helps explain the disability on other than formal terms), and discovering and using parents' preferred forms of communication (written, informal meetings, video or audio tapes).

Historical, Attitudinal, and Perceptual Factors

The success of family collaboration activities is based on partnerships developed and maintained by using the relationship and communication skills described in Chapter 6. Parents of children with learning and behavior problems can be effective change agents for their children; therefore, the question is not whether to involve them, but how to do it (Shea & Bauer, 1985). Although family members may want very much to play a key role in encouraging their children to succeed in school, they may be inhibited by their own attitudes or circumstances. Many parents, while very concerned about their child's education, are fearful and suspicious of schools, teachers, and education in general (Hansen, Himes, & Meier, 1990). They may fear or mistrust school personnel because of their own negative experiences as students. Or they may have experienced an unfortunate history of unpleasant experiences with other professionals, so that current school personnel fall heir to that history.

Parents of children with special needs face many economic and personal hardships. Work schedules and health concerns prevent some parents from participating in school activities (Leitch & Tangri, 1988). Low-income families may have difficulty with transportation and child care, making it hard to attend meetings or to volunteer in school even when they would like to do so (Thurston & Navarrete, 1996).

The single parent, already burdened with great responsibilities, is particularly stressed in parenting a child with special needs. The role can be overwhelming at times. When working with the single parent, school personnel will need to tailor their requests for conferences and home interventions, and to provide additional emotional support when needed (Conoley, 1989).

Many types of disability are very expensive for families, and the impact on the family budget created by the special needs of a child may produce new and formidable hardships. Sometimes families arrive at a point where they feel their other children are being neglected by all the attention to the special needs child. This adds to their frustration and stress. In addition, children with special needs and their families are vulnerable to stereotypes of society about physical, learning, or behavioral disabilities. They feel the impact of their family's dependence on others for services (Schulz, 1987). The ways in which families cope with the frustrations and stress influence their interaction with school personnel. Providing support networks can help them cope with the situation (Morsink, Thomas, & Correa, 1991).

Family members may avoid school interactions because they fear being blamed as the cause of their children's problems. Sometimes teachers do blame parents for exacerbating learning and behavior problems—"I can't do anything here at school because it gets undone when they go home!" But blaming does not facilitate development of mutually supportive relationships. Family members are very sensitive to blaming words and attitudes by school personnel.

Judging attitudes, stereotypes, false expectations, and basic differences in values also act as barriers and diminish the collaborative efforts among teachers and families. It is difficult to feel comfortable with people who have very different attitudes and values. Families and teachers should make every effort not to reproach each other but to work together as partners on the child's team. Educators, including teachers and parents, must abandon any posture of blaming or criticism and move on to collaboration and problem-solving. It is important to remember that it does not matter where a "fault" lies. What matters is who steps up to address the problem.

Collaboration requires respect, trust, and cooperation. However, as noted in Chapter 3 on individual differences and as will be discussed in Chapter 6 on rapport-building, collaboration need not require total agreement. Educators cope with value differences in positive ways when they:

1. Remember that a teacher's place is on the parent's side as a team member working for a common goal—the child's success.
2. Become aware of their own feelings of defensiveness. Taking a deep breath and putting the feelings aside will help them continue building positive relationships. If that is not possible, they should postpone interactions until the defensiveness can be handled.

3. Remember that the focus must be on the needs and interests of families and their children, not on their values. It is important to attack the problem, not the person.
4. Accept people as they are and stop wishing they were different. This applies to parents as well as to their children.
5. Remember that most families are doing the best they can. Parents do not wake up in the morning and decide, "I think today I will be a poor parent."
6. Respect family rights to values and opinions. Different values do not mean better or poorer values. It is not possible to argue family members out of their values, and teachers do not have the right to do so.
7. Demonstrate the qualities of open-mindedness and flexibility.

Bridges to Successful Home-School Collaboration

Friendly, positive relationships and honest, respectful communication can help bridge the barriers in home-school collaboration. The goal of collaboration is to promote the education and development of children by strengthening and supporting families. Keeping this in mind, consultants will remember that collaboration is not the goal, but the means to the end. Strategies that have proved to be sturdy bridges to circumvent barriers are focusing on family strengths; using appropriate communication skills; and promoting positive roles for family members.

Focusing on Family Strengths

It is an unfortunate situation for collaborative consultants that the traditional emphasis in education, health, and mental health is the illness-based, or pathology-based, model of human problems (Berg, 1994; Leviton, Mueller, & Kauffman, 1992). The philosophy of family-focused services and collaboration emphasizes the empowerment approach, rather than focusing on what is going wrong. Instead of focusing on the child's or family's problem, collaborators focus on family members and the strength of their experiences. This encourages the developmental progress of the child as well as healthy reactions to problems and crises, and competent life management (Waters & Lawrence, 1993).

Using Appropriate Communication Skills

Chapter 6 describes communication skills that are important in building and maintaining collaborative relationships with adults in the lives of students with special needs. Consultants will want to use rapport-building skills to build trust and confidence in the collaborative relationship and to recognize and reduce their own language and communication barriers. Those who communicate with family members should use these guidelines:

- Be aware of voice tone and body language.
- Be honest and specific.
- Give one's point of view as information, not as the absolute truth.
- Be direct about what is wanted and expected.

- Do not monopolize the conversation.
- Listen at least as much as talk.
- Do not assume one's message is clear.
- Stay away from educational or psychological jargon.
- Attack the problem, not the person.
- Focus on positive or informational aspects of the problem.
- Have five positive contacts for every "negative" one.
- Always be honest, not soft-pedaling reality.

Promoting Positive Roles for Family Members

Family members play a range of roles from purveyor of knowledge about the child to advocacy and political action. No matter what role is undertaken by individual family members, educational consultants should remember that families are

- Partners in setting goals and finding solutions;
- The best advocates and case managers for the child with special needs;
- Individuals with initiative, strengths, and important experiences; and
- The best information resource about the child, the family, and their culture.

Within any role along the wide continuum of family members, the consultant must respect and support the courage and commitment of family members to struggle with the challenges of daily living faced by all families. Recognizing, supporting, and reinforcing interventions with and on behalf of the child with special needs will promote an increased sense of competency and help create a safe, nurturing environment for children, while maintaining the unique cultural and ethnic characteristics of their family unit (Berg, 1994; Waters and Lawrence, 1993).

Supporting and reinforcing families in their chosen roles is not always easy. Members in multi-problem families often are viewed as having defective or faulty notions of parenting, no problem-solving skills, and an array of psychopathology (Berg, 1994). Even when families have different values and expectations, and face risk factors such as poverty or drug/alcohol involvement, Waters and Lawrence (1993) recommend that professionals focus on strengths. Educational consultants can think of this as the "hero" approach, which recognizes that slaying dragons is courageous. Noting what Joseph Campbell (1990) calls the courageous and natural engagement in the battles in life journeys will help educators recognize the heroic battle instead of counting dragon heads. Figure 4.2 lists other suggestions for developing bridges to overcome barriers in collaboration.

Developing Home-School Partnerships

There is a great variation in individual practices for home-school collaboration. Effective collaboration efforts depend on attitude of teachers, their beliefs about the family role and the efficacy of family involvement, and their comfort level and communication skills. Educators may believe in family partnerships, but they may not know how to involve family members in a systematic and egalitarian manner.

FIGURE 4.2 Suggestions for Building Bridges to Successful Home-School Collaboration

- Keep in mind that the family usually has concerns and issues that have nothing to do with you personally and that you may not know about.
- Be sensitive to the language levels, vocabularies, and background of the family and adjust your language, but be yourself.
- Get enough information, but not more than you need. You don't want to appear "nosy."
- Focus discussions on factors you can control.
- Find out what has been tried before—ask advice.
- Listen so that you are completely clear about the family's concerns.
- Honor confidentiality.
- Remain open to new approaches and suggestions. Each family is different.
- Set concrete, measurable goals. Communication is clearer and measures of success are built in and promote collaboration.
- Wait until the family asks for help or until a good relationship is established before making suggestions.
- Help families solve their own problems and allow them to become, or develop the skills to become, their child's own case manager.

(Adapted from PEATC, 1991b)

Parent involvement is usually conceptualized from the parent's perspectives (Wanat, 1997). In her study with 57 parents, Wanat (1997) found that parents did not distinguish between involvement at school and at home, and they had succinct ideas about what constituted meaningful involvement. One parent in her study summarized legitimate parent involvement as "everything you do with the child because education involves a lot more than just sitting at school." It would be well for education consultants to remember this statement when they work collaboratively with parents.

The crucial issues in successful learning are not between home *or* school, and parent *or* teacher, but the relationship between each pair of variables (Seeley, 1985). When school personnel collaborate with family members, they nurture and maintain partnerships that facilitate shared efforts to promote student achievement. The more that family members become partners with teachers and related services personnel, the smoother and more consistent the delivery of instruction to the student can be (Reynolds & Birch, 1988). As families and teachers plan together and implement plans of action, they find that working as a team is more effective than working alone (Shea & Bauer, 1985). Each can be more assured that the other is doing the best for the child (Stewart, 1978).

Five Steps for Collaborating with Families

Five basic steps will assist school personnel in developing successful home-school partnerships:

Step 1: Examining one's own values
Step 2: Building collaborative relationships
Step 3: Initiating home-school interactions

Step 4: Individualizing for parents

Step 5: Evaluating home-school collaboration

Step 1: Examining One's Own Values. Value systems are individualistic and complex. They are the result of nature and the impact of experiences on nature. People need to apply information and logic to situations that present values different from their own. Kroth (1985) provides an example. He notes that a significant amount of research indicates a positive effect on children's academic and social growth when teachers use a daily or weekly report card system to communicate with parents or guardians. This information provides logical support for interaction among teachers and family members on a regular, planned basis. However, in spite of the evidence, many teachers do not use the system.

School personnel must guard against setting up a climate of unequal relationships. It is vital to recognize that parents are the experts when it comes to knowing about their children, no matter how many tests educators have administered to students, or how many hours they have observed students in the classroom. If professional educators are perceived as *the* experts, and the *only* experts, false expectations may create unrealistic pressure on them. Some family members find it difficult to relate to experts. So a beautiful "boulevard of progress" becomes a one-way street of judging, advising, and sending solutions. (Refer to communication roadblocks in Chapter 6.)

The first step in collaborating with families is to examine one's own values. Figure 4.3 is a checklist for examining values and attitudes toward parents and other family members.

Communicating messages of equality, flexibility, and a sharing attitude will facilitate effective home-school collaboration. The message that should be given to parents of students with special needs is, "I know a lot about this, and *you* know a lot about that. Let's put our information and ideas together to help the child."

The checklist in Figure 4.4 serves as a brief self-assessment to test congruency of attitudes and perceptions with the two-way family collaboration discussed earlier. Inventorying and adjusting one's own attitudes and perceptions about families are the hardest parts of consulting with them. Attitudes and perceptions about families and their roles in partnerships greatly influence implementation of the consulting process.

School personnel also must keep in mind that family members are not a homogeneous group; therefore, experiences with one family member cannot be generalized to all other parents and families. There is evidence that mothers and fathers react differently to their exceptional children (Levy-Shiff, 1986). Furthermore, parental stress seems to be related to the child's developmental age and parental coping strengths (Wikler, Wasow, & Hatfield, 1981).

Step 2: Building Collaborative Relationships. The second step in collaborating with families is building collaborative relationships. As will be emphasized in Chapter 6, basic communication and rapport-building skills are essential for establishing healthy, successful relationships with family members. To briefly set the stage, these are the most important skills for educators in interacting with families:

- Responsive listening
- Assertive responding
- Mutual problem-solving

FIGURE 4.3   Examining Own Values

Instructions: Rate belief or comfort level, from 1 (very comfortable or very strong) to 5 (very uncomfortable or not strong at all).

How comfortable do you feel with each?

____ parents or others who are overly protective

____ teachers who think they are never wrong

____ families who send their children to school without breakfast

____ teachers who get emotional at conferences

____ teachers who do not want mainstreamed students

____ open discussions at family meetings

____ parents who have lost control of their children

____ volunteers in the classroom

____ conflict

____ being invited to students' homes

____ using grades as a behavior management tool

____ family members who call every day

____ teachers who do not follow through

____ students attending conferences

____ principals attending conferences

____ parents who do not allow their children to be tested

____ different racial or ethnic groups

____ family members who do not speak English

____ others who think special needs children should be kept in self-contained classrooms

____ teachers who think modifying curriculum materials or tests is watering down the lessons

____ family members who drink excessively or use drugs

____ administrators who do not know your name

____ criticism

How strongly do you believe the following?

____ Family members should be able to call you at home.

____ Newsletters are an important communication tool.

____ Family members should volunteer in the classroom.

____ General classroom teachers can teach students with special needs.

____ All children can learn.

____ Family members should come to conferences.

____ Resistance is normal and to be expected in educational settings.

____ Children in divorced families have special problems.

____ Family resistance is often justified.

____ Teacher resistance is often justified.

____ Family influence is more important than school influence.

____ Medical treatment should never be withheld from children.

____ Children with severe disabilities are part of a supreme being's plan.

____ Sometimes consultants should just tell others the best thing to do.

____ Consultants are advocates for children.

____ Teachers should modify their classrooms for children with special needs.

____ It is a teacher's fault when children fail.

____ Consultants are experts in educating special needs children.

____ Some people do not want children with special needs to succeed.

Do you think all teachers, administrators, counselors, psychologists, parents, grandparents, social workers, and students would have responded as you did? What happens when members of the same educator team have different views?

FIGURE 4.4   Self-Assessment of Attitudes and Perceptions Concerning Families and Family Collaboration

1. I understand the importance of parent involvement.	1 2 3 4 5
2. I recognize the concerns parents may have about working with me.	1 2 3 4 5
3. I recognize that parents of students with special needs may have emotional and social needs I may not understand.	1 2 3 4 5
4. I recognize and respect the expertise of families.	1 2 3 4 5
5. I feel comfortable working with families whose values and attitudes differ from mine.	1 2 3 4 5
6. I am persistent and patient as I develop relationships with families.	1 2 3 4 5
7. I am comfortable with my skills for communicating with families.	1 2 3 4 5
8. I am realistic about the barriers for me in working with families.	1 2 3 4 5
9. I find it difficult to understand why some families have the attitudes they have.	1 2 3 4 5
10. I recognize that some family members will have problems interacting with me because of their experience with other teachers.	1 2 3 4 5

Prudent teachers avoid words and phrases that may give undesirable impressions of the children or the special needs with which they are concerned (Shea & Bauer, 1985). They listen for the messages given by parents and respond to their verbal and nonverbal cues.

In communicating with families, school personnel must avoid jargon that can be misunderstood or misinterpreted. Some professional educators seem unable, or unwilling, to use jargon-free language (Schuck, 1979). Choices of words can ease, or can inhibit, communication with parents, and professional educators must respect language variations created by differences in culture, education, occupation, age, and place of origin (Morsink, Thomas, & Correa, 1991).

Teachers and administrators often find that one of the most important but difficult aspects of developing relationships with parents is listening to them. The challenge lies in listening to parents' messages even though they might disagree strongly with family members, and their attitudes and values might differ significantly from those of the families. Although the quality of the interaction should be a primary focus in parent relationships, the numbers and variety of initiated communications are important as well. Hughes and Ruhl (1987) found that most teachers averaged fewer than five parent contacts per week, but 27 percent averaged from 11–20 parent contacts per week. Phone calls, introductory and welcoming letters, newsletters, school-to-family calendars, and notepads with identifying logos all have been used effectively by educators to initiate partnerships. Each note, phone call, conversation, or conference, whether taking place in a formal setting or on the spur of the moment at the grocery store, should reflect willingness and commitment of school personnel to work with parents as they face immense responsibilities in providing for the special needs of their child.

An effective partner-educator provides support and reinforcement for family members in their family roles. In addition to listening to family members and recognizing their expertise, it is crucial to support parents by giving them positive feedback about their efforts toward the child's education. Many parents spend more time with their children who have disabilities than with those who do not (Cantwell, Baker, & Rutter, 1979). Families often get very little reinforcement for parenting, particularly for the extra efforts they may expend in caring for children with special needs.

Too many families hear very few positive comments about their children. They may feel guilty or confused because of their children's problems. Examples of support and reinforcement that teachers use include thank-you notes for helping with field trips, VIP (Very Important Parent) buttons given to classroom volunteers, supporting phone calls when homework has been turned in, and Happygrams when a class project is completed. It is important for teachers to arrange and encourage more regular, informal contacts with parents. Family members often report being put off by the formality inherent in some scheduled conferences, particularly when they are limited to 10 minutes, as they often are, with another child's family waiting just outside (Lindle, 1989).

One innovative program is the Trans*Parent* Model (Bauch, 1989) in which teachers use a computer-based system called Compu-Call that stores messages in a computer. It directs the autodialer to place calls either to all families or to specific groups. The purpose of these calls can be to describe learning activities, explain homework assignments, or suggest ways that families can support the child's home study. Parents call any time from anywhere and get the information they need. The system enables families to help children keep up who are having problems or have an extended absence from school.

Family members often become frustrated when they do not understand the subjects their children are attempting to master. A program of Family Math encourages parents and children to work together as a team in evening sessions involving a "hands-on" approach to learning math concepts and logical thinking (Lueder, 1989). Family literacy programs that are established in some communities enable parents to help children with their school work (Nuckolls, 1991). Some schools have set up an evening computer literacy program in which families can learn together and reinforce each other as they gain skills in educational technology. Parents are not the only ones who put energy and time into such programs. The programs require a level of school personnel involvement that challenges the staff and pushes them to the limit. But the positive ripple effect of having family members play more active roles in their child's education makes the effort worthwhile.

Step 3: Initiating Home-School Interactions.
Parents, regardless of their educational background and socio-economic status, want their children to be successful in school. Even parents who are considered "hard to reach," such as non-traditional, low-income, and low status families, usually want to be more involved (Davies, 1988). Most, however, wait to be invited before becoming involved as a partner in their child's education. Unfortunately, many have to wait for years before someone opens the door and provides them the *opportunity* to become a team member with others who care about the educational and social successes of their children. Parent satisfaction with their involvement is directly related to perceived opportunities for involvement (Salisbury & Evans, 1988). They are more motivated to carry on when they are aware that the results of their time and energy are helping their child learn. School personnel who are in a position to observe these results can provide the kind of reinforcement that parents need so much.

Student Collaboration.   The student has the greatest investment and the most important involvement in a planning conference (Hogan, 1975). It seems counterproductive to engage in plan sessions for an individualized program without involving that student as a member of the team. Shea and Bauer (1985) stress several benefits from having students participate in conferences for their individualized programs:

- Awareness that parents and teachers are interested in them and working cooperatively;
- Information by teachers and family members that informs them about their progress;
- Feeling of involvement in the efforts toward personal achievement;
- A task-oriented view of improving their performance.

Shea and Bauer recommend discussing advantages of the student's participation with family members. If there are strenuous parental objections, the issue should be explored for reasons and possible impact on the student's success in school.

Equal Partnership Model.   Teachers use interviews, checklists, and more complex assessment instruments to solicit information about parent needs. If school personnel plan workshops, classes, and materials that are not based on family interests and needs, a message is communicated that educators know more about their needs than they do. Then the family involvement is not a true partnership. An example of a needs and interests assessment is included in Figure 4.5.

The equal partnership model stresses the importance of providing opportunities for family members to use their strengths, commitment, and skills to contribute as full partners to the education of their children. This relationship is not based on a deficit model of blame and inequality. Families appreciate having their special efforts recognized, just as teachers do.

Tools for assessing parent strengths are similar to those for assessing needs. Interviews and checklists are useful in determining what types of contributions families can bring to the partnership. These assets can be conceptualized along four levels of involvement (Kroth, 1985) from strengths which all family members have, to skills that only a few family members are willing and able to contribute. For example, all parents have information about their children that schools need. At more intensive levels of collaboration, some family members are willing and able to tutor their children at home, come to meetings, help make bulletin boards, and volunteer to help at school. At highest levels of collaboration, only a few parents can be expected to lobby for special education, serve on advisory boards, or conduct parent-to-parent programs. A number of parent advocates of children with learning and behavior disorders have made impressive gains in recent decades toward state and national focus on the rights of children with special needs. They have formed organizations, identified needs, encouraged legislation, spoken for improved facilities, and supported each other through crises. In many instances they have involved pediatricians, community agency leaders, and businesses in special projects for children with special needs.

By considering family member strengths as well as needs and interests, educators will be focusing on the collaborative nature of parent involvement. An example of a strengths assessment form is provided in Figure 4.6.

FIGURE 4.5   Family Needs Assessment

Families! We want to learn more about you so that we can work together helping your child learn. Please take a few minutes to respond to these questions so your voice can be heard. It will help the Home-School Advisory Team develop programs for families, teachers, and children.

Check those items you are most interested in.

____ 1. Family resource libraries or information centers
____ 2. Helping my child learn
____ 3. Support programs for my child's siblings
____ 4. Talking with my child about sex
____ 5. Helping with language and social skills
____ 6. Mental health services
____ 7. Talking with another parent about common problems
____ 8. Respite care or babysitters
____ 9. My role as a parent
____ 10. Classes about managing behavior problems
____ 11. Making my child happy
____ 12. Managing my time and resources
____ 13. Making toys and educational materials
____ 14. Reducing time spent watching television
____ 15. What happens when my child grows up
____ 16. Recreation and camps for my child
____ 17. State-wide meetings for families
____ 18. Vocational opportunities for my child
____ 19. Talking to my child's teacher
____ 20. Talking with other families
____ 21. Learning about child development
____ 22. Things families can do to support teachers
____ 23. Home activities that support school learning
____ 24. Information about the school and my child's classes
____ 25. Helping my child become more independent
____ 26. Others?

_____

_____

_____

Thanks for your help!

Name of family member responding to this form:

_____

Child's name: _____

FIGURE 4.6   Strengths Assessment for Family Members

Families! We need your help. Many of you have asked how you can help provide a high-quality educational program for your children. You have many talents, interests, and skills you can contribute to help children learn better and enjoy school more. Please let us know what you are interested in doing.

_____ 1. I would like to volunteer in school.
_____ 2. I would like to help with special events or projects.
_____ 3. I have a hobby or talent I could share with the class.
_____ 4. I would be glad to talk about travel or jobs, or interesting experiences that I have had.
_____ 5. I could teach the class how to _____.
_____ 6. I could help with bulletin boards and art projects.
_____ 7. I could read to children.
_____ 8. I would like to help my child at home.
_____ 9. I would like to tutor a child.
_____ 10. I would like to work on a buddy or parent-to-parent system with other parents whose children have problems.
_____ 11. I would like to teach a workshop.
_____ 12. I can do typing, word-processing, phoning, making materials, or preparing resources at home.
_____ 13. I would like to assist with student clubs.
_____ 14. I would like to help organize a parent group.
_____ 15. I want to help organize and plan parent partnership programs.
_____ 16. I would like to help with these kinds of activities:

At school _____

At home _____

In the community _____

Your comments, concerns, and questions are welcome. THANKS!

Name: _____

Child's Name: _____

How to Reach You: _____

Family Involvement in IEP Planning.   The Individual Education Plan (IEP) or Individual Transition Planning (ITP) conference can be a productive time or a frustrating experience. Parents may be emotional about their child's problems, and teachers might be apprehensive about meeting with the parents (Reynolds & Birch, 1988). A number of researchers have found that too little parent involvement in team decision-making, particularly related to IEP and ITP development, is a major problem in special education programs (Pfeiffer, 1980; Boone, 1989).

School consultants will improve school-home collaboration in these areas if they provide family members with information and preparation for the meeting. Consultants can communicate with family members by phone, letter, or informal interview to inform them about

- Names and roles of staff members who will attend;
- Typical procedure for such meetings;
- Ways they can prepare for the meeting;
- Contributions they are encouraged to make;
- Ways in which follow-up to the meeting will be provided.

Figure 4.7 (Dettmer, 1994) outlines ways parents can be involved in IEP, ITP, or IFSP development and implementation before, during, and after the IEP conference. The lists could be used for conferences or meetings with them.

Osborne and deOnis (1997) suggest five actions for schools to take to involve families in the education of students:

- Actively welcome families in overt ways (such as posting signs).
- Invite and support a range of involvement activities.
- Break down existing barriers such as negative school recollections.
- Educate parents and the community about school policies and procedures.
- Keep parent informed with all communication formats available.

When parents and teachers work together as equals, they have more opportunities to express their own knowledge and can come to respect each others' wisdom. Siblings need information about disabilities, opportunities to talk about their feelings, time to hear about the experiences of other siblings of children with disabilities, people with whom to share their feelings of pride and joy, and ways to plan for the future (Cramer et al., 1997).

Kay and Fitzgerald (1997) suggest parents and teachers collaborate on action research to systematically explore a problem or issue. They believe this partnership helps parents and teachers learn more about each others' perspectives and can lead to alliances that result in making improvements in programs and schools. Project DESTINY in Vermont used monthly parent-support groups, enhancing teachers' attitudes and skills at working cooperatively with parents, and involving parents in weekly planning meetings at school to empower parents of students with emotional and behavioral disabilities (Cheney, Manning, & Upham, 1997). Timberland Elementary School in Fairfax County, Virginia, used multilingual parent liaisons to build a bridge between the school and neighboring families in need (Halford, 1996). The parent liaison begins with home visits. The goal is to help families address their problems and foster an environment that is supportive of their children's learning. The Best Practice Project in Chicago (Daniels, 1996) generated genuine teacher-parent partnerships that supported learning for children and leadership development for parents and teachers. Whether collaborative efforts are ongoing communication or complex family-involvement programs, underlying all types of involvement are trusting and respecting educators.

Step 4: Individualizing for Families. Special education professionals are trained to be competent at individualizing educational programs for student needs. Nevertheless, they

FIGURE 4.7 Checklist for Families in Developing IEPs

Throughout the year:

Read about educational issues and concerns.

Learn about the structure of the local school system.

Observe your child, noting work habits, play patterns, and social interactions.

Record information regarding special interests, talents, and accomplishments, as well as areas of concern.

Before the conference:

Visit the child's school.

Discuss school life with the child.

Talk with other families who have participated in conferences to find out what goes on during the conference.

Write down questions and points you would like to address.

Review notes from any previous conferences with school staff.

Prepare a summary file of information, observations, and products that would further explain the child's needs.

Arrange to take along any other persons that you feel would be helpful in planning the child's educational program.

During the conference:

Be an active participant.

Ask questions about anything that is unclear.

Insist that educational jargon and "alphabet soup" acronyms be avoided.

Contribute information, ideas, and recommendations.

Let the school personnel know about the positive things school has provided.

Ask for a copy of the IEP if it is not offered.

Ask to have a follow-up contact time to compare notes about progress.

After the conference:

Discuss the conference proceedings with the child.

Continue to monitor the child's progress and follow up as agreed on.

Reinforce school staff for positive effects of the planned program.

Keep adding to the notebook of information.

Be active in efforts to improve schools.

Say supportive things about the schools whenever possible.

may assume that all parents have the same strengths and needs, thereby overlooking the need to individualize parent involvement programs (Schulz, 1987; Turnbull & Turnbull, 1982). By using the assessments discussed earlier, and taking care to avoid stereotypes and judgments, they will be more able to involve parents as partners instructing their child's learning program.

Christensen and Cleary (1990) confirm that successful home-school consultation includes mutual problem identification, mutual monitoring of effects of involvement, and active sharing of relevant information. Successful work with parents calls for establishing respectful and trusting relationships, as well as responding to needs of all partners. The degree to which parents are placed in an egalitarian role, with a sense of choice, empowerment, and ownership in the education process, is a crucial variable in successful collaboration (Cochran, 1987; Peterson & Cooper, 1989).

When school consultants and collaborators solicit information from parents, they should use the communication skills discussed in Chapter 6. Interviews must not seem like interrogations. The types of questions consultants ask are important in preserving respectful relationships. Inappropriate types of questions would be yes-or-no questions, "why" questions, forced-choice questions, double-binds that result in no-win responses, and questions that solicit agreement with the educator.

On the other hand, questions that are appropriate for parent interviews explore feelings and focus on the what, when, where, and how dimensions of child learning and behavior. Only questions that provide essential information and nurture the collaborative spirit should be asked. Figure 4.8 demonstrates inappropriate questions restated in a more appropriate manner.

Families from Culturally Diverse Populations.   At times the consultant's communication and collaboration skills are challenged by ethnic and cultural differences. Language and cultural differences can be barriers that must be overcome by understanding the knowledge and skills needed to provide "culturally competent" services (Cross, 1988).

FIGURE 4.8   Appropriate/Inappropriate Questions to Ask Parents

Appropriate	*Inappropriate*
I'd like to hear your thoughts on Ramona's progress.	I think Ramona is doing much better, don't you?
What problems do you have with Jim's teacher?	Why don't you like Jim's teacher?
What thoughts have you had about you and Kay talking with a counselor?	When are you and Kay going to see a counselor?
What are some strategies we can work on to make sure Sherry gets to her first hour class?	Don't you think you should curtail Sherry's late nights on weekdays?
What is the history of Lionel's hearing problems?	Didn't you take Lionel to the doctor about his persistent earaches?
What kinds of concerns do you have?	Do you have any questions?
What are the behaviors that you worry about?	What do you mean, he is always in trouble?
What does the scene look like when it happens?	Just what went on to make her do that?

Lynch and Hansen (1992), Huff and Telesford (1994), and Cross (1988) suggest that school personnel use these strategies when collaborating with families from diverse cultural groups:

1. Acknowledge cultural differences and become aware of how they affect parent-teacher interactions.
2. Examine one's own personal culture, such as how one defines family, desirable life goals, and behavior problems.
3. Recognize the dynamics of group interactions such as etiquette and patterns of communication.
4. Explore the significance of the child's behavior in relationship to his or her culture.
5. Adjust collaboration to include culturally specific activities.
6. Learn about the families. Where are they from and when did they arrive? What cultural beliefs and practices surround child-rearing, health and healing, and disability and causation?
7. Recognize that some families may be surprised by the extent of home-school collaboration expected in the United States.
8. Learn and use words and forms of greetings in the families' languages.
9. Work with cultural mediators or guides from the families' cultures to learn more about the culture and facilitate communication between school and home. Examples are: relative, church member, neighbor, or older sibling.
10. Ask for help in structuring the child's school program to match home life, such as learning key words and phrases used at home.

Well-publicized policies at the district level encouraging home-school collaboration are vital in providing opportunities for minority family members to become full partners with teachers, but effective structures and strategies often do not exist (Chavkin, 1989; Lynch & Stein, 1987). Lightfoot (1981) suggests that traditional methods of parent involvement such as Parent Teacher Association (PTA) meetings, open house, or newsletters permit little or no true collaboration, constructing instead a "territory" of education which minority parents are hesitant to invade. Concern, awareness, and commitment on the part of individuals in the educational system are beginning steps in collaboration between teachers and families who have language, cultural, or other basic differences.

Step 5: Evaluating Home-School Collaboration.   Evaluation of efforts to provide opportunities for collaboration in schools can indicate whether families' needs are being met and family strengths are being utilized. Evaluation also shows whether needs and strengths of educational personnel are being met. Assessment tools used after a workshop, conference, or at the conclusion of the school year allow school personnel to ask parents, "How did we do in facilitating your learning of the new information, or accessing the new services?" Some teachers use a quick questionnaire, to be completed anonymously, to see whether the activity or program fulfilled the goals of the home-school collaboration. If data show that the activity gave families the information they needed, provided them with the resources they wanted, and offered them the opportunities they requested, educators know whether to continue with the program, offer the activity again, or modify the plans.

Educators also should evaluate their own involvement with families. This means assessing the use of family strengths and skills to facilitate educational programs with children who have special needs. Did teachers get the information they needed from families? How many volunteer hours did parents contribute? What were the results of home tutoring upon the achievement of the resource room students? What changes in family attitudes about the school district were measured? Chapter 8 contains information about procedures for evaluating collaboration efforts. Note again that the purpose of family collaboration is to utilize the unique and vital partnership on behalf of their children.

In proposing guidelines for interagency collaboration, Melaville and Blank (1991) have several useful suggestions for successful home-school collaboration:

- Involve all key players.
- Choose a realistic plan or strategy.
- Establish a shared vision.
- Agree to disagree on some issues and processes.
- Make promises you can keep.
- Keep your "eyes on the prize."
- Build ownership for all individuals and units.
- Avoid technical difficulties (language problems, getting hung up on paperwork or details).
- Share the success.

Home-school collaboration is mandated, it is challenging, and it is rewarding. Students, schools, and families are strengthened with appropriate outreach efforts and partnership activities when they are based on the values and practices of the family-focused approach. Educators have two choices in collaborating with families—to see school as a battleground with an emphasis on conflict between families and school personnel, or to see school as a "homeland" with the kind of environment that invites power sharing and mutual respect and collaboration on activities that foster student learning and development (Epstein, 1995).

Tips for Family-Focused Collaboration

1. Establish rapport with families early in the year. Call right away, before problems develop, so that the first family contact is a positive one.
2. Invite families to school to talk about their traditions, experiences, hobbies, or occupations.
3. Send home "up slips," putting them in a different format from the "down slips" that families sometimes receive, and have conferences with families because the student is *performing well* in the classroom.
4. When sharing information with families, "sandwich" any necessary comments about problems or deficits between two very positive ones.
5. During interaction with families, notice how your actions are received, and adapt to that.

6. When interacting with families, never assume anything.
7. When several staff members will be meeting with family members, make sure each one's role and purpose for being included in the meeting is understood by the parents.
8. Introduce families to all support personnel working with the child.
9. Some family members shy away from being handed sample work, preferring to have the work laid out on a surface to view without forced attention. Do not continue talking when they are reading their child's work.
10. Send out monthly newsletters describing the kinds of things the class is doing, and school news or events coming up. Attach articles families would be interested in. Have a "Family Corner" occasionally, for which families provide comments or ideas.
11. Encourage volunteering in the classroom, to read stories, help with art lessons, listen to book reports, or give a lesson on an area of expertise such as their job or a hobby.
12. Invite families to help students find resource materials and reference books on research topics in the library.
13. Send follow-up notes after meetings. Put out a pamphlet about home-school collaboration in IEP planning conferences.
14. Provide classroom teachers with handouts that can be used during conferences.
15. Have a Home Book notebook of pictures, activities, and stories about class that students take turns sharing at home.
16. Put a Family Board at the entrance of the building for posting ideas of interest to families, examples of class activities, and pictures.
17. Invite parents and siblings, sitters, and grandparents to all class parties.
18. Write thank-you notes for suggestions families provide.
19. Have families from other countries or culture groups talk to students about their customs and culture.
20. Ask families what their family goals are, and discuss how those goals can be met by the classroom curriculum.

CHAPTER REVIEW

1. The variable with the most significant effect upon children's development is family involvement in the child's learning. Although educational professionals come and go in children's lives, and school settings change often for many students, families are the link of continuity in the lives of most children. They are the decision-makers for their children, whose futures are largely dependent on the continued ability of their parents to advocate for them.

2. Educators must be partners with families of students with special needs. While this is a demanding and challenging responsibility, educators are committed to such a partnership because it fulfills a legal right of families. Research confirms the benefits of the partnership for children, families, and schools. Involvements mean teacher involvement as well as family involvement. This becomes collaboration and mutually respectful, committed teamwork.

3. Educators and families face barriers to home-school collaboration, including under-utilization of services, lack of cultural competency, and differing attitudes, history, values, culture,

and language. Examining their own culture and values as potential barriers to understanding will enable them to address diversity during collaboration.

4. Educational consultants have successfully used the bridges of focusing on family strengths, using appropriate communication skills, and promoting positive roles for family members. These are considered empowerment strategies which recognize and promote family competence.

5. Educators must clarify their own values in order to respect the values of others. Checklists and structured value-clarification activities help educators identify their specific values about education, school, and home-school collaboration.

6. Using rapport-building skills and communication skills such as responsive listening, assertive responding, and mutual problem-solving will convey respect for family members and willingness to collaborate with them. Patience and calm persistence are needed.

7. Educators should provide a variety of opportunities for families to become involved with the school. These opportunities should be based on family strengths, expertise, and needs. Family strengths represent contributions that they can make to the partnership. The needs of parents are those interests and needs they have concerning their families.

8. Home-school collaboration can be evaluated using informal or formal assessment methods to determine the effects of the program on children's learning and behavior, as well as family members' attitudes and behaviors, and the attitudes and behaviors of school personnel.

TO DO AND THINK ABOUT

1. Brainstorm to identify family characteristics that would be encouraging to a consultant or teacher who has students with learning and behavior disorders. Then develop plans for interaction and involvement with families that would cultivate those characteristics.

2. Identify roadblocks in these three interactions. Then suggest what could and should have been said differently by the teacher in scene A, by the parent in scene B, and by the consultant in scene C.

   Scene A. *PARENT:* What's this about suspending my child from your class for three days? I thought you people were supposed to be teaching kids instead of letting them sit and waste time in the principal's office.

   TEACHER: You're being unreasonable. You don't understand our rules and neither does your child. Your child needs to learn some manners and plain, old-fashioned respect!

   Scene B. *TEACHER:* I'm calling to tell you that your son caused a disturbance again in my class. I would like you to meet with me and his counselor.

   PARENT: He's always been an active kid. Can't you people learn to handle active, curious children without always dragging us parents into it?

   Scene C. *PARENT:* How can I get Bobby to settle down and do his homework without a battle every night? It's driving us crazy.

   CONSULTANT: I'm glad you're concerned, but I think he will be O.K. if you just keep on him. Don't worry, he's a bright kid and he'll snap out of this phase soon. Just be glad your other three aren't dreamers like he is.

3. Plan a booklet that could be used by consultants to improve home-school communication and collaboration. Report on what will be included, how it can be used, and how it will be helpful.

4. Reflect upon the often-told story about three bricklayers being asked what they were doing. The first retorted, "I'm laying bricks, so don't bother me." The second responded, "I'm making a wall, that's what." But the third, with purpose gleaming in his eyes, replied, "Why, we're building a cathedral." Then propose ways educators can build functional but beautiful relationships with family members, and not just go through the required motions.

FOR FURTHER READING

Berg, I. K. (1994). *Family-based services: A solution-focused approach.* New York: W. W. Norton.

Elkind, D. (1994). *Ties that stress: The new family imbalance.* Cambridge: Harvard University Press.

Gorman, J. C., & Balter, L. (1997). Culturally sensitive parent education: A critical review of quantitative research. *Review of Educational Research, 67*(3), 339–369.

Ingoldsby, B. B., & Smith, S. (1995). *Families in multicultural perspective.* New York: The Guilford Press.

Martin, R. (1991). *Extraordinary children—ordinary lives.* Champaign, IL: Research Press.

Sue, C. W., & Sue, D. (1990). *Counseling the culturally different: Theory and practice* (2nd ed.). New York: Wiley.

5 Problem-Solving Strategies

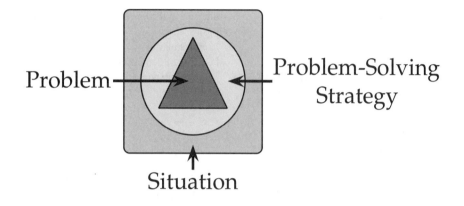

Problem ← | → Problem-Solving Strategy

↑ Situation

A structured format for consultation will help ensure successful teamwork. Using a planned consulting process is like preparing food according to a recipe. After fundamental processes have been mastered, we can adapt the procedures to just about any setting, preference, or creative impulse. In similar fashion, a basic "recipe" for consultation can be adapted to any school context, grade level, content areas, or special learning need.

A collaborative consultation structure does not necessitate rigidity. On the contrary, having general outlines for the interaction will promote flexibility because the basic procedures can be carried out efficiently, leaving more time available for attention to individual needs. When consulting teachers, classroom teachers, support personnel, and parents complement and reinforce each other in using proven problem-solving methods and strategies, schools are better places for learning.

Focusing Questions

1. What are fundamental components in a problem-solving process?
2. What interfering themes affect educators' ability to serve student needs?
3. In what ways are communication, cooperation, and coordination needed in the collaborative consultation process?

4. Why is problem identification so important in collaborative consultation?
5. What ten basic steps should be included in the consultation process?
6. What kinds of things should consultants and consultees say and do during their professional interaction?
7. What group problem-solving tools and techniques are particularly helpful for consultants and collaborators?

Key Terms

benchmarking
brainstorming
buzz groups
circle response
compare and contrast
concept mapping
creative problem solving (CPS)
follow-up

huddle groups
idea checklist
interfering themes
jigsaw
lateral thinking
POCS (problem, option, consequence, solution)
problem identification

problem-solving process
process for consultation
reciprocal teaching
role play
TalkWalk

The Problem-Solving Process

Educators must exercise perception and judgment in order to ascertain student needs, set reasonable goals, and select the most efficient means of addressing those needs and goals (Lanier, 1982). This will require problem-solving skills. Problem-solving ability comes more naturally and easily to some than to others. There is not any one specific formula or "recipe." Furthermore, problem-solving skills, particularly as used by groups, can be improved with training and practice.

Pugach and Johnson (1995) suggest two general categories for problem-solving in the context of teacher collaboration: (1) schoolwide problems, and (2) specific student problems. Full inclusion is an example of schoolwide problem-solving undertaken in a collaborative way by all school staff. Specific student needs are the more common type of issue that teachers deal with in a problem-solving mode. However, both categories of problems provide an opportunity to broaden the educational climate for students with special needs.

Pugach and Johnson (1995) also suggest that another important outcome of collaborative problem-solving on a system-wide basis is development of a support structure for teachers to improve classroom instruction. For this kind of professional development, it is helpful to begin with a study of a fundamental problem-solving process. Gordon (1977) outlines several general components that are important for solving problems effectively:

- Identification and definition of the problem
- Generation of alternative solutions
- Evaluation of alternative solutions

- Decision-making
- Implementing the decisions
- Following up to evaluate the solution

These components include the basic elements of the problem-solving processes most frequently employed in a wide variety of business and professional areas.

At this point it will be helpful to try out the thought-problem concept introduced in an earlier chapter to picture the problem-solving process. One graphic illustration of the problem-solving process could be pictured as a step-wise procedure (see Figure 5.1). Graphic representations and metaphors are useful when discussing collaboration and teamwork with consultees and with administrators who assist with consultation structures.

Communication, Cooperation, and Coordination in Problem-Solving

Communication, cooperation, and coordination are basic ingredients of good consultation. A problem-solving process that reflects high levels of each of these will allow educators to share expertise bearing on the problem. Learning and behavior problems are not always outcomes of student disabilities. Many students are simply "curriculum disabled" (Conoley, 1985), needing a modified or expanded approach to existing curriculum so they can function successfully in school (Pugach & Johnson, 1990). In order to modify the learning environment both in school and at home, educators must identify those aspects of students' curriculum that are interfering with their development.

Interfering Themes.   Consultation provides an arena in which to address four interfering themes that can restrict an educator's ability to facilitate student development. These interfering themes, identified by Caplan (1970), include:

> lack of knowledge about students' needs;
> lack of skills in dealing with the needs;
> lack of confidence in using appropriate strategies; and
> lack of objectivity in assessing the situation.

For example, teachers might demonstrate lack of knowledge by over- or under-identifying students for special education because of stereotypical thinking. They would show lack of skill by failing to modify curriculum for those with disabilities, or by inappropriately using a strategy such as cooperative learning. Lack of confidence shows up in resistance to new plans and inflexibility toward new ideas. Lack of objectivity surfaces when educators equate student situations to another situation in their own lives or to former students and their situations.

During collaboration, consultants should use every opportunity to reinforce the efforts and successes of classroom teachers and also convey a desire to learn from them and their experiences. Too often, classroom teachers, as ones occupying the lowest position in a hierarchy of specialists (Pugach, 1988), and parents, who can be somewhat

Scenario 5

The setting is the office area of an elementary school, where a special-education staff member has just checked into the building and meets a fourth-grade teacher.

CLASSROOM TEACHER: I understand you are going to be a consulting teacher in our building to work with learning and behavioral disorders.

CONSULTING TEACHER: That's right. I hope to meet with all staff very soon to determine your needs and work together on plans for addressing those needs.

CLASSROOM TEACHER: Well I, for one, am glad you're here. I have a student who is driving me and my other twenty-four students up the wall.

CONSULTING TEACHER: In what way?

CLASSROOM TEACHER: Since she moved here a few weeks ago, she's really upset the classroom system that I've used for years.

CONSULTING TEACHER: Is she having trouble with the material you teach?

CLASSROOM TEACHER: No, she is a bright child who finishes everything in good time, and usually correctly, I might add. But she's extremely active, almost frenetic as she busy-bodies around the room.

CONSULTING TEACHER: What specific behaviors concern you?

CLASSROOM TEACHER: Well, for one thing, she tries to help everyone else when they should be doing their own work. I've worked a lot on developing independent learning skills in my students, and they've made good progress. They don't need to have her tell them what to do.

CONSULTING TEACHER: So her behavior keeps her classmates from being the self-directed learners they can be?

CLASSROOM TEACHER: Right. I have to monitor her activities constantly, so my attention is diverted time after time from students I'm working with. She bosses her classmates in the learning centers and even when they play organized games outside. At this rate she will have serious difficulties with peer relationships.

CONSULTING TEACHER: Which of those behaviors would you like to see changed first?

CLASSROOM TEACHER: Well, I need to get her settled into some activities by herself rather than bothering other students.

CONSULTING TEACHER: What have you tried until now to keep her involved with her own work?

CLASSROOM TEACHER: We use assertive discipline in this school, so when she disrupts, I put her name on the board. By the way, the parents don't like this at all.

CONSULTING TEACHER: We could make a list of specific changes in behavior you would like to see and work out a program to accomplish them…There's the bell. Shall we meet tomorrow to do that?

CLASSROOM TEACHER: Sounds good. I'd like to get her on track so the class is more settled. Then the other children will like her better and she will be able to learn other things, too. And the parents will be happier as well. We could meet right here tomorrow if that's O.K. with you. (CLASSROOM TEACHER to herself.) This consulting process may be just what we need!

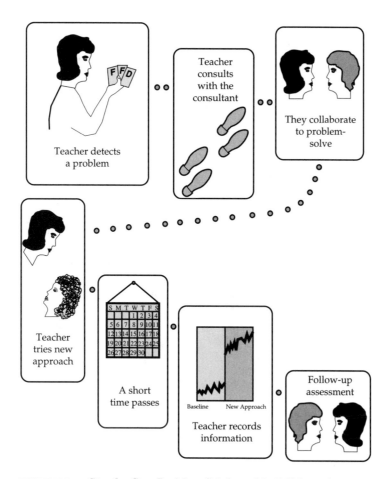

FIGURE 5.1   Step-by-Step Problem-Solving with Collaboration
(By J. M. Loeb)

removed from the school setting, are overlooked as possibilities for solutions when learning and behavior problems are explored.

When communicating and cooperating with consultees to identify the learning or behavior need, it is important that consultants avoid sending messages intimating that classroom teachers and parents are deficient in skills that only special education teachers can provide (Friend & Cook, 1990; Huefner, 1988; Idol, Paolucci-Whitcomb, & Nevin, 1986). Nurturance of communication skills and cooperative attitudes will encourage feelings of parity and voluntariness among all school personnel and parents during the problem-solving process. Students who are assigned to resource settings in other schools for part of the week or school day may have teachers in each setting who never communicate about those students and their programs. This is a serious drawback of some cluster group arrangements in which students travel from one school to another, with no planned interaction among school personnel taking place.

Coordination of collaborative effort is a necessity. Special education teachers who cannot identify basal reading curriculum used in various levels, and classroom teachers who cannot identify the nature of instruction taking place in the resource room, make problem identification more difficult (Idol, West, and Lloyd, 1988). They may even intensify the problem. All parties must think about their own roles in the problem situation and endeavor to learn from each other by interacting, deferring judgment, and coordinating their services.

A team approach is a productive way to assess the context, conditions, interfering themes, and circumstances surrounding the student's needs and the school programs designed to meet those needs. It has been noted that astronomers from all parts of the world collaborate often because there is no one place from which every part of their "work area," the sky, can be observed. This analogy applies to educators and parents as they address each child's total needs in the cognitive, affective, physical, and social domains.

Goals are the building blocks of decision-making. Without goals, decision-making is like a hammer without nails. Educators have long-range and short-term goals. Students have Individual Education Plans (IEPs) with yearly goals and short-term goals. Both school goals and student goals should be used for making decisions in educational environments. A goal motivates action and provides direction for that action. Reviewing the goals helps educators stay focused and sort out activities and problems that are important from those that are not. As some wise person said, "It is hard to get there if you don't know where 'there' is."

The POCS Method of Problem-Solving

The value of communication, cooperation, and coordination in collaborative problem solving can be accentuated by using the POCS method of problem solving (Thurston, 1987):

> *problem* identification (P)
> generating *options* (O)
> determining the *consequences* (C)
> planning the *solution* (S)

A worksheet of POCS (problem, options, consequences, and solution) for taking notes on ideas generated is helpful for consultants as a problem-solving guide (see Figure 5.2).

The Problem.   The first and most critical step in the POCS method of problem solving is to identify the problem (Schein, 1969; Bolton, 1986). The most sophisticated teaching methods and the most expensive instructional materials are worthless if the student need is misidentified or overlooked. It can even be argued that inaccurate definition of the problem situation has potential for iatrogenic results. These hurt more than help, just as identifying an illness incorrectly can delay help or prescribing inappropriate medication might be seriously counterproductive.

FIGURE 5.2   The POCS Method of Problem-Solving

Problem: _____

_____

Expected Outcome: _____

_____

Options	*Consequences*

1._____   _____

2._____   _____

3._____   _____

4._____   _____

5._____   _____

6._____   _____

Chosen Solution: _____

_____

Responsibilities and Commitments: _____

_____

Follow-up Date and Time: _____

_____

(by Linda P. Thurston)

Problem identification requires special emphasis, if the consultation process is to produce results. In problem identification, consultation variables such as interview skills, flexibility, and efficiency have greatest impact on problem solving (Bergan & Tombari, 1976). Consultants who are skilled in problem analysis are most able to identify appropriate target behaviors and develop workable interventions (Bergan & Tombari, 1976). Information on the student's behaviors, discrepancies between current and desired performance, and baseline data are needed to determine the level of potential target behaviors (Polsgrove & McNeil, 1989).

When information about student needs is multisourced, it can give a more accurate perspective on learning and behavior problems, the settings in which they are demonstrated, severity and frequency of the problems, and persons who are affected by those behaviors (Polsgrove & McNeil, 1989). The need for multiple sources of information to help solve problems will be discussed in the section on the ten-step consultation process.

Obtaining information from multiple sources requires effective communication skills by all who can contribute information. Communication is such an important aspect of successful school consultation that it is addressed separately in Chapter 6. Expressing thoughts and feelings with clarity and accuracy entails effective listening and appropriate assertiveness. The problem will never be solved if all parties think they are working on different issues. Problems are like artichokes—they come in layers. Only after the outside layers are stripped away can problem solvers get to the heart of the matter. Good listening facilitates movement to the heart of the problem.

Options.   Problem solving also involves generating options to solve the problem. Brainstorming, or thinking of many solutions without judging or criticizing, is important in order not to get stuck in routines and answers. Some consultants find it helpful to encourage the person who "owns" the problem to make the most suggestions. For example, if the problem is making a decision about post-secondary education for a student with learning disabilities, the student and the parents should be encouraged to generate the most options. This is important for several reasons. When people participate in decision making, they feel more ownership toward the results than when the decision is forced on them. Also, as explained by Johnson and Johnson (1987), people are more apt to support decisions they helped create than those imposed on them, regardless of the merit of the ideas.

An important second reason for prompting the owner of the problem to give initial suggestions is that a consultant should avoid giving advice and being presented or perceived as the expert. Several researchers have shown that the nonexpert model of educational consulting is more effective in special education (Margolis & McGettigan, 1988; Idol-Maestes, Lloyd, & Lilly, 1981). The suggestions and opinions of others need to be listened to with respect and fully understood before additional suggestions are offered.

Finally, teachers and others are more likely to be resistant if the problem-solving process is perceived as advice giving by the consultant. Problems that come up in school consultation often reveal the need for changed classroom practices. This can engender resistance that will not yield to an "I'm the expert and you're not" model. Advice giving and hierarchical structure may be unintentionally communicated if consultants promote the options generated as being their ideas.

If a consultant is regarded as *the* expert, there is pressure on that consultant, and false expectations are created. It is hard to win in this kind of situation. The best practice for the consultant is to communicate equality, flexibility, and a sharing attitude. Three questions assess the equality that is or is not present in a professional consulting relationship:

- Does the consultant recognize the consultee's expertise and opinion?
- Does the consultant encourage the consultee to generate ideas and make decisions?
- Do consultees feel free to *not* do as the consultant might recommend?

Eager, competent consultants who are ready to solve problems and produce quick results, instant cures, and dramatic increases, too often jump in and try to solve problems alone. Consultees may react with resistance, negativism, or hostility by hiding their feelings, withdrawing, or blaming others if things do not work out. (Resistance will be discussed in greater detail in Chapter 6.)

It is difficult for consultants to avoid the "quick fix." But the quick fix is inappropriate (DeBoer, 1986). It is demeaning to the one who has been struggling with the problem. Others need to feel that the consultant fully understands their unique situation and the source of their frustrations before they are ready to participate in problem-solving and listen to the suggestions of colleagues. Consultants must listen before they can expect to be listened to, treated with parity, or approached again voluntarily by consultees.

All learning situations and all students are unique. In response to a question about classroom management, a high school teacher replied, "I don't know all the answers, because I haven't seen all the kids." While students and situations may appear similar in some ways, the combinations of student, teacher, parents, and school and home contexts are unique for each problem.

Furthermore, in many cases, people with problems already have their answers. They just need help to clarify issues or an empathic ear to face the emotional aspects of the concern. If people keep talking, they often can solve their own problems. Joint problem identification and idea generating assure that professional relationships are preserved, professional communication is enhanced, and professionals maintain a greater feeling of control and self-esteem.

Good consultants do not solve problems—they see that problems get solved. So they facilitate problem-solving, and "nix the quick fix." As Gordon (1977) asks, whose problem is it? Who really owns the problem? Busy consultants do not need to take on the problems of others, and such action would inhibit consultees from learning and practicing problem-solving skills. Everyone who owns a part of the problem should participate in solving it. That may involve collaboration among several people—teachers, administrators, vocational counselors, students, parents, and others. Consultants and consultees should focus on the problem rather than on establishing ownership for the problem. All individuals will need to attend carefully to minimizing roadblocks and maximizing assertion and listening skills.

Consequences. Effective consultants facilitate problem-solving in such a way that all members of the group feel their needs are being satisfied and an "equitable" social and professional relationship is being maintained (Gordon, 1977). Members of the problem-solving team work together to evaluate all the suggestions made, with each discussing the disadvantages and merits of the suggestion from his or her own perspective. Agreement is not necessary at this point, because the barriers and merits important to each person are taken into account. Honest and open communication, good listening skills, and the appropriate level of assertiveness are vital at this step.

Solutions. The problem-solving group selects a workable solution all are willing to adopt, at least on a trial or experimental basis. The consultant promotes mutual participation in the decision. Group members more readily accept new ideas and new work methods when they are given opportunity to participate in decision making (Gordon, 1977). Many times a complex problem can be solved as each person in the group discovers what the others really want or, perhaps, fear. Then solutions can be formulated to meet the goals and protect the concerns of all involved.

Better decisions are made with a cool head and a warm heart (Johnson, 1992). Johnson suggests asking oneself if the decision helps meet the *real* need. Real needs are based on reality, not illusion or wishful thinking, and on personal and professional goals. Next, one should ask, What information do I need? Do I have enough information to create options I may not have realized before this? Have I thought of the consequences of each option? Have I *really* thought through the options? Taking time to ask all the necessary questions is a key to Johnson's (1992) decision-making process. "Better decisions often depend on seeing, at the time, what becomes obvious to you later" (Johnson, p. 50, 1992). Asking many questions helps make options and choices obvious.

Problem-Solving Roles.   In collaborative problem-solving, whether using the POCS method or another effective method, the role of the consultant is to facilitate interaction and teamwork. This involves good listening, assertive responses, and successful resolution of conflicts, which will be discussed in greater detail in Chapter 6.

Consultants, consultees, support staff and others involved in collaborative interaction will assume one or more of a variety of functions during the process. These can include, but are not limited to, interaction role functions such as *initiator* of the process, *convener* of the meeting, *information gatherer, questioner, timekeeper, energizer, elaborator, innovator, integrator, humor dispenser, alternative opinion seeker, red-flag waver, standards/regulations adherent, gatekeeper, implementation designer* for the plan, *harmonizer, summarizer, evaluator* of the activity. Consultation encourages collective thinking for creative and imaginative alternatives and allows all involved to have their feelings and ideas heard and their goals met. The ultimate goal for effective problem-solving is to provide the best education possible for students with special needs.

The Ten-Step Process for Consultation

Now that the fundamentals of problem identification, options, consequences, and solution finding have been discussed, it is appropriate to coordinate these activities into a structured consultation process. The ten-step process outlined in Figure 5.3 can help consultants and consultees communicate, cooperate, and coordinate their efforts as they collaborate to identify educational problems and design programs for students' needs.

Step 1: Preparing for the Consultation

As consultants plan and prepare for consultation and collaboration, they focus on the major areas of concern. They prepare helpful materials and organize them in order to use collaborative time efficiently. It is useful to distribute information beforehand so that valuable interaction time is not consumed reading new material. But consultants must take care to present the material as tentative and open to discussion. Of course, it is not always expedi-

FIGURE 5.3   The Ten-Step Process for Consultation

1. Prepare for the consultation.
   1.1 Focus upon major topic or area of concern.
   1.2 Prepare and organize materials.
   1.3 Prepare several possible actions or strategies.
   1.4 Arrange for a comfortable, convenient meeting place.

2. Initiate the consultation.
   2.1 Establish rapport.
   2.2 Identify the agenda.
   2.3 Focus on the tentatively defined concern.
   2.4 Express interest in the needs of all.

3. Collect information.
   3.1 Make notes of data, soliciting from all.
   3.2 Combine and summarize the data.
   3.3 Assess data to focus on areas needing more information.
   3.4 Summarize the information.

4. Isolate the problem.
   4.1 Focus on need.
   4.2 State what the problem is.
   4.3 State what it is not.
   4.4 Propose desirable circumstances.

5. Identify the problem.
   5.1 Encourage all to listen to each concern.
   5.2 Identify issues, avoiding jargon.
   5.3 Encourage ventilation of frustrations and concerns.
   5.4 Keep focusing on the pertinent issues and needs.
   5.5 Check for agreement.

6. Generate solutions.
   6.1 Engage in collaborative problem-solving.
   6.2 Generate several possible options and alternatives.
   6.3 Suggest examples of appropriate classroom modifications.
   6.4 Review options, discussing consequences of each.
   6.5 Select the most reasonable alternatives.

7. Formulate a plan.
   7.1 Designate those who will be involved, and how.
   7.2 Set goals.
   7.3 Establish responsibilities.
   7.4 Generate evaluation criteria and methods.
   7.5 Agree on a date for reviewing progress.

8. Evaluate progress and process.
   8.1 Conduct a review session at a specified time.
   8.2 Review data and analyze the results.
   8.3 Keep products as evidence of progress.
   8.4 Make positive, supportive comments.
   8.5 Assess contribution of the collaboration.

9. Follow up on the situation.
   9.1 Reassess periodically to assure maintenance.
   9.2 Provide positive reinforcement.
   9.3 Plan further action or continue the plan.
   9.4 Adjust the plan if there are problems.
   9.5 Initiate further consultation if needed.
   9.6 Bring closure if goals have been met.
   9.7 Support effort and reinforce results.
   9.8 Share information where it is wanted.
   9.9 Enjoy the communication.

10. Repeat consultation as appropriate.

(Peggy Dettmer, Norma Dyck, & Kari Woods)

ent to plan in depth prior to consultations. Sometimes they happen informally and without notice—between classes, during lunch periods, or on playgrounds. While educators will want to accommodate these occasions for interacting with colleagues, they also need to look beyond them for opportunities to engage in more in-depth sessions.

They will want to provide convenient and comfortable settings for the interaction, arranging seating so there is a collegial atmosphere with no phone or drop-by interruptions. Serving coffee and tea can help set congenial climates for meetings.

Step 2: Initiating the Consultation

Consultants need to exert much effort in this phase. When resistance to consulting is high, or the teaching staff has been particularly reluctant to collaborate, it will be difficult to establish first contacts. This is the time to begin with the most receptive staff members in order to build in success for the consulting program. Rapport is cultivated by addressing every consultee as special and expressing interest in what each one is doing and feeling. Teachers should be encouraged to talk about their successes. The consultant needs to display sensitivity to teachers' needs and make each one feel important. The key is to *listen*.

The consultant will want to identify the agenda and keep focusing on the concern. It is helpful to have participants write down their concerns before the meeting and bring them along. Then the consultant can check quickly for congruence and major disagreements.

Step 3: Collecting Information

The data should be relevant to the issue of focus. However, data which might seem irrelevant to one person may be the very information needed to identify the real problem. So the consultant must be astute in selecting appropriate data that include many possibilities but do not waste time or resources. This becomes easier with experience, but for new consultants, having too much information is probably better than having too little.

Since problem identification seems to be the most significant factor in planning for special needs, it is wise to gather sufficient data from multiple sources. A case-study method of determining data sources and soliciting information is particularly effective in planning for students who have special learning and behavior needs. See Figure 5.4 for a case-study framework that includes up to sixteen data sources to provide information for problem-solving. When a number of these sixteen are tapped, the central problem becomes much more clear and more easily addressed.

Step 4: Isolating the Problem

As discussed earlier, the most critical aspect of problem-solving is identifying and defining the problem at hand. Bolton (1986) emphasizes that consultants and consultees must define the problem by focusing on the need, not the solution. Without problem identification, problem-solving cannot occur (Bergan & Tombari, 1976). Consultants can help isolate what the problem is, and what it is not. After the problem has been identified and stated, collaborators should propose desired circumstances related to that problem.

Step 5: Identifying Concerns Relevant to the Problem

All concerns and viewpoints relevant to the problem should be aired and shared. A different viewpoint is not better or worse, just different. An effective consultant keeps participants focusing on the student need by listening and encouraging everyone to respond. However, a certain amount of venting and frustration is to be expected and accepted. Teachers and parents will demonstrate less resistance when they know they are free to

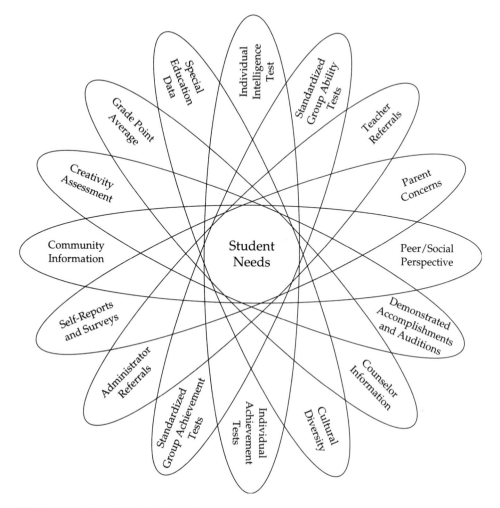

FIGURE 5.4 Case Study Information

express their feelings without retaliation or judgment. Consultants should remain nonjudgmental and assure confidentiality, always talking and listening in the consultees' language.

As information is shared, the consultant will want to make notes. It is good to have everyone look over the recorded information from time to time during the consultation as a demonstration of trust and equality, as well as a check on accuracy. (A log format for recording information and documenting the consultation is provided in Chapter 7.)

Step 6: Generating Solutions

Now is the time for creative problem-solving. If ideas do not come freely, or if participants are blocking productive thinking, the consultant might suggest trying one or more of the techniques described later in the chapter. A problem-solving technique not only unleashes ideas, it sends a message about the kind of behavior that is needed to solve the problem. "Straw votes" can be taken periodically if that helps the group keep moving toward solutions. "Thinking outside the box" and combining ideas are desirable processes at this stage. Two productive activities are to have brief discussions focusing on benefits and on concerns. These two sharing periods should be initiated with the word stems "I like…" (where the benefits are shared), and "I wish…" or "How to…?" (where the concerns are shared). At this stage, the group should modify, dismiss, or problem-solve each concern.

Step 7: Formulating a Plan

After solutions have been generated, wishes and concerns aired, and modifications made, the revised solution is ready to be formulated into a plan. Participants must remain on task. They need to be reinforced positively for their contributions. Consultants will want to have suggestions available for sharing, but defer presenting them so long as others are suggesting and volunteering. They must avoid offering solutions prematurely or addressing too many issues at one time. Other unhelpful behaviors are assuming the supervisor/expert role, introducing biases, and making suggestions that conflict with existing values in the school context.

As the plan develops, the consultant must make clear just who will do what, and when, and where. Evaluation criteria and methods that are congruent with the goals and plan should be developed at this time, and arrangements made for assessment and collection of data on student progress.

Step 8: Evaluating Progress and Process

This step and the final two steps are frequently overlooked. Consultation and collaboration experiences should be followed by assessment of student progress resulting from the collaborative plan, and also by evaluation of the consultation process itself. Several figures in Chapter 8 are useful for this purpose.

The consultant will want to make positive, supportive comments while drawing the interaction to a close, and at that time can informally evaluate the consultation with consultee help or formally evaluate by asking for brief written responses. This is a good time also to plan for future collaboration.

Step 9: Following Up the Consultation

Of all ten steps, this may be the most neglected. Ineffective consultation often results from lack of follow-up service (Neel, 1981). It is in the best interest of the client, consultee, consultant, and future possibilities for consultation to reassess the situation periodically. Participants will want to adjust the student's program if necessary, and initiate further consultation if the situation seems to require it. Informal conversations with consultees at this point are very reinforcing. During follow-up, consultants have opportunities to make consultees feel good about themselves. They can make a point of noting improved student behaviors and performance, especially those that relate to the classroom teacher's efforts.

Also, they may volunteer to help if things are not going as smoothly as anticipated, or if consultees have further needs. As stressed in an earlier chapter, the sweetest words a consultee can hear are, "What can I do to help you?" However, this question *must* be framed in the spirit of: "What can I do to help you *that you do not have the time and resources to do?*" and *not* as, "What can I do for you that you do not have the skill and expertise to accomplish?" Consultants should follow through immediately on all promises of materials, information, action, or further consultation, and reinforce things that are going well. They also need to make a point of noting improved student behaviors and performance, especially those that relate to the classroom teacher's efforts.

Step 10: Repeating the Consultation If Needed

Further consultation and collaboration may be needed if the plan is not working, or if one or more parties believes the problem was not identified appropriately. On the other hand, consultation also may be repeated and extended when things are going well. The obvious rationale here is that if one interaction helped, more will help further. This is reinforcing for processes of consultation, collaboration, and teamwork. It encourages others to participate in the consultation and collaboration activity.

What to Say during the Consultation

The ten-step consultation procedure, committed to memory or stapled into a plan book, is a good organizational tool and a reassuring resource for the consultant, particularly for those engaging in their first consultations. Of course, the consultant does not want to parrot points from an outline as though reading from a manual for programming a video-cassette machine! But by practicing verbal responses that are helpful at each step, it will become more natural and automatic to use facilitative phrases when the need arises. For example:

1. *When planning the consultation* (The comments in this step are made to yourself.)
   (What styles of communication and interaction can I expect with these consultees?)
   (Have I had previous consultations with them and if so, how did they go?)
   (Do I have any perceptions at this point about client needs? If so, can I keep them under wraps while soliciting responses from others?)
   (What kinds of information might help with this situation?)

2. *When initiating the consultation* (In this step and the rest of the steps, say to the consultee—)
   You're saying that…
   The need seems to be…
   May we work together along these lines…?
   So the situation is…
   I am aware that…
   What can we do in regard to your request/situation…?

3. *When collecting information*

Tell me about that...

Uh-huh...

What do you see as the effects of...?

So your views/perceptions about this are...

Tell me more about the background of...

Sounds tough...

To summarize our basic information then,...

4. *When isolating the problem*

The major factors we have brought out seem to be...

What do you perceive is the greatest need for...?

What circumstances have you noted that may apply?

Are there other parts to the need that we have not considered?

So to summarize our perceptions at this point...

Are we in agreement that the major part of this issue is...?

5. *When identifying the concerns*

You say the major concern is...

But I also hear your concern about...

You'd like this situation changed so that...

How does this affect your day/load/responsibility?

You are concerned about other students in your room...

You're feeling...because of...

This problem seems formidable. Perhaps we can isolate part of it...

Perhaps we can't be sure about that...

If you could change one thing, what would you change first?

6. *When generating possibilities*

How does this affect the students/schedule/parents?

Do we have a good handle on the nature of this situation?

We need to define what we want to happen...

How would you like things to be?

What has been tried so far?

What happened then?

How could we do this more easily?

Could we try something new such as...?

What limitations fall upon things we might suggest?

Let's try to develop some ideas to meet the need...

Your idea of...also makes me think of...

7. *When formulating a plan*

    Let's list the goals and ideas we have come up with...

    So, in trying...you'll be changing your approach of...

    To implement these ideas, we would have to...

    The actions in this situation would be different, because...

    We need to break down the plan into steps.

    What should come first? Next...

    When is the best time to start with the first step?

8. *When evaluating progress*

    Have we got a solid plan?

    One way to measure progress toward the goals would be...

    Some positive things have been happening...

    How can we build on these gains?

    Now we can decide where to go from here...

    In what ways did our getting together help?

    I can see [the student] progress every day...

    You're accomplishing so much with...

    How could I serve you and your students better?

9. *When following up and interacting with colleagues*

    How do you feel about the way things are going?

    We had set a time to get back together. Is that time still O.K., or should we make it sooner?

    I'm interested in the progress you have observed.

    I'm following up on that material/action I promised.

    I just stopped by...

    Since we bumped into each other...

    I wondered how things have been going for you...

    How are things in your corner of the world these days?

    I'm glad you've hung in there with this problem.

    You've accomplished a lot, which is easy to overlook when one is with it every day...

    You know, progress like this makes teachers look very good!

10. *When repeating the consultation*

    Should we have another go at discussing...?

    Perhaps we overlooked some information that would help...

    We got so much accomplished last time.

    How about getting together again to...?

    That's a fine progress report.

    Would another plan session produce even more fantastic results?

What to Consider If Group Problem-Solving Is Not Successful

There is no universal agreement on what makes consultation effective, and little empirical support exists to guide consultants as to what should be said and done in consultation (Gresham and Kendell, 1987; Heron and Kimball, 1988). However, the ten steps outlined in this chapter have worked well for many consultants and consulting teachers. If this method of ten steps does not work, consultants should ask several questions:

- Were feelings addressed?
- Was the problem defined accurately?
- Did all parties practice good listening skills?
- Were the nitty-gritty details worked out?
- Were all participants appropriately assertive?
- Was the consultation process evaluated?
- Was there follow-up to the consultation?
- Were any hidden agendas brought to light and handled?
- Could any other problem-solving tools facilitate the process?

Tools to Facilitate Group Problem-Solving

The collaborative format of working together and drawing on collective expertise is widely practiced in the business and professional world. In their efforts to use the best ideas of bright, innovative minds, astute business managers employ a number of group problem-solving techniques. These techniques allow individuals to extend their own productive thinking powers and enhance those of their colleagues by participating in structured group problem-solving activities. Such techniques, often utilized in business and industry, are yet to be promoted to any great extent in educational settings, where autonomy and self-sufficiency have traditionally been valued more than collaboration and teamwork.

Several easy and convenient problem-solving techniques suitable for group participation are: brainstorming, lateral thinking, concept mapping, idea checklists, and creative problem-solving. Others are: jigsaw, reciprocal teaching, compare-and-contrast, role play, benchmarking, and TalkWalk. Many teachers incorporate these kinds of group problem-solving activities into curriculum planning for their students but overlook the potential that the techniques can contribute to carrying out other responsibilities more effectively and pleasurably.

Brainstorming

Brainstorming is a mainstay of creative problem-solving methodology. It facilitates generating many unique ideas. When a group is brainstorming, participants should be relaxed and having fun. There are no right or wrong responses during the process, because problems seldom have only one right approach. No one may critique an idea during the brainstorming process. All ideas are accepted as plausible and regarded as potentially valuable.

APPLICATION **5.1**

The Ten-Step Consulting Process

1. Select one or more of the following situations and simulate a school consultation experience, using the ten-step process and any of the application phrases that seem appropriate:

Situation A: A ninth-grade student is considered lazy by former teachers, has failed several courses, and cannot grasp math concepts. He has difficulty locating information but can read and understand most material at his grade level. He is never prepared for class, seldom has pencil and paper, and loses his assignments. Yet he is pleasant, seemingly eager to please, and will try things in a one-to-one situation. His classroom teachers say he will not pass, and you have all decided to meet about this. How will you, the learning disabilities consulting teacher, address the situation?

Situation B: You are attending a conference on behalf of a third-grade student who is emotionally disturbed and classified as borderline educable mentally handicapped. You believe she should be served in a general classroom with supportive counseling service and reevaluated in a year. The other staff participants feel she should have special education placement with inclusion into music, art, and physical education. The mother is confused about the lack of agreement among school personnel. How will you address the concerns of all in this situation, particularly the mother?

Situation C: A sixth-grade student's mother is known as a perfectionist. Her son did not receive all As on the last report card, and she has requested a conference with you as gifted program facilitator, the classroom teacher, the principal, and the school psychologist. As gifted program facilitator, how will you address this situation?

Situation D: A first-year kindergarten teacher has learned that one of her students will be a child with cerebral palsy. Although the child's history to date has included continuous evaluation, home teaching, group socialization experiences, special examinations, and therapy sessions as well as family counseling for three years, the teacher is nervous about her responsibilities with this child. As the speech pathologist, how will you build her confidence in caring for the kindergartner's language needs and her skill in helping the little girl to develop her potential?

2. As a team effort with colleagues who share your grade level and subject area, construct a scenario to demonstrate the ten-step collaborative school consultation process at your teaching level and in your content area(s)…Role-play it for others, stopping at key points—for example, after problem identification and after formulation of the plan, to ask others what they might do at that point…If several promising alternatives are suggested, try each one and follow it to its conclusion. What techniques worked best? How did individual differences influence the consultation? Were these individual differences used constructively, and if not, what could have been done instead?

Each idea is shared and recorded. In large group sessions, it is most efficient to have a leader for managing the oral responses and a recorder for getting them down on a board or chart visible to all.

APPLICATION **5.2**

Positive and Not-So-Positive Consultations

Assess which of the following consultation contacts were positive and which were not so positive. Why were the positive consultations successful? Why were some of them less successful than the consultant and consultee wished? What might have been done to improve the outcome? What still might be done?

1. Primary level teachers and I sat down and discussed what materials they thought would be good to order and place in the resource room, for their use as well as mine. Everyone had a chance to share needs, express opinions, and make recommendations.
2. An undergraduate asked me about my student teaching and substituting days. She was feeling very down and unsure of her teaching abilities. I reassured her by telling of some things that had happened to me (and why). I encouraged her to find a dependable support system, and gave her some ideas and things to think about.
3. A kindergarten child was staffed into my program, but the teacher wouldn't let me take her out of "her" class time. So I arranged to keep the child after school. The first night I was late coming to fetch the child, and the teacher blew up about it.
4. The music teacher asks students who cannot read to stand up in class and read, and then pokes fun at them. I approached the teacher about the situation, but the teacher wanted nothing to do with me, and after that made things worse for the students.
5. One of the teachers I have spent several weeks with stopped me in the hall yesterday to ask for an idea to use in her class that next hour. Before she finished putting her question into words, she thought of an idea herself, but she still thanked me!
6. In visiting with the principal about alternatives for altering classroom assignments, it ended with his screaming at me for finding fault with his staff, which I had not done.
7. I give a sticker every day to a student with learning disabilities if he attends and does his work in the resource room. His classroom teacher complained to the principal because "other students work hard and don't get stickers."
8. I participated in a parent conference in which the parent wanted to kick the daughter out of the house and into a boarding school. It ended with the daughter agreeing to do more work at home, and the mother agreeing to spend one special hour a week just with her daughter.

Rules for brainstorming are

1. Do not criticize any ideas at this time.
2. The more wild and zany the ideas, the better.
3. Think up as many ideas as possible.
4. Try to combine two or more ideas into new ones.
5. Hitchhike (piggyback) on another's idea. A person with a hitchhike idea should be called on before those who have unrelated ideas (Osborn, 1963.)

This technique is useful when the group wishes to explore as many alternatives as possible and defer evaluation of the ideas until the options have been exhausted. People

APPLICATION **5.3**

Using the Brainstorming Technique

A brainstorming session might be held for the following situation:

A first-grade student has read just about every book in the small, rural school. The first-grade teacher and gifted program facilitator brainstorm possibilities for enhancing this student's reading options and augmenting school resources as well.

---

who cannot resist the urge to critique ideas during brainstorming must be reminded that evaluation comes later. Leaders should call on volunteers quickly.

When the flow of ideas slows, it is good to persevere a while longer. Often the second wave of thoughts will contain the most innovative suggestions. Each participant should be encouraged to contribute.

Creative Problem-Solving

The creative problem-solving approach developed by Osborn (1963) and Parnes (1992) begins with identifying the "mess" to be addressed, and proceeds through five more stages—data-gathering, problem-finding, idea-finding (which uses the brainstorm tool), solution-finding, and acceptance-finding. This process lends itself well to the structure and demands of collaborative staff meetings for defining students' needs and determining strategies to serve those needs.

A cogent application of using CPS methods to include students with severe disabilities in general education classroom activities is described by Giangreco (1993). Detailed examples of curriculum activities generated through CPS, and an instrument for evaluating the effectiveness of this tool, are included.

Lateral Thinking

The conventional method of thinking is vertical thinking, in which one moves forward mentally by sequential and justifiable steps. Vertical thinking is logical and single purposed, digging down more deeply into the same mental hole. Lateral thinking, on the other hand, digs a "thinking hole" in a different place. It moves out at an angle, so to speak, from vertical thinking to change direction, attitude, or approach so that the problem can be examined in a different way (deBono, 1973).

Lateral thinking should not replace vertical thinking, but complement it. While many educators emphasize vertical thinking at the expense of more divergent production, both are necessary to arrive at creative solutions for complex problems. The ability to use a lateral thinking mode by suspending judgments and generating alternatives should be cultivated by school personnel.

APPLICATION **5.4**

Using the Lateral-Thinking Technique

Lateral thinking might be used in this situation:

A high school student with learning disabilities has a serious reading problem, but teachers in several classes are not willing to make adjustments. The teachers have not discussed any problems with you, the resource teacher, recently but the student has. How might you as consultant, and student as consultee, think of ways to approach the situation and modify classroom practices to help this student succeed? To think laterally, the consultant might regard the teachers as clients and consult with the student about ways of reinforcing teachers when they *do* make things easier. The student would be modifying the behavior of teachers, rather than a vertical thinking approach of asking teachers to modify student behavior.

Concept Mapping

Concept mapping (referred to by some as mind mapping, semantic mapping, or webbing) is a tool for identifying concepts, showing relationships among them, and reflecting on the degree of generality and inclusiveness that envelops them (Wesley & Wesley, 1990). The technique allows users to display ideas, link them together, elaborate on them, add new information as it surfaces, and review the formulation of the ideas. The process begins with one word, or issue, written on paper or the chalkboard and enclosed in a circle. Then other circles of subtopics, ideas, words, and concepts are added to that central theme by lines or spokes that connect and interconnect where the concepts relate and interrelate. More and more possibilities and new areas open up as the webbing grows. Relationships and interrelationships that can help verbalize problems and interventions are recorded for all participants to see. If the concept map is not erased or discarded, the process can go on and on as more ideas are generated and added.

Concept mapping is being taught to students at all grade levels for reading comprehension. Buzan (1983) offers strategies for mind mapping in which learning techniques such as note taking can be structured to show interrelationships easily. Many students in gifted programs have been introduced to the concept of webbing to focus on a problem of interest and plan an independent study. Sometimes college students are encouraged to try mind mapping by combining lecture notes and text reading to study for exams. Concept mapping is a powerful tool. It is useful not only for enhancing individual learning, but for leading to more meaningful and productive staff development (Bocchino, 1991).

Idea Checklist

Checklists that suggest solutions for problems can be created from sources such as college texts, teaching manuals, and instructional media manuals. More unusual checklists include the referral agency listings, gift catalog descriptions, instructional resource center guides,

APPLICATION **5.5**
Using the Concept-Mapping Technique

A classroom teacher has agreed to work with a student new to the district and identified as behavior disordered. The student has acceptable social skills in some instances and is friendly and cooperative. But he also requires individual instruction, is working about two years below grade level, and makes threats impulsively to other students. On one occasion he brought a weapon to school. During previous visits with the teacher, she indicated that things were going well. Now, in the middle of November, she asks to see you, as the consultant for behavioral disorders, immediately. She is upset, saying things such as "It just isn't working," and "I've tried so hard," but she has not described the problem. How might concept mapping or webbing help in this situation?

---

and even various Yellow Pages directories. Asking a question such as "How can we help Shawn improve in math proficiency?" and scanning a Yellow Pages section or an off-level teaching manual may generate new ideas. Several chapters of this book contain checklists.

Benchmarking

Benchmarking was developed in the business world as a method for finding world class examples of products, services, or systems and holding them up as standards to meet or exceed (Sparks, 1991). Data are collected, analyzed, and used to make appropriate changes in the local situation. School personnel, for example, might search out benchmark examples of excellent inclusionary programs, preassessment procedures, or professional-development activities for improving or restructuring their own programs.

Other Collaborative Activities

Several collaborative activities that Brown (1994) presents for children's learning are just as promising for facilitating interchange, reciprocity, and a community of learning among adults. They include Jigsaw, reciprocal teaching (Brown, 1994), TalkWalk (Caro & Robbins, 1991), compare-and-contrast, and role play (Dobson, Dobson, & Koetting, 1985).

Jigsaw.   Participants in this learning method developed by Aronson (1978) undertake independent, collaborative research on a topic of mutual interest. The technique can be used by a school faculty, a school district staff, or other group of teachers and area specialists to find background material and possible alternatives for solutions to academic and behavioral problems. The group decides on the central theme(s) of the issue and several subtopics. Then the large group divides into smaller groups. Each small group conducts research on one subtopic and shares that knowledge by teaching it to others. In this way all have a part in the problem-solving. Time and energy of busy professionals are maximized. Most important, a collaborative synergy develops that improves their ability to problem-solve in other situations.

APPLICATION **5.6**

Using the Idea Checklist

A high school sophomore, seventeen years old and in the educable mentally handicapped program, is ready for a vocational training program. As EMH resource teacher, you believe the Vocational Rehabilitation Unit's four-month job-training program would be the most appropriate program for the student. However, the parents feel very protective of their son and are concerned that the environment will be noncaring. They resist suggestions that he leave their home. How might an idea-checklist process help during this consultation?

Reciprocal Teaching.   In reciprocal teaching, six or so participants form a group and each member takes a turn leading a discussion about an article, video, position paper, staff development presentation, or other material they need to understand. The leader begins with a question and summarizes the discussion at the end. Clarification for understanding and predictions about future content can be requested by the leader when appropriate (Brown, 1994). With this technique, group cooperation helps ensure understanding by all members, with the less well-informed learning from those who are better informed.

Compare-and-Contrast.   Each small group identifies terms and phrases that define differing perspectives of an issue—for example, reading methods, math methods, tracking or mainstreaming, inclusion or pull-out programs, graded or ungraded systems. Feedback to the large group and organization of resulting lists complete the interaction, with all leaving the session more informed and reflective about the issues.

Role Play.   Participants have specific parts to play. At a critical part in the interaction the leader stops the players and has the whole group explore options that would be possible from that point.

TalkWalk.   In this form of small-group interaction, the participants engage in collegial dialogue focused on instructional and curricular issues while they walk together in an open environment (Caro & Robbins, 1991). The fresh air, physical and mental exercise, and exploration of ideas leads to free thinking and expression. This technique can be used as part of a workshop or simply as an informal arrangement among colleagues. Caro and Robbins suggest that groups of two or three work best. TalkWalk gives educators the opportunity to share expertise and help each other solve classroom problems.

Other possibilities include interviews, interrogator panels, readers' theater, structured controversies with participants assuming different positions on controversial issues, and the lecture/presentation format.

Interaction Formats

Collaborating consultants will want to know a variety of group formats for stimulating interaction among professionals. (See Figure 5.5.) Some of the most useful ones are:

- *Buzz groups.* Buzz groups work well in a group of 50 or fewer. This format ensures total participation and is easy to set up. The leader presents a topic or problem, provides minimal directions for subgrouping by twos or threes, and invites everyone to consider all aspects of a problem in the time allowed. The main disadvantage is a high noise level if the physical space is small.
- *Huddles.* Huddles work best with groups of five or six discussants. The leader arranges the groups, defines the topic, announces the time limit (six minutes works well), and gives a two-minute warning when time is expiring. Each group designates its own reporter. The leader usually passes from group to group facilitating and encouraging if needed. In this structure the participants tend to build on colleagues' contributions. The reporting process can vary, from a simple "most important points" to ranking of major points, to a written summary that is collected by the leader.

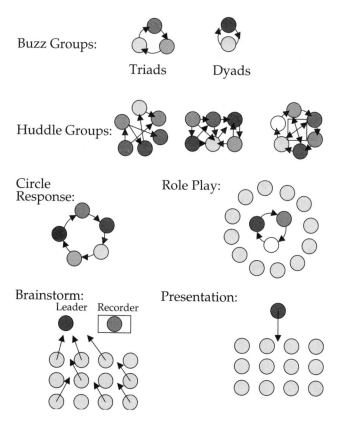

FIGURE 5.5   Interaction Structures

- *Circle response.* Small groups of collaborators sit in a circle. The designated leader begins by stating or reiterating the topic. The response pattern moves to the left, with each taking a turn or saying "I pass." At the end of a stipulated time, the leader summarizes the ideas and integrated thinking of the group.

Tips for Problem-Solving Strategies

1. Have materials and thoughts organized before consultations and develop a list of questions that will help ferret out the real problem.
2. Be prepared for the meeting with a checklist of information typically needed. Do not be afraid to say that you do not have *the* answer. If it is something you should know, find out when you can and get back to the person who asked.
3. Have strategies and materials in mind that may be helpful to the situation but do not try to have all the answers. This discourages involvement by others.
4. Do not offer solutions too readily and try not to address too much or too many topics at once.
5. Avoid jargon and shun suggestions that conflict with policies or favored teacher practices.
6. Make it a habit to look for something positive about the teacher, the room, and the student and comment on those things. Use feedback as a vehicle that can provide *positive* information, not just negative comments.
7. Don't try to "fix it" if it is not "broken."
8. Don't wait for the consultee to make the first move. But do not expect that teachers will be enthusiastic or flattered to have questions asked about their classrooms and teaching methods.
9. When a teacher asks for advice about a student, first ask what the teacher has already observed. This gets the teacher involved in the problem and encourages ownership in serving the student's special need. Whenever possible, use the terms *we* and *us*, not *I*.
10. Know how to interpret test results and how to discuss those results with educators, parents, and students.
11. When possible, provide parents with samples of the child's schoolwork to discuss during the conference. Have a list of resources ready to share with parents for help with homework, reinforcements, and study tips. When providing materials, explain or demonstrate their use and then keep in touch so that no problems develop.
12. Maintain contact with teachers during the year. You may find that the teacher has detected an improvement that is directly related to your work, and this reinforcement will be valuable for you and your own morale.
13. Remember that minds, like parachutes, work best when they are open.

CHAPTER REVIEW

1. While many variants of a problem-solving process exist, basic steps are similar for all. They include identifying the problem, generating options, analyzing consequences, and develop-

ing plans for solutions. When these steps have been taken, implementation of the plan and follow-up activity can occur.

2. Themes that can be detrimental to serving individual needs of students are lack of knowledge, lack of skills, lack of confidence, and lack of objectivity.

3. Communication, cooperation, and coordination are vital components of effective group problem-solving.

4. Problem-identification is the most critical phase of problem-solving. Information from multiple sources, and collaborative input by a team of educators, will help identify the real problem and facilitate its solution.

5. Ten important steps in a problem-solving collaborative consultation are planning; initiating the consultation; collecting information; identifying the problem; generating options and alternatives; formulating a plan; evaluating progress; following up; interacting informally; and repeating the consultation if necessary.

6. Consultants will benefit from practicing key phrases to use during each phase of the interaction.

7. Divergent production of ideas during problem-solving can be enhanced by the use of techniques and tools such as brainstorming, lateral thinking, concept mapping, and idea checklists, jigsaw, reciprocal teaching, compare-and-contrast, and incomplete sentences. Teachers often use these techniques with students but overlook their possibilities for contributing to professional activity. Collegiality and collaboration are enhanced by the use of a variety of interaction formats such as buzz groups, huddle groups, circle responses, role plays, panels, and interviews.

TO DO AND THINK ABOUT

1. When consultants introduce themselves to consultees, what are four or five things they can mention about themselves in order to develop rapport?

2. Discuss at least five things a consultant does *not* want to happen while consulting and collaborating, along with the conditions that might cause these unwanted events, and how the conditions might be avoided or overcome. Who has the most control over whether these unwanted events will or will not happen?

3. For a challenging assignment, select a school issue or student problem and create a method for engaging in consultation by designating a system, perspective, approach, prototype, mode, and model, as discussed in Chapter 3. Carry out the consultation as a role-play or simulation, using the ten steps and verbal responses suggested in this chapter. In a "debriefing" session with your colleagues, discuss which parts of the consultation process were most difficult, some possible reasons, and what could be done to make the consultation successful.

FOR FURTHER READING

Beebe, S. A., & Masterson, J. T. (1994). *Communicating in small groups: Principles and practices* (4th ed.). New York: Harper Collins.

Buzan, T. (1983). *Use both sides of your brain.* New York: E. P. Dutton.

Corey, M. S., & Corey, G. (1992). *Groups: Process and practice* (4th ed.). Pacific Grove, CA: Brooks Cole.

Davis, G. A. & Rimm, S. B. (1989). *Education of the gifted and talented.* Englewood Cliffs, NJ: Prentice Hall. Chapters 10, 11, and 12 on creativity and thinking skills.

deBono, E. (1973). *Lateral thinking: Creativity step by step.* New York: Harper & Row.

Osborn, A. F. (1963). *Applied imagination: Principles and procedures of creative problem-solving.* New York: Charles Scribner.

Starko, A. (1995). *Creativity in the classroom: Schools of curious delight.* White Plains, NY: Longman.

6 Communication Processes

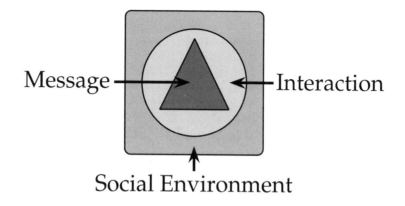

Communication is one of the greatest achievements of humankind. A vital component of human relationships in general, it is also the foundation of cooperation and collaboration among educators.

Communication involves talking, listening, managing interpersonal conflict, and addressing concerns together. Components for successful communication are understanding, trust, autonomy, and flexibility. People who can communicate effectively do so by withholding judgmental behavior and minimizing efforts to control others (Lippitt, 1983).

While problems and conflicts are unavoidable elements of life, good communication skills facilitate problem-solving and resolution of conflicts. On the other hand, ineffective communication creates a void that breeds misunderstanding and distrust. Elements of trust, commitment, and effective interaction are critical for conflict-free relationships (Lippitt, 1983). Effective communication becomes a foundation for cooperation and collaboration among school personnel and parents.

Focusing Questions

1. What is a primary reason people fail at work?
2. What are key components of the communication process?

3. How does one establish rapport in order to facilitate effective communication?
4. What are major verbal and nonverbal skills for communicating effectively?
5. What are the primary roadblocks to communication?
6. How can a school consultant be appropriately assertive and cope with resistance when the need arises?
7. What techniques and skills are useful for conflict management?
8. What are effective methods of dealing with negativity and resistance?

Key Terms

assertiveness	high-context communication	Responsive Listening Checklist
body language	low-context communication	roadblocks to communication
communication	nonverbal communication	verbal communication
conflict management	rapport	
empathy, empathic	resistance	

Communication for Effective School Relationships

People typically communicate in one form or another for about 70 percent of their waking moments. They spend about 10 percent of that time writing, 20 to 40 percent speaking, and 45 to 65 percent listening (Bolton, 1986). Unfortunately, as many as eight out of ten people who fail in their work roles do so for one reason—they do not relate well with others (Bolton, 1986).

Teachers manage many kinds of relationships in their work with children with special needs. Some relationships grow throughout the year or over several years, others are established and stable, while still others are new, tentative, and tenuous. No matter what the type of relationship, and no matter whether it is with families, colleagues, paraprofessionals, or other human service providers, communication is the key to successful relationships.

A supportive, communicative relationship among special education teachers, general classroom teachers, and parents is critical to the success of mainstreamed children with special learning needs. Trends in education emphasize the necessity for greatly strengthened communication among all who are involved with the student's educational program. Special educators must model and promote exemplary communication and interaction skills if they are to serve as consultants and team members for helping mainstreamed students succeed (Dickens & Jones, 1990).

Consulting is not a one-person exercise. A consultant will pay a high price for a "Rambo" style of interaction ("My idea can beat up your idea," or "I'm right and that's just the way it is"). Communication that minimizes conflict and enables teachers to maintain self-esteem may be the most important and most "delicate" process in consulting (Gersten et al., 1991.) Unfortunately, development of communication skills is not usually included in the formal preparation of educators. Because the development and use of "people skills"

Scenario 6

The setting is the hallway of a junior high school in midafternoon, where the general math instructor, a first-year teacher, is venting to a colleague.

MATH TEACHER: What a day! On top of the fire drill this morning and those forms that we got in our boxes to be filled out by Friday, I had a disastrous encounter with a parent.

COLLEAGUE: Oh, one of those, huh?

MATH TEACHER: Jay's mother walked into my room right before fourth-hour, and accused me of not doing my job. It was awful!

COLLEAGUE: (frowns, shakes head)

MATH TEACHER: Thank goodness there weren't any kids around. But the music teacher was there to see me about next week's program. This parent really let me have it. I was stunned, not only by the accusation, but by the way she delivered it. My whole body went on "red alert." My heart was pounding, and that chili dog I had for lunch got caught in my digestive system. Then my palms got sweaty. I could hardly squeak out a sound because my mouth was so dry. I wanted to yell back at her, but I couldn't!

COLLEAGUE: Probably just as well. Quick emotional reactions don't seem to work very well in those situations. I found out the hard way that it doesn't help to respond at all during that first barrage of words. Sounds like you did the right thing.

MATH TEACHER: Well, it really was hard. So you've had things like this happen to you?

COLLEAGUE: Um-humm. I see we don't have time for me to tell you about it, because here come our troops for their next hour of knowledge. But I can tell you all about it later if you want. Come to my room after school and we'll compare notes—maybe even plan some strategies for the future just in case. And, by the way, welcome to the club!

---

is the most difficult aspect of collaboration for many educators, more and more educators are stressing the need for specific training in consulting and communication skills to serve special needs students.

Challenges of Communication

Communication requires three elements:

- A message;
- A sender of the message, and
- A receiver of the message.

Semantics play a fundamental role in both sending and receiving messages. A person who says, "Oh, it's no big deal—just an issue of semantics" is missing a major point. The semantics frequently *are* the issue and should never be taken for granted. The vital role of semantics in consultation, collaboration, and teamwork was introduced in Chapter 2 and will be important in this chapter, with its focus on communication skills.

In order to communicate effectively, the message sender must convey the purpose of the message in a facilitative style with clarity to the receiver. Miscommunication breeds misunderstanding (Ozturk, 1992). A gap in meaning between what the message sender gives and what the message receiver gets can be described as distortion at best, or as communication trash in severe cases. A person may send the message, "You look nice today," and have it understood by the receiver as, "Gee, then I usually don't look very good." A classroom teacher wanting to reinforce the learning disabilities teacher might say "Gerry seems to get much better grades on tests in the resource room," but the resource teacher may hear, "You're helping too much and Gerry can't cope outside your protection."

Vague semantics, distorted messages, and psychological filters disrupt the message as it passes (or doesn't pass) between the sender and the receiver. Examples of filters are differing values, ambiguous language, stereotypes and assumptions, levels of self-esteem, and personal experiences. Static from preconceived ideas works constantly to prevent people from hearing what others are saying and provide only what people want to hear (Buscaglia, 1986). This can be demonstrated with the well-known game of "Gossip." Players stand in a long line or a circle, while one of them silently reads or quietly receives a message. Then that person whispers the message to the next one, and that message continues to be delivered to each one in turn. After passing through the filters of many people and stated aloud by the very last one, the message in most cases is drastically different from the original message. The game results are usually humorous. Real-life results are not always so funny.

Ethnic and Gender Differences in Communication

Language is the window through which the reality of others' experiences is revealed. Gender and ethnicity are other factors that may cloud that window and lead to systematic misjudgments in interpreting communication. Misunderstanding may not be due simply to miscommunication. Other factors such as the sex or cultural background of the sender or the receiver may be responsible. Examples of gender differences in conversational style affecting both sender and receiver of the message are discussed by sociolinguist Deborah Tannen (1994; 1991). Her research describes differences in communication styles between females (both girls and women) and males (both boys and men):

- Amount of time listening versus talking
- Interrupting
- Physical alignment during conversation
- Use of indirectness and silence
- Topical cohesion

For example, men's and boys' conversations tend to be diffuse, while those of women and girls are tightly focused with minimal topics. Educational consultants should be aware that communication style differences may lead them to be misunderstood or cause them to misunderstand their consultees.

The caveat for gender also applies to cross-cultural interactions. Most consultants are aware that different languages or different dialects may have different words for the same object. Some languages have no direct translations for terms we use in education and so must be translated indirectly.

Conversational style is a major component of ethnicity (Tannen, 1994). Different cultures use silence, interruption, proximity, eye contact, facial expression, and intonation to communicate ideas and feelings that consultants may not perceive. For example, in the Midwest it may be considered rude to interrupt; however, overlap or simultaneous group talk is the norm in some ethnic cultures or regional areas of the United States. The Athabaskans in Alaska value silence highly and devalue what they perceive as excessive talk (Scollon, 1985). Unwary educational consultants in such cases could lose much esteem for engaging in consultations as they might do elsewhere. As discussed specifically in Chapter 3 and elsewhere throughout the book, consultants will continue to be challenged by the cultural diversity of collaborators. Increasing diversity of colleagues, families, and communities requires that educational consultants recognize and continuously consider the impact of culture on communication in their work.

In order to be effective communicators, senders and receivers of messages need skills that include rapport-building, responsive listening, assertiveness, tools for dealing with resistance, and conflict-management techniques. After effective communication skills have been cultivated, consultants and consultees are able to engage more effectively in collaborative problem-solving.

Other powerful roadblocks to communication are: Too much sending, not enough receiving; excessive kindness (Fisher, 1993); reluctance to express negative information (Rinke, 1997); and inadequate feedback, that is, the sender does not find out if the message has been received, acknowledged, or understood (Fisher, 1993). When consultants use roadblocks, they are making themselves, their feelings, and their opinions the focus of the interaction, rather than allowing the focus to be the issues, concerns, or problems of the consultee. When they set up roadblocks, listeners do not listen responsively or encourage others to communicate clearly, openly, and effectively. Because it is so easy to inadvertently use a communication block through speaking, it is wise to remember the adage, "We are blessed with two ears and one mouth, a constant reminder that we should listen twice as much as we talk." Indeed, the more one talks, the more likely a person is to make errors, and the less opportunity that person will have to learn something.

Inappropriate use of terms and labels can erect roadblocks to communication. Educators should adhere to the following points when speaking or writing about people with disabilities ("Guidelines for Reporting," 1996):

1. Do not focus on the disability, but instead on issues affecting quality of life for them, such as housing, affordable health care, and employment opportunity.
2. Do not portray successful people with disabilities as superhuman, for all persons with disabilities cannot achieve this level of success.
3. Do not use generic labels such as "the retarded" or "the deaf," but say people with mental retardation or people who are deaf.
4. Emphasize abilities and not limitations, such as "uses a wheelchair," rather than "wheelchair-bound."

5. Terms such as "physically challenged" are considered condescending, and saying "victim of" is regarded as sensationalizing.
6. Do not imply disease by saying "patient" or "case" when discussing disabilities resulting from prior disease.
7. Show people with disabilities as active participants of society.
8. Use proper terms—for example, cleft lip and not hare lip, a person with cerebral palsy and not spastic (the muscles being spastic, not the people), stroke survivor and not stroke victim.

Acceptable, contemporary terminology facilitates active listening and improves verbal communication.

Skills for Communicating

Five major sets of skills are integral to successful communication:

- Rapport-building skills
- Responsive listening
- Assertion skills
- Conflict management skills
- Collaborative problem-solving skills

Rapport building is the first step in establishing a collaborative relationship. Responsive listening skills enable a person to understand what another is saying and to convey that the problems and feelings have been understood. When listening methods are used appropriately by a consultant, the consultee plays an active role in problem-solving without becoming dependent on the consultant.

Assertion skills include verbal and nonverbal behaviors that enable collaborators to maintain respect, satisfy their professional needs, and defend their rights without dominating, manipulating, or controlling others. Conflict management skills help individuals deal with the emotional turbulence that typically accompanies conflict. Conflict management skills also have a multiplier effect of fostering closer relationships when a conflict is resolved. Collaborative problem-solving skills help resolve the conflicting needs so that all parties are satisfied. Problems then "stay solved," and relationships are developed and preserved. Problem-solving was discussed in Chapter 5.

Rapport-Building to Enhance Communication

Collaboration with other professionals that is in the best interest of students with special needs often means simply sitting down and making some joint decisions. At other times, however, it must be preceded by considerable rapport building. Successful consultation necessitates good rapport between the participants in the consulting relationship. Johnson and Johnson (1987a) contend that it is more difficult to reject ideas offered by persons who are liked and respected than by those who are disliked. It is important to keep in mind that both the consultant and the consultee should provide ideas toward solving the problem. Respect must be a two-way condition for generating and accepting ideas. Rapport building is vital for building an appropriate consultation climate.

When we take time to build positive relationships with others that are based on mutual respect and trust, others are more likely to:

- Want to work with us
- Care about our reactions to them
- Try to meet our expectations
- Accept our feedback and coaching
- Imitate our behavior

We are more likely to:

- Listen to and try to understand their unique situations
- Accept them as they are and not judge them for what they are not
- Respond appropriately to their concerns and criticisms
- Advocate for, and support and encourage them in their efforts on behalf of, students with special needs

What behaviors are central to the process of building a trusting, supportive relationship? When asked this question, many teachers mention trust, respect, feeling that it is O.K. not to have all the answers, feeling free to ask questions, and feeling all right about disagreeing with the other person. People want to feel that the other person is *really* listening. Respecting differences in others is an important aspect of building and maintaining rapport. Although teachers and other school personnel are generally adept at recognizing and respecting individual differences in children, they may find this more difficult to accomplish with adults. Accepting differences in adults may be particularly difficult when the adults have different values, skills, and attitudes. Effective consultants accept people as they really are rather than wishing they were different. Rapport building is not such a formidable process when the consultant respects individual differences and expects others either to have this respect or to develop it (Margolis & McGettigan, 1988).

Responsive Listening Skills

Plutarch said, "Know how to listen and you will profit even from those who talk badly." Shakespeare referred to the "disease" of *not* listening. Listening is the foundation of communication. A person listens to establish rapport with another person. People listen when others are upset or angry, or when they do not know what to say or fear speaking out will result in trouble. People listen so others will listen to them. Listening is a process of perpetual motion that focuses on the other person as speaker and responds to that other person's ideas, rather than concentrating on one's own thoughts and feelings. Thus, effective listening is *responsive listening* because it is responding, both verbally and nonverbally, to the words and actions of the speaker.

Listening responsively and empathically is associated with the development of trust and understanding (Margolis & Brannigan, 1986; Nichols & Stevens, 1957) and with effective consulting practices (Gutkin & Curtis, 1982). It improves relationships, promotes exploration of prospective solutions (Egan, 1982), minimizes resistance (Murphy, 1987), and fosters collaboration (Idol-Maestas, Lloyd, & Lilly, 1981). Although most people are convinced of the importance of listening in building collegial relationships and preventing and solving problems, few are as adept at this skill they would like or need to be. There are several reasons for this. First, most people have not been taught to listen effectively. They have been taught to talk—especially if they are teachers, administrators, or psychologists. Educators are good at talking and regard it as an essential part of their roles. But effective talkers must be careful not to let the lines of communication get tangled up in a tendency to talk too much or too often.

Reasons for Listening.   Listening helps keep the "locus of responsibility" with the one who owns the problem (Gordon, 1977). Therefore, if one's role as a consultant is to promote problem-solving without fostering dependence on the part of the consultee, listening will keep the focus of the problem-solving where it belongs. Listening is important in showing empathy and acceptance, two vital ingredients in a relationship that fosters growth and psychological health (Gordon, 1977).

Responsive, effective listening enables you to gather information essential to your role in the education of children with special needs. It helps others feel better, often by reducing tension and anxiety, increasing feelings of personal well-being, and encouraging greater hope and optimism. This kind of listening encourages others to express themselves freely and fully. It enhances your value to others, and often contributes significantly to positive change in others' self-understanding and problem-solving abilities.

Listening can prevent or minimize misunderstandings that occur in schools when educational roles are overloaded with responsibilities. It is very difficult for one person to understand the variety and complexity of another's problems. The receiver of a communication cannot know the sender's experiences or the nuances of the message. Katz and Lawyer (1983) define communication as the exchange of meaning that allows each to influence the other's experience. Listening helps one person "experience" the other's attitudes, background, and problems.

If listening is so important, why is it so hard? First, as discussed earlier, people often are not taught to listen and do not develop the skills needed to be effective listeners. Also, people may be hesitant to listen because they think listening implies agreeing. However, listening is much more than just hearing.

Listening is difficult also because it is hard to keep an open mind about the speaker. Openness certainly is important in effective communication. Consultants must demonstrate tolerance toward differences and appreciation of richly diverse ideas and values while they are engaged in consulting relationships. A consultant's own values about child rearing, education, or the treatment of children with special needs become personal filters that make it difficult to really listen to those whose values are very different. For example, it may be hard to listen to a consultee parent who thinks it is appropriate for a very gifted daughter to drop out of school at the age of sixteen to help on the family farm because "She'll be getting married before too long and farm work will prepare her to be a wife better than schoolwork ever can." It takes discipline to listen to comments such as this when your mind is reacting negatively and wants to put together some very pointed arguments. A good rule of thumb to remember in such cases is that "when we add our two cents' worth in the middle of listening, that's just about what the communication is worth!" (Murphy, 1987).

Feelings of the listener also act as filters to impede listening. Listening is very hard work. If the listener is tired or anxious or bursting with excitement and energy, it is particularly hard to listen carefully. While listening is demanding and difficult, it is vital for the collaborative relationships that are an integral part of the school consultation process. Improving listening skills can help establish collaborative relationships with colleagues, even those with whom it is a challenge to communicate. When consultants and consultees improve their listening skills, they have a head start on solving problems, side-stepping resistance, and preventing conflicts.

There are three major components of responsive listening:

- Nonverbal listening (discerning others' needs and observing their nonverbal gestures)
- Encouraging the sending of messages (encouraging others to express themselves fully)
- Showing understanding of the message (reviewing what they conveyed)

Nonverbal Listening Skills. Responsive listeners use appropriate body language to send out the message that they are listening effectively. Some body language cues reflect ethnic background (Schein, 1969). Hall (1981) discusses a wide range of nonverbal cues that must be understood in order to interpret messages correctly. The high-context communication identified by Hall (1981) relies heavily on nonverbals and group understanding (Sue & Sue, 1990). An example is the communication that develops between twins. Another example is the shortened communication by people who know each other well and can omit much verbal communication without loss of meaning. Low-context communication puts greater reliance on the verbal part of the message.

Studies in kinesics, or communication through body language, show that the impact of a message is about 7 percent verbal, 38 percent vocal, and 55 percent facial. The eyebrows are particularly important in conveying messages. Nonverbal listening behavior of a good listener is described by Tony Hillerman in his 1990 best-seller *Coyote Waits:* "Jacobs was silent for awhile, thinking about it, her face full of sympathy. She was a talented listener. When you talked to this woman, she attended. She had all her antennae out. The world was shut out. Nothing mattered but the words she was hearing" (Hillerman, 1990, pp. 148–149).

Nonverbal listening may be particularly difficult for those people who do several things at once, such as watch a television show and write a letter, or talk to a colleague and grade papers, or prepare supper while listening to a child's synopsis of the day. This is because nonverbal components of listening should demonstrate to the speaker that the message receiver is respecting the speaker enough to concentrate on the message and is following the speaker's thoughts to find the *real* message. Careful listening conveys attitudes of flexibility, empathy, and caring, even if the speaker is using words and expressions that cloud the message. A person who is attentive leans forward slightly, engages in a comfortable level of eye contact, nods, and gives low-key responses such as "oh," and "uh-huh," and "umm-humm." The responsive listener's facial expression matches the message. If that message is serious, the expression reflects seriousness. If the message is delivered with a smile, the listener shows empathy by smiling.

The hardest part of nonverbal listening is keeping it nonverbal. It helps the listener to think about a tennis game and remember that during the listening part of the "game," the ball is in the speaker's court. The speaker has the privilege of saying anything, no matter how silly or irrelevant. The listener just keeps sending the ball back by nodding, or saying "I see" or other basically nonverbal behaviors, until he or she "hears" the sender's message. This entails using nonverbal behaviors and "listening" to the nonverbal as well as the verbal message of the sender. The listener recognizes and minimizes personal filters, perceives and interprets the filters of the sender, and encourages continued communication until capable of understanding the message from the sender's perspective. Responsive listeners avoid anticipating what the speaker will say and *never* complete a speaker's sentence.

After listeners have listened until they really hear the message, understand the speaker's position, and recognize the feelings behind the message, it is their turn to speak. But they must be judicious about what they do say. Several well-known, humorous "recipes" apply to this need.

- Recipe for speaking—stand up, speak up, then shut up.
- Recipe for giving a good speech—add shortening.
- It takes six letters of the alphabet to spell the word *listen.* Rearrange the letters to spell another word that is a necessary part of responsive listening. (Did you get *silent?*)
- In the middle of listening, the *t* doesn't make a sound.

Verbal Listening Skills. Although the first rule of the good listener is to keep your mouth shut, there are several types of verbal responses that show that the listener is following the thoughts and feelings expressed by the speaker. Verbal responses are added to nonverbal listening responses to communicate that the listener understands what the other is saying from that speaker's specific point of view. Specific verbal aspects of listening also keep the speaker talking. There are several reasons for this that are specific to the consulting process:

- The consultant will be less inclined to assume ownership of the problem.
- Speakers will clarify their own thoughts as they keep talking.
- More information will become available to help understand the speaker's point of view.
- Speakers begin to solve their own problems as they talk them through.
- The consultant continues to refine responsive listening skills.

Three verbal listening skills that promote talking by the speaker are inviting, encouraging, and questioning cautiously. Inviting means providing an opportunity for others to talk, by signaling to them that you are interested in listening if they are interested in speaking. Examples are "You seem to have something on your mind," or "I'd like to hear about your problem," or "What's going on for you now?"

Verbal responses of encouragement are added to nodding and mirroring of facial responses. "I see," "Uh-hum," and "Oh" are examples of verbal behaviors that encourage continued talking. These listener responses suggest: "Continue. I understand. I'm listening." (Gordon, 1977)

Cautious questioning is the final mechanism for promoting continued talking. Most educators are competent questioners, so the caution here is to use minimal questioning. During the listening part of communication, the message is controlled by the speaker. It is always the speaker's serve. Intensive and frequent questioning gives control of the communication to the listener. This is antithetical to the consulting process, which should be about collaboration rather than power and control. Questions should be used to clarify what the speaker has said, so the message can be understood by the listener—for example "Is this what you mean?" or "Please explain what you mean by 'attitude problem.'"

Paraphrasing Skill.   Responsive listening means demonstrating that the listener understands the essence of the message. After listening by using nonverbal and minimal verbal responses, a consultant who is really listening probably will begin to understand the message of the speaker. To show that the message was heard, or to assess whether or not what was "heard" was the same message the sender intended and was not altered by distortion, the listener should paraphrase the message. This has been called active listening (Gordon, 1977) and reflective listening (Bolton, 1986). Paraphrasing is an even more intricate skill than skills discussed earlier. It requires the listener to think carefully about the message and reflect it back to the speaker without changing the content or intent of the message.

There is no simple formula for reflecting or paraphrasing, but two good strategies are to be as accurate as possible and as brief as possible. A paraphrase may begin in one of several ways: "It sounds as if…" or "Is what you mean…?" or "So, it seems to me you want (think) (feel)…" or "Let me see if I understand. You're saying…" Paraphrasing allows listeners to check their understanding of the message. It is easy to mishear or misinterpret the message, especially if the words are ambiguous. Correct interpretation of the message will result in a nod from the speaker, who may feel that at last someone has really listened. Or the speaker may correct the message by saying, "No, that's not what I meant. It's this way…" The listener may paraphrase the content of the message. For example, "It seems to me that you're saying…" would reflect the content of the message back to the speaker. "You appear to be very frustrated about…" reflects the emotional part of the message. It is important to use the speaker's words as much as possible in the paraphrase words and to remain concise in responses. By paraphrasing appropriately, a listener demonstrates comprehension of the message or receipt of new information. This aspect of hearing and listening is essential in communication, and in assertion, problem-solving, and conflict management as well.

Just by recognizing a consultee's anger, sadness, or frustration, a consultant can begin to build a trusting relationship with a consultee. The listener doesn't necessarily have to agree with the content or emotion that is heard. It may appear absurd or illogical. Nevertheless, the consultant's responsibility is not to change another's momentary tendency; rather, it is to develop a supportive working relationship via effective communication, paving the way to successful cooperation and problem-solving while avoiding conflict and resistance.

Parents often comment that they have approached a teacher with a problem, realizing they didn't want a specific answer, but just a kindly ear—a sounding board, or a friendly

FIGURE 6.1   Responsive Listening Checklist

	Yes	No
A. *Appropriate Nonverbals*		
1. Good eye contact	_____	_____
2. Mirrored facial expression	_____	_____
3. Body orientation toward other person	_____	_____
B. *Appropriate Verbals*		
1. Door openers	_____	_____
2. Good level of encouraging phrases	_____	_____
3. Cautious questions	_____	_____
C. *Appropriate Responding Behaviors*		
1. Reflected content (paraphrasing)	_____	_____
2. Reflected feelings	_____	_____
3. Brief clarifying questions	_____	_____
4. Summarizations	_____	_____
D. *Avoidance of Roadblocks*		
1. No advice-giving	_____	_____
2. No inappropriate questions	_____	_____
3. Minimal volunteered solutions	_____	_____
4. No judging	_____	_____

(Thurston, 1989)

shoulder. Responsive listening is important in establishing collaborative relationships and maintaining them. It is also a necessary precursor to problem-solving in which both parties strive to listen and get a mutual understanding of the problem before it is addressed.

So when is responsive listening to be used? The answer is—*all* the time. Use it when establishing a relationship, when starting to problem-solve, when emotions are high, when one conversation doesn't seem to be getting anywhere, and when the speaker seems confused, uncertain, or doesn't know what else to do.

This complex process may not be necessary if two people have already developed a good working relationship and only a word or two is needed for mutual understanding. It also may not be appropriate if one of the two is not willing to talk. Sometimes "communication postponement" is best when you are too tired or too emotionally upset to be a responsive listener. When a consultant cannot listen because of any of these reasons, it is not wise to pretend to be listening, while actually thinking about something else or nothing at all. Instead, a reluctant listener should explain that he or she does not have the energy to talk about the problem now, but wishes to at a later time, for example: "I need a chance to think about this. May I talk to you later?" or "Look, I'm too upset to work on this very productively right now. Let's talk about it first thing tomorrow." Figure 6.1 summarizes responsive listening skills that help avoid blocked communication.

Roadblocks to Communication

Roadblocks (Gordon, 1977) are red flags to interaction, halting the development of effective collaborative relationships. They may be verbal behaviors or nonverbal behaviors that send out messages such as, "I'm not listening," or "It doesn't matter what you think," or "Your ideas and feelings are silly and unimportant." Roadblocks discourage the speaker and erode feelings of being able to handle problems, complete tasks, or live up to standards (Gordon, 1977).

Responsible school consultants most assuredly do not intend to send blocking messages. But by being busy, not concentrating, using poor listening skills, or allowing themselves to be directed by filters such as emotions and judgment, well-meaning consultants inadvertently send blocking messages.

Nonverbal Roadblocks. Nonverbal roadblocks include facing away when the speaker talks, displaying inappropriate facial expressions such as smiling when the sender is saying something serious, distracting with body movements such as repetitively tapping a pencil, and grading papers or writing reports while "listening." Interrupting a speaker to attend to something or someone else—the phone, a sound outside the window, or a knock at the door—also halts communication and contributes in a subtle way toward undermining the spirit of collaboration.

Verbal Roadblocks. Gordon (1977) lists twelve verbal barriers to communication. These have been called the "Dirty Dozen," and they can be grouped into three types of verbal roadblocks that prevent meaningful interaction (Bolton, 1986):

- Judging
- Sending solutions
- Avoiding others' concerns

The first category, judging, includes criticizing, name-calling, and diagnosing or analyzing why a person is behaving a particular way. False or nonspecific praise, and evaluative words or phrases, send a message of judgment toward the speaker. "You're not thinking clearly," "You'll do a wonderful job of using curriculum-based assessment!" and "You don't really believe that—you're just tired today," are examples of judging. (Notice that each of these statements begins with the word "you.") Avoiding judgment about parents or others helps teachers avoid deficit-based thinking, which hurts everyone it touches (Lovett, 1996). Nonjudgmental communication conveys interpersonal equity (Gibb, 1974), which is a vital component of a collaborative relationship.

Educators are particularly adept with the next category of verbal roadblocks—sending solutions. These include directing or ordering, warning, moralizing or preaching, advising, and using logical arguments or lecturing. A few of these can become a careless consultant's entire verbal repertoire. "Not knowing the question," Bolton (1986, p. 37) says, "it was easy for him to give the answer." "Stop complaining," and "Don't talk like that," and "If you don't send Jim to the resource room on time…" are examples of directing or warning. Moralizing sends a message of "I'm a better educator than you are." Such communication usually starts with "You should…" or "You ought to….". When consultees have problems, the last thing they need is to be told what they *should* do.

Avoiding others' concerns is a third category of verbal roadblocks. This category implies "no big deal" to the message receiver. Avoidance messages include reassuring or sympathizing, such as "You'll feel better tomorrow" or "Everyone goes through this stage," or interrogating to get more than necessary information thereby delaying problem solving. Other avoidance messages include intensive questioning in the manner of the Grand Inquisition, and humoring or distracting, "Let's get off this and talk about something else." Avoiding the concerns others express sends the message that their concerns are not important.

Advising, lecturing, and logical argument are all too often part of the educator's tools of the trade. Teachers tend to use roadblock types of communication techniques frequently with students. The habits they develop cause them to overlook the reality that use of such tactics with adults can drive a wedge into an already precarious relationship. Consultants must avoid tactics such as assuming the posture of the "sage-on-the-stage," imparting wisdom in the manner of a learned professor to undergraduate students, lecturing, moralizing, and advising. Unfortunately, these methods imply superiority, which is detrimental to the collaborative process.

Assertiveness

By the time the consultant has listened effectively and the collaborative relationship has been developed or enhanced, many consultants are more than ready to start talking. Once the sender's message is understood and emotional levels are reduced, it is the listener's turn to be the sender. Now the consultant gets to talk. However, it is not always easy to communicate your thoughts, feelings, and opinions without infringing on the rights, feelings, or opinions of others. This is the time for assertiveness.

Being assertive involves achieving your goals without damaging the relationship or another's self-esteem (Katz & Lawyer, 1983). The basic aspects of assertive communication (Sundel & Sundel, 1980; Alberti & Emmons, 1974; Thurston, 1987) are

> Use an "I" message instead of a "you" message.
> Say "and" instead of "but."
> State the behavior objectively.
> Name your own feelings.
> Say what you want to happen.
> Express concern for others.
> Use assertive body language.

Open and honest consultants say what they want to happen and what their feelings are. That does not mean they always get what they want. Saying what you want and how you feel will clarify the picture and assure that the other(s) won't have to guess what you want or think. Even if others disagree with the ideas and opinions, they can never disagree with the feelings and wishes. Those are very personal and are expressed in a personal manner by starting the interaction with "I," rather than presenting feelings and opinions as truth or expert answer.

In stating an idea or position assertively, consultants should describe the problem in terms of its impact on the consultant, rather than in terms of what was done or said by the other person. "I feel let down" works better than "You broke your part of the agreement." If a consultant makes a "you" statement about the consultee which the consultee thinks is wrong, the consultant will only get an angry reaction and the consultant's concerns will be ignored.

Concern for Others during the Interaction. Expressing concern for others can take many forms. This skill demonstrates that although people have thoughts and feelings which differ from those of others, they can still respect the feelings and ideas of others. "I realize it is a tremendous challenge to manage thirty-five children in the same classroom." This statement shows the consultant understands the management problems of the teacher. As the consultant goes on to state preferences in working with the teacher, the teacher is more likely to listen and work cooperatively. The consultee will see that the consultant is aware of the problems that must be dealt with daily. "It seems to me that…" and "I understand…" and "I realize…" and "It looks like…" are phrases consultants can use to express concern for the other person in the collaborative relationship. If the consultant cannot complete these sentences with the appropriate information, the next step is to go back to the listening part of the communication.

How to Be Concerned and Assertive. Assertive people own their personal feelings and opinions. Being aware of this helps them state their wants and feelings. "You" sentences sound accusing, even when that is not intended, which can lead to defensiveness in others. For example, saying to a parent, "You should provide a place and quiet time for Hannah to do her homework," is more accusatory than saying, "I am frustrated when Hannah isn't getting her homework done, and I would like to work with you to think of some ways to help her get it done." Using "and" rather than "but" is very important in expressing thoughts without diminishing a relationship. This is a particularly difficult assertion skill. To the listener the word "but" tends to erase any preceding phrase and prevents the real message from coming through.

It is important to state behavior specifically. By describing behavior objectively, a consultant or consultee sounds less judgmental. It is easy to let blaming and judgmental words creep into language. Without meaning to, the speaker throws up a barrier that blocks the communication and the relationship.

Assertive communication includes demonstrating supportive body language. A firm voice, straight posture, eye contact, and body orientation toward the receiver of the message will have a desirable effect. Assertive body language affirms that the sender owns his or her own feelings and opinions but also respects the other person's feelings and opinions. This a difficult balance to achieve. Body language and verbal language must match or the messages will be confusing. Skills for being assertive are listed in Figure 6.2.

What we say and how we say it have a tremendous impact on the reactions and acceptance of others. When consultants and consultees communicate in ways that accurately

---

APPLICATION **6.1**

Communicating Positively

Compare the first statement with the second one:

1. "I would like to have a schedule of rehearsals for the holiday pageant. It is frustrating when I drive out to work with Maxine and Juanita and they are practicing for the musical and can't come to the resource room."
2. "When you don't let me know ahead of time that the girls won't be allowed to come and work with me, I have to waste my time driving and can't get anything accomplished."

In reflecting on these statements, which one is less judgmental and accusatory? Can these two contrasting statements create differing listener attitudes toward the speakers? For many listeners the judgmental words and phrases in the second sentence ("you don't let me know," "won't be allowed," "waste my time") sound blaming. They introduce a whole array of red flags.

---

reflect their feelings, focus on objective descriptions of behavior and situations, and think in a concrete manner about what they want to happen, assertive communication will build strong, respectful relationships. Assertive communication is the basis for solving problems and resolving conflicts.

The Art of Apologizing. Sometimes, despite good communication skills and careful relationship-building and problem-solving, consultants make errors and mistakes. Good consultants never blame someone else for communication breakdowns; they accept

FIGURE 6.2 Assertiveness Checklist

	Usually	Sometimes	Never
1. Conveys "I" instead of "you" message			
2. Says "and" rather than "but"			
3. States behavior objectively			
4. Says what he/she wants to have happen			
5. States feelings			
6. Expresses concern			
7. Speaks firmly, clearly			
8. Has assertive posture			
9. Avoids aggressive language			

responsibility for their own communication. This is demonstrated when a consultant says "Let me explain in a different way" instead of "Can't you understand?" Good consultants also use the art of apologizing.

One of the biggest misconceptions in the area of consultation and collaboration is that apologizing puts consultants and teachers at a disadvantage when working with colleagues and parents. It is simply not true that strong, knowledgeable people never say they're sorry. In fact, apologizing is a powerful strategy because it demonstrates honesty and confidence. Apologizing offers a chance to mend fences in professional relationships. Some suggestions from psychologist Barry Lubetkin (1996) about how to apologize include allowing the person you've wronged to vent her or his feelings first, apologize as soon as possible, don't say "I'm sorry, but…," and say it once and let that be enough. Most importantly, apologies are empty if you keep repeating the behavior or the mistake.

Managing Resistance, Anger and Negativity

Communication is the key to collaboration and problem-solving. Without back-and-forth discussions, there can be no agreement. Problem-solving often breaks down because communications break down first, either because people are not paying attention or because they misunderstand the other side, or because emotions were not dealt with as a separate and primary issue. In problem-solving it is critical to separate the person from the problem. Consultants need to deal with emotions, as well as any errors in perceptions or communication, as separate issues which must be resolved on their own. Emotions may take the form of resistance, anger, or negativity; and emotions may become barriers of effective communication when they are experienced by the consultant or the consultee. Sometimes, regardless of how skillful and diplomatic people are in dealing with the emotions of others, they run into barriers of resistance in their attempts to communicate with others.

It is estimated that as much as 80 percent of problem solving with others is getting through the resistance. Resistance is a trait of human nature that surfaces when people are asked to change. A wise person once suggested, "How can we ask others to change when it is so hard to change ourselves?" Resistance often has nothing to do with an individual personally or even with a new idea. The resistance is simply a reaction to change of any kind. It requires new ways of thinking and behaving (Margolis & McGettigan, 1988). Change implies imperfection in the way things are being done, and this makes people defensive.

Why Educators Resist

As discussed in Chapter 1, teachers value their autonomy (Parish & Arends, 1983). They tend to interpret instructional modifications for exceptional learners as limits on their freedom to make instructional decisions (Truesdell, 1988). When people experience such threats to their freedoms, they often demonstrate resistance (Hughs & Falk, 1981).

It is human nature to be uncomfortable when another person disagrees. It is also human nature to get upset when someone resists efforts to make changes, implement plans, or modify systems to be more responsive to children with special needs. The need for change can generate powerful emotions. Most people are uncomfortable when experiencing the strong emotions of others. When someone yells or argues, the first impulse is to become defensive, argue the other point of view, and defend your own ideas. Although a school consultant may intend to remain cool, calm, and collected in the interactions that involve exceptional children, occasionally another individual says something that pushes a "hot button" and the consultant becomes upset, angry, or defensive.

Special education consulting teachers who have been asked to describe examples of resistance toward their roles provide these examples:

> Consultees (classroom teachers) won't share how they feel.
> They act excited about an idea, but never get around to doing it.
> They won't discuss it with you, but they do so liberally with others behind your back.
> They may try, but give up too soon.
> They take out their frustrations on the students.
> They are too quick to say that a strategy won't work in their situation.
> They dredge up a past example where something similar didn't work.
> They keep asking for more and more details or information before trying an idea.
> They change the subject, or suddenly have to be somewhere else.
> They state that there is not enough time to implement the strategy.
> They intellectualize with a myriad of reasons it won't work.
> They are simply silent.

When resistance spawns counter-resistance and anger, an upward spiral of emotion is created that can make consulting unpleasant and painful. Bolton (1986) describes resistance as a push, push-back phenomenon. When a person meets resistance with more resistance, defensiveness, logical argument, or any other potential roadblock, resistance increases and dialogue can develop into open warfare. Then the dialogue may become personal or hurtful. Nobody listens at that point, and a potentially healthy relationship is damaged and very difficult to salvage.

How to Deal with Resistance

An important strategy for dealing with resistance and defensiveness is to handle your own defensiveness, stop pushing so that the other person will not be able to push back, delay reactions, keep quiet, and *listen*. This takes practice, patience, tolerance, and commitment. It is important to deal with emotions such as resistance, defensiveness, or anger before proceeding to problem-solving. People are not inclined to listen until they have been listened to. They will not be convinced of another's sincerity and openness, or be capable of thinking logically, when the filter of emotions is clouding their thinking.

Negative people and negative emotions sap the energy of educational consultants. Reactions to negative people, to conflict, and to resistance can block communication and ruin potentially productive relationships. It is important to remember that negative people are not going to change. The person who has to change is the consultant.

The first step is to find an antidote to one's reaction to negative thinking and to deal first with one's own emotional reaction. According to William Ury of the Program on Negotiation at Harvard Law School, one of the keys to working with difficult people is controlling your own behavior (Ury, 1991). Instead of reacting, you need to regain your mental balance and stay focused. So his suggestion is, don't react.

The natural reaction to resistance, challenges, and negativity is to strike back, give in, or break off the communication. A negative reaction to resistance leads to a vicious cycle of action and reaction and leads to communication and relationship breakdowns.

Ury (1991) suggests two strategies for curbing one's own natural reactions to resistance and negativity. First is to "go to the balcony." This means distancing oneself from the action–reaction cycle. Step back and take a deep breath and try to see the situation objectively. Imagine yourself climbing to the balcony overlooking the stage where the action–reaction drama has been taking place. Here, you can calmly look at the situation, with a detached or third-party perspective. Going to the balcony means removing yourself from your natural impulses and emotions. Remember, when your "hot buttons" get pushed or when you find yourself getting emotional and reacting, instead of acting, go to the balcony!

Another strategy Ury (1991) suggests is to keep your eyes on the prize. Dealing with emotional and difficult situations in collaborative efforts usually diverts us from our goals and causes distress, so always keep your mind on the larger picture. In the collaborative consultant's case, the prize is optimal developmental and educational outcomes for students with special needs. If we remember that the communication process is crucial to the relationships among the stakeholders in a student's education, we will remember that diversions are worth dealing with and the eventual outcome is well worth the process.

Consultants must "hear their way to success" in managing resistance. This may take five minutes, or months of careful relationship building. Colleagues cannot always avoid disagreements that are serious enough to create anger and resistance. A comment or question

APPLICATION **6.2**
Managing Resistance

Construct a problem situation involving another person that could happen, or *has* happened, in your school context and interact with a colleague to try these communication techniques:

Dismiss the negativity with "You may be right," and keep moving forward. Be assertive, i.e., "I am bothered by discussing the negative side of things." Ask for complaints in writing (because some people don't realize how negative they sound). Ask for clarification, also, by suggesting that the person describe the problem and clarify the desired outcome. This leads people to thinking about positive actions. Don't defend attacks, and invite criticism and advice instead. Ask what's wrong. Look for interests behind resistance, negativity, and anger by asking "why" questions. Tentatively agree by saying "that's one opinion."

Switch roles and try another episode. Then have a debriefing session to critique the interactions.

delivered in the wrong manner at the wrong time may be the "hot button" that triggers the antagonism. Consider remarks such as these:

> "If you want students to use good note-taking skills, shouldn't you teach them how to take notes?"
>
> "Not allowing learning disabled students to use calculators is cruel."
>
> "Why don't you teach in a way that accommodates different learning styles?"
>
> "You penalize gifted students when you keep the class in lockstep with basal readers."

Such remarks can make harried, overworked classroom teachers defensive and resentful. If an occasion arises in which a teacher or parent becomes angry or resistant, responding in the right way will prevent major breakdowns in the communication that is needed.

Conflict Management

Conflicts are a part of life. They occur when there are unreconciled differences among people in terms of needs, values, goals, and personalities. If conflicting parties cannot give and take by integrating their views and utilizing their differences constructively, interpersonal conflicts will escalate. School consultants and collaborators are not exempt from the dysfunction that often accompanies conflict. So it is important for them to develop tools for transforming vague and ambiguous sources of conflict into identified problems that can be solved collaboratively. Lippitt (1983) suggests that conflict, as a predictable social phenomenon, should not be repressed, because there are many positive aspects to be valued. Conflict can help clarify issues, increase involvement, and promote growth, as well as strengthen relationships and organizational systems when the issues are resolved. Gordon (1977) contends it is undesirable to avoid conflict when there is genuine disagreement, because resentments build up, feelings get displaced, and unpleasantries such as backbiting, gossiping, and general discontent may result.

Reasons for Conflict among Educators.   Teachers, administrators, and parents face many possible occasions for conflict when they are involved with educating children who have special needs. Some conflicts occur because there is too little information or because misunderstandings have been created from incorrect information. These instances are not difficult to resolve because they require only the communication of facts. Other areas of conflict arise from disagreement over teaching methods, assessment methods, goals, and values. Parent goals and teacher goals for the exceptional student may differ significantly, and support personnel may add even more dimensions to the conflict. For example, if a child is instructed by the reading specialist to read more slowly, urged by the learning disabilities teacher to read more rapidly, required by the classroom teacher to read a greater amount of material, and ordered by the parent to get better grades or *else,* effective communication is tenuous or nonexistent, and conflict is inevitable.

Perhaps the most difficult area of conflict relates to values. When people have differing values about children, education, or educator roles within the learning context, effective communication is a challenging goal. As discussed earlier in this chapter, rapport building, listening, and paraphrasing are significant in building relationships among those whose values conflict. The most important step is to listen courteously until a clear message about the value comes through, demonstrating respect for the value even if it conflicts with yours. Then it is time to assert your own values and, along with the other person, try to reach a common goal or seek a practical issue on which to begin problem-solving.

How to Resolve Conflicts in the School Context.   Some conflicts, particularly those involving values, are difficult to prevent and may seem at the time to be unresolvable. However, if all can agree to common goals or common ground for discussion, conflicts can be resolved.

When emotions or conflict inhibit the communication process, Fisher, Ury, and Patton (1981) suggest first listening responsively and acknowledging what is being said. The other side appreciates the sense of being heard and understood, and the consultant will gain a vivid picture of their interests and concerns. They also suggest the strategy of focusing on interests rather than positions as a way to circumvent potential conflicts during the communication process.

Gordon (1977) and many others suggest that conflict resolution can follow one of three paths:

- I win, you lose.
- You win, I lose.
- I win, you win.

The first two paths are frequently taken because people fear conflict and wish to avoid it. The third path, with the win/win outcome, is hard because those involved must confront their emotions and the emotions of others, and work diligently to turn conflict into cooperation. This method focuses on needs rather than solutions. It is based on two-way communication with lots of listening. During conflict situations, the immediate purpose of interaction is improving communication, not changing points of view.

"Always think win/win" is one of Stephen Covey's (1989) seven habits of highly effective people and is a crucial element of effective relationships and problem-solving in educational and community settings. If you can't come to a true win/win agreement, Covey suggests, it is better to go for no deal at all. This allows you to preserve the relationship and the possibility for a win/win pact in the future. Win/win agreements flow from solid relationships, and taking time to develop a strong level of trust is essential for mutual collaboration. We must resist the urge to succeed at the expense of the other person. This forms a relationship that is open to success on both sides in the future.

Covey (1989) suggests a four-step process for the win/win approach:

1. Try to see the situation from the other person's perspective.
2. Identify the key issues and concerns involved.
3. Make a list of the results that you would consider a fully acceptable solution.
4. Look for new options to get those results.

Resolving conflicts within an "everybody wins" philosophy requires listening skills described earlier in the chapter to find common ground. In dealing with emotions of the speaker, the listener must concentrate with an open mind and attend to the speaker's feelings as well as the facts or ideas that are part of the message. The listener must strive to hear the whole story without interrupting, even if there are strong feelings of disagreement. Conflict usually means that intense emotions are involved. Only by concentrating on the message with an open mind can all parties begin to deal with the conflict. Emotional filters often function as blinders. If the emotions cannot be overcome, the best tactic is to postpone the communication, using assertive responses to do so.

Listening establishes a common intent and develops a starting attitude. Listening to one who is upset helps that person focus on a problem rather than an emotion. Listening lets people cool down. Bolton (1986) calls this the spiral of resistance, suggesting that if one listens with empathy and does not interrupt, the speaker's anger or high emotion will dissipate. Without saying a word, the listener makes the speaker feel accepted and respected.

It is hard to argue with someone who does not argue back. It is hard to stay mad or upset with someone who seems to understand and empathize. Each time a person listens, a small victory for the advancement of human dignity has been achieved (Schindler & Lapid, 1989). Only after emotions are brought into the open and recognized can all parties involved move on to seek a common goal.

Barriers to communication among educators and families may sometimes be specific conditions such as learning disabilities. When education consultants work with parents, paraprofessionals, or other adults who may have a learning disability such as ADHD, as discussed in Chapter 3, some suggestions for improving communication are:

- Break large tasks or bodies of information into smaller ones.
- Give information in a very structured manner.
- Offer "organizational tools" such as notes, colored files or flyers for color coding, paper for taking notes or printed notes.
- Be very careful about being critical.
- Offer plenty of positive feedback, when warranted.
- Encourage them to tape meetings or instructions.
- Communicate frequently and offer information in smaller segments.
- Frequently test the accuracy of communication by asking them to repeat or rephrase what was said.

The initial intent for resolving a conflict should be to learn. This enables all factions to increase mutual understanding and think creatively together. Most people could agree to such a start because it does not address goals or values. It does not even require agreement that a problem exists. It simply establishes the intent to learn by working together. Establishing intent for dialogue should follow the reduction of emotional responses. Of course, as discussed earlier, it is important to avoid roadblocks at all stages of the process.

Consultants and consulting teachers must put aside preconceived notions about their own expertise and learn from those who often know the student best—parents and classroom teachers. Such consultees respond positively to open-ended questions that let them know they are respected and needed. When consultants open their own minds, they unlock the potential of others.

After listening constructively, consultants need to help establish ground rules for resolving the conflict. The ground rules should express support, mutual respect, and a commitment to the process. Again, this requires talking and listening, dialoguing, and keeping an open mind. It is important not to dominate the dialogue at this time and, by the same token, not to let the other person dominate the conversation. This part of the communication might be called "agreeing to disagree," with the intent of "agreeing to find a point of agreement." It is important to share the allotted interaction time equitably and in a way that facilitates understanding. Consultants must use precise language without exaggerating points, or, as discussed earlier, flaunting "educationese" or taking inappropriate shortcuts with jargon and "alphabet soup" acronyms.

Dealing with conflict productively also requires asserting your ideas, feelings, or opinions. While listening enables the consultant to understand the speaker's perspectives, wants, and goals, assertion skills allow consultants to present their perspective. This often follows a pattern of listen—assert—listen—assert—listen, and so on, until both parties have spoken and have been heard.

Although there may be resistance after each assertion, it will gradually dissipate so that *real* communication and collaboration can begin to take place. Only after this process has happened can collaborative goal setting and problem-solving occur. Figure 6.3 summarizes useful steps for managing resistance and conflict.

There is a well-known story of a man who had three sons. He stipulated in his will that the oldest son should inherit half his camels, the middle son should get one-third of the camels, and the youngest should be the new owner of one-ninth of his camels. When the old man died, he owned seventeen camels. But the sons could not agree on how to divide the camels in accordance with their father's will. Months and months of bitter conflict went by. Finally the three young men sought the advice of a wise woman in the village. She heard their complaints and observed their bitterness and felt sorry that brothers were fighting and putting the family into turmoil. So she gave the brothers one of her camels. The estate then was divided easily according to the father's wishes. The eldest took home nine camels, the second put six camels beside his tent, and the youngest took home two camels. The men were happy, the father's last wishes were honored, and the wise woman took her own camel back and led it home.

Conflict management is the process of becoming aware of a conflict, diagnosing its nature, and employing an appropriate problem-solving method in such a way that it simultaneously achieves the goals of all involved and enhances relationships among them. If the consulting relationship is treated as a collaborative one in which each person's needs are met (the win/win model), then feelings of self-confidence, competence, self-worth, and power increase, enhancing the overall capacity of the system for responding to conflict in the future (Katz & Lawyer, 1983). The win/win relationship is based on honesty, trust, and mutual respect—qualities stressed earlier as vital to a successful consulting relationship. Win/win allows all involved parties to experience positive outcomes. The model works best when all parties use effective communication skills (Fisher & Ury, 1981).

The opposite of successful conflict management is avoiding conflict, ignoring feelings, and bypassing the goals of others. The relationship becomes adversarial, if it is not

FIGURE 6.3   Checklist for Managing Resistance and Conflict

A. *Responsive Listening*

   1. Had assertive posture   _____

   2. Used appropriate nonverbal listening   _____

   3. Did not become defensive   _____

   4. Used minimal verbals in listening   _____

   5. Reflected content   _____

   6. Reflected feelings   _____

   7. Let others do most of the talking   _____

   8. Used only brief, clarifying questions   _____

B. *Assertiveness*

   9. Did not use roadblocks such as giving advice   _____

  10. Used "I" messages   _____

  11. Stated wants and feelings   _____

C. *Recycled the interaction*

  12. Used positive postponement   _____

  13. Did not problem-solve before emotions were controlled   _____

  14. Summarized   _____

  15. Set time to meet again, if applicable   _____

already so, because for someone to win, another must lose. When conflicts are approached with responsive listening and dealt with honestly and openly, the underlying problem or need can be resolved.

When engineers stress collaboration, they often use the bumblebee analogy. According to the laws of aerodynamics, bumblebees cannot fly. But as everyone knows, they do. By the same token, some might say that groups cannot function productively because of the conflicts, personal agenda, and individual preferences that exist among the members. But they do. Groups of people play symphonies, set up businesses, write laws, and develop IEPs for student needs. An understanding of adult individual differences, styles, and preferences, as discussed in Chapter 3, will encourage participants in consultation and collaboration to listen more respectfully and value differences among colleagues. This knowledge, when combined with responsive listening, avoidance of roadblocks, and assertiveness, will enable consultants to deal with resistance and conflict productively. Conflict management puts these skills to practical use in educational settings of school and home.

Educational consultants maximize their effect on the lives and education of children with special needs by using good communication skills. They should always keep in mind the ancient rule we instill in children for crossing the street: "Stop, Look, and Listen." For the collaborative school consultant it means:

- Stop talking, judging, and giving advice.
- Look at the long-term outcome of good communication (keep eyes on the prize).
- Listen to parents, colleagues, and others who work in collaboration for children with special needs.

The stop, look, and listen rule sets up consultants for success—in establishing collaborative relationships, in developing rapport, in dealing with conflict and emotions, and in solving problems.

Tips for Communicating Effectively

1. Avoid communication roadblocks. Research shows that positively worded statements are one-third easier to understand than negative ones (Rinke, 1997).
2. Listen. This helps dissipate negative emotional responses and often helps the other person articulate the problem, perhaps finding a solution then and there.
3. Use assertion. Say what you feel and what your goals are.
4. Be aware of your "hot buttons." Knowing your own responses to certain "trigger" behaviors and words will help you control natural tendencies to argue, get defensive, or simply turn red and sputter.
5. Attend to nonverbal language (kinesics, or body language) as well as to verbal language when communicating.
6. Don't "dump your bucket" of frustrations onto the other person. Jog, shout, practice karate, but avoid pouring out anger and frustration on others. Instead, fill the buckets of others with "warm fuzzies" of empathy and caring.
7. Develop a protocol within the school context for dealing with difficult issues and for settling grievances.
8. Deal with the present. Keep to the issue of the current problem rather than past problems, failures, or personality conflicts.
9. Use understanding of individual differences among adults to bridge communication gaps and manage conflicts in educational settings.
10. Advocate for training that focuses on communication, problem solving, and conflict management.

CHAPTER REVIEW

1. The primary reason people fail at work is because of communication problems. It is too often assumed that communication skill develops with no special attention to the complexities of social interaction.

2. The sender, the message, and the receiver are three key components of the communication process. Each component is vital. When a message is missent or misheard, many distortions occur which prevent open, honest communication. This happens because of differences in values, language, attitudes, perceptions, gender, ethnicity, and history of sender and receiver.

3. Rapport-building requires respect for differences in others, trust, feeling all right about not having all the answers, and being comfortable even when there is disagreement.

4. Major skills in effective communication are responsive listening, asserting, managing conflict, and collaborative problem-solving. Both verbal and nonverbal components are included in these skills. The skills form the basis of a respectful, egalitarian relationship and a successful team on behalf of the student with special needs. They pave the way to effective problem-solving and mutual collaboration.

5. Communication can be hampered by verbal roadblocks and nonverbal roadblocks. Verbal roadblocks include responses which are judging, responses that send solutions, and responses that avoid the concerns of others. Nonverbal roadblocks include body language that conveys lack of empathy and concern.

6. Assertive communication allows speakers to state their own views, feelings, and opinions without impeding the ongoing consulting process. Assertiveness means stating one's wants or feelings by starting sentences with "I," using "and" rather than "but," and showing concern for the other person. Resistance sometimes occurs when a speaker is assertive. This resistance is a natural reaction to the request for change. It can be managed by using a combination of assertiveness and responsive listening.

7. Conflict arises when members of educational teams have different feelings, values, needs, and goals. Conflict resolution should follow a win/win model if collaborative efforts are to be maintained. Listening instead of arguing, establishing ground rules, and seeking a common goal will help bring teams to the problem-solving stage without any "losers."

8. Negativity and resistance are residuals of disagreements and unwanted change. Consultants will want to remain calm and listen, using strategies such as "going to the balcony" and "hearing their way to success."

TO DO AND THINK ABOUT

1. Discuss the following:

What roadblock does each of these comments set up?

> What you need is more activity. Why don't you develop a hobby?

> You are such a good friend. I can count on you.

> Let's talk about something more positive.

> I know just how you feel.

> Why did you let her talk to you that way?

Which of these lines create resistance and defensiveness?

> What you should do is…

Do you want to comment on this?

Everyone has problems like that.

That's a good thought.

You mean you'd actually do that?

Let's change the subject.

What should I do?

What assertive statements could be made for each situation?

A colleague talks to you about his personal problems and you can't get your work done.

The para-educator comes in late frequently.

During a committee meeting one member keeps changing the subject and getting the group off task.

A colleague wants to borrow some material but has failed to return things in the past.

During a phone conversation with a wordy parent, you need to get some information quickly and hang up soon.

The class next door is so rowdy that your class can't work.

2. Discuss these basic assumptions about communication for consultation and add more to the list.

The reactions of others depend on your actions, word choices, body language, and listening skills.

People generally want to do a good job.

People have a powerful need to "save face."

No one can force another person to change.

Learning to communicate, be assertive, and facilitate conflict resolution is awkward at first.

3. During initial attempts at paraphrasing, the process often feels and sounds awkward and phony. What might be done about that?

4. Practice the following situations:

expressing anger in constructive ways;

getting the interaction back on task;

stating a contrasting view to a supervisor-type;

recommending a better way of doing something;

asking again, and again, for materials you loaned some time ago and you need now.

5. Restate the following message so the language is assertive but nonthreatening to the receiver.

"You penalize gifted students when you keep the class lockstepped in the basal texts and the workbooks."

"If you want students to use good note-taking skills, you should teach them how to take notes."

"Not allowing students to use calculators is poor teaching practice and terribly outmoded."

"It is not fair to insist that learning disabled students take tests they cannot read."

FOR FURTHER READING

Bolton, R. (1986). *People skills: How to assert yourself, listen to others, and resolve conflicts.* New York: Simon and Schuster.

Fisher, R. & Ury, W. (1981). *Getting to yes: Negotiating agreement without giving in.* New York: Penguin.

Hall, E. T. (1959). *The silent language.* New York: Doubleday.

Rinke, W. J. (1997). *Winning management: 6 fail-safe strategies for building high-performance organizations.* Clarksville, MD: Achievement Publishers.

Smith, D. K. (1996). *Taking charge of change: 10 principles for managing people and performance.* Reading, MA: Addison-Wesley Publishing Co.

7 Managing Time and Technology

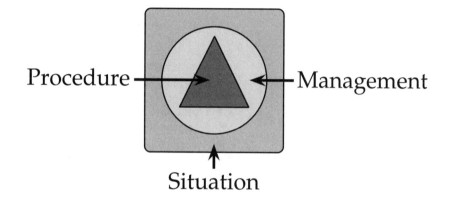

Procedure ← → Management

Situation

Schools are bustling arenas of activities that often seem to have little to do with books and studies. Not only do school personnel teach students in academic settings, they also feed them, transport them, keep records, counsel and advise, dispense materials and resources, address social and health problems, and much, much more. If the services of various school-related roles such as librarian, speech pathologist, school psychologist, social worker, nurse, were included, the list of responsibilities would be even more daunting.

In this complex hubbub the demands on educators for efficiency, expertise, and accountability can be overwhelming. Stress and fatigue take a toll, with burnout and attrition from the field an all too frequent result. Nevertheless, role-related stress can be minimized and heavy responsibilities controlled by managing time and resources wisely and by organizing technology efficiently.

Focusing Questions

1. What aspects of their roles cause school personnel to be vulnerable to stress and burnout?

2. What organizational techniques can help consultants and collaborators perform their roles effectively?
3. What procedures for conducting meetings, interviews, and observations contribute to consultation and collaboration success?
4. How can collaborating school consultants manage records and resources efficiently?
5. How can telecommunications and electronic networks make consultation, collaboration, and teamwork more efficient and effective?
6. What time-consuming routine tasks in collaborative settings can be done more efficiently with the use of technology?
7. How can consultants provide leadership in schools to assure effective use of technology for needs of students with disabilities in general classrooms?

Key Terms

attrition	local area network (LAN)	stress management
burnout	observation	technology-infused
consultation log or journal	scan	environments
electronic bonding	shell or template	telecommunications
electronic bulletin board	single agenda meetings	time management
electronic mail (e-mail)	(SAM)	wide area network (WAN)
emerging technology	software	word processor
FAX	SpecialNET	
interview	spreadsheet	

Stress, Burnout, and Attrition

Rising costs, public criticism, low morale, and an avalanche of regulations and paperwork create pressures on educators that erode their ability to prepare students for a successful future. Some remain in the profession and juggle their daily routines within a burgeoning agenda of reform and mandates. Others burn out and leave the profession. Still others simply "fizzle out," "rust out," or "coast out." The latter go through the motions of their profession in lackluster fashion, just getting by until retirement age arrives or opportunity for a better situation comes along. These educators create situations that are particularly penalizing for students who have special needs and are the most vulnerable to effects of uninspired teaching.

Burnout disproportionately affects those in human service professions (Maslach, 1982). High levels of emotional exhaustion and depersonalization, when accompanied by low feelings of personal accomplishment, signal burnout for teachers, social workers, nurses, and others who serve people's needs. They feel used up and exhausted physically, emotionally, and attitudinally. Truch (1980) describes the condition as being "chronically miserable."

As advocates for children with special learning and behavior needs, special education teachers may set unreasonably high expectations for themselves and others. Lack of role clarity, and discrepancy between their own role perceptions and the expectations of

Scenario 7

CONSULTANT: Mr. Wilcox, please.

SECRETARY: I'm sorry, but Mr. Wilcox is in a meeting right now. May I take a message?

CONSULTANT: This is Ms. Spencer, the school psychologist in Centennial School. I need to speak with him about one of the students in his class. (The consultant makes similar calls to team members with similar results.)

Later that day:

WILCOX: I'm returning a call to Ms. Spencer.

SECRETARY: I'm sorry, but Ms. Spencer is away from her desk. May I ask her to return your call?

WILCOX: Yes, please do.

Later that day:

CONSULTANT: Mr. Wilcox, please.

SECRETARY: I'm sorry, but Mr. Wilcox is away from his desk. May I ask him to return your call?

CONSULTANT: No, I will try to reach him later, thank you.

---

others, contribute to this syndrome (Bensky, Shaw, Gouse, Bates, Dixon, & Beane, 1980). Dettmer (1982) identifies lack of recognition and reinforcement for their work, along with heavy responsibilities without much decision-making authority, as additional stressors for special education personnel. There may be a cyclical or reciprocal relationship between teacher stress and student behavior (Shaw, Bensky, & Dixon, 1981). For example, short term results of teacher stress such as irritability, inability to concentrate, disorganization, and poor management of work flow can affect the behavior and performance of students.

The overwhelming responsibilities and pressures of working with special needs students make teachers particularly vulnerable to stress and burnout, and the severity varies by service-delivery model. In a study of more than 600 special educators in the midwest, Zabel and Zabel (1982) found that consulting teachers rank higher in emotional exhaustion and depersonalization than those in other service deliveries. The researchers propose that this occurs because consulting teachers serve large geographic areas, many students, and a wide range of expectations by others. They have multiple bosses, heavy caseloads, and a position that provides fewer feelings of personal accomplishment.

Minimizing Stress of Professional Responsibilities

Stress results from actions or situations that place special physical or psychological demands on a person. When the stressors cannot be balanced by one's coping mechanisms, an imbalance or disequilibrium is created (Sapolsky, 1994). Medical research has shown that under stress a person's body responds in a stereotypical pattern (Selye, 1993). The body senses the stressor and prepares for "flight or fight." It responds by releasing hormones into the bloodstream that activate the autonomic nervous system. Energy is mobilized by increased heart rate, respiration rate, and other physical reactions. Because this alarm stage cannot be sustained for prolonged periods of time, the body draws on reserves of energy. When stress is diminished, the body recuperates and resistance to stress is increased. However, if stress does not diminish, exhaustion occurs, which brings negative physical and psychological effects.

Burnout can come about from physical and emotional exhaustion. Prolonged stress or the buildup of stressors causes fatigue and frustration. Up to 50 percent of educators have indicated they may leave the profession because of burnout (Raschke, Dedrick, & DeVries, 1988), and burnout disproportionately affects special education teachers and others in helping professions (Maslach, 1982; Pines & Aronson, 1988). There are three basic components of burnout:

1. Emotional exhaustion ("I'm tired and irritated all the time. I am impatient with my students and colleagues.")
2. Depersonalization ("I am becoming emotionally hardened; I start to blame the students or their families for all the problems.")
3. Reduced accomplishment ("I feel like I'm not making a difference for my students.")

The result is attrition, alienation, cynicism, and physical problems such as heart disease, hypertension, ulcers, headaches, and psychosomatic illnesses.

Stressors that cause stress reactions are many and varied. For the consultant, stressors could be a new special education regulation, a change in job description, an angry parent, or a student who is behaving in a violent manner. Most educators do have a vast repertoire of coping skills, and we all know that stress in general is a normal life event. It helps us learn and grow. People who have experienced stress probably are more likely to have good coping skills and to be understanding of others under stress than people who have not. However, prolonged periods of stress may eventually lead to maladaptive responses such as depression, anger, anxiety, decreased ability to concentrate, distractibility, overeating, or excessive use of alcohol or drugs. Busy, committed educators will never be able to reduce or eliminate all the stressors in their lives, but they can develop some positive coping strategies so that a balance between stress and coping can be achieved and burnout can be avoided.

Developing positive adaptive strategies is crucial to maintaining emotional and physical health. Although stress is unavoidable, certain behavioral, physical, and cognitive strategies can be used to reduce the impact of stress and reduce burnout. Stress-management strategies such as time management, good nutrition, routine exercise, setting goals and priorities, relaxation, positive self-direction, spiritual development, seeking social support, and developing a positive attitude are helpful. The techniques individuals use depend on their preferences, lifestyle, and skills. Consultants and consultees must learn to "work smarter, not harder" to accomplish goals for students who are at risk of failure in school. Consultants also must take care of themselves so they do not lose their commitment and enthusiasm, and students with special needs do not lose their good, caring teachers.

Building mutually supportive networks will minimize, if not eliminate, feelings of isolation and helplessness in the demanding role of school consultant. It helps to talk things out with others and get a new perspective when tackling complex responsibilities inherent in meeting special needs. A support system is an effective outlet for frustration and provides a backup in times of crisis. One special education staff makes a commitment to meet each Friday at a centralized place for lunch and lively conversation. Ground rules stipulate there will be no talking about students, schools, or staff in that public place. The camaraderie and conviviality of the weekly event, looked on favorably by district administrators, provide an effective support system for teachers whose roles invite stress.

One of the most all-encompassing strategies is thinking positively. Planning and actively carrying out this intention can reduce stress.

APPLICATION **7.1**

Strategies for Reducing Stress

What if burnout has happened or is at least in the glowing embers stage? What if you feel low self-esteem, and emotional and physical exhaustion now? These strategies may help.

1. Talk to someone, give a positive comment, share ideas.
2. Pretend you are O.K. Remember that problems in life are inevitable, demonstrating that we are alive and still functioning. Smile. Stand up straight and walk with a bouncy step. Wear bright, happy clothes—a funny tie, or long, dangling earrings shaped like dinosaurs or pea pods or clowns.
3. Sit in the warm, fresh air. Natural light helps the body function better.
4. Laugh out loud. Each person should have his or her "laugh ration" every day for mental and physical health. Listen to a comedy tape. Read a joke book. Watch children play.
5. Move, stretch, walk, jog. Mild exercise gets the blood flowing and transports more oxygen throughout the body, helping you feel alert and alive.
6. Play energetic, happy music. Classical music is best. Listening to sixty-cycle music such as that by Bach, Handel, and Mozart has been shown to increase alpha brain wave, the relaxation wave length (Douglass & Douglass, 1993). On the other hand, rock music is tiring and tends to drain energy away.
7. Break the routine. Take a different route when driving to work. Let everyone cut in front of your car and feel smug about it. Rearrange your schedule or your furniture. Take a vacation if you can and when you do, leave worries and cares behind. Give yourself over to relaxation and rejuvenation.
8. Schedule appointments with yourself. Keep a jar of little treats on your desk, such as encouraging statements, or envelopes with a $5 bill inside, to be good to yourself every now and then.
9. Use reminders to help remember these and other prevention and intervention strategies. They could be colored ribbons, stick-on happy faces, ads from magazines, letters to yourself. Put the reminders on your tote bag or briefcase, on your watch, calendar, or rear view mirror.
10. Remind yourself often that prevention and remediation of stress and burnout are the concern of the individual, not family or friends or colleagues. Each must become aware of the factors and variables in his or her own personal formula of strategies for keeping the flame of motivation alive.

Management of Time

When school consultants are asked about the biggest obstacle to their role, the majority respond, "Time!" Time is indeed a critical factor in the plans and purposes of educators, particularly for school consultants and consultees in their complex roles. Studies have shown that school consultants have time pressures from attending meetings, preparing and planning, administering tests, communicating, observing, evaluating, and problem-solving (Tindal & Taylor-Pendergast, 1989; Nelson & Stevens, 1981). Time is a precious, unrenewable commodity, with many school consultants prone to "timelock" in which claims on time have grown so demanding that it seems impossible to wring one more second out of the crowded calendar (Keyes, 1991). Personality differences and cultural diversity affect the value and use of time, and everyone responds to pace and pressure in a different way.

Caseload is a critical factor in managing time and arranging schedules. One consultant devoted 76.8 hours over 13 weeks to just one case. The experience of Idol (1988) and others suggests that special education consultants should serve a maximum of 35 students. Those having both direct and indirect service roles should have their ratios classified for each category, and students receiving consultation services as well as direct services should be counted twice. The solution, if there is one, lies in how we choose to use the time available to us.

Time management is really self-management. Time is not adaptable, but people are. An ancient Chinese proverb says, "You cannot change the wind, but you can adjust the sail." Time-management skills can be learned and improved. Because time management is about choices, it is very personal, and the best management plan for one is not the choice of another. A generic five-step plan is useful for practicing time management:

1. Analyze your current use of time.
2. Establish your goals and priorities.
3. Plan your time and your work.
4. Use positive time-management techniques.
5. Review results and reinforce yourself for success.

Most consultants, when asked specifically how they use their time, rely on memory or perceptions. However, to make significant improvements in time management, busy consultants must accurately observe *and record* their use of time. Time logs are a valuable way to observe personal use of time. Consultants may choose to use a diary time log, recording everything they do, when they do it, and how long it takes. Another option is to record time in 15-minute segments, or use a matrix which lists times of the day in segments and lists elements of the consulting role. The matrix can be used to check off quickly those responsibilities that were being done in each segment, and time spent on each activity can be totaled at the end of the day. When recording use of time, remember to begin early in the day, not waiting until the end of the day to try to remember it all.

It is helpful to review long-term goals daily. They should be posted on the desk, the wall, or in a planner. This simple activity, according to Douglass and Douglass (1993), helps one stay focused and "sort out all the trivia that fills your days." Long-term goals should be subdivided into short-term goals, weekly goals, and daily goals. To minimize the gap between long-term and short-term goals, Douglass and Douglass (1993) suggest:

1. Keep a master "to do" list with priority codes that match the items to your goals.
2. Assign a due date to each project. Due dates keep tasks from being put off and foster a sense of completion when accomplished.
3. Estimate time required to complete the task or the project.

Time-management practices encourage efficient use of abilities and strengths. The purpose of time management is not to get *everything* done, but to accomplish professional and personal goals (Maher, 1985). Being busy is not the same as being productive. Time management is a skill that can be learned and improved.

Finding Time for Collaboration and Teaming

Managing time and schedules in order conduct consultation and collaborate effectively is one of the biggest challenges for school consultants. Research by Cawelti (1997) reveals that teachers report their instruction improves most when they work in teams. But they need to have the time available in order to do that. Many educators believe outcomes-based education and performance-based assessment are promising innovations for schools, but acknowledge that each requires additional teacher plan time, while how to accomplish that is as yet unresolved. Three examples from comments by teachers as reported by Voltz, Elliott, Jr., and Cobb (1994) are less than optimistic:

> Our schedules are so tight, there is no time during the regular school day for planning together or discussion.
> Timing is the greatest problem. There is just no time for classroom teachers and resource teachers to communicate....
> ...when the resource teacher and I needed to confer and we had to do it on our own time...we had an essential conference with the resource teacher in the lavatory and me on the floor outside the door, talking through the door...(p. 534).

These findings are consistent with a number of other studies investigating barriers to consultation, collaboration, and teaming (Davis, 1983a; Idol-Maestas & Ritter, 1985; Fullan & Miles, 1992). Time emerges as the key issue inherent in every school-change analysis for the past decade (Raywid, 1993), with successful schools differing from unsuccessful ones in the frequency and extent to which teachers interact and collaborate about materials and instruction.

Raywid found that approaches to finding time included freeing up existing time, restructuring or rescheduling time, using existing time better, or buying time. Examples from her research (1993) include:

■ Teachers sharing the same lunch period with their plan period after lunch, which results in 90 minutes of shared time per day.

APPLICATION 7.2

Using Time Wisely

Physicists define time as nature's way to keep everything from happening at once. By planning time and managing time-wasters, educators can be more productive and less stressed. These strategies are helpful:

1. Make a "to do" list. Some make monthly, weekly, and daily lists. Others divide their lists into professional and personal categories. Still others designate categories such as meetings, direct service, observation, and others. Each time you make your list, do it at the same time of day and on the same kind of paper. Write down all that needs to be done and plan all activities, even those such as talking with friends or playing with the family.

   Then prioritize the list. Lakein (1973) suggests "ABC-ing" the list, with A as top priority. It is not good to let others' priorities become *your* A priorities. Designate as A priorities only those which must be done, regard B priorities as "nice if done," and treat C jobs as "maybe later." You might even end up with a D or Z pile, which you could regard as your "so what?" list. Some jobs turn into "so-whats" if left untended for long enough, and then they can be discarded.

2. Learn to say "No." Avoid saying "Well…," or "I'll think about it." Perhaps the very worst response is, "I will if you can't find anyone else," for there will be little doubt as to who will end up doing it! Say "No," give a brief reason, and offer an alternative if one comes to mind easily. If it does not, try these responses, "Yes, if you will do something for me," or "This is so important that it needs more attention than I can give it now," or "Please take a number and be seated, because I'm inundated right now." Saying "No" is a difficult social skill that should be practiced until it feels comfortable and guilt-free.

3. Rearrange your personal schedule. If you are most alert at 6:00 a.m., get up earlier than usual and do the most difficult tasks at your peak-efficiency time. If you are least efficient at 8:00 p.m., then write letters, talk with friends, iron, fix a broken towel rack, or anything that does not take your best effort. Trying to do difficult tasks at low-efficiency times is frustrating and often requires doing the task over.

4. Plan for bits of time. Keep "can do" lists for periods of 5 minutes, 15 minutes, and 30 minutes. When waiting for a meeting to start, or classes to begin, do something on your list. This is a good chance to get some C-priority things done. It is also reasonable at times to sit and think, read a mystery, or listen to music. Time spent relaxing is not wasted time.

5. Delegate. This is the perfect solution for C priorities, if a helper is available. Teachers are habituated into functioning autonomously, but at times others may be just waiting for a chance to contribute and develop their own skills. Performing delegated tasks can be good learning experiences for students.

6. Break mountains of work into molehills. Do a task analysis or break down the job into smaller steps that you can complete with satisfaction. This is a reinforcing process, and after enough small steps have been taken, the job is done. To practice this process, think about a task that has needed doing for awhile—cleaning out files, organizing a parent-volunteer program, painting the living room. Then conduct a task analysis of the job. Carve that job into small, manageable steps. Put deadlines on the steps. Finally, put the first step on your "to do" list for tomorrow. Then you have a firm start toward accomplishing it.

7. Set deadlines and time limits. Plan a treat for accomplishing a task by deadline. Time limits help get things done efficiently, help overcome procrastination, and prevent simple tasks

from becoming major projects. It prevents letting the intentions to clean out one drawer become major cleaning of the whole desk, file cabinet, and bookshelves.

8. Organize the desk and office area. MacKenzie (1975) describes the "stacked desk syndrome," in which the desk is so cluttered with things-not-to-forget that one cannot find things, concentrate, or work efficiently.

9. Handle the C tasks. If they can't be delegated or ignored, try putting them on the extraminutes list. If that is not an option, consider bartering, pooling resources, and consolidating activities.

10. Overcome procrastination. Entire books have been written about this phenomenon, but most of us put off reading them! Several previous suggestions will help break the procrastination habit. The hardest part is simply getting started on a task. Do a more pleasant step first or have a friend do the first step with you. Think hard about the cost of putting things off.

11. Take less time to do routine things. For example, make a list of tasks that require attention once a month, twice a month, weekly, and daily. Look at the list. What would happen if the daily list became a weekly list, the weekly list moved to semi-monthly, and the twice-monthly to once a month? Probably nothing drastic. It may not be necessary to vacuum weekly, or wash twice a week, or grade every worksheet, or communicate with parents weekly. If so, fine, but if not, do it less often and use that time to work on A activities or special activities for students and colleagues.

12. Get a "Do Not Disturb" sign, and use it adamantly, without guilt. Some teachers have had great success making and using work-status cubes for their desk *and* even encouraging their students to do the same. Faces on one's cube can convey messages such as "Do Not Disturb," "I need help," "This is not a good day, so be patient, please," or "May I help someone?"

13. Plan time for yourself. Busy educators often devote much time and energy to taking care of others while neglecting themselves. Take time to relax, visit with others in the building, talk to a child, read a book, go for a walk, sketch a picture.

14. Plan rewards to reinforce one's own efficiency and measurable progress toward goals. Many teachers are quite goal directed but fail to build self-rewards into their planning schedules (Davis, 1983b).

- Teachers interacting while students leave the building a few hours weekly to perform community service.
- Substitutes hired with money saved by increasing class sizes by one or two students.
- Day-long staff development for 3 to 5 days per year in some districts.
- Compensatory time for teachers participating in 2- to 3-day planning sessions during breaks between terms.
- Staff-development days, from as many as 5 or more instructional days waived by state legislatures.
- Lengthened instructional days.
- Special talents and skills programs provided by specialists, or hobby days for students while teachers meet to collaborate and plan.
- University personnel working in partnership to provide activities that free up teachers to interact.

Raywid stresses that teachers cannot be expected to give up time for working together when they are exhausted at the end of the school day, or when they have their own personal activities, or when they are uncomfortable about the way their class might be handled in their absence.

Other educational leaders offer additional strategies for creating time to collaborate. These include working with the Parent-Teacher Organization to implement volunteer substitute-teacher programs that free up teachers, revising school schedules to provide shared planning time, releasing teachers who collaborate from other school duties such as lunch and bus supervision, providing other supervisors for times such as assemblies and student activities, and implementing peer-tutoring programs across classes. Many innovative ideas are available for carving out time to collaborate and team; however, the ideas themselves require significant amounts of time to plan, implement, and coordinate effectively.

Techniques for Meetings, Interviews, and Observations

Who has not winced at the thought of yet another meeting? Meetings, interviews, and classroom observations take precious time as well as physical and mental energy. Tremendous amounts of collective time and energy are wasted when many people are trapped in unproductive meetings. Educators who seem to work harder rather than smarter should set goals for conducting group interactions that are efficient and productive for all.

Conducting Efficient Meetings.   Consulting educators are busy, but classroom teachers may be the most overextended of all. Many classroom teachers find that the total time for having all their students together for a class period is appallingly short. Consultation and collaboration will be accepted more readily when consultees know that consultants respect their time and their students' time. So a meeting should be planned only if it promises to contribute significantly in serving client needs.

The first rule of thumb in planning an efficient meeting is to ask, "Do we really need to have this meeting?" If the answer is *not* a resounding "Yes," then the business probably can be handled a more efficient way, perhaps by memo, phone, e-mail, or brief face-to-face conversations with individuals. Good reasons for having a meeting are:

- Meeting legal obligations (such as an IEP conference).
- Problem-solving with several people representing a variety of roles.
- Brainstorming so that many ideas are put forth.
- Reconciling conflicting views.
- Building a team to implement educational decisions.

Unnecessary meetings waste school time. They also erode participants' confidence in the value of future meetings that may be called. Sigband (1987) recommends that meetings be held only when there is verifiable need, basing each meeting on an overall purpose and series of objectives. Only people who can make a definite contribution need to be there. An agenda should be prepared, and the meeting room and any needed equipment should be ready. Most important, the meeting must begin on time and end on time, or early if possible.

Preparing for the Meeting.   Leaders or chairs of meetings will be more prepared and organized if they follow a planning checklist. See Figure 7.1 for an example. The planning sheet should include general planning points such as date, time, participants, and goals. Checklists designed to stipulate preparations for the room and to note participant needs also will be useful.

Participants.   After determining a need for a meeting, leaders and chairs will want to request attendance from only those who can contribute. They should keep the group as small as possible, adhering to the rule of thumb that the more people involved, the shorter the meeting should be. Experts on group interaction recommend that the maximum for problem-solving is five, for problem identification about ten, for hearing a review or presentation as many as thirty, and for motivation and inspiration as many as possible. If a

FIGURE 7.1   Checklist to Prepare for Meetings

Date: _____   Place: _____

Time: _____   Topic: _____

Participants: _____

Goals for Meeting: _____

_____

_____

Preparation for Room: Preparation for Participants:

_____ Overhead projector   _____ Nametags

_____ Screen, bulbs, cord   _____ Pads and pens

_____ Chalkboard, chalk   _____ Handouts

_____ Charts, pens, tape   _____ Agenda

_____ Tape recorder, tapes   _____ Ice-breaker activity

_____ Podium, lectern   _____ Map of location

_____ Tables, chairs   _____ Refreshments

_____ Breakout arrangements   _____ Follow-up activity

_____ Other?   _____ Other?

Room Arrangement: _____

_____

_____   (Sketch of Room)

_____

_____

group includes more than six people, it is likely that not everyone will have an opportunity to speak.

Agenda.   Chairpersons for meetings should develop an agenda that reflects the needs of all participants. With an agenda distributed beforehand, participants will be more productive and less apprehensive. Sometimes leaders of large-group meetings draw upon a teaching technique of placing a short, high-interest activity, relating to the topic but needing little explanation, on the chalkboard or overhead screen. Participants focus on the task as they arrive, thereby becoming centered on the meeting topic as they do so. Meetings are more effective when participants can anticipate the task. (See Figure 7.2 for an example of a pre-meeting communication to prepare participants.)

It is important to allocate time for each item on the agenda. Estimating the time needed for each item will allow the chair to monitor progress during the meeting. It is counterproductive to focus too long on early items and fail to get to the last ones. If more important items are placed far down the agenda and time becomes short, it might even

FIGURE 7.2   Checklist to Prepare Participants

Date: _____   Place: _____

Time Start: _____   Time End: _____   Topic: _____

Roles: Facilitator: _____

Recorder: _____

Timekeeper: _____

Other Participants: _____

Agenda for Meeting: _____

_____

_____

_____

_____   Minutes of Prior Meeting Attached _____

_____   Advance Preparation Needed _____

_____   Next Planned Meeting _____

At the Meeting

Action	Person(s) Responsible	Target Date	Done

appear that they have been put there by the convener to avoid action or decision-making. Consultants seeking to build collaborative interactions among their colleagues will not want that to happen.

Seating Arrangements.   Comfortable chairs and seating arrangements that facilitate inter-action are important factors in the success of a meeting. Full-size chairs (not kindergarten furniture) with a little padding, but not too much, should be provided. For best interaction, there should be an arrangement where all can face each other. A circle for six to ten people, a U-shape with peripheral seating if there is to be a visual presentation, and a semi-circle of one or more rows for large groups work well (Lawren, 1989).

Participant Responsibilities.   Along with the responsibility of each participant to interact and help problem-solve, brainstorm, or decide, three other responsibilities are important—chair, recorder, and timekeeper. In many cases the consultant will take care of all three roles, particularly if the meeting includes only two or three people. However, if the meet-ing is long, or the issues are complex and there is much discussion and brainstorming, it is efficient for the chair to ask another participant to record the plans and decisions.

During the Meeting.   Whether the meeting involves two or twenty persons, all partici-pants should be made to feel that they have important contributions to make. All should listen attentively to each other, think creatively and flexibly, and avoid disruptive commu-nication such as jokes, puns, sarcasm, or side comments (Gordon, 1974). Talking and whispering in subgroups can be particularly distracting. Ironically, some teachers who will not tolerate such behavior by their students in the classroom are the biggest offenders. Astute group leaders have various ways of handling this disagreeable occurrence. They might go over to the offenders and stand alongside or between them, direct questions to them, or request a response from them. Each participant in a meeting should be thinking at all times, "What will help move us ahead and solve the problem," and "What does the group need and how can I help?" (Gordon, 1974).

Minutes of the Meeting.   Sometimes a committee is accused of keeping minutes to waste hours! Minutes should reflect the group's decisions about what is to be done, by whom, and by what date, but need not include each point of the discussion. Minutes are a record for naming those who will have a responsibility, for describing plans and decisions, and for listing projected dates for completion of tasks. This is an important aspect of the consulta-tion which should not be slighted.

Assessment of the Meeting.   Some time should be reserved at the end of the meeting to discuss progress made and to evaluate the effectiveness of the meeting. If a meeting agenda becomes sidetracked, leaders should redirect the group's attention by making a point to refocus the discussion (Raschke, Dedrick, & DeVries, 1988).

Compromise for consensus is not always the best solution. It may reflect a weak deci-sion, a watered-down plan, or failure by some participants to express their concerns as firmly as they should. During the meeting leaders should encourage opposing views so that they do not surface later when the matter has been closed. If any participant wishes to dissent, the time to do so is in the meeting, not in hallways after the matter has been decided. Of course, many consultations and collaborations involve only two individuals—consultant and consultee. But procedures recommended for groups of several or more are often pertinent to interactions between only two individuals as well.

Single Agenda Meetings (SAM).   When educators have a single topic that can be handled in a quick meeting before or after school, they can structure the meeting with a single agenda meeting (SAM) process. After becoming familiar with this process, team members will be able to have short SAM meetings without much ado. However, they should not try to squeeze a large agenda or issue into the SAM format. (See Figure 7.3.)

Conducting Effective Interviews

School consultants often need to interview school personnel, community resources, and family members to plan programs for helping students with special needs. Interviewees can provide information for case studies and formulation of learning goals. They help generate options and alternatives for special needs, and provide data for program evaluation.

Successful interviews require effective communication skills (see Chapter 6), and postures of onedownsmanship, parity, and cooperativeness. Queries such as "Tell me more," and "Could you expand on that," and "Let me see if I understand what you are saying," are examples of the responsive listening and paraphrasing that help to elicit the most useful information.

The interviewer should take notes, allowing interviewees to look them over at the conclusion of the interview. If a tape-recording is desired, the interviewer must ask permission beforehand to make one. Some feel it is best to avoid taping, because respondents are often less candid if their comments are being recorded.

FIGURE 7.3   Single Agenda Meetings (SAM)

Date and Time

Problem Statement: _____

_____

1. Background information	5 minutes
2. Possible solutions (each individually writes ideas)	5 minutes
3. Share and select solution	12 minutes
4. Assign action items and schedule next meeting	5 minutes

(1995, Curriculum Solutions, Inc., used by permission)

Interviews must be conducted ethically, collegially, and for a purpose not attainable by less intrusive, time-consuming methods. Keys to a successful interview by the school consultant are asking the right questions and valuing the expertise of the interviewee. A follow-up interaction soon after the interview session is affirming and reassuring, thus facilitating further collaboration.

Making Prudent Observations

Consultants often need to observe a student, groups of students, or an entire program in operation. This is not an easy professional task. Consultants who go into classrooms to observe can expect some discomfort and anxiety on the teacher's part. There may be latent resentment because the consultant is free to visit other classrooms, something many teachers would like but are rarely given the opportunity to do.

Consultants can facilitate the process of observation and ease the minds of those being observed in several ways. First, they should provide a positive comment upon entering the room, and then sit unobtrusively where the teacher has designated. They should avoid getting involved in classroom activities or helping students. Effective observers can blend into the classroom setting so they are hardly noticed. Regular visits minimize the likelihood of having students know who is being observed and for what reason. It is a sad thing to hear a student say, "Oh, here's that learning disabilities teacher to check up on Jimmy again." Records of behaviors must be done in code so that the physical aspects of writing, watching, and body language of the consultant do not reveal the intent of the observation. Each consultant should develop a personal coding system for recording information. Sometimes observers watch the targeted student for one minute, and then divert their attention to another student for one minute, continuing the process with other peers. In this way the student's behavior can be compared with that of classmates. The consultant may teach a lesson and have the classroom teacher observe. This can be helpful for both consultant and consultee.

An observer should exit the room with a smile and a supporting glance at the teacher. Then very soon after the observation, the observer will want to get back to the classroom teacher with positive, specific comments about the classroom, feedback on the observation, and suggestions for entering into problem-solving. Although consultants do not observe in classrooms for the purpose of assessing teacher behaviors and teaching styles, it would be myopic to assume that they do not notice teaching practices which inhibit student success in that classroom. When the practices seem to be interfering with student achievement, the consultant might ask the consultee in a non-threatening, onedownsmanship way whether the student achieved the goals of the lesson. If not, is there something the teacher would like to change so this could occur? Then what might the consultant do to help?

To avoid gathering inaccurate information, consultants will want to make repeated observations. In doing so they can use the opportunity to obtain additional information on antecedents to the problem (Cipani, 1985).

Achieving rapport with a consultee, while targeting a teaching strategy for possible modification, requires utmost finesse by consultants. The observer should make an appointment as soon as possible for providing feedback and continuation of the problem-solving.

Management of Consultation Records and Resources

A prominent space scientist commented that physicists can lick anything, even gravity, but the paperwork is overwhelming. Special education teachers can relate to that. They cite excessive paperwork and record-keeping, along with insufficient time in which to do it, as major causes of stress and burnout. Writing and monitoring IEPs, individual pupil record-keeping, and completion of records and forms rank high as major usurpers of their personal and professional time (Davis, 1983a). Components of the IDEA reauthorization will require even more. When asked to estimate the amount of time they spend performing their responsibilities, resource teachers often overestimate the time spent on direct pupil instruction and staffings and underestimate their preparation for instruction and clerical duties such as record-keeping.

Nevertheless, if teaching is to be an important service profession, careful record-keeping is essential. Record-keeping must be written into the consultant's role description as an important responsibility, with time allowed for its accurate completion. Who would want to be treated by a doctor who did not write down vital information after each visit, or a served by lawyer who failed to record and file important documents? The key for educators is to manage their paperwork so that it does not manage them. Developing efficient systems and standardized forms for record-keeping will help educators, and consultants in particular, work smarter and not harder.

Using a Consultation Log

One of the most important formats for consultants to develop is a consultation log or journal. Consultants can record the date, participants, and topic of each consultation on separate pages, along with a brief account of the interaction and the results agreed on. Space should be provided for follow-up reports and assessment of the consultation. (See Figure 7.4 for a sample format.) Records should be kept for the time spent in consultation and any positive results accomplished, if consultation is to gain credibility as an essential educational activity. Although consultants cannot control the type of records required, they can exercise a good bit of control over processes and procedures for collecting and using information (Davis, 1983a).

One caution is due in regard to consultation logs. Important points of the discussion about student needs and progress might be entered in the log. However, no diagnostic classification or plan that necessitates parent permission should be recorded (Conoley & Conoley, 1982). Confidentiality of the information must be preserved. Consultants will want to develop procedures for coding that will ensure confidentiality, yet identify pertinent information efficiently.

Memos

A consultation memo is a communication tool and also a record of that communication. It should be as brief as possible and very clear, or it will confound rather than convey the

FIGURE 7.4 Consultation Log Format

Client (coded): _____ Consultee (initials): _____

Initiator of Consultation: _____

General Topic of Concern: _____

_____

Purpose of Consultation: _____

_____

_____

Brief Summary of Consultation: _____

_____

_____

_____

Steps Agreed On—By Whom, by When: _____

_____

_____

_____

Follow-up: _____

_____

Most Successful Part of Consultation: _____

_____

Consultation Areas Needing Improvement: _____

_____

Satisfaction with consultation process (1 = least, 5 = most)

1. Communication between consultant and consultee   _____

2. Use of collaborative problem-solving   _____

3. Consultee responsiveness to consultation   _____

4. Effectiveness of consultation for problem   _____

5. Impact of consultation on client   _____

6. Positive ripple effects for system   _____

message (Cleveland, 1981). Receivers will pay more attention to a memo that synthesizes the information and expresses it in simple terms. Jargon, acronyms, excess verbiage, and cryptic sentences are to be avoided. Contrary to some practice, memos should be drafted and then rewritten in best form, rather than dashed off hastily and flung into a mailbox. This is particularly relevant to electronic memos, which will be discussed in a later section. The writer should put the message simply, telling just enough and no more, have facts (times, dates, meeting rooms, descriptions, names) accurate, stick to the point and make the memo as grammatically correct and aesthetically pleasing as possible without spending hours at the task.

Consultants will find it helpful to include a personalized logo on the memo forms they use to communicate with consultees. This logo identifies the consultant at a glance. A busy recipient immediately recognizes its source and can make a quick decision about the need to respond now or at a later time. It personalizes professional interaction by providing a bit of information about the consultant, a humorous touch, or the creative element that educators enjoy and appreciate. A carefully designed logo can promote consultation, collaboration, and team effort in a positive light.

Another item that improves consultant efficiency is the professional card. Business cards have been a mainstay for communicating basic information in many professions and can be useful in education as well. Administrators can increase the visibility of their staff and enhance staff morale as well, by providing them with attractive, well-designed professional cards. Educators find these cards helpful when they interact with colleagues at other sites, or when they attend conferences and conventions. The cards are convenient for quickly jotting down requests for information. They help build communication networks among colleagues with similar interests, and even promote one's own school district.

Organizing a Consultation Notebook

Consultants often use a looseleaf notebook divided into sections with index tabs. The sections can be categorized by buildings served, students served, or teachers served. One very organized consulting teacher had a section of "Best Times to Meet with Teachers," listing days and times available for every teacher with whom she collaborated. Each consultant will want to develop the style that works best in his or her school context and role. Figure 7.5 is a list of suggestions for a special education consultant's notebook sections. Figure 7.6 shows a different format used by a consulting teacher for learning and behavioral disabilities. Consultants may not want or need all of these sections, and may come up with others of their own they would like to include. Personalization for the role and school context again determines its usefulness.

A primary responsibility of the consultant is to ensure confidentiality of information for both student and staff. This can be accomplished in at least two ways—coding the names with numbers or symbols while keeping the code list in a separate place, and marking person-specific files as confidential. A "Confidential" rubber stamp prepared for this purpose can be used to alert readers that the information is not for public viewing. These practices, along with the usual protection of information and data, and the practice of seeing that the recorded information is as positive and verifiable as possible, are common-sense rules that should be sufficient for handling all but the most unusual cases.

FIGURE 7.5   Consultation Notebook Format

Appointments:	One for week, one for year.
"To-do" lists:	By day, week, month, or year as fits needs. List commitments.
Lesson plans:	If delivering direct service, outline of activities for week.
Consultation logs:	Chart to record consultation input and outcomes (Figure 7.4)
Phone call log:	Consultation time by phone.
Observation sheets:	Coded for confidentiality.
Contact list:	Phone numbers, school address, times available.
Faculty notes:	Interests, social and family events and dates, teaching preferences of staff.
Student list:	Coded for confidentiality, birth dates, IEP dates, other helpful data.
Student information:	Anecdotal records, sample products, events, awards, interests, birthdays, talents.
Medication records:	If part of responsibilities.
Materials available:	Title, brief description with grade levels, location.
Services available:	School and community services for resources.
State policies:	Guidelines, procedures, names and phone numbers of agencies/ personnel.
School policies:	Brief description of school policies regulations, handbook.
Procedural materials:	Forms, procedures, for standard activities.
Evaluation data:	Space and forms to record data for formative and summative evaluation (see Chapter 8) and coded if confidential.
Idea file:	To note ideas for self and for sharing with staff and parents.
Joke and humor file:	To perk up the day, and for sharing with others.
Three-year calendar:	For continuity in preparing, checking, and updating IEPs.
Pockets:	For carrying personalized memos, letterhead, stamps, hall passes, paper, professional cards.

An itinerant consulting teacher who serves several schools may want to prepare a simple form stating the date, teacher's name and child's code, along with the topic to be considered, for each school. The list can be scanned before entering the building, so that no time is lost in providing the consultative or teaching service. Some consulting teachers block off and color-code regular meeting times and teacher responsibilities. This practice permits a clearer picture of available consultation times. Another helpful strategy is development of a comprehensive manual that includes standard procedures and forms used in the school district and required by the state.

Consultation Schedules.   The consultant schedule is a vital tool. It not only allows the consultant to organize time productively, but demonstrates to administrators and other school personnel that the school consultant is goal-directed, productive, and facilitative.

FIGURE 7.6 Consulting Teacher's Notebook

Table of Contents

1. Student Information
   - 1.1 Personal Information
   - 1.2 Student Profiles
   - 1.3 A Quick Look at IEPs
   - 1.4 Student Schedules
   - 1.5 Medication Records
2. School Information
   - 2.1 Faculty-Staff Roster(s)/Faculty Notes
   - 2.2 Master Schedule(s)
   - 2.3 School Calendar(s)
   - 2.4 School Policies/School Handbook(s)
3. Calendars
   - 3.1 Daily To-Do Lists
   - 3.2 Personal Calendars (Weekly, Yearly)
   - 3.3 IEP Review Dates
   - 3.4 Three-Year Evaluation Dates
4. Forms
   - 4.1 Personal Motif Memos
   - 4.2 Consultation/Collaboration Request
   - 4.3 Observation Sheets
   - 4.4 Weekly Teacher Progress Report
   - 4.5 Consultation Logs
5. Lesson Plans
   - 5.1 Weekly Lesson Plans
   - 5.2 Student Matrix Worksheet
   - 5.3 Class Co-planning Sheet
   - 5.4 Unit Co-planning Sheet
   - 5.5 Co-teaching Planning Sheet
6. Consultation/Collaboration
   - 6.1 Advantages of Consultation/ Collaboration
   - 6.2 Tips for Consultation/Collaboration
   - 6.3 Completed Consultation Logs
   - 6.4 Consultation Evaluation Forms
   - 6.5 Personal Journal
7. Resource Listing

Elizabeth Jankowski

Schedules should be left with secretaries of all buildings assigned to the consultant, and posted in teacher workrooms so that colleagues have easy access to the information.

Consultations and collaborative experiences can be keyed on the consultant's schedule with code letters for efficiency. One consulting teacher uses this code in her notebook:

- **ID** informal discussion, spontaneous meeting
- **PM** planned, formal meeting
- **PC** phone conversation
- **MM** major meeting of more than two people
- **FT** follow-through activity
- **SO** scheduled observation

Standardized forms are helpful for collecting and using basic information. The forms that produce multiple copies may be more expensive in the short run, but can save valuable time and energy in the long run. The time spent on developing systems and standardizing conventional forms will be well-spent. It frees up more time and energy for individualizing and personalizing the instruction for special needs of the students.

Commercial resources are available which provide sample letters and forms adaptable to a variety of educational purposes, from writing a letter of congratulations to answering concerns and criticisms (Tomlinson, 1984). Although educators will not want to use these patterns verbatim, they can get a "jump start" in preparing some of the more difficult communications.

Coordination and organization of student files, consultation logs, school procedures, and schedules will necessitate more time for paperwork at the outset, but once the procedures are set up, they will be time-efficient and cost-effective in the long run.

Organizing and Distributing Materials

Many school districts now have extensive instructional resource centers where school personnel can check out a variety of material for classroom use. Even with the busiest resource center in full operation, consultants usually have their own field-related materials and information about special areas that teachers want and need. With little or no clerical help, and often little storage space available beyond the seats, floor, and trunk of their own vehicles, traveling school consultants need to develop a simple, orderly check-out system for loaned materials, or soon the consultant will have little left to use and share.

Materials belonging to the schools should be marked with a school stamp, and personal materials should be labeled with a personal label. Library pockets and check-out cards facilitate check-out and return. The consultant should keep an up-to-date inventory of available materials within both personal and school libraries that are loanable and specific to student needs. Before traveling to a school, the consultant can scan the check-out file for due dates, and stop by classrooms or put memos into message boxes asking for their return. Efficient consultants leave request cards so school staff can let them know of their needs. They also periodically assess the usefulness of their materials by querying teachers and students who used them. These kinds of interactions build positive attitudes toward collaboration and teamwork, promote the effectiveness of school consultation, and extend the ripple effect of special services.

Technology for Enriching Collaboration

Technology is revolutionizing the processes of consultation, collaboration, and teamwork in school settings. Educators in technology-rich environments are able to engage in many of their collaborative efforts continuously throughout the day without leaving their classrooms or offices. Information can be exchanged instantly rather than waiting until a later time or day for face-to-face meetings. Technology, of course, does not eliminate the need for face-to-face interaction; rather, it frees the team members' time together to deal with major issues instead of day-to-day background information. It improves the efficiency of other routine tasks such as writing, material development, or data collection, so more time will be available for collaborative activities.

Many definitions of technology have been documented. One that encompasses a wide range of applications comes from the International Technology Education Association's 1993 issue of *The Technology Teacher,* quoting Wright and Lauda:

Technology is a body of knowledge and actions, used by people, to apply resources in design-ing, producing, and using products, structures, and systems to extend the human potential for controlling and modifying the natural and human-made (modified) environment.

Using technology as a team may be a major reason that full inclusion of students with disabilities in general classroom settings is a feasible option (Lipsky, 1994; Male, 1994). Educators who are concerned about students with special needs can be powerful influences in providing leadership for the use of technology in inclusive classrooms to accommodate the special instructional needs of all students.

Technology can improve achievement and self-esteem of many students with dis-abilities and can be a powerful motivator for students who have experienced failure and frustration in school. It can empower students with disabilities by enabling them to accom-plish things never before thought possible:

Telecommunications and multimedia technologies such as interactive video bring the world into the classroom. Electronic communication devices allow students to speak and add their voices to those of their classmates. Adapted computers provide access to instruction in myriad subject areas from learning to count to calculus (Lewis, 1993, p. 3).

Technology for Managing Consultation and Collaboration

The commercial marketplace of the 1990s embraces the use of emerging technologies for managing organizations and delivering their services. "Electronic bonding" is a means of teaming through technology. Interdisciplinary teams that cross organizational boundaries, sometimes even including customers and vendors, use technologies such as electronic mail, broadcast FAX, teleconferencing and video conferencing to communicate with one another consistently and quickly. Digital pagers and cellular phones make team members accessible regardless of their location and mobility. Information is gathered rapidly and exchanged through databases and electronic bulletin boards.

Walls of classrooms can be opened and expanded through technology. Consider the common stumbling block to collaboration—the need for time. Computers and telecommu-nications are major time-savers in many ways:

- Messages sent at the convenience of one party while others read and respond to them at their convenience.
- Databases and information on student progress stored in a file-server and accessed by any team member at a convenient time.
- Notes added by team members that keep everyone on the team apprised of informa-tion or items of concern.
- Computer adaptation of assignments by teachers or resource personnel for meeting students' needs.
- Copies of special instructions or worksheets sent by a consultant in one building to a teacher in another by way of computer FAX.

The possibilities are unlimited. Lewis (1993) states "...technology can increase teacher's professional productivity and reduce the amount of time that must be spent in non-instructional classroom duties" (p. 126).

Telecommunications and Electronic Networks

Computer networks and electronic mail might be the most useful applications of technology for school consultants. Wires or cables can link computers within the building, known as a local area network (LAN), or outside to other areas, known as a wide area network (WAN). Users share software and communicate with one another in an efficient manner. With electronic networks, a consultant could prepare an adapted lesson or test and send it to the classroom where needed. The adapted lesson or test would be "waiting" for the teacher or students in the classroom to access at the appropriate time without the presence of the consultant. Conversely, a student might prepare a product in the classroom and send it to the consultant for review and feedback. So a computer network allows monitoring of student work and makes feedback to the student more immediate.

Another advantage of the electronic network is facilitation of interaction among the users, in this case consultants, co-teachers, or team members. In some systems users can work simultaneously with the same program. For instance, team members could use a word processor to collaborate in developing a lesson plan, with each team member accessing the work of others and making changes or adding notes. This reduces the number of time-consuming, face-to-face meetings for team members with a comparable or even better outcome.

Electronic mail (e-mail) is another use of the network that saves time and makes collaboration more efficient. The scenario at the beginning of this chapter illustrates the needed change in accessibility that could be realized if electronic mail would replace irritating "phone tag" with efficient communication. E-mail allows information prepared on one computer to be sent by network to another computer. When all members of a collaborative team are connected to the e-mail system and regularly access it, a message can be sent to one or more persons faster than it takes to walk down the hall to speak to those individuals.

Although it is possible for individuals to arrange for e-mail, most educators have the e-mail service facilitated through internal networks set up by the school system. This ensures that all district e-mail participants are using the same or compatible systems. Some advanced e-mail systems are capable of providing real-time conferencing. An IEP conference or team-planning meeting could use such a system, thus saving the time and expense of everyone traveling to a single location. Messages can be designed more carefully than those delivered by phone and left in the voice-mail box. If team members could have only one of the technologies discussed in this chapter, e-mail might be the one of choice.

E-mail is not a substitute for face-to-face interaction and conversations. Some think it can make us inappropriately reactive rather than proactive. It also requires the use of e-mail etiquette in selecting appropriate recipients and in refraining from entering anything there that we would not want disclosed. Neither should complex issues or immediate needs be handled in this way.

Electronic Scheduling Programs

Many consultants find a scheduling program useful. These programs are electronic calendars in which appointments and other commitments are entered. One special advantage is the way the program can handle recurring appointments. For example, if a team planning meeting is scheduled for 2:00 Friday afternoons, the consultant can enter that information; the program will automatically write in meeting reminders on the appropriate dates. Another advantage is the ability to view and print out daily, weekly, or monthly calendars. These calendars can be shared through the network if desired. Sharing privileges can be customized to allow one or many individuals the right to view or schedule appointments for all or part of a colleague's calendar.

Information Services

Consultants, teachers, and students can use computers with modems to engage in communication with large host-computer information systems. These systems offer a variety of options to users, ranging from electronic bulletin boards to conferencing capabilities. Potential uses for consultants and teachers include library searches and information bulletins relating to special needs of students with disabilities. Special bulletin boards can be created to address unique audiences. It is even possible to create local bulletin boards that are used by teachers in a single building or school district. A creative consultant or teacher might consider developing such a bulletin board where ideas that have worked in other classrooms can be shared with fellow teachers and consultants.

Information bulletin boards can be interesting to special educators. One for co-teachers and others involved in school consultation is "LRE" (least-restrictive environment for education). Other bulletin boards relate to relevant topics such as assistive devices, various categories of disability, parent information, recruitment/retention, and transition from school to work. The Handicapped Users' Database on CompuServe contains a reference library as well as information about computer products designed for users with disabilities. The Disabilities Forum is a bulletin board where people with or interested in disabilities can exchange information. The IBM/Special Needs Forum focuses on special education applications for IBM-compatible computers (Lewis, 1993). Technology specialists and many librarians in a school district usually can provide currently available information services and bulletin boards.

Internet Resources

Consultants can find a wide array of useful information and resources through Internet searches. The following are a few sites that we have found relevant for our purposes.

http://www.hood.edu/seri/serihome.htm
SERI: Special Education Resources on the Internet (SERI) is a collection of Internet-accessible information resources of interest to those involved in the fields related to special education. This collection exists in order to make on-line special education resources more easily and readily available in one location. This site will continually modify, update, and add additional informative links.

http://www.usoe.k12.ut.us/sars/inclusion/inclusion.html
Utah's statewide inclusion project.

http://www.ldanatl.org/positions/inclusion.html
LDA's position paper on full inclusion of all students with learning disabilities in the regular education classroom, 1993.

http://schoolnet2.carleton.ca/sne/index2.html
Select "SEARCH" and enter the term inclusion to locate listings of several sites.

http://www.cec.sped.org/
Council for Exceptional Children home page.

http://members.aol.com/CurrSol/CSIhome.html
Curriculum Solutions, Inc. home page.

http://www.cef-cpsi.org/
Creative Education Foundation.

http://www.connix.com/~hypercog/add.html
Born to Explore! The Evolution of ADD & Creativity

FAX Communication

FAX (facsimile) machines represent yet another form of technology that can enhance the consultation and collaboration processes. Many school buildings have at least one FAX machine. Consultants who serve more than one building can make efficient use of the machines by sending letters, reports and other written products for use in another building, city, or state, over telephone wires. As previously noted, computers on an electronic network can FAX a document directly from a computer, without requiring a printout.

Monitoring Student Records

Databases and other types of management software can help teachers keep track of important information. Databases are most useful for organizing large amounts of information. Being equivalent to electronic filing cabinets, they allow great flexibility in sorting and retrieving data. For example, a consultant might set up a database file on a caseload of students. That file would be made up of individual records, each containing a separate entry for categories selected, such as name, address, phone, age, grade, type of disability, parents' name(s), address, and phone number. Once the format is established, the consultant or an assistant can enter the information for each record. It then can be searched and sorted for different types of reports. This search-and-sort capability is what gives databases flexibility, an advantage over traditional paper-filing systems.

Grades and Attendance Records

Several software programs are available to manage records of students' grades. Most allow the teacher to enter students' scores, determine the weight of each assignment or quiz, and set standards for assigning grades. Final grades can be computed automatically. Many programs provide options for printing class rosters, grade reports by student or by assignment, and summary statistics and graphs. If special software is not available to a teacher or consultant, a standard spreadsheet can be used to accomplish many of these purposes.

Individual Educational Plans

Many special educators use computers to assist in the laborious process of writing Individual Educational Plans (IEPs). Software programs for producing IEPs have been developed and are available commercially. These programs are special types of databases tailored to the needs of special education professionals. The programs usually contain an IEP shell and a collection of suggested annual goals and short-term objectives. Although the availability of these goals and objectives can alleviate much of the drudgery of writing IEPs, this is also the source of most of the criticism of computerized IEPs. Critics argue that the goals and objectives provided in the software are often isolated skills that are not relevant to an individual student or are inconsistent with the local school curriculum. However, effective software does not require use of the goals and objectives provided in the program. It allows the IEP team to develop others if they wish. Some systems even enable users to generate administrative reports and notices to teachers and parents.

Assessment and Evaluation

Assessment and evaluation issues in collaboration and consultation will be discussed more fully in Chapter 8. The data gathered in these processes can be stored in database or spreadsheet applications. They can be readily summarized in various formats, including meaningful graphs and charts. However, when educators store confidential information in computers, *careful steps must be taken to protect confidentiality of student information.* This issue is a major concern if data are to be shared with team members by way of computer networks. Computer technicians should be consulted to determine the safest and most efficient ways to make files secure.

Test-Scoring.   One of the most time-consuming parts of the assessment process is scoring standardized tests. Many test-developers provide software programs to assist in this task. "These programs are quick, accurate, and an excellent way for busy teachers to save time" (Lewis, 1993, p. 134). Monitoring Basic Skills Progress, by PRO-ED, Inc., is an example of a program that assists educators in generating, administering, and scoring probes that monitor student progress when using the Curriculum-Based Measurement techniques to be discussed in Chapter 8. The results are graphed by computer over time so progress can be compared with the expected rate of improvement. The program also analyzes the results and makes recommendations about possible changes in instruction.

Consultants and collaborating teachers need to monitor student performance on computer tasks, especially when use of computers is specified on a student's IEP. Integrated learning systems (ILS) can be beneficial for this purpose. These systems provide instructional software for students and management tools for teachers. They are available in subject areas such as reading, writing, language arts, math, and science. Teachers or consultants can easily monitor student progress and prescribe individualized activities based on the results of previous performance. These systems are growing in popularity with school districts as a measuring tool for Outcomes Based Education (OBE). When available, and when relevant to student goals, these systems should be chosen by teachers and consultants for students in inclusive classrooms. Teachers and/or consultants then can refer to such data to make collaborative decisions about student progress and make changes as may be appropriate. If the software does not have built-in record-keeping capability, the student or paraprofessional can be taught to enter data in a database or spreadsheet that can then be used to prepare summaries or graphs. A skilled consultant can provide valuable assistance to the classroom teacher in making these decisions and setting up the record-keeping tools.

Portfolios.   Use of portfolios is yet another way to monitor and evaluate student progress and document consultation activities. However, organizing and maintaining portfolio information can be very time-consuming. The convenience of filing information on a computer should not be overlooked. Products developed on the computer are easily filed. Other products and information can be scanned into the computer to be added to the portfolio. It is even possible with some computers to add audio and video products. Many interesting possibilities exist for the innovative educator and students.

Several formats for recording consultation activities are discussed in this chapter and in Chapter 8. This type of information could be kept on the computer and would be more efficient than the paper-pencil format. Some of the information such as date, time, or name of student could be automatically entered, and the information searched and sorted in various ways, to provide valuable information for making decisions about students and collaboration processes. For example, if one wanted to know how many times a certain consultant or service provider worked with the student during the year, the data could be sorted to have all the entries for the service provider appearing together. Later, if one wanted to know who provided services on a particular date, the information could be sorted by the date field. Data can be sorted to produce valuable reports for making decisions about programs and services for students. Data also can be added to larger information bases for more extensive district-wide reports. Figure 7.7 illustrates a form that could be used in a classroom to record services provided for students with special needs. Figure 7.8 shows the information when recorded in a database and sorted by a service provider.

Significant advances in technology-based assessment within special education have been made as a result of the Technology-Related Assistance for Individuals with Disabilities Act of 1988 (Greenwood, 1994). A special issue of *Exceptional Children* (October/November, 1994) that addresses this topic is but one example of its importance:

> Advances in software design enable expert-level assessment knowledge to be employed automatically in the context of data collection, data analysis, decision making, and prescription. Advances in the portability of computers (notebook and subnotebook computers) support classroom observational assessments by practitioners using quality instruments that routinely integrate data collection and numerical analyses with observer training and reliability assessment (Greenwood, 1994).

FIGURE 7.7   Service Provider Log

Student	Francisco, W.		Teacher	P. Webber

Date	Time	Service Provider	Comments
9-16-99	9:46 a.m.	N. Carney	Scripted paper for English
9-16-99	1:46 p.m.	L. Baker	Checked points earned, made
			suggestion to teacher
			about time-on-task
9-18-99	9:15 a.m.	K. Foster	PT—Worked on small motor
			during handwriting activity
9-18-99	1:44 p.m.	N. Carney	Helped with math instruction.
			Difficult. Try more manipulatives.
9-19-99	2:27 p.m.	N. Carney	Paraprofessional helped him
			with math. Spoke to
			teacher about next week's work.

Adapting Materials and Tests

Another time-consuming activity for co-teachers and consultants is adapting written products for individuals with disabilities, as discussed in Chapter 9. A common example is to adapt a worksheet used to supplement a math or science lesson. It is often felt there are too many work items for students with disabilities to complete in one sitting. Moreover, the graphic material might be distracting from the relevant stimuli and needs to be removed. The old-fashioned way to deal with this situation is to make a copy of the worksheet, cut it apart with scissors, and paste it back together in a more usable format. However, if a scanner and computer with graphics software are available, the project can be completed more efficiently. The worksheet is scanned into the graphics program. The "cut and paste" function of the program is used to eliminate portions that are distracting or too difficult. Then the remaining portions are rearranged as needed and the "new" worksheet printed out. This approach allows for making different adaptations for many different students in a relatively short amount of time.

Text also can be scanned into the computer if OCR software is installed. A consultant might scan a teacher-made test, for example, and then make adaptations as needed. The print can be enlarged or more space provided between items. Even better, if a classroom

FIGURE 7.8   Service Provider Log Sorted by Service Provider

Student: *Francisco, W.*   **Teacher:** *P. Webber*

9/18/99   *9:15 AM*   **Service Provider:** *K. Foster*

Comments:

 PT—Worked on small motor during handwriting activity

9/16/99   *1:46 PM*   **Service Provider:** *L. Baker*

Comments:

 Checked points earned, made suggestion to teacher about time-on-task

---

9/19/99   *2:27 PM*   **Service Provider:** *N. Carney*

Comments:

 Paraprofessional helped him with math. Spoke to teacher about next week's work.

9/18/99   *1:44 PM*   **Service Provider:** *N. Carney*

Comments:

 Helped with math instruction. Difficult. Try more manipulatives.

9/16/99   *9:46 AM*   **Service Provider:** *N. Carney*

Comments:

 Scripted paper for English

---

teacher prepares the test on the computer, the file can be shared with a consultant or co-teacher to make the adaptations.

There are a number of software programs that can be used to develop written tests. Test banks often accompany classroom texts. Teachers and consultants might find that the use of such programs is an efficient way to adapt a classroom test. For example, some software can produce several types of tests—matching, true-false, completion, and multiple choice. When questions have been typed into the program, they can be easily transferred from one of the formats to another. Other software can create paper-and-pencil tests as well as quizzes that students take at the computer.

Preparing Reports and Other Written Products

Word processors and desktop publishing programs are a *must* for busy consultants and other team members. Once text has been entered in a word processor, it can be changed easily, edited, added to, modified, or reformatted. This capability is particularly useful for routine writing such as consultation logs, letters to parents, memos to other team members, assessment reports, and newsletters and classroom materials with adaptations made for specific students with disabilities.

Consultants and collaborating teachers might want to develop "shells" or "templates" for frequently used products. A shell or template is a word processing file that contains portions of a document that do not change. For example, most of the forms and checklists recommended in this text could be scanned in or retyped to form shells. McLoughlin and Lewis (1990) suggest a shell for assessment reports. Permanent information would include the title, spaces for identifying information and headings such as Reason for Referral, Test Behavior, Results, and Recommendations. Brief descriptions of commonly administered tests could be included in the shell and simply omitted if not appropriate for a particular report. Male (1994) provides an example of a shell for homework assignments. When using a shell, the file is loaded into the word processor and relevant information is added before saving the file under a new name.

Integrated software that combines word processing and database may be the most powerful tool for enhancing personal productivity of school personnel (Male, 1994). Software of this type allows the user to create a database such as the student information previously described. Any part or all of these data can be merged (or inserted) into word processing documents such as form letters or reports. Once the data for each student have been entered, a consultant can print out any lists needed. Academic or behavioral progress reports can be prepared for specific parents, or for all the parents in the caseload, with personalized information inserted automatically by the computer (Male, 1994).

Planning for Use of Technology

Consultants should provide leadership in schools to assure effective professional use of technology and to accommodate the needs of students with disabilities in general classrooms in three important ways:

- Participating in school-wide planning groups;
- Providing a role model in the use of technology; and
- Engaging in collaborative activities where technology is being used.

As one can see from the vast array of technology applications discussed in the preceding pages, there are many decisions to make about what, when, and how to invest in emerging technology. Right now, most schools do not have technology-rich environments to support consultation and collaboration. Thoughtful planning and investment decisions are needed to ensure that team members have the right technologies in their classrooms and offices for both managing and instructional purposes.

Many decisions in education are based on reactions to problems or historical trends (Cain, 1985). This decision-making method does not work well for decisions about technology because of the rapid pace of change in the technology itself. Instead, a holistic and visionary method of planning is needed. Cain recommends a planning process for technology use in which individuals responsible for different program elements are brought together to pose certain questions, such as those in Application 7.3.

APPLICATION **7.3**

Envisioning Computer Technology

Ask a team of educators the question, "What is your vision of computer technology in this school district 5, 10, or 20 years in the future?" (Remember, the team needs to include the technology specialist as well as the teachers, consultants, and administrators.) Participants are then charged with the task of breaking down the path to achieve that vision into smaller attainable projects. The smaller projects and futuristic vision can be revisited and adjusted from year to year to reflect changes that develop in the industry or school district.

The entire process of technology planning: (1) looks forward, not backward; (2) looks across all disciplines; and (3) includes applications for professional collaboration as well as instructional and student uses.

Tips for Managing Time and Technology

1. At the end of the year, write thank-you notes to school personnel you have worked with, including principals, secretaries, and custodians. When writing notes to colleagues, sign your name in a distinctive color on pads of an individualized design. Send a note on a "reminder" memo, and staple a bag of nuts, or a Valentine cookie, or a doughnut, to it. Remember those who collaborate with you in special ways by delivering a treat to their room along with a brief note of appreciation.

2. Color-code folders for schools if you serve several. Use a file box with a card for each day to list reminders, and a schedule book. Keep an idea file of filler activities.

3. Use tubs for storage of materials. Plan ahead and put materials in the tub for one week, one month, a season, or a thematic unit.

4. Have a retrieval box in a certain place for receiving borrowed items that are returned. Keep a check-out catalog so you will know where your materials are. When materials are due, remove due-cards for the buildings where you will be that week and collect the materials while there.

5. Listen to conversations in the workroom, lunchroom, and faculty meetings. When a topic surfaces for which you have materials, offer to share. Prepare a list of instructional material that is for loaning and distribute it. Make sure grade level and sample objectives of the material are given.

6. Don't schedule yourself so tightly that you have no time for informal interactions and impromptu consultation. These can open the door for more intensive and productive collaboration. Also, be even more protective of colleagues' time than you are of your own, and make good use of it.

7. Furnish treats often. (For very nutrition-conscious schools, make the treats vegetables or fruit.)

8. Make concise checklists for procedural activities, such as general items to tell parents at conferences, or items to tell new students and their parents.

9. If doing a demonstration lesson, give the classroom teacher a paper stating the activity name, type of activity it is, and learning objectives. State your name at the bottom and specify that it comes from "Consultant ___'s Lesson Plan," thereby establishing your identity.

10. Go to classroom teachers and ask *them* for help in their area of expertise. Ask for a copy of something you have seen that would be a good addition for your file, but be sure they mean for you to use it or share it before you do so.

11. Generate alternatives to having more and more meetings, try them out, and get input from colleagues on their value. When a meeting *is* needed, and it promises to be a difficult one, on the night before the meeting try visualizing a successful one in which everything goes very well.

12. Visit other schools and take notes on organizational systems and management techniques that could be incorporated into your system. Then prepare a summary sheet for colleagues on your return.

13. Find time to collaborate by exploring innovative ways of "making" more time and using it wisely. Schedule common lunch or preparation periods; in large districts increase class size by just one and use surplus funds to hire substitutes; have teachers match a period of early dismissal time with their contribution of equal time; have students involved in community service one afternoon a week while teachers meet.

14. Develop ways of working smarter, not harder, such as having information-exchange pools with other teachers, sharing learning centers and packets with colleagues in other attendance centers, and gathering free resources from commercial business and industry.

15. Make a weekly plan called "completion focus," and in that week curtail interferences, get reports up-to-date, grade papers, and on Friday get rid of everything that really doesn't matter anyway.

16. Before sending confidential information through electronic networks make sure steps have been taken to keep hackers and other would-be "technology thieves" from gaining access to the information.

17. Constantly monitor your habits of protecting confidential information. Make sure you do not leave information in files accessible to individuals who are not authorized to see them. When you use e-mail, be careful when selecting addresses for mail. It is very easy to accidentally include an unauthorized person. Most breaches of confidentiality result from carelessness of people, and not from lack of technology safeguards.

18. Consult a technology specialist on a regular basis to remain current in the ever-changing uses of technology.

19. Join or form a computer user's group to learn from one another about new uses for computers.

CHAPTER REVIEW

1. Stress that is encountered in many human service roles can lead to burnout and subsequent attrition from the field. Positive attitudes, health maintenance, supportive networks, realis-

tic goals, relaxation, environmental changes, and taking control of one's life will minimize stress and help prevent burnout, fizzle out, rust out, and coast out among consultants and teachers.

2. Careful management of time and energy decreases stress and increases productivity for those in consultative roles. School personnel will want to establish goals to manage their resources, identify and remediate time-wasters, use positive time-management strategies, and take good care of themselves.

3. Meetings, interviews, and observations must be kept as efficient and positive as possible. With careful planning each of these activities can be more productive for consultants and collaborators. It is important to provide a comfortable meeting environment, prepare an agenda, keep minutes of decisions and plans, and assess the success of the meeting. When consultants observe in classrooms, they should demonstrate caring attitudes and provide positive support for those being observed.

4. Record-keeping systems and resource-management systems are necessary for busy consultants who serve many schools. Consultants must keep records and materials in order, maintain confidentiality, and be on the lookout for helpful material with which to consult and collaborate. Consulting journals and notebooks are tools that facilitate management of complex responsibilities. Personalized touches for memos and messages help develop rapport with consultees.

5. Telecommunications and electronic networks are possibly the most valuable elements of technology that can revolutionize the way consultants and collaborating teachers engage in collaborative activities.

6. Many time-consuming, routine tasks such as organizing schedules, keeping and sorting records, adapting materials, and developing IEPs can be done more efficiently with the use of technology.

7. Consultants should provide leadership in schools to assure effective professional use of technology and to accommodate the needs of students with disabilities in general classrooms by participating in school-wide planning groups, being a role model in the use of technology, and engaging in collaborative activities where technology is being used. Planning should include applications for professional collaboration as well as instructional and student uses.

TO DO AND THINK ABOUT

1. Discuss some record-keeping and managerial tasks that most people really do not like to do, such as preparing income tax returns, and consider ways the activities could be made less unpleasant and more manageable. Then consider how these techniques could be used creatively by school consultants.

2. Describe The Perfect Meeting. What would need to be done in order for this meeting to transpire?

3. Design a weekly and daily planning sheet that has space for stating goals, listing activities in categories, prioritizing the list, and estimating times for accomplishing the activities. Try your planning sheets, and share them with others if you found them helpful.

4. Conduct a time analysis to diagnose time-management problems you may have. Use one of the methods described in this chapter or develop your own.

5. Create ideas for the following management tools, and if your present situation warrants, construct them and try them out:

   A logo for personalized note pads or memo sheets that will identify you and feature school consultation in a positive, collaborative spirit

   An observation checklist that would work in your school situation

   A consultation log or journal format to record the consultation and follow through, as well as a brief assessment of the consultation

   A table of contents for a notebook in which to organize information, data, and material needed to carry out the school consultation role

   A system for cataloging materials to be shared with consultees, and for checking the material in and out

6. Survey your school building to determine the extent to which staff members are using telecommunications and electronic networks to engage in their collaborative activities. Then think about how you can get involved in this type of collaboration in your building. Or, interview a person who uses electronic networks extensively and write a plan for yourself to learn more about that use for your work.

7. Develop "shells" or "templates" on your computer for some of the forms suggested in other chapters of this text.

8. Develop a database that would be helpful to you as a consultant or co-teacher. Enter real or imaginary data and practice sorting it and preparing reports that would be useful to you.

9. Use a computer to adapt instructional material or a test.

10. Create a computerized portfolio for yourself.

11. Read a journal article about ways to promote development of information literacy.

12. Describe what you would want in a technology-infused inclusive environment if money were no object.

13. Consult a technology specialist in your school district and discuss the possibilities for expanding the uses of technology to facilitate consultation, collaboration, and teamwork in your school.

14. Join or form a computer user's group to learn about new uses for computers from one another.

FOR FURTHER READING

Blackhurst, A. E. (1997). Perspectives on technology in special education. *Teaching Exceptional Children, 29*(5), 41–48.

Collins, C. (1987). *Time management for teachers: Practical techniques and skills that give you more time to teach.* West Nyack, NY: Parker.

Davis, W. E. (1983). *The special educator: Strategies for succeeding in today's schools.* Austin, TX: PRO-ED. Chapter 2 on burnout, chapter 5 on meetings, chapter 6 on paperwork, record-keeping, and time management, and chapter 8 on ethical, legal, and professional dilemmas.

Douglass, M. E., & Douglass, D. N. (1993). *Manage your time, manage your work, manage yourself.* New York: AMACOM.

Educational Leadership (November, 1997), *55*(3). Topical issue on Integrating Technology into Teaching.

Exceptional Children (October/November, 1994). Special Issue: Technology-Based Assessment Within Special Education, *61*(2).

Geisert, P. G., & Futrell, M. K. (1995). *Teachers, computers, and curriculum: Microcomputers in the classroom* (2nd ed.). Boston: Allyn & Bacon.

Jusjka, J. (1991). Observations. *Phi Delta Kappan, 72*(6), 468–470.

Keyes, R. (1991). *Timelock: How life got so hectic and what you can do about it.* New York: Harper Collins.

Kozoll, C. E. (1982). *Time management for educators,* Fastback #175. Bloomington, IN: Phi Delta Kappa Educational Foundation.

Kurland, D. J., Sharp, R. M., & Sharp, V. F. (1997). *Introduction to the INTERNET for education.* Belmont, CA: Wadsworth.

Land, M., & Turner, S. (1997). *Tools for schools: Applications software for the classroom* (2nd ed.). Belmont, CA: Wadsworth.

Lewis, R. B. (1993). *Special education technology: Classroom applications.* Pacific Grove, CA: Brooks/Cole.

Lippet, G., & Lippitt, R. (1978). *The consulting process in action.* San Diego: University Associates. Chapter 5 on ethical dilemmas and guidelines for consultants.

MacKenzie, A., & Waldo, K. C. (1981). *About time: A woman's guide to time management.* New York: McGraw-Hill.

Maher, C. A. (1982). Time management training for providers of special services. *Exceptional Children, 48,* 523–528.

Majsterek, D., & Wilson, R. (1993). Computer-assisted instruction (CAI): An update on applications for students with learning disabilities. *LD Forum, 19*(1), 19–21.

Male, M. (1994). *Technology for inclusion: Meeting the special needs of all students* (2nd ed.). Boston: Allyn & Bacon.

Newman, J. E. (1992). *How to stay cool, calm and collected when the pressure's on: A stress control plan for business people.* New York: American Management Association.

Phi Delta Kappan. (1992, December). A Special Section on "Technology in the Schools," *74*(4).

Sapolsky, R. (1994). *Why zebras don't get ulcers: A guide to stress, stress-related diseases, and coping.* New York: W. H. Freeman.

Sugai, G. (1986). Recording classroom events: Maintaining a critical incidents log. *Teaching Exceptional Children* (1986, Winter), 98–102.

Teaching Exceptional Children (May/June 1997), *29*(5). Topical issue.

8 Assessment and Evaluation

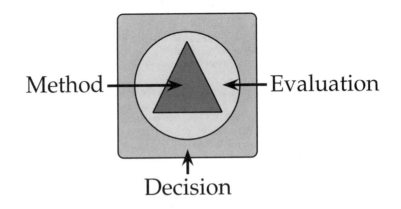

Method — Evaluation

Decision

Setting goals and evaluating the achievement of those goals are integral parts of education. This was most vividly illustrated in the requirements of Public Law 94-142 stipulating the development of individual education programs (IEPs). The basic philosophy that supports IEP development and evaluation is also the backbone of all good program development. A critical part of any educational program is the evaluation plan. Without such a plan, it is impossible to determine whether or not the goals have been achieved.

A collaborative school consultation program requires evaluation just as any other educational program does. Indeed, evaluation is particularly important in programs which strive for abstract skills and intangible outcomes.

Focusing Questions

1. How are evaluation data helpful in developing and improving consultation programs? Who will want to see data from the consultation program for accountability and planning purposes?
2. When should evaluation plans for school consultation and collaboration be developed? When should evaluation procedures for consultation be implemented?

3. Why do school consultants need to evaluate aspects of classroom environments that might affect student behavior? What are classroom environments that might affect student behavior? What are variables that might affect assessment?
4. What are the important processes in consultation? How can the effectiveness of these processes be evaluated? How might objective information be obtained to help consultants improve specific process skills? Are there parallels to the way teachers gather data about student skills?
5. What is the important content of consultation? What types of data might be collected to document the effectiveness of using this content?
6. What data might a consulting teacher collect about student (or client) progress that could be included as part of an evaluation plan? How might that type of information indicate whether or not the consulting teacher is doing a good job in the consultation?
7. How can a consultation program be justified, considering all possible sources of information available in the school and other information that might be gathered for this purpose?
8. What skills and competencies are needed by collaborative consultants?
9. What ethical considerations guide the practice of collaborative school consultation?

Key Terms

accountability	evaluation	rating forms
assessment	evaluation plan	self-assessment
behavioral observation	formative evaluation	self-monitoring of behavior
Curriculum-Based Assessment	ongoing systematic	summative evaluation
Curriculum-Based	assessment	
Measurement	outcomes-based education	
ethics of consultation	portfolio assessment	

Assessing and Evaluating the Consultation

Assessment and evaluation—the words produce apprehension and uneasiness over the use of tests, observations, and rating scales. Who has not dreaded the prospect of having one's work and progress evaluated? Yet in these days of accountability, evaluation is an essential part of professional responsibilities. Consultants cannot know if the consultation activities are effective unless they conduct some type of evaluation. Administrators and policymakers cannot support their programs unless meaningful data are available.

In the early 1990s Fuchs, Fuchs, Dulan, Roberts, and Fernstrom (1992) conducted a literature review on consultation effectiveness from 1961 to 1989. They found that the majority of the investigations used group designs, were conducted in the behavioral consultation areas, and used student or teacher behavior rather than student achievement as the criterion for consultation success. These researchers called for more databased studies of consultation effectiveness and for analysis of student achievement rather than teacher involvement, enjoyment,

Scenario 8

The setting is the conference room of a special education program office where the principal, the director of special education, the special education consulting teacher, and a parent are seated.

PRINCIPAL: Mrs. James, I have asked Mrs. Garcia, our director of special education, and Mr. Penner, our special education consulting teacher, to meet with us today to help address your questions. I've explained to them that you're concerned about the new program for your daughter. As I understand your concerns, you feel she is not learning as much as she did last year when she went to the resource room for special help. Is there anything you would like to add?

PARENT: Well, I don't like to complain, but I just don't understand this new way of doing things for her. I was glad when she qualified for special education, because I thought she would finally get some help. Now she isn't getting it any more. Besides that, I wonder how this consulting program affects the other children. As you know, I am president of the local Parent Teachers Association, and questions about the special education program have come up at several of our meetings. I told parents I would try to get more information from you.

CONSULTING TEACHER: I've been working closely with your daughter's classroom teacher this year, and we've worked out some special learning activities in the classroom such as cooperative learning. She loves that, and when she needs a little extra help, we've arranged for a sixth-grade girl to tutor her. Besides that, she goes to the resource room for math.

SPECIAL EDUCATION DIRECTOR: I understand the placement team agreed to all these special experiences at the IEP meeting last spring.

PARENT: Yes, I know we agreed to try them, but I don't think they are working. I'd like more evidence that this is the right way to educate children who have learning problems.

PRINCIPAL: Mr. Penner, do you have data that we can show Mrs. James?

CONSULTING TEACHER: Well, I could get some test scores from teachers, I guess.

SPECIAL EDUCATION DIRECTOR: Our consultation program is rather new. I believe it is already producing some positive outcomes, but it's evident that we must provide more documentation of the results. We'll need a more structured evaluation plan to get the appropriate data for assessing our results.

PRINCIPAL: I agree. Thank you for being involved with your daughter's program Mrs. James, and thanks for helping us to think through what we need to do. After we do some further work on this topic, may we call on you to collaborate with us on developing a more specific plan?

---

and satisfaction. They observed that many of the studies treated teachers, not students, as the clients. More knowledge is needed on what situation calls for which type of consultation, and on how the consultation process can have more appeal for teachers.

Conoley and Conoley (1982) articulate the critical importance of evaluation to consultants with the following statement:

It will make little difference to a consultee organization if the consultant does everything with textbook perfection. The decision-makers are interested in positive outcomes in terms of cost, increased services, or staff feedback. Consultants must be prepared not only to provide assistance to others who are planning, implementing, and evaluating programs (i.e., program consultation) but must also *give priority* [emphasis added] to such activities in their own service delivery systems. (p. 82)

Engaging in an on-going systematic assessment process is the best way to make sure appropriate decisions are made.

Components of Consultation Evaluation

A model of consultation evaluation is shown in Figure 8.1. The model features the accumulation of information for two primary purposes—formative evaluation and summative evaluation. Formative evaluation is used when making decisions to modify, change, or refine a program during its implementation. Summative evaluation documents the attainment of program goals and is used most often by administrators in determining whether or not programs should be started, dropped, maintained, or chosen from among several alternatives (Scriven, 1967; Popham, 1988; Posavac & Carey, 1989).

Data gathered during formative evaluations are often included as part of summative evaluations (Tuckman, 1985). The key in selecting evaluation procedures is to consider the

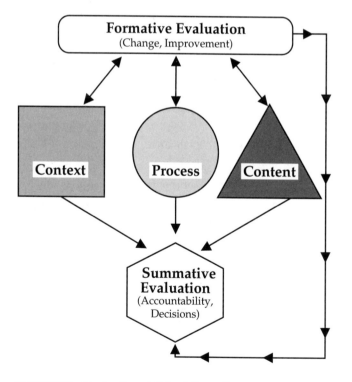

FIGURE 8.1   Evaluation of School Consultation

purposes of assessment—the questions that need to be answered. Formative assessments provide information for making changes and improvements. The focus is upon individual concerns and the local school context. Summative evaluations are used to make decisions about program goals; therefore, they require collection of data from larger groups. Formative and summative evaluations also differ in the audiences to whom the results will be targeted and the way in which those results will be communicated (Popham, 1988). We propose that a good consultation evaluation will include context, processes, and content of consultation. These three elements are used for both formative and summative purposes. Examples of questions that might be answered in each situation are presented in Figure 8.2.

Evaluation of Consultation Context. Formative evaluation of the context yields information about all elements that are expected to have an impact on the effectiveness of the consultation, such as students, teachers, family, or home and classroom environments. This information helps in selecting and modifying consultation processes and content, and is particularly useful during the initial stages of a consultation episode. Summative evaluation of context provides information to help decide whether or not the program should be continued in a particular school or district.

Evaluation of Consultation Processes. Formative evaluation of consultation processes provides information about skills and procedures that the consultant should develop or improve during the consultation process. Summative evaluation of processes gives information that demonstrates whether or not the skills and procedures used by the consultant were appropriate and effective.

Evaluation of Consultation Content. Formative evaluation of the content of consultation provides information about effectiveness of the interventions planned by the consultant and consultee and, when the interventions are not effective, provides data to guide school personnel in making program changes. Summative evaluation of content indicates whether or

FIGURE 8.2   Purposes of Assessment and Evaluation

Focus on:	**FORMATIVE** Change/improvement	**SUMMATIVE** Accountability
Context *Program success*	*Development/change* What program aspects should be changed to fit this school and community?	*Status decisions* Should the consulting program continue next year?
Process *Consultation skills*	*Growth/development* What interpersonal management skills need to be changed?	*Self-analysis* Do I have the skills to be an effective consultant?
Content *Student/client progress*	*Growth/progress* Are achievement and behavior improving?	*Placement decisions* Does the student need more or less restrictive service?

not the student is receiving the appropriate level or type of service. For example, a student might need more in-depth psychotherapy than the school counselor can provide.

Developing an Evaluation Plan

Consultants should identify data-collection methods clearly in the initial stages of program development and at the beginning of each school year thereafter. A consultant who does not determine how to evaluate the program until the end of the school year will be working harder, not smarter. Summative evaluation procedures should be extensive enough to document achievement of each annual goal. This language probably sounds familiar, for that is exactly what is required when an IEP is developed. The similarity is not coincidental. Principles guiding IEP development must guide all good program development.

Once goals are determined, consultants can begin to list the types of data needed and determine ways of obtaining the data. Much of the data will exist within classrooms, in student files, or in school computer data banks. The challenge is to know what is needed and plan a strategy for collecting and summarizing the data in a meaningful, time-efficient way.

Example of an Evaluation Plan

Anita, a certified learning disabilities teacher, was excited about the prospects for the coming school year. Her school had set goals to address the educational needs of students at risk and to decrease the number of students labeled as disabled. Since many of these formerly labeled students were placed in LD programs, she volunteered to change her program delivery model to consultation and collaboration, with only limited resource room services. It was a challenge for which she hardly knew where to begin.

Anita had studied literature on consultation and collaboration and she knew that the first step was to think through the program goals. She also knew it would be important to gather appropriate data so she and her administrators could decide whether or not their goals were met by this program change. She carefully considered the types of data that she would gather throughout the school year in order to make a good decision about the effectiveness of the program. As she thought about her evaluation plan, she also wanted to make sure she continued to improve her consultation skills during the year. So she included several goals that addressed that need.

Her plan is shown in Figure 8.3.

Components of a Good Evaluation Plan

The evaluation plan should contain at least one measure to document achievement of each program goal and a projected time line for gathering the information. Many different sources of information should be used, including but not limited to:

- Direct observations of behavior
- Portfolios of student work
- Long-term projects

FIGURE 8.3   Consultation Evaluation Plan

Program Goals	Evaluation Procedures	Dates
Student progress in general classroom, with grades no less than D.	Curriculum-Based Measurement Grade reports Student portfolios	Daily 9-wks on-going
Increase in skills of teachers for teaching special needs students.	In-service evaluation	Each session
Student use of study skills classroom.	Classroom observation Teacher reports	9-wks 9-wks
Positive interaction with peers and teachers in classroom settings.	Classroom observation Behavior rating scale	on-going 9-wks
Parent satisfaction with child's school experiences.	Questionnaire	Dec.–May
Teacher satisfaction with consultation services.	Self-assessment checklists and rating forms	9-wks
Teacher use of suggested materials and methods in teaching.	Classroom environment Checklist	Sep., Jan., May
Consultant use of effective communication and problem-solving.	Videotapes, behavior rating form, consultation verbal analysis system	9-wks
More student service with less labeling.	Consultation activity report Consultation log	Daily By need

- Logs and journals of consultation activities
- Interviews
- Videotaped conferences
- Anecdotal records
- Student grades

Assessment methods and procedures should be as objective and unbiased as possible. Sometimes unbiased opinions and objectivity are not easily attained. For example, a consultant might ask consultees to complete checklists such as the ones presented in this chapter, but respondents may not be willing or able to offer objective opinions. As noted in earlier chapters, lack of objectivity was cited by Caplan (1970) as theme interference in working with the special needs of students. Consultees sometimes give high ratings indiscriminately. This failure to discriminate may be due to fear of the consequences of being truthful (such as losing a colleague's friendship) or not knowing enough about the questioned behavior to offer a constructive opinion. High ratings are of little benefit for evaluation, and if inaccurate, they may be another example of an iatrogenic effect, compounding problems rather than creating solutions. For these reasons, consultants need information from multiple sources, in different circumstances within the context, and at varying times throughout the school year.

The following points list key elements in developing an effective evaluation plan:

1. It should be an ongoing process.
2. Multiple sources of information should be used.
3. Valid and reliable methods of gathering information should be used.
4. It should be limited to gathering data that will answer pertinent questions and document attainment of consultation goals.
5. It should be realistic, diplomatic, and sensitive to multicultural considerations.
6. Legal and ethical procedures, including protection of rights of privacy, should be followed.
7. Anonymity of respondents should be maintained whenever possible.
8. It should be cost-effective in time and money. For example, whenever possible, existing data should be used.

Evaluating the Context of Consultation

Contextual evaluation is a relatively new conceptual framework through which consultants can examine their efforts. This approach to evaluation grew in importance as part of the educational reform of the 1980s. It is based on the premise that educational events occur in a context and the elements of the context play important parts in determining whether or not educational processes result in the desired outcomes (Field & Hill, 1988).

Contextual evaluation acknowledges the interdependence of all aspects of the school experience, including teachers, parents, students, administrators, classroom environment, school facilities, policies, procedures, and legal requirements. Contextual evaluation should consider the impact of students on teachers as well as the impact of teachers on students. It must assess the effect of teachers on consultants as well as the effect of consultants on teachers. It also should provide information on the professional interactions among individuals involved within the consultation environment(s).

Contextual evaluation is discussed here as it might be applied by individual consultants or collaborators. Administrators interested in a more extensive discussion of contextual appraisal for special education evaluation will find the work of Field and Hill (1988) a helpful reference.

Part I of this book discusses many contextual elements that play a part in school consultation, including societal values, legal requirements, community climate, home environment, school reform movements, teacher attitudes, and student characteristics. That information can provide background for appraising all elements when evaluating a consultation program. Evaluators will want to give careful attention to environmental factors that are related to student outcomes (Ysseldyke & Christenson, 1987). These factors include

- ■ *School district conditions* such as teacher-pupil ratio, extent of emphasis on basic skills, amount of homework, emphasis on test taking, or grading policies;

- *Within-school conditions* such as class size, school ambience, leadership from the principal, cooperative environment, collaborative staff relations, degree of structure, or classroom rules and procedures; and
- *General family characteristics* such as socio-economic status, educational level, use of out-of-school time, and peer groups outside the school.

Assessment of student characteristics and general classroom conditions is needed in order for a consultant to determine whether or not any mismatch between student characteristics and classroom situation is a factor in the problem. If the classroom environment is a problem, analysis of the information can be used to formulate appropriate solutions. Information about student progress will be discussed later under content of consultation, because student academic and behavior change is the most valid measure of the effectiveness of content.

Assessment of Classroom Environments

The major contextual element to be assessed is the classroom learning environment in which the student is expected to function. Bender (1988) suggests that educational placement teams conduct extensive evaluations of every classroom in the building at least every five years, keeping the information available for the use of preassessment team members, consultants, and other school staff. He articulates the importance of this type of assessment information for consultants:

> …some of the most useful services presently performed by special education consultants depend on knowledge about the standard functioning of general classrooms. When a consultant visits a class to observe the student and to consult, prior knowledge of what general types of strategies are commonly used in that class is likely to greatly enhance the consultant's ability to make meaningful strategy suggestions. (Bender, 1988, p. 19)

Other reasons for including this type of assessment in the evaluation plan are: (1) it is recognized that planning for instruction based on student learning styles and characteristics alone has been unsuccessful (Bender, 1988; Bursuck & Lessen, 1987; Ysseldyke & Christenson, 1987); (2) research on effective instruction now provides useful information for determining which elements of the classroom environment should be evaluated (Bursuck and Lessen, 1987; Ysseldyke and Christenson, 1987); and (3) the assessment has the potential to help classroom teachers better understand their own needs in facilitating learning for students with special needs (Bender, 1988).

Classroom elements (Bender, 1988) that should be assessed appear in Figure 8.4. This list of elements will be helpful for consultants who wish to prepare their own checklists or rating forms. The forms should be completed by classroom teachers and discussed in consultations with the teacher. Other sources of rating forms and checklists that can be used for this purpose are cited in the section for further reading.

Evaluating the Process of Consultation

One of the most important reasons for conducting process evaluation is to glean information for professional development. According to some authorities, self-assessment and

FIGURE 8.4   Classroom Elements to Be Assessed

Teaching Strategies and Approaches

Analysis in this category determines types of effective teaching practices used by the teacher, such as:

1. Precision teaching
2. Cooperative learning
3. Self-monitoring
4. Peer tutoring
5. Use of learning strategies
6. Use of alternative or supplementary reading materials, alternative testing and grading strategies

Typical Modifications Made in the Classroom

Analysis in this category includes strategies for effective teaching behaviors, such as:

1. Pacing
2. Monitoring
3. Providing feedback and follow-through
4. Using alternative presentation modes, including visual and auditory presentations
5. Alternative classroom organizations
6. Use of cognitive organizers for reading
7. Use of individualized instruction

Unusual Aspects of the Local Curriculum

Elements assessed in this area include:

1. Average achievement levels of the school
2. Type of curriculum presented to students in prior years
3. Reading level of classroom texts

---

self-direction are preferred methods of professional development for teachers (Bailey, 1981). The rationale for self-assessment applies even more to school consultants than to teachers, because in most school contexts there will be few, if any, opportunities for consultants to receive any assistance from administrators or supervisors. Without some type of self-assessment, a consultant may perpetuate ineffective processes and the quality of the consultation may decline over time. The value of engaging in self-assessment of one's consultation is illustrated by this journal entry of a graduate student in consultation:

> Before involvement in the consulting project at this university, I had never seriously examined my communication skills. The videotaping has been the hardest for me; however, I have come to realize the importance of it and I have gained a better insight into areas that can be improved.
>
> The first videotape recording was a real eye-opener, revealing lack of skill in handling resistance. The second recording surprised the consultee, as she realized that during the consultation she had thought of a solution to the problem for herself. The third videotape

revealed more areas in need of work: Conflict resolution, assertiveness, and controlling facial responses. I feel I did a good job of using the problem-solving technique, and the best part was to hear two consultees say they were going to use it themselves in problem situations. They feel it helped them focus on the problem and think of real solutions. It gave them a base from which to work.

Setting time limitations is something I'm not comfortable doing. I would rather allow the consultee enough time to work through feelings and identify the issues. However, looking back over my consultation log, I see that six of the consultations took more than 45 minutes and might well have concluded earlier if I had set time limits.

Now that I have identified this baseline of strengths and weaknesses, I have set the following goals to achieve by the end of the school year:

1. Reduce resistance from consultees to no more than 95% of the time.
2. Resolve conflicts at least 80% of the time.
3. Use assertive behavior during consultation 100% of the time.
4. Eliminate inappropriate facial responses. I will videotape consultation episodes every nine weeks and tabulate the target behaviors to see if I am making progress in reaching my goals. In addition, I will use a simplified version of the Consultant Behaviors Checklist to get feedback from my consultees every nine weeks. I will periodically interview consultees after consultation episodes to gather more immediate feedback about the target behaviors I am trying to improve.

Consultant Self-Assessment Procedures

While many individuals engage in some self-appraisal or mental reflection, few do so systematically. Thus, the assessment or appraisal might not lead to meaningful improvement. Effective self-assessment should consist of a systematic, comprehensive program in which the consultant can gain information that leads to improvement or to a change of behavior.

The following suggestions for developing a self-assessment program are adapted from the work of Bailey (1981).

1. *Gain a philosophical overview of self-assessment.* Understand that self-assessment is not synonymous with the accountability required by administrators. Its purpose is personal change and improvement, and you should not share the results with supervisors unless you want to. The activities may not be easy to do, and some are rather time-consuming. They require selection of objective methods to gather data, in order to be most effective. Data should be collected in several consulting sessions with different types of consultees and various problem situations.

2. *Use media for self-assessment.* An objective way of gaining feedback about your behavior is to monitor it through use of audio- or videotaped material. Students in consulting preparation programs have been reluctant initially to use this type of feedback, but most are grateful later for its helpfulness. These tips for preparing and analyzing videotapes are helpful:

2.1 Set the consultee at ease by explaining the purpose of the videotape recording.
2.2 Do a few "trial runs" before involving a consultee, in order to become comfortable with the video camera and accustomed to seeing yourself on tape.

2.3 Don't focus on traits that have nothing to do with the quality of consultation. Taping distorts your voice and visual image, so don't worry about them.

2.4 Observe or listen to the tape several times, each time focusing observations on just one or two behaviors.

2.5 Tabulate behavior using a systematic observation method so the information can be interpreted meaningfully and progress followed objectively.

2.6 Be sensitive to the rights of privacy of the consultee. Arrange the seating during a videotape-recording session so that you face the camera and the consultee's back is to the camera.

2.7 Do not show the tape to an audience without receiving signed permission from the consultee.

3. *Identify the important consultation skills to be observed.* Merely watching and listening to oneself with the help of media will not provide enough information to guide personal development. Specific skills must be designated for recording the observation. Checklists and rating forms such as the Consultant Behaviors Checklist (Figure 8.5) can be used to identify behaviors to observe while viewing or listening to the taped consulting sessions. These checklists were developed from lists of important consulting behaviors described by researchers in the field.

4. *View or listen to taped consulting sessions and tabulate observation data.* Systematic behavioral observation techniques discussed later in this chapter are useful for observing consultant behavior, just as they are useful in observing student behavior in the classroom. Tabulate only one or two behaviors in each viewing, perhaps starting with a verbal behavior such as the number of times you said "O.K." or a nonverbal behavior such as looking away from the consultee. After tabulating the target behaviors, summarize strengths and behaviors that should be improved.

5. *Write down goals and objectives.* Prioritize the behaviors needing change and write behavioral objectives for them. Remember to state some type of criterion such as saying "O.K." no more than two times in a 20-minute consultation session. Include dates for achievement of each objective.

6. *Select strategies to help make the needed changes.* Formulate the strategies from material presented in other chapters of this text.

7. *Gather feedback and chart progress in achieving goals.* Periodic checks to determine whether or not you are making progress in the self-selected area for change is essential. It is very easy to believe falsely that the change has taken place if this step is bypassed. If goals focus on verbal skills, audio tapes probably will be sufficient for follow-up data, but if they include nonverbal skills, use of videotapes should continue. Perhaps it would be most efficient to reevaluate consultation skills at every marking period for students. The advantage of using consultee feedback is that consultee information can be contrasted with the consultant's own information. If there is much discrepancy between the two sets of information, causes of the discrepancy need to be determined.

8. *When a criterion is met, a self-reward is due for a job well done!* The objective data can be shared with a supervisor. The consultant may wish to chart consultation growth just

FIGURE 8.5   Consultant Behaviors Checklist

Consultant _____   Observer _____   Date _____

	yes	needs work	does not apply
1. *Welcome*			
Sets comfortable climate	____	____	____
Uses commonly understood terms	____	____	____
Is nonjudgmental	____	____	____
Provides brief informal talk	____	____	____
Is pleasant	____	____	____
2. *Communication Exchange*			
Shares information	____	____	____
Is accepting	____	____	____
Is empathic	____	____	____
Identifies major issues	____	____	____
Keeps on task	____	____	____
Is perceptive, providing insight	____	____	____
Avoids jargon	____	____	____
Is encouraging	____	____	____
Gives positive reinforcement	____	____	____
Sets goals as agreed	____	____	____
Develops working strategy	____	____	____
Develops plan to implement strategy	____	____	____
Is friendly	____	____	____
3. *Interpretation of Communication*			
Seeks feedback	____	____	____
Demonstrates flexibility	____	____	____
Helps define problem	____	____	____
Helps consultee assume responsibility for plans	____	____	____
4. *Summarizing*			
Is concise	____	____	____
Is positive	____	____	____
Is clear	____	____	____
Sets another meeting if needed	____	____	____
Is affirming	____	____	____

as student progress growth is documented. Charts tell the story much more quickly than a list of numbers or a narrative description. Self-assessment should be an on-going process propelled by realistic expectations.

Records of Consultation Activities

Administrators are interested in more than how effectively consultants communicate or engage in problem-solving. They want to know about practical issues such as how the consultant uses time, how many consultees have been helped, the types of problems addressed, and whether or not the consultation services were helpful to the consultees.

Consultants should keep records of consultation activities in order to answer these types of questions. The consulting log in Chapter 7 is a useful form for documenting these data. Those who want to develop their own forms would find the work of Tindal and Taylor-Pendergast (1989) a helpful reference. It may be productive also to check with one's administrator to find out what specific information would be most desired. Busy consultants should not spend time collecting information that is not wanted or needed.

> One special education consultant in an inclusive school avoided the confusion that resulted from many people going in and out of each classroom every day by devising a system to record these activities. In each classroom she placed record forms that were completed by each person who went into the classroom to consult or provide special services to a student with disabilities. These individuals were asked to "log in" by entering the date, time, name, and a brief comment regarding the student(s) with disabilities during the time in the classroom. Later, the data were sorted in various ways for final reports.

Evaluating the Content of Consultation

The content of consultation consists of the problem solutions, instructional techniques, or behavioral interventions selected through the consultation process. The content can be judged effective if the goals of the consultation are achieved. In school consultation the goals usually address improved achievement or behavior.

Assessing Student Academic Performance

School consultants need training in the traditional approach of examining students through use of formal and informal testing procedures to identify their special learning needs. Skill in observing classroom performance, as differentiated from performance in a testing situation, is also necessary. The most functional approach to making these observations is Curriculum-Based Assessment (CBA).

Curriculum-Based Assessment (CBA).   It is important to identify accurately the student's current level of performance in the classroom and monitor progress in a systematic, on-going manner. Standardized tests are not designed for this type of monitoring. Curriculum-Based Assessment is the most appropriate approach for the purpose (Bender, 1988; Bursuck & Lessen, 1987; Deno, 1987; Wang, 1987).

"There is nothing new about Curriculum-Based Assessment. In many respects it is like coming home to traditional classroom instruction" (Tucker, 1985, p. 199). What *is* new are more precise and practical ways of examining student progress in the classroom curriculum. The basic concept of CBA is use of the actual curriculum materials, or the course of study adopted by a school system, in making the assessment (Tucker, 1985). CBA differs from traditional testing, which uses material representing a composite of items taken from many different curricula. While standardized tests tell us how students perform in relation to a large reference group, CBA tells us how students perform in the classrooms where they are expected to function. Since most school consultants will be addressing problems that occur in general classrooms, they will need this type of information to formulate good solutions to problems and to document effectiveness of their efforts.

Consultants can choose among several ways to conduct CBA. Figure 8.6 illustrates the purposes for some of these ways to conduct CBA. Although teacher-made tests and criterion-referenced tests provide information about content mastery, portfolios and Curriculum-Based Measurement provide information to monitor progress in larger domains over time. All the procedures have valid uses. The method chosen will depend on the circumstances within the school and should be the most valid, reliable, and efficient method for a given purpose. Although Curriculum-Based Measurement meets these criteria, it is limited to measurement of basic skills and cannot be used to monitor many other valuable educational goals. Caution should be taken in adopting commercially prepared CBA measures because they probably will not be accurate measures of the curriculum in a particular school. Criterion-referenced tests that accompany the textbooks adopted by school personnel would be appropriate CBA measures for a consultant to use.

Some school districts and states require a type of CBA for all students. A term commonly used for this practice is *outcomes-based education* (OBE). OBE requires schools to state the outcomes they expect from their efforts. These outcomes are often stated as processes as well as products. Although school districts might state very broad outcomes, such as "all students will be good communicators in a complex world," the outcomes become more narrow as they are stated at the building and classroom levels. For special

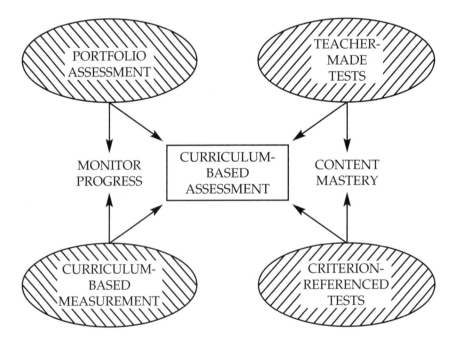

FIGURE 8.6   Purposes of Various Types of CBA

educators, the IEP is an outcomes-based document for a single individual. For a school that utilizes the principles of outcomes-based education, the information generated for that program might be sufficient for evaluation needs. The consultant would need only to gain access to the information as it applies to the program being evaluated.

Other CBA measures are informal reading inventories (assuming the reading materials are taken from school texts), and mastery tests in content subject matter. "CBA is the ultimate in 'teaching the test,' because the materials used to assess progress are *always* drawn directly from the course of study" (Tucker, 1985, p. 200). The disadvantages of teacher-made CBA procedures are the time it takes teachers to develop them, and lack of knowledge about reliability and validity of the measures (Fuchs, Fuchs, & Hamlett, 1990).

Many special educators are familiar with approaches to evaluation of student learning such as Precision Teaching (Lindsley, 1964) and Data-Based Instruction (Mercer & Mercer, 1993). These approaches require specification of observable and measurable objectives which can be recorded as the number of correct and incorrect movements or responses per minute. One-minute probes are given daily and the scores are plotted on charts. The charts are analyzed frequently to observe trends indicating whether instructional program changes are needed. A variation of this approach was developed and refined at the University of Minnesota (Deno, 1987). This CBA system is called Curriculum-Based *Measurement* (CBM), emphasis added to differentiate it from other forms of CBA.

Deno (1987) specified two distinctive features of Curriculum-Based Measurement: (1) the procedures possess reliability and validity to a degree that equals or exceeds that of most achievement tests; and (2) growth in each curriculum area is measured on a single global task performed repeatedly across time. This approach differs significantly from criterion-referenced testing, which uses many different tasks, each measuring a different skill in a sequence. CBM has been widely researched in elementary schools using different types of curricula. It measures effectively the growth in academic areas of reading, writing, math, and spelling. The research has not singled out particular situations where it is most appropriate, but CBM is likely to be more useful than criterion-referenced tests for students in classrooms where whole language instruction is being used, because of its emphasis on global measures. It is very appropriate for use with students who have learning problems. It might also be an attractive approach to use with gifted students when basic skill development is of less interest to the evaluator than progress on more global measures.

A major disadvantage of CBM is the time needed to keep records and chart results. However, this process can be facilitated by use of computer software that automatically generates, administers, and scores tests; saves student scores and responses to the items on the tests; graphs scores; and automatically analyzes the student's rate of progress in comparison to the goal line (Fuchs, Hamlett, & Fuchs, 1990).

Portfolio Assessment.   Other types of student performance, including sample worksheets, copies of projects, extra-credit reports, and samples of artwork, can be collected to help document the content of consultation. Evaluation of such products is an alternative that has much potential for assessing a wide range of student abilities and needs. A number of educational pioneers are leading the movement toward alternative assessment by promoting portfolios as a means for attesting to student progress over time (Maeroff, 1991).

Many classroom teachers guide students in developing "working portfolios" and "showcase portfolios." The first is used to monitor progress toward specified goals (usually defined mutually by the student and teacher); the second presents the "best" of the products pulled from the working portfolio to show to parents, other teachers, and future employers. Special educators should consider preparing another working portfolio referenced to IEP goals. CBM charts and teacher-made tests can be part of the portfolio, but the strength of using the portfolio is the opportunity to present products such as writing samples, tape-recorded spoken language samples, and observation data that do not lend themselves to being tested in traditional ways.

Paulson, Paulson, and Meyer (1991) describe the portfolio as a purposeful collection of student work that exhibits efforts, progress, and achievements in one or more areas. They propose that students participate in selecting the contents to put into their portfolios, and in developing the criteria for selection and for judging merit. Such processes are arenas for involving students in collaborative experiences to improve their learning and productivity.

A portfolio is larger and more elaborate than a report card, but smaller and more focused than a trunkful of artifacts (Valencia, 1990). A convenient storage device is the expandable file folder. This is to be a working folder; therefore, it should be easily accessible to the student owner and the teacher. Suitable products to be added to the portfolio, after self-assessment by the student and consultation with the teacher, might include: progress charts; completed learning packets; artwork; a student-made book; lists of mastered vocabulary or spelling words; notes on informal conversations; research reports; clever doodles; original songs; creative writing samples; descriptions of good deeds and helpful behavior; an autobiography; journal entries; tests; records of scores; teacher observational notes; audio- or videotapes; solutions to problems; and much more. It is helpful to have a summary sheet, table of contents, or other organizing format. The construction of this format provides another valuable opportunity for the teacher and student to collaborate and discuss learning.

Portfolio assessment is a procedure that focuses on both process and the product of learning. It is authentic in purpose and task, multidimensional, and contributes to an ongoing learning process. The material can be continuously evaluated, streamlined, and sent with the student from grade level to grade level as visible evidence of growth and improvement. It provides an effective vehicle for partnership in learning between teacher and student and contributes valuable support material for staffings and parent conferences.

Problems to be overcome in using this alternative form of assessment center around the additional work, storage space, patience, and time for teacher interaction with each student. A school consultant can ease the load of a teacher who wishes to use portfolio assessment by working as a team member to consult with students as they reflect on their work, and by collaborating with the teacher to develop ways of organizing and using the procedure.

Portfolios must provide some measure of objectivity to be reliable indicators of growth or progress toward goals in a working portfolio. Teachers need to guide a systematic process of securing samples to put into the portfolio. For example, writing samples might be gathered once each month, dated, and placed in chronological order in the portfolio. Then the samples can be easily viewed to show progress toward the goal. Additional objectivity and evaluation are provided with use of a rubric. Rubrics are lists for standards or outcomes that guide the evaluation process. They are often in the form of rating scales.

APPLICATION 8.1

Collaborating for Portfolio Use

Consulting teachers can assist with the process of initiating student portfolio development by:

1. Reading research, attending workshops on portfolio development, and then sharing the information with colleagues.
2. Developing and disseminating "how-to" sheets on portfolio assessment.
3. Demonstrating an example of a well-prepared portfolio.
4. Conducting staff-development sessions on portfolios. For example, staff might have a brainstorming session on what to include in portfolios, how to assess the products, and how to use the portfolios most constructively.
5. Helping teach students how to develop tables of contents, organize their portfolios, and critique their work.
6. Getting parents involved in and enthused about portfolio development.
7. Assisting teachers with development of criteria and expectations for portfolios to encourage consistency in the school and district.
8. Helping teachers and students locate resources needed for portfolios.

Figure 8.7 provides an example of a rubric for the product, process, and content of writing. Ideally, the rubric is completed and discussed in a conference between the student and teacher at regular intervals during the school term. The completed rubrics are kept in the portfolio for future reference and modified as growth takes place (Swicegood, 1994).

Implementation of a portfolio assessment system in collaboration with students and colleagues includes the following steps:

1. Inform students and involve them.
2. Determine types of contents to be included (with flexibility for adding new types that may be determined later).
3. Prepare formats to organize portfolio contents, such as a table of contents or a summary sheet.
4. Determine criteria for evaluating the contents.
5. Determine the final destination of the portfolio and its contents.

Maintaining Student Academic Records. If consultants have been using curriculum-based assessment and systematic behavioral observation procedures, a summary of the information can provide a summative record of consultation content. This information can report the number of goals met or not met, student grades or test scores, and interviews with teachers and parents.

As suggested earlier, one disadvantage of collecting and maintaining records generated by types of assessment such as student portfolios is the amount of space needed for filing them. Minner, Minner, and Lepich (1990) illustrate this point by stating, "If a teacher had a caseload of 15 students and each student worked in four academic content areas, the

FIGURE 8.7   Example of Rubric for Portfolio Assessment

WRITTEN EXPRESSION RUBRIC				
	EMERGING	**GROWING**	**MASTERED**	**EXPANDED**
WRITING PRODUCT				
Handwriting				
Grammar				
Spelling				
Capitalization				
Paraphrasing				
WRITING PROCESS				
Idea generation				
Brainstorming				
Organization of ideas				
Editing skills				
Error correction				
Final draft				
WRITING CONTENT				
Sentence development				
Paragraph organization				
Paragraph development				
Overall length of writing				
Use of words				
Fluency of writing				
Variety of purposes				

COMMENTS:

teacher would collect over 2,000 work samples in an academic year if he or she collected only one sample per week in each area" (pp. 32–33). The volume of papers would be even greater for a consultant who wished to monitor the progress of a caseload of thirty or more students. One solution to this dilemma is to require students to keep their own portfolios of their work (Wolf, 1989). This strategy seems especially valuable for use by consultants for gifted and talented students in content areas of art, music, design, written expression, computer programming, and other subjects which do not lend themselves easily to conventional forms of assessment.

Another method involves collaboration among classroom teacher, special education consultant, *and student* to develop criteria for assessing portfolio products, selecting the best or most representative ones, and removing others. Thus the portfolio volume is reduced while the student is gaining valuable self-assessment skills. Students skilled in using computers can store their products in a computer file.

Assessing Student Behaviors

Finding solutions to classroom behavior problems constitutes one of the major content areas of consultation. Consultants will need to gather objective information to document behavior changes. Systematic behavior observations, as well as subjective measures such as rating scales and checklists, should be used for this purpose.

Behavior Observations.   Many students with learning and behavior problems, as well as some gifted and talented students, demonstrate social difficulties, lack of motivation, poor work habits or other behaviors that need to be monitored as part of the consultation

---

APPLICATION **8.2**

Developing a Teacher Portfolio

Educators who plan, develop, and maintain their own portfolios derive several benefits from the activity. They model the process for their colleagues who are not yet participating in this assessment technique and they demonstrate to students the value and importance they place upon portfolios. The portfolio can be presented as an example of their productivity when they are evaluated by a supervisor or an administrator. Last, but not to be overlooked—it can be fun.

Possibilities for portfolio products abound. A few are lesson plans that worked well; videotapes of classroom activity highlights; sample tests; effective worksheets or packets; an original teaching or grading technique; sketch of an unusual bulletin board so it won't be forgotten; list of professional books read; any articles published in newsletters, newspapers, or other professional outlets; documentation of consultation episodes (coded for confidentiality); descriptions of team teaching activities; photos of special class sessions; original computer software that worked well; a highly effective management technique; notes from parents or students that were reinforcing; goals for the semester or school year; special achievements by students. The list could go on and on.

evaluation program. Researchers studying general classroom settings have identified emotional, social, and work skills important for success in that setting (Bursuck & Lessen, 1987; Fad, 1990; Wood & Meiderhoff, 1989). These data can be used to develop a checklist or rating scale most appropriate for your level of service. An alternative is to use one of several commercially developed rating scales and checklists that are available—for example, the Walker Problem Behavior Identification Checklist (Walker, 1976) or the Behavior Problem Checklist (Quay & Peterson, 1987). Caution should be exercised when selecting from existing rating scales, so that those chosen will be appropriate for the classroom situation in which they are to be used.

Several individuals, such as classroom teachers, parents, teacher aides, or peer tutors, can be asked to complete the rating scales. There are two advantages in asking the classroom teacher. First, the behaviors to observe can be more closely targeted. Second, teachers can be encouraged to focus attention on behaviors not previously considered. Bursuck and Lessen (1987) emphasize that a combination of behavioral observation by a consultant and completion of a behavior checklist by the teacher will be preferable to either one alone.

It is not sufficient to observe that the student does not pay attention or is noisy. The educator needs to know precisely the rate and frequency of the behaviors and under what conditions the student displays the behaviors. Systematic, direct observation of the student in the environments in which the problems occur is the best assessment procedure for gathering the information.

Data collected on specific behaviors can help collaborators set goals, plan programs, and evaluate interventions. In preassessment and problem-solving, it is much easier to deal with "is at least 15 minutes tardy 85 percent of the time," or "screams and kicks heels on the floor an average of six times per day," or "writes 90 percent of the 4s, 5s, and 7s backward," than it is to work collaboratively on problems described as "irresponsible," "aggressive," and "has problems writing numbers."

Consultants may select from among several types of ongoing measurement of behavior when they wish to observe a student's behavior in the classroom, on the playground, or in the halls. There are many excellent resources about the methodology of behavior observation (Alberto & Troutman, 1990; Wolery, Bailey, & Sugai, 1988; Rusch, Rose, & Greenwood, 1988).

Documenting Changes in Student Behavior.   Several methods of behavior measurement are useful for consultants:

- frequency recording,
- interval recording,
- time sampling,
- duration.

Each method begins with identifying and defining a specific, concrete behavior or a set of behaviors to be observed.

Behavior should be defined so precisely that when measured by two different people, the numbers will be virtually the same, assuring reliability of the measurement. Two people measuring "aggression" or "irresponsibility" would not be likely to have very high interrater reliability of the measurement! Sometimes it will take several visits to the classroom to develop an observable and measurable definition of the behavior.

Frequency recording determines the number of times the event happens. It is used to measure discrete behaviors that can be discriminated, such as swearing in class or episodes of crying. Consultants will want to observe in the environment in which the behavior occurs for a number of times to get a representative sample of the behavior. It may be necessary to spend time in the classroom before observation, so that the student becomes accustomed to the observer's presence and is not "on best behavior." Then the measurement will be more realistic. Teachers and students themselves can record frequency of specific behaviors. Trial recording is a variation of frequency recording. This method adds the dimension of recording the opportunities a student has to perform a behavior. For example, if the observer uses frequency recording to measure "compliance with teacher instructions," it will be necessary to know how many teacher instructions were presented before a compliance rate or percent can be obtained. A tally mark could be made on the data sheet for every instruction, and those that are followed would then be circled. A sample data sheet for frequency recording is provided in Figure 8.8.

In interval recording and time sampling, the observation period is marked into intervals such as fifteen-second sections, two-minute sections, or ten-minute sections. Although the measure is more precise with smaller sections of time (intervals), it is not always possible to do this when the observer is teaching the class or leading a discussion. For interval recording, the observer would mark whether or not the behavior in question occurred during the interval. Did Jay spit at another student during that five-minute period (mark +), or refrain from doing so (mark -)? Did Tracy work on the workbook lesson during the interval (mark +), or did she get up and wander around, look out the window, or comb her hair (mark -)? After the observation period, the consultant or teacher should divide the number of intervals in which the behavior occurred by the total intervals observed to get a percent of intervals (or time) that the behavior in question happened.

Time sampling is similar to interval sampling, and usually is easier because it does not require looking at the student for the entire observation period. After the observation time is divided into blocks of time (intervals), the observer only marks whether or not the behavior is occurring at the end of the interval. For example, at the end of fifteen seconds, the observer checks to see if Ryan is carving on the desk, the learning materials, or his flesh with a pencil, pen, or some other instrument. If so, the observer would mark +, and if not, the observer would mark -. Although some teachers might wish to stop Ryan's behavior rather than measure it, for the purposes of behavior observation, an observational posture rather than a disciplinary posture is needed. A percent of intervals is reported in order to describe the behavior.

Duration recording requires using a watch or clock to measure how long a behavior occurs. This type of behavior measurement is often used with time on task, time in seat, or time required to complete an assignment or task. The observer starts the stopwatch or notes the time the behavior begins and ends. Using a stopwatch to measure accumulated time performing a specific behavior is an alternative to interval recording or time sampling.

When such measures are used to assess a behavior, and used again after an intervention to reassess the same behavior, observed changes can be very obvious and dramatic.

FIGURE 8.8   Sample Data Sheet for Frequency Recording

Student _____   Observer _____

Dates _____   Time _____   Place _____

Definition _____

_____

_____

_____

Date	Time		Behavioral Episodes Tally	Total
	Start	Stop		

Then the results of collaboration are precise. It is a real boost to a collaborative partnership when a student's homework completion rate soars from 10 percent to 85 percent, or when the number of times a student puts on her coat independently changes from zero percent of opportunities to 100 percent after some work at home by parents.

Audio- or Videotape Records.   Another possibility for accumulating records of student behavior, particularly social behavior in the classroom, is the use of audio- or videotaped sessions (Minner et al., 1990), which can be part of a student's portfolio. "Teachers have told us that tapes are especially useful when showing parents how their son or daughter has progressed" (p. 33). This approach to data collection, while very effective, is often difficult to arrange. The suggestions discussed for using videotapes in self-assessment are applicable for this situation. Consultants should be very cautious about protecting the confidentiality of the observed student as well as other students in the classroom.

Skills and Competencies for Collaborative Consultation

A consultant wears many hats. Consultants are context systems analysts, process specialists, and content information banks, as well as role models and educational leaders. Consulting and collaborating require flexibility, adaptability, resilience, and the tolerance for delayed reinforcement or none at all. A person in this role is called on to diagnose, problem-identify, problem-solve, prescribe, evaluate, and follow-up, but all as part of a team whose members do not always understand or want to understand each other. Therefore, effective school consultants are knowledgeable about special education and general education curriculum and methods. They recognize and value adult differences among colleagues. They understand how schools function, and have a panoramic view of the educational scene. They are diplomatic at the same time as they are innovators.

Successful school consultants relate well to teacher colleagues and staff members, administrators, students, and parents. They have good communication skills, a patient and understanding demeanor, and assertiveness when it is needed. The consultant links people with resources, refers people to other sources when necessary, and teaches when that is the most appropriate way to serve student needs. A consultant is self-confident, but if running low on resources and ideas, the consultant may even find a consultant for himself or herself!

Perhaps most of all, the consultant is a change agent. As one very experienced consulting teacher put it, "You have to be abrasive enough to create change, but pleasant enough to be asked back so you will do it some more" (Bradley, 1987). The ideal consultant encourages other educators, including parents, to help students with special needs succeed in school. Most encouraging of all, consultation, collaboration, and teamwork among educators in schools and at home can nurture the potential and productivity of all students. See Figure 8.9 for a composite of characteristics demonstrated by effective school consultants and collaborators. Then use Figures 8.10 and 8.11 as rating instruments to evaluate collaborative school consultation.

Ethics of Consulting and Collaborating

Consultation and collaboration in the school setting require particular emphasis on ethical interaction for several reasons:

- Special needs of students are involved.
- Confidential data must be shared among several individuals.
- Consultants are out and about much more than classroom teachers, interfacing with many people in several buildings.
- Parent permission is not always required, but many of the issues to be dealt with approximate the sensitivity of issues that do necessitate parent consent.
- Consultants have complex roles with many demands upon them, but they often receive little or no training in how to adapt to those roles.

FIGURE 8.9   Characteristics of Effective School Consultants and Collaborators

Facilitative	Personable	Knowledgeable	Organized
Reflective listener	Considerate	Skilled in content area(s)	Prioritizes
Assertive	Thoughtful	Up-to-date with information	Efficient
Visible	Communicative	Resourceful	Manages time
Nonjudgmental	Self-assured	Skilled in process area(s)	Can say no
Properly persistent	Reliable	Can develop networks	Documents
Open to ideas	Goes extra mile	Knows procedures	Ethical
Flexible	Perceptive	Knows legislation	Schedules
Patient	Sensible	Creative	Decisions
Confidential	Self-reliant	Innovative	Available
Unbiased	Positive thinker	Knows regulations	Shares material
Diplomatic	Caring	Skilled in leadership	Punctual
Objective	Sensitive	Applies research	Seeks the best
Avoids roadblocks	Empathic	Conducts staff development	Personable
Puts forth effort	Determined	Desires to learn	Professional
Admits mistakes	Hard-working	Knowledge-linker	Friendly
Gives compliments	Kind	Advocating	Sincere
Brief when need be	Calm	Respectful	Dependable
Approachable	Participates	Responsive	Tactful
Recognizes feelings	Spokesperson	High energy level	Cooperative
Courageous	Open-minded		

- "Consultation" implies power and expertise until the collaborative spirit can be cultivated.
- Consultants may be asked on occasion to act inappropriately as a middle person, or to form alliances, or carry information, and they must respond ethically.
- Adults often have difficulty adapting to individual differences in teaching styles and preferences of colleagues, and many of them demonstrate resistance.

The persuasive aspects of consultation require a close, careful look at ethical practice (Ross, 1986). Ethical consultation is implemented by adhering to principles of confidentiality in acquisition and use of information about students, families, and individual school settings. It also includes a high regard for individual differences among colleagues and the constructive use of those differences to serve students' needs, concern and empathy for all, onedownsmanship in the consultative role, and mutual ownership of problems and rewards in the school environment.

Consultants and collaborators should review legal requirements relating to confidentiality, such as the Family Educational Rights and Privacy Act of 1974 (Buckley Amendment), and truth-in-testing laws within states that legislate them. Requirements such as these stipulate the need for confidentiality of student data and regulate parental access to information about their children.

FIGURE 8.10   Consultee Assessment of Consultation and Collaboration

Please evaluate your use of the consulting teacher service provided in the _____
program by providing the following information. Respond with:

1 = Not at all   2 = A little   3 = Somewhat   4 = Considerably   5 = Much

1. The consulting teacher provides useful information.   _____
2. The consulting teacher understands my school environment and teaching situation.   _____
3. The consulting teacher listens to my ideas.   _____
4. The consulting teacher helps me identify useful resources that help my students'   _____
    special needs.
5. The consulting teacher explains ideas clearly.   _____
6. The consulting teacher fits easily into the school setting.   _____
7. The consulting teacher increases my confidence in the special programs.   _____
8. I value consulting and collaborating with the consulting teacher.   _____
9. I have requested collaboration time with the consulting teacher.   _____
10. I plan to continue seeking opportunities to consult and collaborate with the   _____
    consulting teacher.

Other comments: _____

Hansen, Himes, and Meier (1990) present several suggestions for school consultants
to follow in order to exercise ethical behavior in their roles:

1. Promote professional attitudes and behaviors among staff about confidentiality and
    informed consent.
2. Take care with the quality of information entered in written records.
3. Take care in discussing problems of children and their families.
4. Focus on strengths of clients and share information only with those who need it to
    serve the student's needs.

School consultants will be more successful in their roles and more widely accepted
by their professional colleagues if they base consultation, collaboration, and teamwork on
a code of consultation ethics that includes the following recommendations:

- Avoid any activity that might embarrass colleagues.
- Do not violate confidences or carry tales.
- Limit the consultative activities to things for which one is trained.
- Take care not to distort or misrepresent information.
- Openly share helpful data, but only in ways that protect the rights of students and
  families.
- Make as few remarks about specific teaching practices as possible.

FIGURE 8.11 Checklist for Evaluating Collaborative Consultation

Dear _____,

Please take a few minutes to help me improve my consulting skills by completing this checklist.

Any additional comments you wish to make will be greatly appreciated. Thank you!

_____(name)_____

	A Strength	O.K.	Needs Improving
1. Helped me to be comfortable collaborating.	____	____	____
2. Communicated clearly.	____	____	____
3. Used our time productively.	____	____	____
4. Listened well.	____	____	____
5. Asked facilitating questions.	____	____	____
6. Showed understanding of my role.	____	____	____
7. Demonstrated flexibility.	____	____	____
8. Presence/time not disruptive.	____	____	____
9. I want to work together again.	____	____	____
10. Other comments:			

Marty Schneider

- Know when to stay in the consultation and when it would be best to get out and seek another approach.
- Be open to new ideas and knowledge.
- Give colleagues the benefit of wanting to help.
- Leave therapy to therapists who are trained for it.
- Maintain good records that provide confidentiality.
- Keep consultative channels and doors open.
- Refrain from taking issues personally.
- Above all, advocate for the child, letting student needs guide one's actions and decisions.

Several well-known maxims apply to the implementation of planful, efficient, collegial, and ethical practices for consultation:

"Keep your words sweet, for you may have to eat them."
"Better to bend than to break."
"Only a fool would peel a grape with an ax."
"Eagles do not hunt flies."
"What breaks in a moment may take years to mend."

APPLICATION **8.3**

Evaluation of Consultation

1. Teacher involvement in consultation and collaboration must not be perceived as a sign of weakness or inadequacy. Instead, consultees should be commended for taking advantage of services provided to help both educators and students succeed.
2. Involvement in consultation and collaboration is to be rated as a strength on the performance evaluations of school personnel by administrators and supervisors.
3. Involve school personnel in developing and implementing consultation practices and assessing their outcomes.
4. Conduct self-assessment of consultation and collaboration. Self-assessment is a sometimes painful but always necessary practice for the consultant. The Consultation Log in Chapter 7 includes a brief self-assessment.
5. Videotaping, having a colleague observe and report, and often just reflecting upon one's habits are all potentially helpful ways of growing professionally. Reflection leads to insights about oneself, prompting changes in self-concept, changes in perception of an event or person, or plans for changing some behavior (Canning, 1991). One speech/language pathologist analyzed her emerging consultation skills this way:

In my early perception of consulting I viewed myself as the expert. Experience has taught me I am not. Expert language usually is understood by very few. Knowing how to frame good questions is an invaluable tool. I used to think I knew what was best for the child. Experience again has shown me this is not so—we must all get our respective "what's bests" on the table and mediate. I felt that I needed to have all the workable solutions to the problem at hand, but this was assuming too much. I thought everyone likes and respects the "expert" and wants his or her help. I now perceive my task as one of earning the right to become part of the planning for any child. This means I must be as knowledgeable as possible, not only in my own field, but about the total environment (physical and mental) of each child. I am still learning that effective intervention takes time and careful planning.

6. Other self-assessment questions the consultant can ask include:

   - What solutions have I offered for discussion?
   - What documentation have I gathered to support my opinions?
   - Can I list the questions I want to ask the consultee?
   - Can I listen and work cooperatively on the problem?
   - Can I be honest about my feelings toward the student, the problem, and the personnel involved?
   - Will I follow through on the plan?
   - Will I document the efficacy of the plan?
   - Will I try new methods and strategies?
   - Will I persist in the plan?
   - Will I give feedback to the consultee about the situation?
   - Am I willing to ask for help or advice?

7. As a consultant, portray oneself as assistant to the teacher.
8. Become more visible, visiting each classroom and making positive comments about what is going on there.

(continued)

9. Always have an ear open to opportunities to help out and use those opportunities to become more established as a consulting teacher.
10. Be realistic and understanding about the demands that are placed upon classroom teachers, administrators, and parents in fulfilling *their* roles.
11. Be realistic about what consultants can do.
12. Keep school personnel wanting more consultation services, making them so valuable that if taken away from the schools, the role and its services would be missed.
13. "Advertise" consultation successes.
14. Keep providing benefits for them. Again, "What can I do for you and your students that you do not have time or resources to do?" is the operative question.
15. Identify ways for parents, as consultees, to be partners for their children.
16. Create and nurture many opportunities for special education programs and related services to interface with general education programs.
17. Institute communication networks among staff, parents, and advocacy groups.
18. Demonstrate strategies, methods, and materials to any who will listen.
19. Identify successful, exemplary consultation and collaboration practices, *especially* when they occur in your school district!
20. Share newest trends and techniques in a nonpatronizing way.
21. Work with a group of collaborating colleagues to write a guide on the use of consultation and collaboration. Present it to new faculty members and periodically conduct refresher sessions for all professional-development activities.
22. Send notes of appreciation to consultees regularly.
23. Do not expect a uniformly high level of acceptance and involvement from all, but keep aiming for it.

Tips for Assessing and Evaluating

1. Evaluate consultations in order to improve upon effectiveness.
2. Suggest to teachers a variety of evaluation tools for monitoring student progress.
3. Acknowledge that less-than-desirable consultations occur occasionally, and build on the experience.
4. Share results of evaluation with key groups as appropriate—consultees, administrators, decision makers, parents—maintaining confidentiality and rights of privacy for those involved.
5. Celebrate even small gains in consultation success.
6. Promote instances of high-quality consultation and collaboration, not just the frequency and time spent in the activities.

CHAPTER REVIEW

1. An evaluation program is essential for documenting the effectiveness of any educational program. Evaluation is necessary to make program improvements and to defend the quality of the program to administrators and other decision makers.

2. During the initial stages of program development, consultants should create a plan for ongoing evaluation. Formative and summative information of the context, processes, and content of consultation must be gathered in the most efficient manner possible. Methods of gathering data should come from multiple sources and should be as objective and unbiased as possible.

3. Consultants should evaluate the context that has the most impact on student performance, with emphasis on student characteristics and their relationships to classroom environmental conditions. Context evaluation is used primarily for formative evaluation and should include careful appraisal of classroom setting demands.

4. Formative and summative evaluation should include evaluation of consultation processes. Consultants need to engage in systematic self-assessment, in order to gain information for improving their consultation skills, because it is not likely most will have the administrator feedback and monitoring needed for professional growth in this area. They should also keep careful records of their activities, to justify the program to decision makers.

5. No matter how good the processes of consultation may be, the program will not be effective unless students make progress in learning or behavior goals. The content of the consultation must work. It will be critical for consultants to keep records of student achievement and behavior change, in order to document the effectiveness of the program.

6. Data collected on learning achievement and specific behaviors can help collaborators set goals, plan programs, and evaluate the effectiveness of interventions. The desired student behavior should be defined precisely. Data collection methods from which to select include Curriculum-Based Assessment, student portfolio assessment, frequency recording, interval recording, time sampling, duration recording, and audiotape and videotape records.

7. Consultation effectiveness is three-dimensional. Consulting will be a great success if it results in:

   ■ Consultee satisfaction;
   ■ Problem resolution for the client's need(s); and
   ■ A strengthened consultation system.

8. Collaborative school consultation requires skills and competencies of communication, empathy, diplomacy, organization, problem-solving, assessment, resourcefulness, and much more.

9. Ethical and conscientious considerations must guide consultants in every consultative and collaborative effort. The primary aim of any school interaction is the welfare of the student.

TO DO AND THINK ABOUT

1. Evaluation is an essential aspect of education. While classroom teachers assume responsibility for evaluating student learning, it is administrators who usually are responsible for evaluating the effectiveness of programs and educational methods such as school consultation. Discuss how the role of school consultants requires that they become actively involved in evaluating consultee satisfaction, problem resolution, and the strength of the consultation system.

2. Name several consumer and decision-making target groups within a school district who are likely to ask for data to support a consultation program. What would be the most effective formats for presenting the data to each target group for its purposes?

3. Study the evaluation model in Figure 8.1 and the example of one consultant's plan described in this chapter. Then develop an evaluation plan for consultation service during the coming school year in your school setting.

4. Work with a group of other consultants or teachers. Have each person make a copy of one of the checklists or rating scales of classroom environment cited in this chapter's section for further reading. Collaborate to compare the rating scales, and create a rating scale that would be useful in a typical school setting.

5. Conduct a self-assessment of consultation skills. Give careful attention to each step of the process as described in this book. Make an effort to videotape the consultation in a real or simulated experience at least every nine weeks throughout an entire school year. Chart behavioral data to demonstrate progress on at least two specific objectives.

6. Use the Consultation Log in Chapter 7 for at least six weeks. Meet with other consultants to modify the forms as needed, and then use the revised forms for the remainder of the school term.

7. Read the references about Curriculum-Based Measurement cited in the section for further reading. Then work with other consultants and teachers to see if this type of assessment could be implemented in a way that would be beneficial to all involved.

8. Practice using the behavior observation techniques described in this chapter. Refine those that are most useful to you.

9. Reflect on characteristics and competencies a collaborative school consultant should have. Terms presented in Figure 8.9 may be helpful for this. Then write a job description for this role at the grade level(s) and curricular area(s) in which you are most interested. Suggest how you would publicize and promote your job description to attract the best applicants for the position.

FOR FURTHER READING

Behavior Observation

Cautela, J. R., Cautela, J., and Esonis, S. (1982). *Forms for behavior analysis with children.* Champaign, IL: Research Press.

Hall, R. V., and Houten, R. V. (1980). *The Measurement of behavior.* Austin, TX: PRO-ED.

Maag, J. W. (1989). Assessment in social skills training: Methodological and conceptual issues for research and practice. *Remedial and Special Education, 10*(4): 6–17. Discusses criticisms of assessment of social skills training, and suggests procedures to improve this type of assessment.

Checklists and Rating Scales of Classroom Environments

Bender, W. N. (1988). The other side of placement decisions: Assessment of the mainstream learning environment. *Remedial and Special Education, 9*(5): 28–33.

Renzulli, J. S., and Reis, S. M. (1985). *The schoolwide enrichment model: A comprehensive plan for educational excellence.* Mansfield Center, CT: Creative Learning Press. Contains figures, charts, checklists, and text for assessing enrichment activities, process development, and independent study for gifted and talented students.

Salend, S. J., and Viglianti, D. (1982). Preparing secondary students for the mainstream. *Teaching Exceptional Children, 14:* 137–140.

Wood, J. W., and Miederhoff, J. W. (1989). Bridging the gap. *Teaching Exceptional Children, 21*(2): 66–68.

Ysseldyke, J. E., and Christenson, S. I. (1987). Evaluating students' instructional environments. *Remedial and Special Education, 8*(3): 17–24.

Comprehensive Classroom Assessment Programs

Bursuck, W. D., and Lessen, E. (1987). A classroom-based model for assessing students with learning disabilities. *Learning Disabilities Focus, 3*(1): 17–29. Describes the elements of Curriculum-Based Assessment and instructional design, a well-designed, comprehensive system utilizing academic probes, work habit perception check, and environmental inventory.

Steele, J. (1982). *The class activities questionnaire.* Mansfield Center, CT: Creative Learning Press. Evaluates skills and factors related to the instructional climate that indicate the presence of enrichment opportunities for students. Obtains feedback from both teachers and students.

Ysseldyke, J. E., and Christenson, S. I. (1987). Evaluating students' instructional environments. *Remedial and Special Education, 8*(3): 17–24. Discusses the rationale for assessing a student's instructional environment and describes The Instructional Environment Scale (TIES), a set of assessment tools produced by PRO-ED.

Contextual Appraisal of Special Education Programs

Field, S. L., and Hill, D. S. (1988). Contextual appraisal: A framework for meaningful evaluation of special education programs. *Remedial Education, 9*(4): 22–30. Explains the importance of contextual appraisal for special education programs. Of primary interest to administrators.

Curriculum-Based Assessment

The next four references, a set of short papers, explain different aspects of CBM, such as how to develop and administer measurement devices, how to graph performance and practical suggestions for teachers when using the system.

Deno, S. L. (1987). Curriculum-based measurement. *Teaching Exceptional Children, 20*(1): 41–47.

Fuchs, L. S. (1987). Program development. *Teaching Exceptional Children, 20*(1): 42–44.

Tindal, G. (1987). Graphing performance. *Teaching Exceptional Children, 20*(1): 44–46.

Wesson, C. L. (1987). Increasing efficiency. *Teaching Exceptional Children, 20*(1): 46–47.

Fuchs, L. S., Fuchs, D., and Hamlett, C. L. (1990). Curriculum-Based Measurement: A standardized, long-term goal approach to monitoring student progress. *Academic Therapy, 25*(5): 615–632. Provides a reasonably detailed description of how CBM can be used to help teachers formulate effective instructional programs using the charted data to make relevant decisions.

Portfolio Assessment

Edyburn, D. L. (1994). An equation to consider: The portfolio assessment knowledge base + technology = The Grady Profile, *LD Forum, 19*(4): 35–38. Discusses a software package for using the computer for portfolio assessment.

Swicegood, P. (1994). Portfolio-based assessment practices. *Intervention in School and Clinic, 30*(1): 6–15. Provides an overview of portfolio assessment practices and their application for students with disabilities.

Evaluation of Consultation Processes

Conoley, J. C., and Conoley, C. W. (1982). *School consultation: A guide to practice and training.* New York: Pergamon Press. Contains more than a half-dozen forms to be used or adapted for gathering consultee feedback about the effectiveness of the consultation process.

Work Habits and Social Skills

Fad, K. S. (1990). The fast track to success: Social behavioral skills. *Intervention in School and Clinic, 26*(1): 39–43. Reports the results of a survey of classroom teachers to identify the social and behavior skills considered essential for classroom survival. The author lists the ten most critical skills. A helpful resource for developing behavior checklists.

9 Planning for Inclusion

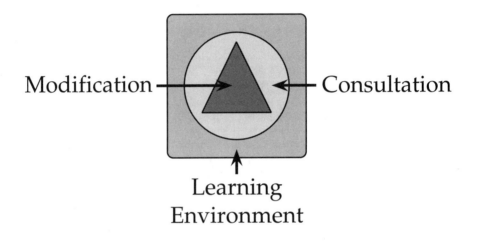

If you don't take time to plan, don't plan to have successful inclusion. All persons in inclusive schools must plan together in a variety of ways to assure a good educational experience for all students and to avoid unnecessary tension. This chapter provides suggestions for:

- *Planning to Begin Inclusion.* "In order to do inclusion right, it must be done slowly, with a great deal of planning" (Working Forum on Inclusive Schools, 1994, p. 4). All individuals who work in the school must participate in the planning processes.
- *Planning Lessons.* Individual teachers have always developed lesson plans, much of it "in their heads"—not written down. Co-teachers, however, need a process that helps them put in writing the lesson plans that map out the essential elements of the lessons.
- *Planning for Individuals.* Special educators are required by law to prepare plans for individuals (IEP). They need a method of communicating the plan to all parties involved in an individual student's instruction.
- *Planning Curriculum Adaptations.* Federal laws require that public schools make reasonable accommodations and modifications for students with special needs, and that inclusive schools make these adaptations for all students who need them. Accommodations refer to a variety of supports for enabling the individual to accomplish outcomes specified for all other students in the classroom. Modifications involve changing curriculum outcomes. Many authors use these two terms interchangeably.

A major role of the special educator in inclusive classrooms is to plan these adaptations and modifications for individual students in the classroom.

■ *Planning Remediation.* Some students with disabilities need intensive remediation in specific skills such as reading, writing, or math. Teachers may need to use specialized techniques not conducive to general classroom instruction. Consultants need to develop remedial plans that specify skills to remediate, teaching techniques to use, persons responsible for implementing the techniques, when the remedial instruction will take place, and where it will be provided.

■ *Planning Instructional Support.* It is neither possible nor necessary for special educators or therapists to be present in inclusive classrooms for every instructional activity. They must support the classroom teachers when not physically present in the classrooms by: Supervising paraeducators in the classroom; teaching students self-advocacy behaviors, study strategies, and classroom survival skills; adapting tests; and monitoring student progress.

Focusing Questions

1. Why is it important to engage in school-wide planning with all stakeholders before beginning inclusion programs?
2. How does planning for co-teaching differ from typical teacher lesson planning?
3. What are some common approaches for co-teaching?
4. How do cooperative learning techniques benefit inclusion?
5. Why is it important to inform classroom teachers about the goals and objectives on a student's IEP?
6. Who can qualify for curriculum adaptations and what are options to consider?
7. What kinds of accommodations are appropriate for paraeducators to provide?
8. What is assistive technology? What is its value in inclusive programs?
9. What are appropriate curriculum modifications for students with disabilities and students with high ability?
10. How can remedial instruction be used with inclusion programs?
11. What other instructional supports will benefit students placed in inclusion programs?
12. Why is it essential for special education teachers to monitor student classroom performance frequently in inclusive schools?

Key Terms

accommodations
adaptations
assistive technology
classroom enrichment
cooperative learning
co-planning
co-teaching
curriculum compacting
enrichment
flexible pacing
IEP

inclusion
Interactive Lesson Planning Model
modifications
monitoring student progress
para (paraprofessional, paraeducator)
Parallel Teaching
peer tutoring
remedial instruction

scaffolding
self-advocacy
stakeholders
Station Teaching
Strategies Intervention Model
study strategies
Teach and Monitor
Team Teaching
technology
TREAT Program

Scenario 9

The setting is the LD teacher's office (once the resource room where LD students came for special instruction in the former "pull-out" program). The principal arrives first, followed by a behavioral disorders (BD) teacher, two learning disabilities (LD) teachers, a speech pathologist, and a counselor. Teacher A assumes the facilitator role, teacher B functions in the recorder role, and the speech pathologist has the timekeeper role (with these roles being rotated in subsequent meetings).

TEACHER A (facilitator):   Who has agenda items today?

PRINCIPAL: I want to discuss CBM and a discipline policy procedure.

TEACHER A (facilitator):   How much time do you need for your agenda item?

TEACHER A (facilitator):   (Writes the agenda item and time needed—varying anywhere from 1 to 10 minutes—on a form.)

TEACHER C: I need ideas for working with Jason.

TEACHER A (facilitator):   (Continues to write agenda items and time needed as each person states them...).

TEACHER A (facilitator):   All right, let's start with item 3—Jason.

TEACHER C: I'm concerned about Jason because he can't read the fourth-grade materials. He has a wonderful background in science and social studies. I really think his problem is that he can't read and write the material used in the classroom.

TEACHER B (recorder):   (Writes the main points of the discussion, pertinent decisions, and future agenda items related to issue.)

SPEECH PATHOLOGIST (timekeeper):   (Starts stopwatch at beginning of each item discussion and notifies when the allocated time has been used.)

TEACHER A (facilitator):   (After most of the items have been discussed, the time allotted for the meeting has almost expired.) I will put the last two items on the agenda for next week. Are there other items for that meeting?

Planning Inclusive Schools

The most effective inclusive schools that we have observed spent at least one year planning and preparing for change. Schools that engage in this planning reap the benefits for years to come. Inclusion practices can take place without extensive preplanning, but the road is rocky and tensions are high for an extended period of time.

Importance of Planning for Inclusion

Who could argue with the ideals of inclusion—a school where every student is respected as part of the school community and where each student is encouraged to learn and achieve as much as possible? Achieving this ideal is a major challenge in many schools. It takes time and effort to plan and put in place all the factors critical for a successful inclusive school. According to some authors (McLaughlin & Warren, 1992), inclusive schools need:

1. A clear school "vision" consistent with inclusive ideals
2. A set of learner outcomes for schoolwide accountability
3. A governance structure that promotes collaboration and school-level flexibility
4. A curriculum that promotes high expectations for all students
5. Professional development that builds collaborative work structures, joint problem-solving, and the sharing of experience

For some schools, none of these factors is in place, and they will need to plan for system-wide change—a whole new way of thinking and working. Other schools may have some of the factors well established. Only a few, rare schools have been completely transformed into inclusive schools. The first step in planning, then, requires school staff to assess their current status. They should ask:

- Which of the five factors are well established in our school?
- Which of the five factors are established but need fine tuning?
- Which of the five factors are not in place?

Once the current status of the school is clearly identified, the planners must describe the inclusive school they would like to become. They need to remember every inclusive school is unique (Working Forum on Inclusive Schools, 1994). They should discuss each factor cited above that is not in place or is in need of fine tuning and decide what to do about it. Once they have agreed on the ideal, they must become realistic and create an action plan that will help them get to where they want to be. This process, which uses the problem-solving processes outlined in Chapter 5, may take considerable time. As a minimum, action plans for each of the five factors should be put into writing specifying the actions, person(s) responsible, and target dates for completing each action.

Creating inclusive schools is a journey, not a destination. Some wonderful ideas on paper simply do not work in practice. Once the original plan is put in place, the planners need to engage in continuous problem-solving processes. They will know their school is inclusive when teachers function differently than they did before the journey began, and all students are making progress in learning. Student learning is the final test of a successful inclusive school.

> Schools will be judged by performance assessment results. Any suggestions for improvement that aren't structured to improve student achievement are a distraction from the larger mission of transforming public education to succeed with every child at a much higher level (*Working Forum on Inclusive Schools,* 1994, p. vii).

Involving All Stakeholders

Stakeholders are all the persons who work in the inclusive school, including teachers, related-services personnel, administrators, parents, and students. The more stakeholders involved in the planning, the higher the probability of success.

Stakeholders must create a plan and make it work. Two types of group-planning efforts must continue as an on-going process of inclusive schools: (1) an inclusion management team with stakeholder representatives, and (2) special-service staff—special education teachers, related-service personnel, and administrators. The first group should meet about four times a year and address global issues related to inclusion. The second group should meet once each week and address student concerns and day-to-day process issues. The scenario at the beginning of this chapter occurred at a special-service staff meeting in one inclusive school. These individuals met at a scheduled time each week and used the systematic meeting format illustrated in the scenario to make best use of that time.

In a contrast school the special-service staff did not meet regularly. As a consequence, they often did not know the other staff members' concerns nor were they helpful in solving one another's problems. This school has one LD teacher and one BD teacher. They divide their loads, with the BD teacher working with half the teachers and the LD teacher working with the other half. Likewise, they divide their student responsibilities, with both special education teachers responsible for both LD and BD students. This is a common inclusion model in elementary schools, but in order for it to work the teachers must communicate with one another regularly to consult about areas in which they do not have a high degree of specialization. Since these teachers do not communicate regularly, it is not surprising that several of the LD students in the BD teacher's caseload have not made progress in the general classroom. When a meeting was organized to discuss the matter, it was clear the LD teacher could have made helpful suggestions if they had been meeting regularly to discuss student needs.

Related-service personnel such as speech therapists, occupational therapists, counselors, or psychologists must not be overlooked. For example, in many inclusive schools these therapists take the child apart from the group and provide individual therapy in the classroom rather than taking the student to another room in the building. This arrangement can cause considerable apprehension on the part of other teachers (Schlax, 1994) and should be part of the discussion during the planning process. Roles of support personnel are discussed further in Chapter 10.

Planning Lessons

Co-teaching (two or more teachers planning and delivering instruction) by special educators and general educators creates new challenges for planning lessons in inclusive schools. Without co-planning, co-teaching often becomes a special educator helping the classroom teacher, or "turn taking" at best. This arrangement brings little satisfaction to the "co-teachers" and is not likely to result in the high-quality student outcomes that educators and parents desire. In a review of ten articles on co-teaching, Reinhiller (1996) proposes that co-teaching is both art and talent, voluntary in nature, and has become widely accepted as an appropriate model for collaboration.

Brody (1994) regards co-teaching as a distinct form of teacher collaboration that can apply also to involvement of more than two teachers who plan, teach, and assess students in a learning community. Brody's three steps for co-teaching include celebrating each other by giving and taking credit; reciprocating expert and learner roles; and developing shared understandings. Teachers can think out loud to each other during the process of instruction.

Typical Lesson Planning

Special educators and general educators in traditional roles plan lessons differently from one another. General classroom teachers usually plan for groups of students, while special education teachers typically plan for individuals. Research conducted by a Joint Committee on Teacher Planning for Students with Disabilities (1995) indicated that general education teachers do not individualize instruction although they might differentiate by planning for *all, most,* and *a few* students. They do not typically engage in a linear planning process going from objectives to activities followed by evaluation methods, even though they usually know how to use that type of planning. They usually start planning lessons by selecting a theme or topic, and then planning content and activities to use with the entire class or large group. Those plans may be followed by consideration of the objectives or specific outcomes for the group and ways to evaluate them.

Special educators, on the other hand, are trained, even required by federal law, to base lesson plans on individualized learner goals. Federal laws for individuals with disabilities require multidisciplinary teams to develop plans for individuals (IEPs). The planning steps are based on traditional, linear lesson-planning models—goals, objectives, activities, and evaluation. This linear process may not be the best way for co-teachers to plan lessons, nor does it reflect the way teachers typically plan lessons (Joint Committee on Teacher Planning for Students with Disabilities, 1995). General classroom teachers obviously are concerned about student learning, but they must keep their groups of students engaged in activities throughout the school day for the sake of classroom order. The challenge for co-teachers is to reconcile the individualized and group-planning processes for the benefit of all students.

Co-planning Lessons

An interactive model for lesson planning that reflects the realities of current classroom contexts and students with special needs included in the classroom is shown in Figure 9.1. The model (Dyck, Pemberton, Woods, & Sundbye, 1996) does not follow the linear approach found in many planning models. The interactive model allows teachers to plan activities, objectives, and assessments concurrently or to plan them in varying orders depending on the situation. Co-teachers can begin planning at any point in the model, or they can choose to use only parts of it. It does not require that each objective be tied to a separate activity, as is usually the case in a linear-planning mode. An activity can address several objectives and assessments. Likewise, one objective can be addressed by several activities and assessments. In all instances, the lesson theme, topic, or goal, often determined by the textbook, is the common element in the plan.

The Interactive Lesson Planning Model presented in Figure 9.1 addresses *nearly all* students, *most* students, and *some* individual students. As a result, the model can be successful when co-teachers plan (Dyck, Pemberton, Woods, & Sundbye, 1996).

Co-teachers using the Interactive Lesson Planning Model answer the following questions when planning a lesson:

- What is the theme, topic, or goal of the lesson?
- What content is in the textbook and/or printed curriculum guide that addresses this theme, topic, or goal?

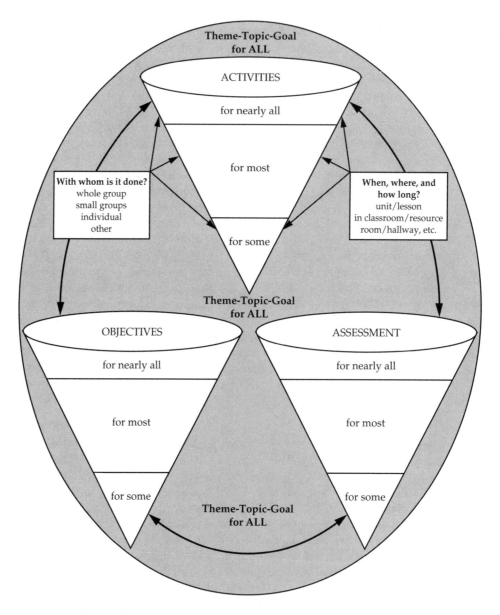

FIGURE 9.1 Interactive Lesson Planning Model

- What of that content is useful to and can be learned by *all* or *nearly all* students in the class?
- What of that content is useful to and can be learned by *most* students in the class?
- What of that content is useful to and can be learned by only *some* individual students in the class?

- Which students cannot benefit from any of that content?
- How will the activities take place—whole group, small groups, individual, etc.?
- Who will be in each group or activity?
- What activities will keep *each* student motivated and busy?
- When, where, and for how long will this lesson plan be taught?
- Who is primarily responsible for each of the activities and assessments?

The answers to these questions form a basis for differentiating activities, objectives, and assessments.

An example of a lesson plan using this process is shown in Figure 9.2. A narrative of the planning meeting follows. References to correlates in the Interactive Lesson Planning Model are noted in brackets. Another example using an elementary classroom is presented in *Teaching Exceptional Children* (Dyck, Sundbye, & Pemberton, 1997).

Narrative for the Co-planning. Lori and Mark decided to co-teach an American history lesson about the Battle at Gettysburg during the Civil War. [*What is the theme, topic, or goal of the lesson?*]

1. Mark provided his lecture materials from past lessons. They reviewed the lecture outlines, textbook materials, and assignments. [*What content is in the textbook and/ or printed curriculum guide that addresses this theme, topic, or goal?*]
2. They discussed what could be eliminated or added to the original lecture and textbook material. Everyone could benefit from the lecture, including Randy who had mental retardation. Most students could read the textbook assignment (pages 254– 263) except Colin, who needed it read aloud and Randy, who couldn't read it at all. [*What of that content is useful to and can be learned by all or nearly all students in the class?*]
3. They decided most students, with the exception of Randy, would benefit from assignments 1 and 3 on page 263 of the textbook. [*What of that content is useful to and can be learned by most students in the class?*]
4. Mark was concerned about the ability of some students with learning difficulties to benefit from some of the content. Lori wondered whether students with high ability would be challenged. They decided to use cooperative learning methods to deal with some of those concerns. Lori would prepare "challenge tasks" which would be required for the students with high ability, although anyone could try to do them. Mark had group-study worksheets they could use, but Lori recommended several changes. Mark thought of some other items that could be eliminated or added to help the students in the class who had learning difficulties.
5. Mark then volunteered to make the revisions since he had the original study worksheets on his computer. [*What of that content is useful to and can be learned by most students in the class? What of that content is useful to and can be learned by only some individual students in the class?*]
6. Although Lori was assigned to be teacher for the course, they decided Mark should present the lecture since he had done it many times previously. However, Lori would be in the class and would feel free to add information whenever it seemed appropriate

FIGURE 9.2   Interactive Lesson Planning Form

Theme, Topic, or Goal: *Battle at Gettysburg*	Date(s): 4/5 – 4/10

ACTIVITIES

WHEN	WHAT	FOR NEARLY ALL	FOR MOST	FOR SOME	WITH WHOM
Mon. & Tues.	Lecture Read pages 254-263	all for lecture	Reading all but Randy	Read aloud to Colin	Mark.
Tues. & Wed.	assignments 1 and 3 on pages 263 of the textbook		all but Randy		Lori & para
Tues. & Wed.	Draw picture showing important people in the battle			Randy	Mark
Thurs.	Cooperative Learning – revised study guides.	all		challenge tasks for high achiv.	Lori & Mark
Friday	Independent Test		all but Randy	read to 3 LD	Lori
Fri.	Test in resource room			Randy	para.

OBJECTIVES

WHEN	WHAT	FOR NEARLY ALL	FOR MOST	FOR SOME	WITH WHOM
by 4/10	State the primary events leading up to the Battle at Gettysburg		all but Randy		
by 4/10	State primary people and events during the battle		all but Randy		
by 4/10	Answer questions about the important outcomes of the Battle			orally for LD and Randy	
by 4/10	Identify pictures of key persons and events in the Battle at Gettysburg			Randy	
by 4/10	Create a product showing the important outcomes of the Battle at Gettysburg			high achieving students	

ASSESSMENT

WHEN	WHAT	FOR NEARLY ALL	FOR MOST	FOR SOME	WITH WHOM
Fri.	Independently take written test		all but 3 LD & Randy		Lori.
Fri.	Take oral test			3 LD	Mark.
Fri.	Draw picture of key people and events			Randy	para.

to help clarify a point. [*How will the activities take place—whole group, small groups, individual, etc.?*]

7. Lori would direct the cooperative learning activities. She had already established teams in the class, and this content would fit in nicely. Mark said he would have his para come into the classroom during that time. It would free him up to consult with another teacher. [*Who will be in each group or activity? What activities will we use to keep EACH student motivated and busy?*]

8. Lori felt the students needed a summative experience that would require them to demonstrate individual accountability. Mark and Lori discussed what the activity would be, and Lori agreed to prepare it (a test). They would divide the tests, each grading half. When the tests were graded, Lori would record the scores in her grade book and Mark would give team rewards. Mark would give the test orally to the students with learning disabilities and prepare a modified test for the para to give to Randy in the resource room. [*Who is primarily responsible for each of the activities and assessments?*]

Co-teaching a Lesson Plan

Co-teaching (sometimes referred to as collaborative teaching or cooperative teaching) involves two or more teachers (usually a general education teacher and a special education teacher) who plan and deliver instruction as equals within one educational setting to one group of students. A key element of co-teaching is the shared responsibility of the teachers in both planning and delivering instruction. Co-teaching usually occurs for a set period of time, such as one class period each day, certain days of the week or, as illustrated in the case above, one lesson topic. Some teachers have been misled to believe that co-teaching is necessary for every inclusion situation and that students should never be taken out of the general classroom for special help. However, co-teaching should only be used when it is the *best* option for meeting the needs of a significant number of students. Friend and Bursuck (1996, pp. 86–87) note: "It is relatively expensive (that is, the cost of two teachers with one group of students) and should be reserved for situations in which the number of students with disabilities in a class justifies the presence of two teachers, or the class is one in which all students with disabilities enroll (for example, in high school, it may be U.S. history)."

Co-teachers must use effective teaching practices well documented by research (ERIC, 1987a; 1987b; Bickel & Bickel, 1986; Morsink et al., 1986), which include:

1. Gain the learner's attention. Use verbal prompts such as "look here" and listen." Maintain 90 percent task engagement during teacher-directed activities.
2. Review relevant past learning. Teacher review, with correcting of homework, is recommended.
3. Communicate the goal of the lesson. Tell what is being learned and why it is important. Keep the goal statement brief.
4. Model the skill to be learned. Proceed in small steps that are not too difficult and give explicit verbal directions. Exaggerate steps as needed to call attention to the critical features.

5. Prompt for correct response. Let students practice with many correct responses. Continue until very high levels of proficiency are demonstrated. The teacher should do each step as the students are doing them, providing modeling and verbal prompts.

6. Check for skill mastery. Students perform the behavior under teacher supervision without prompting. The teacher provides feedback after every trial and watches for many successful repetitions.

7. Close the lesson. Review the skill, discuss what will be in the next lesson, or introduce independent work.

The Plan in Action:
No matter how well the teachers plan, some co-teaching actions must be spontaneous. This reality became obvious as Lori and Mark put their plan into action. Mark presented the lecture while Lori monitored, as planned. Lori spontaneously "jumped in" from time to time to clarify information. At one point she went to the chalkboard and drew a diagram to more clearly illustrate a point that seemed confusing to students. The next day, as planned, Lori took over when the class began team study in the cooperative learning format. She instructed students to get into their teams, gave instructions for team activities, and told how they could earn bonus points. Now the para was monitoring and noticed Randy needed more explanation, so he wrote out the steps for Randy. Once students were engaged in teamwork, Lori and the para "cruised" the classroom, stopping to help individuals or teams as needed and providing positive reinforcement for team effort. Friday, both teachers were present while students took individual tests. The para took Randy to the resource room to help him take his special test while Mark read the test to the students with learning disabilities. He read questions orally for them when needed. He noticed two students having difficulty writing their answers and pulled them aside one-by-one to let them dictate answers to him. Then he asked them to do an additional task while the rest of the class finished their tests. Lori involved the students with high ability in other activities in the center of the classroom when they finished their tests, while Mark continued to monitor the test-takers. Lori and Mark divided the tests to grade as planned.

Preparation for Co-teaching.   Teachers need to prepare the classroom before implementing co-teaching. They need to discuss their views on teaching and learning and resolve any differences. If these differences cannot be resolved, for example, direct instruction versus constructivist learning, it would be best to forego co-teaching. However, the teachers would still need to engage in regular co-planning. They need to also agree on classroom rules and routines during co-teaching. In addition, they should agree on how grades will be assigned to students. Other matters to discuss are the role of paraeducators and substitute teachers during co-teaching, how to inform parents of the new approach, and most important, scheduled planning time at least once per week.

Selecting the Best Approach.   Co-teachers can use one of several approaches to present their lessons. Some examples are Teach and Monitor, Parallel Teaching, Station Teaching, and Team Teaching. Vaughn, Schumm, and Arguelles (1997) and Bauwens and Hourcade (1997) provide descriptions of other co-teaching arrangements.

Teach and Monitor.   One of the most common approaches is for both teachers to be in the classroom during instruction, but one of them takes primary responsibility for lecturing or presenting the lesson. The other teacher helps monitor performance of students and provides additional assistance to those who need it. This approach does not require as much advanced planning as other approaches and is simple to implement. However, the teacher who circulates around the room can easily begin to feel like a "teacher's aide." One parent recently reported a situation where her child came home from school saying they had a new "student teacher" in her room. In reality, the "student teacher" was the special education teacher who was co-teaching in the classroom. This remark is not provided to minimize the role of "student teachers" but to illustrate the point that both teachers might not be recognized as co-equals by the students and as such may not be equally effective in providing instruction. In order to minimize potential limitations of the Teach and Monitor approach to co-teaching, Cook and Friend (1993) suggest that teachers should alternate roles regularly.

Variations of this approach are Speak and Chart or Speak and Add. With Speak and Chart one teacher lectures while the other writes the outline or notes on the chalkboard. With Speak and Add one teacher lectures while the other jumps in to add or clarify points from time to time. Duet is a planned variation of Speak and Add where each teacher takes turns presenting portions of the material in a coordinated fashion. These co-teaching structures often become blended, as the example of Lori and Mark illustrates.

Parallel Teaching.   A second form of co-teaching that is commonly practiced in inclusive schools is parallel teaching (NCERI, 1994). While both teachers co-plan a lesson, they split the class, and each delivers the lesson to a smaller group at the same time. Parallel teaching might also require parallel curriculum, that is, both teachers teach a similar topic but one teacher teaches it at a more advanced level than the other. For example, after having read a story to the entire class, one teacher takes the highest achievers and works on a dramatization of the story, while the other teacher works with the other students on vocabulary meaning and retelling the story sequence.

Station Teaching.   A third method of co-teaching is Station Teaching. This approach occurs when teachers co-plan instructional activities that are presented in "stations" or learning centers. While the teachers are stationed at some of the centers, others require independent work or involvement of peer teachers or paraeducators. Each station presents a different aspect of the lesson and allows teachers to work with small groups of students. This way, each teacher works with all students in the class as they rotate through the stations.

Team Teaching.   This approach is sometimes used as a synonym for co-teaching. However, the NCERI study (1994) identified it as a model where the special education teacher teams up with one or more special education teachers to form a team. This team is responsible for all of the children in the classroom or at a particular level. A variation of team teaching observed in an inclusive school involved ignoring the categorical labels for service of students. Instead, all students identified for special education services were assigned to special educators according to their age or grade-level placement. The special educators, regardless of categorical specialization, were assigned to grade-level teams and assumed primary responsibility for all students with special needs at the assigned grade-level. The special educators met weekly to discuss matters of concern. In addition, each special educator was a member of a grade level team and met regularly to discuss common issues with those team members. The special educators moved in and out of the classrooms at that grade level to co-teach as needed, to adapt materials, or sometimes to present a special lesson. The teaming processes to manage such a system are extensive. According to the teachers involved in the approach, it will not work unless there is *trust* among all the teachers and efficient *teaming* practices. The scenario at the beginning of this chapter provides an example of the system used for team meetings at this school.

Planning Cooperative Learning Lessons

Mark and Lori, in the example above, used cooperative learning as part of their co-teaching method. Bauwens and Hourcade (1997) also describe a set of co-teaching arrangements that involve cooperative learning. Cooperative learning methods have gained widespread attention for use in many classrooms and, if carefully planned, may not require the presence of the special educator in the classroom every day, as illustrated in the scenario above. When used appropriately, the methods result in improved student achievement and improved social relationships at the same time (Johnson & Johnson, 1987b; Lloyd et al., 1988; Madden & Slavin, 1983).

The term *cooperative learning* has become associated with a variety of structured approaches that arrange classrooms so students study in heterogeneous groups to meet academic goals (Johnson & Johnson, 1987b; Slavin, 1986). In most of the models, all students in the classroom are assigned to heterogeneous groups and, under the guidance of the teacher, help one another master content previously presented by the teacher. Students are held individually accountable for the content, with individual performance scores pooled to determine group rewards. Thus, all students are rewarded for helping, sharing, and working together.

Common problems and possible solutions are listed in Figure 9.3. Co-teachers may need to modify cooperative learning activities for students with learning and behavior problems in the classroom. If a modification is made, co-teachers should make sure that these two elements are present (Slavin, 1990):

1. *Group goals or positive interdependence.* The members within a group must work together in order to earn recognition, grades, rewards, and other indicators of group success.
2. *Individual accountability.* All individuals within the group must demonstrate their learning in order for the group to experience success. This accountability could involve individual test scores that are averaged for group recognition or a report in which each person contributes a specific portion. It should not be a single product without differentiated tasks, for that would be disastrous for students with severe disabilities included in the class.

When students with behavior problems are included in the classroom, special educators will need to closely monitor the experiences. The classroom teacher may require assistance to teach social skills needed for successful cooperation. Dishon and O'Leary (1989; 1990) provide useful suggestions for efficient teaching of social skills for cooperative learning.

FIGURE 9.3   Common Problems and Possible Solutions during Cooperative Learning

Learning Problems

Student cannot read and/or write the material.
Have a teammate read material to the student.
Have teammates read material aloud "round robin."
Highlight main ideas and important information.

Student is hearing impaired.
Have team work in area of room with most sound control.
Seat student where lips of team members can be seen.
Provide extra teacher prompting during team study.

Student is visually impaired.
Provide more time to complete assignment.
Seat student where team discussion can be heard easily.
Reinforce efforts of team to explain information.

Student has difficulty making oral presentations.
Have student write and a team member read the report.
Allow student to pre-plan comments by assigning issue.
Have student work closely with another to offer ideas.

Student cannot do any of the group work.
Give different material to study and different quiz.
Form teams by achievement levels (is hard to manage).
Give direct teacher instruction to provide head start.

Behavior Problems

Student cannot get along with other team members.
Give team bonus points based on team cooperativeness.
Move from team to team, reinforcing right behavior.
Ignore the behavior (as team sometimes handles it well).

Student is ostracized by team members.
Use improvement points to provide equal opportunity.
Select the team for that student with care.
Place a sympathetic person on that student's team.

Student refuses to become involved in team study.
Use bonus points often to reinforce involvement.
Make every effort to involve student in the group.
Allow student to work alone, but keep door open.

Student is frequently absent or tardy.
Upon return, have student complete assignment or quiz.
Use late score for individual grade, but not team score.
Give creativity bonus if team copes well with absence.

Parents of high ability students disapprove of the strategy.
Meet with parents to explain cooperative learning.
Stress universal need to learn cooperative strategies.
Promote the concept of developing leadership skills.

Developing and posting class rules for cooperative learning such as those shown in Figure 9.4 will be helpful to all students. Resources for further reading about cooperative learning methods are listed at the end of this chapter.

Planning for Individuals in Inclusive Classrooms

Special educators need a method of communicating information recorded on the IEP (Individualized Education Program as required by IDEA 97) to classroom teachers, paras, and other persons involved in a student's instruction. These individuals can only assume the student should meet the same goals and objectives as most students in the classroom without IEP information to guide them. Dover (1994) suggests putting the student's identifying information and each IEP goal accompanied by the objectives on a one-page form, *A Quick Look at the IEP.* Other information on the IEP should be available to teachers on request.

IEP Requirements

IEP documents must be kept confidential, as required by law. Other documents summarizing student goals and objectives such as *A Quick Look at the IEP* may not be subject to the same legal limits, but the intent of confidentiality should not be violated.

Helping Teachers Use IEP Information

Consultants should devise a way to provide IEP highlights to teachers and paras without violating students' rights. One possibility is to put the information in a "locked" computer file. Only individuals who know the identification code can have assess to the information. Another possibility is to put paper copies in a locked file cabinet in the classroom. The limitation of putting information in locked files is that it can be easily forgotten—*out of sight, out of mind.* Perhaps a periodic e-mail message with the relevant information and a personal note

FIGURE 9.4   Class Rules for Cooperative Learning

Speak to Each Other
  1. Speak softly.
  2. Take turns talking.
  3. Limit talking to the subject of study.
  4. Look at the person speaking—be a good listener.
  5. Ask teammates for help before asking the teacher.
  6. Disagree agreeably.

Help Each Other
  7. Tell your teammates how to find answers when they need help, instead of telling answers.
  8. Encourage everyone on the team to do his or her best work.
  9. Make sure everyone on your team knows the material before you stop working together.
  10. Don't get yourself or another person off task—pay attention to the assigned work.

about the student's progress or lack of it would be a way to keep everyone informed about progress toward meeting IEP goals and objectives.

Planning Curriculum Adaptations

IDEA 97 requires accommodations for individuals who qualify for certain types of carefully defined disabilities. Section 504 of the Rehabilitation Act of 1973 requires public agencies to provide reasonable accommodations for individuals with disabilities, even those who do not qualify for IDEA, such as students with attention deficit disorders or other health impairments. The intent of both laws is to provide access to participation in school programs. Although the "504" and IEP plans may specify accommodations needed by individual students, consultants should help all parties involved in teaching these students in planning and preparing the accommodations.

Many authors use the terms *adaptations, accommodations,* or *modifications* interchangeably. For our purposes, curriculum adaptations involve both accommodations and modifications. Curriculum accommodations are assistive aids and supports that help the student achieve the same outcomes as most other students in the class. Examples of accommodations include reading a test to the student, writing answers dictated by the student, putting text into Braille, and providing sound amplification. Curriculum modifications involve changing the goals, activities, or outcomes for students—for example, reducing the number of spelling words for a student to master.

Consultants in elementary schools should consider using the term "scaffolding" rather than accommodations. Scaffolding, as used by general educators, assumes that the external supports to enable a student to benefit from classroom learning are temporary and will be faded out once the individual no longer needs them. While that is the goal of general educators and is reasonable for some students with disabilities, many individuals with disabilities will need scaffolding or accommodations for a lifetime. Consider the special needs of students who are deaf or hard of hearing.

Several competencies will be needed by both classroom teachers and facilitators for gifted programs, and others typically will be assumed by gifted education specialists as consultants with general education personnel as consultees. Items 1 to 5 should be the responsibility of all teachers, while the leadership for items 6 to 10 rests with gifted program facilitators:

1. Enhance complex thinking and high-order production by students.
2. Recognize and nurture creative potential.
3. Use technology and innovation for general and specialized learning.
4. Use appropriate assessment and reporting techniques for student work and achievement.
5. Consult and collaborate on the teaching team, including parents as educators.
6. Develop, administer, and evaluate appropriate learning programs for very able students.
7. Identify resources (people, places, and things) to optimize learning.
8. Guide and advise high-ability students with their cognitive, affective, and social concerns.

9. Facilitate staff development that enables all school personnel to address needs of highly able and talented students.

10. Advocate for differentiated educational programs that target the needs of highly able students.

Curriculum Accommodations

Curriculum accommodations are assistive aids and supports that help the student achieve the same outcomes as all other students in the class. Here we discuss some of the most common forms of accommodations, para assistance and assistive technology. In addition, we challenge readers with a discussion of multimedia scaffolding, which holds great promise as schools begin to make available powerful computers for student use in classrooms.

Para Assistance.   Over 500,000 paras are employed in public schools in the United States, and increases are anticipated in the coming years (Giangreco, Edelman, Luiselli, & MacFarland, 1997). Many of these paras have become the primary form of accommodation for students with severe or multiple disabilities in inclusive schools. In most instances paras stay in close proximity to the students with disabilities, attending to every need of the student from physical needs, such as toileting, to instructional needs, such as reading aloud, writing answers, and prompting.

While paras make possible educational opportunities previously unavailable to some students, Giangreco et al. (1997) expressed concern about fostering overdependence on adult assistance. These researchers recorded observations of paras' actions in a number of different settings and reported that paras had a tendency to do too much for students in their charge. Paras sometimes spoke when the student was capable of speaking for himself. Sometimes they did not respect the gender identity of the student, for example, taking the students to restrooms of their own gender rather than the restroom of the students' gender. Paras tended to make decisions for the students when they were capable of making their own. Sometimes other students wanted to help the student, and the para did not permit it. Paras assigned to a single student in a classroom tend to "hover" over the student without realizing the "…effects and potential harm to children caused by excessive adult proximity" (Giangreco et al., 1997, p. 16).

Special educators responsible for supervising paras need to clearly define and carefully monitor para roles. "Too often students with disabilities are placed in general education classrooms without clear expectations established among the team members regarding which professional staff will plan, implement, monitor, evaluate, and adjust instruction" (Giangreco et al., 1997, p. 15). The researchers suggested assigning the para as classroom assistants rather than to assist a single student. They noted that when co-teachers failed to plan instruction, as we have recommended, the responsibility often fell on the para, which is clearly beyond a reasonable expectation for a person without teacher training. Likewise, French (1997) observed in her study of inclusion classrooms that the least-trained person (para) usually is responsible for planning and instructing the students who are hardest to teach.

Parents of children with disabilities want their children to become as independent as possible. Supervisors must help paras understand how to use basic instructional methods designed to fade out assistance and encourage students to respond to natural cues so they do not inadvertently strengthen dependence on external supports from adults.

Far too often paras pull the students in their charge away from the group (Giangreco et al., 1997). Supervisors should help paras understand that students need to be physically, programmatically, and interactionally included in classroom activities that have been planned by qualified teachers. Teachers need to make sure they consider the para's role when co-planning lessons. Whenever possible, the para should be included in the planning process.

Special education teachers may be assigned as many as five or six paras who must be supervised. Supervision requires skills somewhat different from consulting, collaborating, or teaching. The supervisor is responsible for the para's actions, and the para is account able to the supervisor. Whereas collaborating teachers mutually develop a teaching plan, the supervisor may tell the para what parts of the plan to implement. French (1997) lists seven functions associated with para supervision:

- Planning
- Managing schedules (prioritize tasks, prepare schedules)
- Delegating responsibilities (assign tasks, direct tasks, monitor performance)
- Orienting (introduce people, policies, procedures, job descriptions, and so on)
- On-the-job training (teach, coach new skills, give feedback)
- Evaluating (track performance, summative evaluating of job performance)
- Managing work environment (maintain communication, manage conflicts, solve problems)

French asks "…Who plans?…If a paraeducator is employed to work under the super vision of a single school professional, then it is obvious who plans—that professional. When a paraeducator is employed to work with a team, it is less obvious, but crucially important, to determine the specific response within the team" (French, 1997, p. 96). The team will need to determine who holds ultimate responsibility for the outcomes, who will be in the best position to direct performance, who will be in the best position to provide training for the assigned duties, and who will be in the best position to observe and docu ment para performance.

The more individuals with whom the para works, the more complex the supervision processes. When paras are in the general classroom most of the school day, it is critical that the classroom teacher be involved in the supervision. In some instances the classroom teacher and special educator may want to co-plan, with the classroom teacher taking major responsibility for supervising the para. If communication processes among all parties are open, this arrangement can work well.

Technology-Based Instruction.   Technology provides another powerful way to help individuals with disabilities to benefit from the inclusive classroom instruction. The uses of technology are changing at such a rapid pace that all educators must continually seek more information about its possibilities. Gardner (1994) observes that "What's 'new' in technology is not always what's hot off the production line—it's the discovery of new and creative ways teachers use technology to deliver instruction to students with disabilities

APPLICATION **9.1**

Obtaining Resources for Curriculum Modification

Write sources listed in this book to get more information about the strategies discussed in the chapter. Work with teachers to determine which of these strategies or skills are most needed by students in your school. Develop a comprehensive plan for including them in a systematic way, and include plans for obtaining training in their use.

through powerful and effective techniques!" (Gardner, 1994, p. 10). For example, Gardner describes ways to use digital camera to enhance written and oral expression.

Technology-based instruction can provide many options and alternatives for the learning programs of students with special needs. All teachers and students can expect to benefit from these learning enhancements, while those with special needs may respond to the particular innovations that deliver stronger representations of the world than traditional approaches to learning now provide. See Chapter 7 for a more extensive discussion of this topic.

Ten general areas most amenable to curriculum accommodation and modification (Munson, 1987) are:

- Instructional level
- Curricular content
- Instructional materials
- Format of directions and assignments
- Instructional strategies
- Teacher input mode
- Student response mode
- Individual instruction
- Test administration
- Grading policies

While curriculum adaptations may seem to be the most logical way of addressing special learning needs, the consultant should be aware that classroom teachers may resist suggestions for modifying their classrooms and curriculum (Ammer, 1984; Zigmond, Levin, & Laurie, 1985). Teachers seem to be most receptive to adapting the format of directions and assignments and making test modifications (Munson, 1987.) Although they view instructional adaptation as desirable, most feel they are not able to do it (Ysseldyke, Thurlow, Wotruba, & Nania, 1990).

Classroom teachers might believe they do not know how to adapt instruction, but the most plausible explanation is that they do not have time to do it. Consultants and collaborators must consider whether or not their suggestions for classroom modifications are reasonable and feasible for the situation. (See Chapter 6 for information about dealing with consultee resistance.)

Many of the resources available for helping teachers make classroom modifications represent the views of special educators rather than the collaborative views of classroom teachers and special education teachers. However, Figure 9.5 contains a list of modifications taken from materials prepared collaboratively by elementary classroom teachers and special education teachers (Munson, 1987; Riegel, 1981). The list is a helpful resource for sharing with classroom teachers during consultations.

FIGURE 9.5   Suggestions for Classroom Modifications

Instructional Level
Let student work at success rate level of about 80%.
Break task down into sequential steps.
Sequence the work with easiest problems first.
Base instruction on cognitive need (concrete, abstract).

Curricular Content
Select content that addresses student's interest.
Adapt content to student's future goals (job, college…).

Instructional Materials
Fold or line paper to help student with spatial problem.
Use graph paper or lined paper turned vertically.
Draw arrows on text or worksheet to show related ideas.
Highlight or color-code on worksheets, texts, tests.
Mark the material that must be mastered.
Reduce the amount of material on a page.
Use a word processor for writing and editing.
Provide a calculator or computer to check work.
Tape reference materials to student's work area.
Have student follow text as listening to taped version.

Format of Directions and Assignments
Make instructions as brief as possible.
Introduce multiple long-term assignments in small steps.
Read written directions or assignments aloud.
Leave directions on chalkboard during study time.
Write cues at top of work page (for example, noun = …).
Ask student to restate/paraphrase directions.
Have student complete first example with teacher prompt.
Provide folders for unfinished work and finished work.

Instructional Strategies
Use concrete objects to demonstrate concepts
Provide outlines, semantic organizers, or webbings.
Use voice changes to stress points.
Point out relationships between ideas or concepts.
Repeat important information often.

Teacher Input Mode
Use multi-sensory approach for presenting materials.
Provide a written copy of material on chalkboard.
Demonstrate skills before student does seat work.

Student Response Mode
Accept alternate forms of information-sharing.
Allow taped or written report instead of oral.
Allow students to dictate information to another.
Allow oral report instead of written report.
Have student practice speaking to small group first.

Test Administration
Allow students to have sample tests to practice.
Teach test-taking skills.
Test orally.
Supply recognition items and not just total recall.
Allow take-home test.
Ask questions requiring short answers.

Grading Policies
Grade on pass/fail basis.
Grade on individual progress or effort.
Change the percentage required to pass.
Do not penalize for handwriting or spelling on tests.

Modifications of Classroom Environment
Seat students according to attention or sensory need.
Remove student from distractions.
Keep extra supplies on hand.

(adapted from development by Munson, Riegel)

Assistive Technology.   Assistive technology means any item or piece of equipment that helps the individual participate in the school activities. It can be as simple as a special pen or as complex as a computer. An excellent resource to assist consultants in making decisions about appropriate assistive technology is *Has Technology Been Considered? A Guide for IEP Teams* (Chambers, 1997) This guide, published by the Council of Administrators of Special Education and the Technology and Media Division of CEC, clarifies many questions that can arise when preparing the IEP and making plans for inclusion. Assistive technology may be needed for positioning or self-care devices for students with physical disabilities; augmentative communication devices for students with communication challenges; environmental controls such as switches that make equipment accessible to the student; listening devices such as hearing aids for individuals with hearing loss; visual aids such as magnifiers, scanners or reading machines for blind students or those with low vision; mobility devices such as wheelchairs and canes that provide mobility; devices for leisure and play such as special balls or swimming-pool lifts; computer access with special switches or keyboards or speech recognition for individuals who cannot use standard computer equipment; and computer-based instruction such as special software for individuals with special cognitive challenges.

When planning for assistive technology, the team should ask and answer these questions:

- What is it we want the student to be able to do within the educational program that he/she isn't able to because of his/her disability?
- What has been tried to serve the special education needs?
- Are the accommodations working; do they address the student's specific needs?
- How do we know they are working?
- If not working, how do we know they are not?
- Do we have the necessary knowledge and resources to meet this student's needs?
- If yes, what and where are the resources?
- If not, where can we get outside assistance?

Once the planning team has made a preliminary decision about needed assistive technology, it can ask another set of questions before making the final decision:

- Will the distracting nature of this device outweigh its benefits for the student?
- Is the device safe and functional for this student?
- Can the student take the device home?
- What will we do if the student abuses the device?
- What will be the annual goal for the IEP?

Examples of IEP goals provided by Chambers (1997) include:

1. Maggie will make oral presentations and participate in class discussions using an appropriately programmed electronic device (device could be specified).
2. Susan will use a computer and printer to complete exercises that other children do with pencil and paper.

3. Using a computer keyboard, Rachel will type 12 words per minute with no errors over 10 or more consecutive trials.

4. Using a word processing program with a spell checker, Tom will compose a three-paragraph paper composed of fifteen or more sentences with a minimum of 80 percent accuracy in the use of spelling, punctuation, and grammar over 5 or more consecutive trials.

Multimedia Scaffolding.   Multimedia lends itself nicely to scaffolding, "…an adjustable and temporary support that can be removed when no longer necessary" (Brown & Palincsar, 1989, p. 411). A familiar example of scaffolding for nonreading students is having an expert reader tape record reading material so students with decoding difficulties can listen to it. Such scaffolding allows the nonreading student to be engaged with the regular classroom curriculum and learn the concepts and principles presented in it. The challenge lies in being able to remove the scaffold so that the students are not always dependent on others. This involves teaching the students how to read for themselves. Another challenge is to provide the right amount of support at the right time—neither too much nor too little. A third challenge involves providing the right kind of support; for example, listening to taped material may not be helpful for some students who have low listening-comprehension skills (Dyck, Pemberton, Woods, & Sundbye, 1996).

Multimedia presentations may be considerably more effective than audio-taped material. For example, your authors had this experience in a local school:

> A fifth-grade teacher was discussing one of her students who couldn't read the classroom text. She said: "I don't know what I will do. I have audio tapes, but I have found students have difficulty attending to them. I guess I can have another student listen to the tape with him. Maybe that will help." We suggested she try a multimedia presentation of the material. Since she didn't know how to use multimedia software, we offered to help her. The presentation would be visual and audio. In addition, we would put in elements that would require the student to interact with the material. Although comprehension wasn't this student's major problem, we would put in more frequent comprehension checks to maintain attention. And, if needed, design a way to make more explicit links between questions and answers.
>
> The project was a resounding success. At the end of the school term the teacher said: "The multimedia presentation saved him! He became a part of the class culture and experienced genuine success."

Teachers trained to use multimedia software such as HyperStudio® report benefits such as:

- Students with specials needs were able to have their individual needs met without leaving the regular classroom or becoming isolated through the use of a curriculum different from the rest of the class.
- Multimedia curriculum adaptations fostered student independence rather than dependence on another student or teacher.
- The multimedia presentations (i.e., shorter reading passages with frequent comprehension questions) were highly motivating for students with behavioral problems.

- Teachers using multimedia presentations were able to incorporate student assessment into the normal process of learning through the software's testing functions. The testing function recorded student responses to questions throughout the learning process.
- Teachers could remove scaffolding such as spoken text or comprehension prompts one at a time as students' reading skills improved.

Curriculum Modifications

Students whose cognitive disabilities prevent them from benefiting from the general classroom curriculum, even with accommodations, need curriculum modifications. Students with mild or moderate cognitive disabilities may need adapted outcomes, while students with severe cognitive disabilities will need different goals or outcomes. Whenever possible, a theme or topic being studied by the rest of the students in the classroom should also be studied by these students.

Adapted Outcomes.   Students with moderate learning and behavior problems can succeed very well in inclusive classrooms but may need adapted outcomes such as reduced number of practice problems or highlighted text. Other examples: in math, the student works on the same concept but the number of required practice problems may be reduced; in social studies the teacher might mark certain parts of the text material that must be read and the remainder skimmed; in science the teacher might limit the number of concepts within a domain to be mastered. In short, these students are expected to master most but not all of the content. Most of the items listed in Figure 9.5 support adapted outcomes.

Different Outcomes.   For students with severe cognitive challenges, the curriculum goals may focus on areas such as social/behavioral development, language development, concept development, basic skills, or self-help skills. For example, if the class is studying plants, but the goals for a particular student have to do with counting and language development, he or she may count, sort, and talk about seeds. These students may also need accommodations to help them attain their goals. The primary reason for their inclusion in the class is to participate in the social context and culture of the group.

Enhanced Outcomes.   Students with high ability in classrooms also need modified curriculum. Several strategies presented in this chapter as effective practices for students with learning and behavior disorders in inclusive classrooms are identified as less appropriate for gifted students (Schatz, 1990; Robinson, 1990). For example, cooperative learning is an effective instructional strategy for a variety of reasons. However, it should not be justified for gifted students through inference that they require remediation in social skills. Nor should it be used to make gifted students available as handy tutors (Robinson, 1990). While occasional peer tutoring can be challenging and rewarding for the gifted student, it should not be used to set very able students up as surrogate teachers for other students.

When gifted students are included in general classrooms, as the majority are for most of their school day, their learning needs also must be considered. Providing appropriate learning environments for them necessitates intensive collaboration and consultation among gifted-program facilitators, classroom teachers, and resource personnel so that classroom modifications and resource adaptations help gifted students develop their learning potential.

Classroom Enrichment.   Since most gifted children in elementary schools spend more time with their classroom teachers than with specially trained resource teachers (Gallagher, 1985), the general classroom curriculum should be enriched and adapted to meet their needs. Classroom teachers are responsible for a wide range of student needs and often do not have the time, resources, and facilities to challenge students who can function two, four, or more grade levels beyond their age peers. They do want bright students to master the basic skills without falling victim to learning gaps that might impede their progress later. They also feel the brunt of parent pressures to provide advanced opportunities, and they wince when their most able students describe lessons and materials as "boring." Some do not feel prepared to teach children who may be as knowledgeable or more so in subjects than they.

The inclusive school will bring added responsibilities for classroom teachers in providing for the learning needs of highly able students as well as needs of students with learning disabilities or behavioral disorders. Van Tassel-Baska (1989) notes four mistaken beliefs that need to be overturned regarding educational programs for gifted students. First, consultants and consultees should not assume that differentiated curriculum must always be different from what all learners receive. Neither do all learning experiences need to be product-oriented. One curriculum package or a single learning strategy will *not* provide all that is needed. Acceleration of content for gifted students is *not* harmful as a general rule. Van Tassel-Baska (1989) promotes a content-based, accelerative curriculum, which contains a process/product/research dimension for in-depth learning and involves exploration of issues, themes, and ideas across curriculum areas. Activities which can be provided through collaborative efforts of consultants, teachers, parents, and resource personnel include:

Flexible pacing (appropriate acceleration in content)

Meaningful enrichment (not busywork or enrichment that is irrelevant to their strong abilities and interests)

Group activities (seminars, special classes)

Individual arrangements (independent study, acquisition of skills in areas needed for pursuing major interests and talents, mentorships, and internships)

Tomlinson (1996) recommends a planning model for academic diversity and talent development that uses a sliding scale of differentiation and adaptation, much like the adjustment bar on an electronic sound machine. Asserting that no one size of hat, shoe, or curriculum fits all students, she adapts curriculum to needs of the very able by designing curriculum flexibility in a number of areas, including abstract representations, leaps of insight, open approaches, greater independence in planning, and quicker pace of study.

Curriculum Compacting.   Curriculum compacting (Renzulli and Reis, 1985) is a strategy that consulting teacher and classroom teacher can plan and implement productively for very able students. Just as teachers condense daily lessons and assignments for children returning to school after an illness, they can compact curriculum for students who learn more quickly and easily than the majority of students. This "buys time" for students to pursue individual interests and independent study in complex areas of regular or accelerated curriculum.

Gifted students need not always accelerate at a fast pace through the curriculum. On occasion they may welcome the opportunity to slow down and study a subject in depth and detail, catching up with the class later by completing regular assignments on a compacted basis at a later date.

Some arrangements needed by gifted and talented students are accessible only outside the school setting. When students leave their school campus for enrichment, or for accelerated course work, group learning experiences, or individual arrangements, special educators and classroom teachers must assume responsibility for collaborating and communicating often to ensure that the students master basic skills and continue to be involved in the life of the school. A list of learning options and alternatives for gifted students is provided in Figure 9.6.

The TREAT Program Model.   The TREAT Program (Treat & Dyck, 1997) provides a successful model that can be used by any elementary classroom teacher to address special needs of students with high ability in the classroom. The TREAT Program follows the steps described in Figure 9.7. The testout option is available for any student who wants to try. The result is that some students are pleasantly surprised to discover they can successfully testout and receive the same positive benefits as the students identified as gifted. Students with less ability benefit because the teacher can provide instruction aimed at their needs without being concerned about overlooking the needs of students with high ability. Classroom teachers can implement the TREAT Program alone, but if they are fortunate enough to have available the resources of a gifted facilitator, the TREAT Program can be greatly enhanced. Gifted facilitators have extensive training in understanding students with high ability and usually have available special materials and guides, creative ideas of their own, and knowledge about other resources available in the school and community. The gifted-program facilitator and classroom teacher should meet regularly (preferably every week) to plan.

Planning Remedial Instruction

Many inclusion programs have put all their resources into co-teaching, accommodations, and modifications, while overlooking the special needs of students with significant basic-skill disabilities in need of remedial instruction. We have observed far too many parents turning to private remedial services, home schooling, or private tutors to help their children who are not getting remediation in the schools. Special educators in public schools must provide this type of instruction for students who need it.

According to a study by Zigmond (1997), half of the students with learning disabilities in inclusive elementary schools made no progress in reading during the school year. Traditional resource rooms are not meeting these needs of students, either. One-fourth of the students in pull-out programs did not make progress in reading during the school year.

FIGURE 9.6   Appropriate Learning Programs for Gifted Students

Exciting, challenging learning activities for gifted and talented students can be provided in the classroom. Collaborators can shop among these very basic enrichment options when working together to plan alternatives for very able students.

- Allow students to testout of already mastered material.
- Compact curriculum to "buy" time for enrichment activity.
- Acquire advanced texts and references for students to use.
- Allow students to study a subject longer than usual.
- Arrange cross-age tutoring between very able students with similar interests and learning styles.
- Facilitate independent study.
- Encourage investigations by a small group of able students working as a team.
- Provide learning packs, modules, mini-courses, and task cards on topics of interest to gifted students.
- Bring in resource speakers to discuss special issues.
- Cultivate and facilitate mentorships.
- Allow dual course work for dual credit.
- Permit extended library or laboratory time.
- Schedule time each day for concentrated, uninterrupted work on a project or reflection on an idea.
- Conduct discussions about complex, appealing topics.
- Prepare resource files of community members who could help in the classroom or behind the scenes.
- Provide instruction to students on learning taxonomies and principles.
- Set up mini-seminars for groups of students who share similar interests and abilities.
- Use biographies of exemplary persons to model for and motivate students.
- Set aside an area where student research projects and creative products are showcased and discussed.
- Introduce the world's wisdom through use of quotes, credos, maxims, fables.
- Conduct problem-solving sessions, using real and hypothetical problems.
- Provide discussion time for moral dilemmas, logic, and ethics.
- Make career information and resource persons available.
- Encourage students to keep idea journals, sketchbooks, and idea files.
- Cultivate student self-assessment of own learning habits and self-evaluation of learning products.
- Use feedback, grading, and reporting alternatives that do not penalize students for selecting harder curriculum.
- Seek outlets for displaying and publishing exemplary student work.
- Arrange for student participation in appropriate competitive activities.
- Provide instruction in "life tools" such as parliamentary procedure, orienteering, interviewing, research.
- Provide opportunities for developing global awareness.
- Arrange independent study or tutorial in a foreign language.
- Provide "how-to" books on various areas of human endeavor.
- Encourage students to read something from each subject area in the library.
- Recognize and respect unusual, creative questions and ideas.
- Provide liberal, in-depth critiques and comments on work.
- Use intrinsic rewards and appeals to reasoning as much as possible for reinforcement.

FIGURE 9.7 The TREAT Program

Testout: Any student in the class is given an opportunity to testout of a study unit.

Revise: The successful student receives a grade of "A" for the unit. The student participates in choosing what to do next and completes a contracted activity as described in steps E, A and T below.

    Enrich: The student may select from enrichment options offered by the teacher from appropriate curriculum.

    Accelerate: The student may be given the option of accelerating the pace of learning subject matter material through advance placement.

    Think-and-Do: The student, with teacher guidance, constructs an independent study in a personally meaningful content area.

Neither situation is acceptable. Inclusion programs must provide intensive remedial instruction in basic skills for some students.

Guidelines for Remedial Instruction

Collaborating teachers must develop remedial plans indicating what skills to remediate, teaching techniques to use, who will provide the instruction, when and where it will be provided. Harris and Sipay (1990) give the following guidelines for planning remedial instruction:

- Tutoring from one to three children at a time produces best results.
- Some students must be given one-on-one tutoring to make any progress.
- A minimum of about 50 instructional hours is necessary for significant improvement.
- Three times a week will produce results, but every day is even better.
- Remedial periods should usually last from 30 to 45 minutes.

Resources for Remedial Lessons

Most special educators in inclusive schools will not have time to provide extensive remedial instruction given all their other responsibilities. Most will need to plan the remediation and direct a para, peer tutor, or volunteer to provide the instruction. Special educators need to acquire a library of resources that provide explicit guidelines for tutors to follow. An excellent resource for this task is *Helping the Struggling Reader: What to Teach and How to Teach It* (Sundbye and McCoy, 1997). This resource provides thirty-nine teaching plans that address varying student needs from learning about sounds and letters, to using print and meaning together, to comprehension. The teaching plans are designed for one-on-one, intensive teaching, but can be adapted for use with small groups as well. An easy-to-use grid helps the teacher match types of reading difficulties with the teaching plans that are most likely to be helpful. Tutors can easily follow the teaching plans selected. The performance records for each teaching plan will help the consultant monitor student progress and make adjustments when needed.

Another resource that goes beyond reading is *Tactics for Teaching* (Lovitt, 1995). One hundred and five tactics are categorized into six sections: reading, writing, spelling, mathematics, classroom management, and self-management. Each tactic provides a brief rationale for the tactic, describes the type of student with whom it would be most appropriate, an outline of procedures for implementing the technique, procedures for monitoring its use, and ways the tactic can be modified in special situations.

Planning Instructional Support

Consultants and collaborating teachers cannot be present in every inclusive classroom for all instruction that takes place, but they can support classroom teachers in many other ways. Consultants can provide invaluable support for classroom teachers by planning for and supervising paras; planning for tutors and other instructional assistants assigned to the classroom; teaching students study strategies, classroom survival skills, and self-advocacy behaviors; adapting tests and other text material; and monitoring student progress.

Planning for Paras

Not only are paras assigned to provide accommodations for students with severe disabilities, they frequently assist in co-teaching lessons. The *Teach and Monitor* approach described above is the most common co-teaching model when paras are involved. Generally, the para is always the monitor when this model is used. Paras often provide much of the prompting, tutoring, and other needed support when the special education teacher cannot be present in the classroom.

Paras assist teachers in preparing materials, especially adaptations for students with special needs. They are not responsible for diagnosing problems or planning interventions, but they can and should be prepared to implement the lesson plans and interventions and to assist professional educators with most of their duties. The responsibility for planning paras' tasks and schedules falls on the teachers to whom they are assigned.

It is one thing to plan for yourself and quite another to organize and plan for another person such as a para. French (1997) provides several examples of forms teachers can use to plan for paras. Teachers who co-plan should clearly specify the para responsibilities, as illustrated in Figure 9.2. They might want to add other instructions on the back side of the planning form to clarify the para role. Explicit instructions might say:

- Cue Melony to take lecture notes.
- Use "Review Notes" tool (Dyck & Pemberton, 1997) while reading textbook assignment.
- Monitor Melony's team closely during cooperative learning and clarify for Melony when needed.

Another type of plan one might prepare with the para is a daily schedule. This plan would list all time periods through the day; where the para will be each time period, such as Room 25, or work room; and what activity or responsibility the para will have, such as "co-teach with Jones" or "adapt Chapter 10 for Willy." Plans of this nature can be printed on paper or put in a computer database where the para and professional can easily add comments and provide feedback to one another.

See Chapters 7 and 10 for more suggestions about managing people resources. No matter how much advance preparation the para has received, teachers to whom a para is assigned must provide orientation and on-the-job training. See Chapter 10 for more information about paras. Teachers may find evaluating paras neither easy nor pleasant, particularly when performance is substandard. See Chapter 8 for more suggestions about evaluating paras.

When we interview teachers, we discover one of their major concerns about supervising paras is time for interaction, planning, observation, and communicating. See Chapter 7 for suggestions about managing time in a school context.

Planning for Peer Tutors and Other Instructional Assistants

Peer tutoring, including same-age and cross-age tutoring, is receiving renewed attention within the inclusion movement. Peer tutoring is more cost effective than other tutoring approaches such as the use of paraprofessionals, computer-assisted instruction, and reduced class size (Jenkins & Jenkins, 1985). The benefits of peer tutoring include improved achievement (for tutors as well as tutees), opportunities to learn responsibility, improved social skills, and enhanced self-esteem of tutors and tutees (Gerber & Kauffmann, 1981; Scruggs & Richter, 1986).

Classroom teachers occasionally are reluctant to implement peer tutoring programs despite obvious benefits, because they must spend time and effort in gaining successful results. Since time, energy, and resources for establishing effective peer-tutoring programs are considerable, consulting teachers can collaborate with teachers to develop the programs. Peer-tutoring programs can be building-wide or limited to one or a few classrooms.

Jenkins and Jenkins (1985) identified the following critical components of a successful peer-tutoring program:

1. Provide highly structured lesson formats for tutors to use during the tutoring session, such as packaged programs with teacher instruction.
2. When possible, use content that correlates with the classroom content. Do not expect the tutor to teach material that has not already been presented by the teacher.
3. A mastery model of instruction is preferred because it provides satisfaction to tutor and tutee.
4. Schedule tutoring sessions frequently for moderate lengths of time (about one-half hour every day at the elementary level and daily one-hour sessions at the secondary level).
5. Provide tutor training and supervision, including feedback and reinforcement to tutors and classroom teachers.
6. Keep daily performance data on instructional objectives (as discussed in Chapter 8 concerning curriculum-based assessment). Other types of information can include daily assignment record, monthly calendar, diary, or log book.

7. Carefully select and pair tutors with learners. The most important selection criteria are individual characteristics such as dependability, responsibility, and sensitivity.

Consideration should be given to personalities and compatibility of the tutor and tutee, congruence of schedules, gender differences (not a critical issue, but perhaps pertinent at the secondary level), tutor knowledge of content to be tutored, interests, and eagerness to participate. More highly skilled tutors are often placed with more difficult-to-teach students (Jenkins & Jenkins, 1985).

One of the most important elements of a good peer-tutoring program is tutor training. The amount and type of training will vary depending on the ages and abilities of the tutors and learners. Training usually addresses topics such as information about the program, tutor responsibilities, measurement procedures, lesson structure, teaching procedures, and personal behavior. The training should include personal relationship skills such as responsive listening, conversing, and praising good effort as described in Chapter 6. It is important that the tutors be instructed in specific procedures which have been experimentally validated to assure maximum learning and minimum frustration.

An example of peer tutoring at the high-school level is the H.E.L.P. room in a Midwestern high school. The program (Here to Encourage the Learning Process) was developed for students who had difficulties keeping up in general education classrooms, but who did not qualify for special education programs. Although a teacher and a paraprofessional staffed the program, peer tutoring was the principal methodology. Tutors were trained over a period of several weeks in communication skills, study skills, observation skills, writing of behavioral objectives, and tutoring skills. Evaluations of the H.E.L.P. program showed positive results. Parents reported that their children are more interested in school, and teachers welcomed the assistance. Students said they were less frustrated and more successful in the classroom (Thurston & Dover, 1990).

Teaching Study Strategies

Students with learning difficulties often show marked improvement in general education classrooms after they have been taught strategies for using information presented in the classroom. Many learning strategies resemble processes more commonly recognized as study skills.

Strategies Intervention Model. Teachers in inclusive high schools can support classroom teachers by teaching all students to use The Strategies Intervention Model (Deshler & Schumaker, 1986). The strategies are techniques, principles, or rules that enable students to learn, solve problems, and complete tasks independently. Deshler and Schumaker (1986) stress the importance of deliberately teaching for generalization across settings. If the special education teacher is collaborating with the classroom teacher, this generalization process will be much more effective than other delivery options. Perhaps the special education teacher will teach the strategies in the resource room, but the regular classroom teacher will want to take over monitoring the generalization. The classroom teacher provides explicit cues that will help the student know when to use a particular strategy and gives periodic probes to determine whether or not the student continues to use the strategy.

Central to the entire generalization process just described are regular cooperative planning efforts between the resource and regular classroom teacher. Regular communication is essential to determine the degree to which the newly-acquired learning strategies are being used in the regular classroom. In addition, in such meetings classroom teachers can be encouraged to cue students to use the strategy at the appropriate time (Deshler and Schumaker, 1986, p. 586).

Teaching Self-Advocacy

Students with special needs should be taught how to communicate their special needs to teachers, employers, and others. The self-advocacy form in Figure 9.8 was prepared by Dyck (1997) to use with secondary-level students in general classrooms. Under ideal circumstances, the special education teacher would prompt the student to take responsibility to give the form to each teacher and pick it up once the teacher has filled in the right-hand column. This responsibility is especially important for students with learning and behavior problems. A good variation is for the classroom teacher to hand out the form the first day of class and ask every student to complete the left-hand column and return it. The teacher then looks over each form, writes responses in the right-hand column, and returns them to the students shortly thereafter. (It is a good idea for the teacher to photocopy the completed forms before returning them to the students.) This process provides an efficient and confidential way for teachers and students to communicate regarding special needs and preferences.

Adapting Tests

Many students with learning and behavior problems have difficulty taking tests on subject matter they have learned. As a student progresses to higher grade levels, the ability to demonstrate knowledge through tests becomes more important. Many consultants at upper grade levels will need to give careful attention to the test-taking skills of mainstreamed students with learning and behavior difficulties.

When students have difficulty taking teacher-made tests in content subjects, consultants should give attention to a number of elements about the nature of the tests and ways to either help students take the tests as written, or collaborate with the teacher to make test adaptations. Lieberman (1984) suggests the first week of each school year, beginning at about the seventh-grade level, should be devoted to teaching study skills and test-taking strategies.

Other suggestions to consider when consulting with classroom teachers about alternative test construction and administration are:

- Give frequent, timed mini-tests.
- Give practice tests.
- Have students test one another and discuss answers.
- Use alternative response forms (multiple choice, short-answer, essay).
- Back up the written tests with taped tests.
- Provide extra spacing between discussion or short-answer items.
- Underline key words in test directions as well as test items.

FIGURE 9.8   Self-Advocacy Form

Name _____   Course _____

What Works for Me:	**What Teacher Accepts:**

Class Presentations
- Allow me to tape record lectures
- Hand out lecture outlines or objectives in advance
- Give me copies of overheads
- Let me sit where I can see and hear the presenter
- _____

Tests
- Give me oral tests
- Record test on tape
- Allow someone to read test to me
- Allow extra time for me to take tests or shorten the test
- Put plenty of space for me to write on tests
- Provide short answer and multiple choice questions
- _____

Study Methods
- Allow more time for reading or shorten assignments
- Let me read an easier book (____ level)
- Provide explanations for acceptable homework form (typed, etc.)
- Check to make sure I understand directions
- I need frequent breaks
- I need a quiet area for study
- Explicitly instruct me to write down my homework assignment in my notebook
- Type handwritten teacher materials
- Use written backup for oral directions
- Allow me to use a calculator
- Allow me to use a word processor with spell check
- Break down long assignments into smaller sections for me to complete
- I learn well in small groups
- I don't learn well in small groups
- I learn well in whole-class presentations
- I need to learn with a "study buddy"
- _____

© 1997 Curriculum Solutions, Inc., used with permission.

- Provide test-study guides featuring a variety of answer formats.
- Provide additional time for students who write slowly.
- Administer tests orally (Mercer & Mercer, 1993).

Teachers are likely to be more resistant to test adaptations than to adaptations of classroom materials. Likewise, even when they believe it is a good thing to do, they are not very likely to make the adaptations themselves (Gajria, Salend, & Hemrick, 1994; Salend, 1994). Consultants can assist classroom teachers in:

- Adapting their tests by adjusting the content to be directly related to the objectives of the class.
- Changing the format so the items are easy to read, more space is allowed for discussion, or the order of items is rearranged to make them more predictable.
- Rewriting directions or providing cues such as highlighting, underlining, and enlarging.
- Providing prompts such as "Start here" or "Look at the sign on this row."
- Adjusting the readability level of the questions.
- Providing outlines or advance organizers.
- Providing spelling of difficult words.
- Allowing students to use outlines, webs or other visual organizers (Salend, 1994).

As teachers become proficient in using more authentic assessment procedures, the need for test modification will lessen. Even then, some type of accommodation is likely to be needed for some students with disabilities.

Adapting Text Materials

Many of the guidelines for adapting tests apply when adapting other text material such as textbooks, study guides, or activity sheets. Before getting started with textbook adaptations, the consultant and collaborating teacher should answer the following questions:

- What are the outcomes or objectives?
- What chapters will be covered and in what order?
- When will the chapters be covered, and in what depth?
- In what setting will the text be used?
- How will the objectives be assessed?
- What is the student's reading problem—decoding, comprehension?
- What are the student's interests, strengths, and prior experiences?

Other points to consider when adapting textbooks are:

- Break the chapter into small study units.
- Limit the number of new concepts presented in one lesson.
- Clarify references that are ambiguous, distant, or indirect in easier terms.
- Rearrange order of events or instructions to proceed in one direction only.
- Set aside units of text not needed for main flow of content.
- Make very difficult sentence structure more simple.
- Rearrange content so the same information is presented with each new example in the same order.

- Add material that
  - — Explains the relevance or significance of information in the text.
  - — Makes the text more interesting to the reader (but be careful about "seductive detail" that can be distracting).
  - — Makes explicit connections between concepts.
  - — Highlights key terms, concepts, or other essential information.
  - — Helps provide clear definitions for technical terms or difficult words.

Monitoring Student Progress

Frequent monitoring is essential in situations where the special education teacher is not providing all the direct instruction to students with special needs. In fact, it might be the most important function performed by the special educator in inclusive schools. Consider the example of Debbie:

> Debbie was now in her second year at an inclusive school. She had sixteen students in her caseload—mostly fourth and fifth graders. Debbie spent at least one hour each day in each classroom where her students were included. In addition, she taught math to several small groups in which her students were included. Although she felt confident her students were making satisfactory progress in basic skills, she wasn't sure. She began using Curriculum-Based Measurement (CBM) procedures, taking reading and math probes once each week (see Chapter 8 for more information about CBM). After a few weeks of charting data she realized four of her students were not making progress in reading. She had not been working directly with these students in reading and did not realize the problems they were having. She immediately took steps to make changes in those students' reading instruction.

Curriculum-Based Assessment (CBA). Curriculum-based assessment (CBA), discussed in Chapter 8, is an appropriate testing tool for use at any grade level but may be most beneficial in elementary schools. It has the most direct application in monitoring growth in basic skill areas such as reading, writing, and mathematics. The consultant or classroom teacher should take frequent measures using the actual materials or content from the classroom.

Monitoring Classroom Grades. Secondary-level teachers can monitor student progress by the number of completed assignments and grades in general classroom courses. This information must be interpreted cautiously, however, because teacher's grading standards vary greatly. Special educators in inclusive schools should discuss with each teacher their grading philosophies and plan a system for grading students with adapted curriculum.

Tips for Co-planning and Co-teaching

1. The processes of restructuring schools is painful. Begin with small steps and don't get discouraged with your first attempts.
2. Co-teaching *requires* co-planning. Co-planning time must be built into the restructured school day. (See Figure 9.9.)
3. Co-teachers need to discuss their philosophies about teaching (content and activities in Chapter 3 being helpful for this purpose).

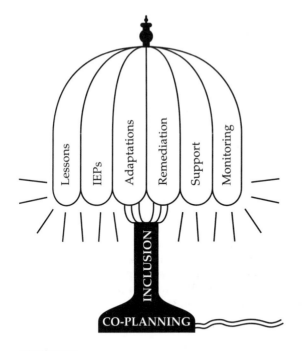

FIGURE 9.9

Cristi Wiegers

4. When co-teaching, clarify classroom rules and procedures such as routines for leaving the room, discipline matters, division of chores such as grading or making bulletin boards (Friend & Cook, 1992).
5. Devise a way to keep track of individuals who are providing services for students, so that monitoring does not become a problem.
6. Rather than just telling classroom teachers about materials modification, *show* them. Give examples or do one for them.
7. Request demonstration lessons from classroom teachers featuring *their* most outstanding teaching techniques.
8. Offer to retype a test for a teacher (to double space, type in large print, or organize it differently) for use with a student who has a learning problem.
9. Before ordering computer software, have students try it out first. This gives them an opportunity to be consultants for teachers, and cultivates student ownership in educational planning and evaluation.
10. When preparing and distributing materials for classroom use, don't just drop them off and run. Help the teacher or student get started, and stay awhile to see how it goes.
11. Keep a supply of materials to send to classrooms for students who need reinforcement, even those with whom you don't work who could use the practice.

12. Have a favorite dozen of successful strategies available for demonstration teaching or sharing.
13. Be understanding of classroom teachers' daily trials with some mainstreamed students. Celebrate with classroom teachers even the smallest student progress.

CHAPTER REVIEW

1. Schools that engage in school-wide planning with all stakeholders reap the benefits for years to come. Planners need to engage in continuous problem-solving processes. They will know their school is inclusive when teachers function differently than they did before the journey began and all students are making progress in learning. Student learning is the final test of a successful inclusive school.

2. Co-teaching (two or more teachers planning and delivering instruction) by special educators and general educators requires co-planning, which differs from group-planning models used by general educators and the linear, individual planning models of special educators.

3. The Interactive Planning Model addresses nearly all students, or most students, or some individual students, as needs dictate. As a result, the model can be successful when co-teachers plan and co-teach lessons using one or a combination of various approaches for presentation of lessons.

4. Because students work together in achieving meaningful objectives, their achievement and social relationships can be improved at the same time.

5. Without information about a student's IEP goals and objectives, classroom teachers, paras, and other persons involved in a student's instruction can only assume the student should meet the same goals and objectives as most students in the inclusive classroom.

6. IDEA 97 and Section 504 of the Rehabilitation Act of 1973 specify who should be eligible for reasonable accommodations in schools.

7. Curriculum adaptations involve accommodations such as assistive technology and curriculum modifications such as easier or more challenging curriculum.

8. Assistive technology means any item or piece of equipment that helps the individual participate in the school activities. It can be as simple as a special pen or as complex as a computer.

9. Students whose cognitive disabilities prevent them from benefiting from the general classroom curriculum, even with accommodations, need curriculum modifications. Students with mild or moderate cognitive disabilities may need adapted outcomes, while students with severe cognitive disabilities will need different goals or outcomes. Whenever possible, a theme or topic being studied by the rest of the students in the classroom should also be studied by these students. Students with high ability need modifications such as enrichment, acceleration, or independent study activities.

10. Most special educators in inclusive schools will not have time to provide extensive remedial instruction given all their other responsibilities. Most will need to plan the remediation and direct a para, peer tutor, or volunteer to provide the instruction. Special educators need to acquire a library of resources that provide explicit guidelines for tutors to follow.

11. Consultants and collaborating teachers cannot be present in every inclusive classroom for all instruction that takes place, but they can support classroom teachers in many other ways such as planning for and supervising paras; planning for tutors and other instructional assistants assigned to the classroom; teaching students study strategies, classroom survival skills, and self-advocacy behaviors; adapting tests and other text material; and monitoring student progress.

12. Frequent monitoring is essential in situations where the special education teacher is not providing all the direct instruction to students with special needs. In fact, it might be the most important function performed by the special educator in inclusive schools because they have no other valid way to make curriculum changes if needed. Curriculum-based measurement is a helpful tool in elementary schools. Teacher grades can be useful in secondary schools.

TO DO AND THINK ABOUT

1. Use the Interactive Lesson Planning Model to co-plan a lesson with another teacher. Consider including the para as part of the instructional staff. Then co-teach the lesson. After teaching, evaluate the processes and think about what you need to do to improve.

2. Interview a para in an inclusive school setting to find out what types of tasks are required of the person each day.

3. Identify a real or hypothetical student with disabilities and provide accommodations for the student during a lesson in the general classroom when you are not present.

4. Develop a plan for implementing a peer-tutoring program that could be used in your school.

5. Select a real or hypothetical situation in which you would be consulting about a student with severe learning disabilities. Draft ideas that might come up for discussion regarding testing and grading. The ideas should be consistent with school policy, and fair and honest for the student.

FOR FURTHER READING

Dyck, N., and Pemberton, J. (1997). *A dozen tools for paras.* Lawrence, KS: Curriculum Solutions, Inc.

Dyck, N., Pemberton, J., Woods, K., & Sundbye, N. (1996). *Creating inclusive schools: A new design for ALL students.* Lawrence, KS: Curriculum Solutions, Inc.

Friend, M., & Bursuck, W. D. (1996). *Including students with special needs: A practical guide for classroom teachers.* Boston: Allyn & Bacon.

Lovitt, T. C. (1995). *Tactics for teaching* (2nd ed.). Englewood Cliffs, NJ: Merrill, Prentice Hall.

Sundbye, N., & McCoy, L. (1997). *Helping the struggling reader: What to teach and how to teach it.* Lawrence, KS: Curriculum Solutions, Inc.

Treat, M., & Dyck, N. (1997). *The TREAT program: Including students with high ability.* Lawrence, KS: Curriculum Solutions, Inc.

Vaughn, S., Schumm, J. S., and Arguelles, M. E. (1997). The ABCDEs of co-teaching. *Teaching Exceptional Children, 30* (2) 42–45.

10 Related-Services and Support Personnel

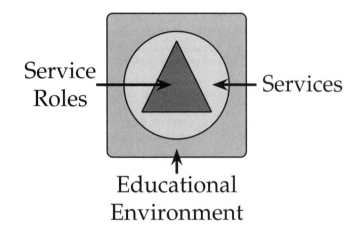

Service Roles → Services → Educational Environment

Resources for learning include people (experts, models, coaches, guides); places (sites, sources); and things (data, materials, artifacts, equipment, and technology systems and procedures). The possibilities are virtually unlimited—local colleges and universities; business, industry, and professions; special-interest groups in the community; city, county, and state agencies; homes with talented parents and grandparents; local service organizations; foreign student exchange; museums; libraries; vocational and technical schools; media; recreation; county extension offices; senior-citizen centers; even classrooms where students help other students. This wealth of resources is a rich pool from which to draw for students' special learning needs.

Consulting and collaborating teachers can be very effective catalysts for learning by finding multiple resources in and beyond school facilities and matching them with students' interests and needs. When consulting and collaborating, they have many opportunities to locate and coordinate the services of mentors, resource speakers, experts, adjudicators, and technology and media specialists.

One important source of assistance in special education programs is the paraeducator. Paras can help students locate and use other resources and special materials, and assist on the teaching team in a variety of ways.

Networking and interaction among general and special education teachers, paras, related-services and support personnel, administrators, and outside individuals and agencies will increase learning and production opportunities for students greatly. In order to obtain even more resources for schools and students, school personnel should consider submitting proposals to funding agencies.

Focusing Questions

1. What can related-services personnel and support personnel contribute to learning programs for students with special needs by collaborating on a team with general and special education teachers?
2. What roles do paras serve within the inclusive, collaborative school?
3. What roles do school administrators and supervisors have in promoting consultation and collaboration among school personnel?
4. How can collaborative consultation solidify needed collaborative links among various agencies of home, school, and community to serve students' special needs?
5. How might school personnel seek out external funding to enhance school environments and learning programs for special needs?

Key Terms

Educational Resources
  Information Center (ERIC)
*Federal Grants and Contracts
  Weekly*
Federal Register

grant funds
home-school collaboration
interagency collaboration
paraeducator/paraprofessional/
  para

related-services personnel
Request for Proposal (RFP)
support personnel
whole-faculty study groups

Related-Services and Support Personnel as Partners in Inclusion

An ancient proverb counsels us that a child's life is like a piece of paper on which every passer-by leaves a mark. Several years ago Bronfenbrenner (1973) stressed that all members of society have the responsibility to teach society's children. A typical community has three kinds of agencies for education—informal, nonformal, and formal (Seay, 1974). Families and neighborhoods are informal agencies for education. Churches, media, and cultural centers are examples of nonformal educator agencies, and schools and universities are considered formal agencies.

Schools are required by the Individuals with Disabilities Education Act (IDEA), and Section 504 of the Rehabilitation Act of 1973, to provide an array of services for students with disabilities. These services, classifiable as informal, nonformal, or formal, range from health and medical services, to physical and occupational therapy, in-home services, transportation, speech pathology and audiology, psychological services, recreation and counseling services, and much more. (See Figure 10.1.) As mandated by P.L. 94-142, multidisciplinary teams determine student eligibility for special education, decide on the most appropriate placement, and monitor progress after placement. Collaboration is essential for identifying the needs or problems, and for exploring modifications that address them.

Services such as those displayed in Figure 10.1 are tapped to provide appropriate education programs for children with disabilities that range well beyond the traditional concept of basic education (Zirkel & Knapp, 1993). Such services must be real and substantial.

Scenario 10

—Adapted from Michelle Berg

The setting is the kitchen of a home where a middle-school student and mother are sitting at the kitchen table.

MOTHER: I see a note here from your teacher saying that you need to make up an important math test you missed yesterday.

CHILD: Uh-huh, I missed it because yesterday was Tuesday.

MOTHER: What does that have to do with the math test?

CHILD: Well, on Tuesdays I'm supposed to see Mrs. Evans, but she wasn't there. So I went to Mr. Bowman instead.

MOTHER: Who is Mrs. Evans?

CHILD: She's the reading teacher. I see her Tuesdays and Thursdays, from 1:30–2:30, but she was sick yesterday.

MOTHER: So you saw Mr. Bowman. Who is he?

CHILD: The special education teacher I see for more help with reading, but mostly with spelling and my workbooks. He got called to another school for a meeting, so he sent me to Jeanette.

MOTHER: Now wait a minute—who is Jeanette?

CHILD: Gee, mom, I thought you told the principal you and dad would keep up with my school program.

MOTHER: I'm *trying*!

CHILD: Anyway, Jeanette is the high school girl who tutors me in reading.

MOTHER: Oh?

CHILD: It's O.K. She's nice. She wants to be a teacher someday. Mrs. Bagley helped me work it out.

MOTHER: And *who* is Mrs. Bagley?

CHILD: The counselor. She says working with Jeanette is good for me, and for her, too.

MOTHER: And just what does Ms. Anderson think about all of this?

CHILD: Uh, who's she?

MOTHER: Your *classroom teacher*!

CHILD: Oh, yeah, I forgot all about her.

(This child's schedule underscores the complexity of the school day and accentuates the need for communication, cooperation, and coordination among an array of school personnel.)

FIGURE 10.1   Related Services/Support Personnel

These roles can assist general and special education classroom teachers and school administrators in providing for students' academic, emotional, social, and physical needs:

Adaptive Physical Education	Parent Counseling Training
Art Therapy	Parent Volunteers
Assistive Technological Devices/Services	Physical Therapy (PT)
Audiology	Reading Specialist
Counseling	Recreational Services
Custodian	School Health Services
Dance Movement/Drama Therapy	School Psychologist
Food Services	Secretarial/Receptionist Services
Media/Library/Technology Specialists	Security Services
Medical Diagnosis	Senior Citizens/Grandparents
Mentors/Apprenticeship Supervisors	Social Work Services
Music Therapy	Special Education Administration/Supervision
Occupational Therapy (OT)	Speech/Language Services
Other Aides	Student Teachers
Paraeducator (para)	Transportation (Bus/Cab Services)

They are defined and determined by how they relate to the student's IEP. Zirkel and Knapp cite numerous court cases, along with the background and outcomes for each case, that describe services school districts must provide. They make several recommendations for schools, including:

1. Do not reject parental requests for related services.
2. Separate related-services obligations under IDEA from those under Section 504.
3. Determine the school's obligation on a case-by-case basis according to the student's defined disability.
4. Distinguish between reasonable benefits and optimal education.
5. Follow due process considerations carefully to avoid grounds for an appeal.

Collaboration in Early Childhood Education for Children with Disabilities

Concern for preschoolers from poverty-level environments and other conditions of disadvantage gained momentum in the 1960s. Passage of Public Law 99-457 in 1986 expanded attention to preschoolers. Public schools now are required to provide special services for children age 3 and above who have disabilities. Public Law 99-457 has gone far beyond classroom concerns to include family, social workers, speech and language pathologists, medical personnel, and other professionals. The law authorizes funding for state grants and for experimental, demonstration, and outreach programs that are multidisciplinary in nature. An increase in services for preschool children with disabilities calls for cooperation among professionals, parents, and other caregivers. Collaboration, consultation, and teamwork are at the heart of these programs.

Early intervention programs for infants and toddlers with disabilities have proliferated following the early childhood legislation. Parents and other caregivers outside the school now play an even more integral part in the education and well-being of these children. Because most disabilities of children in the early intervention programs are severe, services of specialists from several disciplines are essential for serving special needs. Families play an integral part in the therapy through home-based programs. In these programs therapists go into the homes to provide stimulation for the children and guidance and instruction for the parents. Staff and parents must collaborate with all available resources, including health and medical personnel, social services personnel, public school personnel, and community resources such as preschool and day-care centers.

Transition from Preschool to Kindergarten.   While formal programs such as Head Start and Follow Through for young children have been successful in and of themselves, P.L. 99-457 reaches far beyond classroom interventions. Transition from the preschool settings to kindergarten-school programs requires strong, continuous collaboration as educator teams. Preschool teachers should identify essential skills needed in the local kindergarten in order to prepare children for that setting (Beckhoff & Bender, 1989; Salisbury & Vincent, 1990; McCormick & Kawate, 1982). Their contributions to elementary-school programs are invaluable for getting new kindergarten students off to a successful start.

Transition from School to the Adult World

At the opposite end of the continuum from early childhood needs are the needs of students leaving school to enter the world of work and adult living. Awareness of this important transition period for young people with disabilities grew in the 1980s. The transition movement of the 1980s was preceded by two similar movements in the 1960s and the 1970s (Halpern, 1992). During the 1960s a work/study program emerged as an approach to preparing students with mild disabilities for adjustment in their communities. Two flaws of this movement were the funding mechanism that supported it, and the requirement that rehabilitation agencies could not pay for services that were the responsibility of other agencies (Halpern, 1992). The 1970s career education movement was an expansion of the work/study movement. However, it eventually was disowned as a federal initiative, leaving the door open for the emergence of the transition movement during the 1980s.

The goal of transition programs during the 1980s was to assist students with disabilities in obtaining education services to enable them to lead meaningful and productive lives. One of the realities was that no one parent, teacher, or counselor, can provide all the necessary assistance. The emphasis on college-preparatory curriculum that grew out of school reform was appropriate for perhaps only 40 percent of the students (Daggett, 1989; Edgar, 1990; Goodlad, 1984; Pugach & Sapon-Shevin, 1987).

The decade of the 1990s is an important one for making transition approaches work in the local communities (Halpern, 1992). Educational- and social-reform movements have escalated attention on this age-group population of students who have special needs. Schools now are responsible for generating Individual Transition Plans (ITPs) to assess students' career interests and help them focus on career possibilities. Community support is given through vocational transition liaisons, job coaching, work awareness classes, and school employment. Thorough assessment is vital for effective transition, and students with disabilities may need special comprehensive testing (Dragan, 1994).

Without concerted team effort, students with disabilities do not make successful transition to adult life. More than 50 percent remain unemployed or under-employed. Students, parents, teachers, guidance counselors, and other support personnel should contribute to development of the ITP. In order for the transition process to be successful, all parties and agencies are required to work together systematically to plan for it (Clark & Knowlton, 1988; Rusch & Menchetti, 1988). Collaborative consultation has been helpful in providing this support (Sileo, Rude, & Luckner, 1988).

Roles for Related-Services and Support Personnel

Two transition service providers in secondary schools are vocational education teachers and school counselors. Planning is to be coordinated among special education, vocational education, and out-of-school adult service agencies. Students and their families must be collaborating participants in the discussions. IDEA stipulates the need for setting transition goals and interagency linkages and for the integration of these into the IEP. In this way the linkages are made before the student exits the school environment. School administrators are responsible for facilitating the collaboration, outlining roles and responsibilities, and designating resources.

Related-services and support personnel for students also include those serving in areas coordinated with school programs such as transportation, speech pathology, audiology, psychological services, physical and occupational therapy, recreation, counseling, library and media service, medical and school health, social work, parent counseling and training, cultural agencies, and transition-to-work and internship supervisors. Special resource services from outside the school include a multitude of other roles, ranging from Scout leaders, to 4-H leaders, private music and art instructors, and synagogue or church-school teachers. There also are media, speakers, mentors, tutors, judges of events and products, and community partners. Extender services can be provided by libraries, parks, colleges, industries, businesses, and professions. Special activities, managed through clubs, workshops, interests groups, travel, and the like, are an important part of special services for special needs. Doctors and dentists teach and advise within their professional roles. Some request information from school personnel for their medical interventions and welcome interaction with teachers.

A frequently overlooked educational personnel source that more and more schools are learning to value and use is senior citizens, including grandparents of students, to instruct, demonstrate, relate experiences, and model for children and youth. Schools and universities also house a variety of support personnel that can assist with student needs. In addition, they are catalysts for the increasingly popular practice of using community resources to accentuate learning (Dettmer, 1980). Another source for student learning is other students. Cooperative and collaborative learning activities, peer tutoring, and coaching give students opportunities to share their own new knowledge and provide service to others.

Consulting teachers find it helpful to have a resource notebook of potential resource personnel. A school-related group such as the Parent Teacher Organization or Association for Retarded Citizens, committee of teachers, or a students' group seeking a service project, could develop a Community Resources Information Page format for the school and compile individual pages into a Community Resources Notebook. Persons or agencies targeted for inclusion in the notebook could be contacted for their permission to be included and for information to enter on the page. Figure 10.2 shows an example of a resource template. The notebook should be reviewed and updated periodically to keep it current and useful.

Each school also has a number of ancillary personnel without whom school life would be uncomfortable and disorganized. These include people in support roles such as food-service staff, secretaries, transportation staff, paraeducators, custodians, and volunteer aides.

FIGURE 10.2   Community Resources Information Page

Name of Individual or Agency _____

Phone Number _____   Fax _____   E-Mail _____

Address _____

Occupation or Emphasis _____

Area(s) of Expertise/Contribution _____

Preference for Grade Level or Staff Area _____

Preference for Group Size with Which to Work _____

Time of Day Preferred _____

Preference for Day(s) of Week and Month(s) of Year _____

Maximum Times Would Care to Assist in a Year _____

Special Arrangements Needed _____

Special Equipment Required _____

Any Further Clarifications _____

Record of Dates Contributed, with Description of Activities of the Contribution:

_____

_____

For More Information Contact (Resource Personnel) _____

                                                    (School Personnel) _____

Just as the roles of consultant, consultee, and client are interrelated and interchangeable according to the focus of the consultation, the roles and responsibilities of related, support, and ancillary service personnel interrelate and interchange according to the part each plays in the student's education. For example, transportation personnel are integral to the programs of special education students beyond picking them up and delivering them home again. They are a key link between home and school, being the first to see the student in the morning and often the last of the school staff to see them in the afternoon. They transport students from school to school and program to program while adhering to tight schedules and sometimes unpredictable weather and traffic conditions. They can play an active role in a referral process for special education and can also help with intervention programs. They may be involved as partners in reward and reinforcement systems for students or in extending learning activities beyond the classroom.

Transportation staff support by respecting student differences and needs and by collaborating with other school staff for schedules, incentives, and other modifications. One driver of the special education bus displays school work in the bus. She also has a chart for the "Star" bus student of the week. She explains that because it is the special education bus, she wants to make their bus ride special. She makes an effort to collaborate with teachers, adhering carefully to special schedules so students are not late or left stranded at a building.

Sometimes transportation staff might be the consultant, and a teacher for an educable mentally handicapped student could be the consultee who needs information about the student's social interaction or neighborhood environment. A librarian could be a consultant to help a gifted program teacher, as consultee, select and locate resources. The school psychologist could contribute valuable information about the purposes, interpretation, and uses of tests. The training of counselors in both individual guidance and group guidance techniques makes them helpful resources in staff development activities and problem-solving sessions. School nurses and social workers contribute valuable data in consultations and staffings. They are often able to target seemingly insignificant data toward important aspects of problem-identification. An understanding custodian has always been regarded as a teacher's best friend and helpmate in the school setting. This is especially relevant to the special education teacher's responsibilities. Consultants can encourage custodians to be involved in planning and monitoring special programs for students with special needs. All of these examples extend the concept of interchanging consultant, consultee, and client roles, as suggested in Chapter 1.

Related Services in Inclusive Schools

Other chapters have focused on the teacher's restructured role in inclusive schools, but roles of other service personnel also must be modified. When students need services such as physical therapy, occupational therapy, or speech therapy, a decision must be made about where to provide the service. In many inclusive schools the therapist removes the child from the group while providing the service directly in the classroom. This arrangement can cause considerable apprehension on the part of other teachers (Schlax, 1994). These fears can be reduced by having only one therapist at a time working with the child and by integrating therapies with the classroom routine.

The majority of students with special needs are assigned to general classrooms, even though they may attend resource rooms or work with consulting teachers for a portion of the school day. In order to serve their special learning and behavioral needs, support services and classroom extender services must be integrated into their educational programs. Pearce (1996) stresses the need to work with specialists in order to adapt curriculum to special needs. She recommends that special education teachers work with all students in the classroom to plan activities that classroom teachers could not do on their own. Having another teacher alongside may take getting used to, but is well worth the effort when they can get twice as much done.

Sometimes therapists can work with all the students in the class to avoid singling out those with disabilities. When therapies such as physical therapy or occupational therapy require space, it might be possible to provide it in the classroom. Schlax (1994) suggests that the physical therapist and occupational therapist can assist one another by reinforcing common goals for a student whenever each is in the classroom. Speech therapists can often provide discrimination, language expression, or vocabulary lessons to an entire class of students. Many classroom teachers welcome such a partnership, which can occur as a normal part of the classroom routine such as during "show-and-tell".

A group of teachers in a special project to include students with severe disabilities in their general education classrooms reported that the most helpful part of the specialist support they received included: Shared framework and goals; physical presence; validation of the teacher's contribution; and teamwork (Giangreco, Dennis, Cloninger, Edelman, & Schattman, 1993). When problems did appear, they tended to be caused by:

- Separate goals by specialists
- Disruption to the class routine
- Overspecialization in special education practices

Both teacher and consultant needed to consider more fully the context of the regular classroom and the respect of the support for values and needs of that classroom, its students, and its teacher. In this study, which was to analyze the benefits of inclusion for students with severe disabilities, 17 of the 19 teachers reported that they were transformed by their experience. Not only were their attitudes toward the students changed, in some cases the teachers said their attitudes about themselves were changed as well (Giangreco et al., 1993).

Communication, cooperation, and coordination among general educators, special education teachers, support and related personnel, administrators, and ancillary staff will help ensure that collaboration has the best possible likelihood of success as an integral educational process. Several concrete steps can be taken. See Figure 10.3 on integrating efforts when collaborating with specific role groups.

Using Library and Media Resources

Libraries and media centers are repositories of tremendous amounts of information. Conceivably, no other public service center has changed more than the library in the past half-century. It now is a teaching and learning system, a network for interactive learning, a storehouse for artifacts to enhance learning, a workplace for development of interests and skills, and much

FIGURE 10.3   Integrating Efforts through Collaboration

Collaborative consultants can integrate and collaborate with other educators in these ways:

With general education teachers:
1. Establish joint ownership of the student and the learning situation.
2. Respect the views of all.
3. Keep problems "in house."
4. Request regular interaction and feedback from them.

With other special education colleagues:
1. Openly deal with the discomfort of having others give critique and feedback.
2. Arrange and coordinate planned interactions.
3. Together develop support systems.

With support and related-services personnel:
1. Become more knowledgeable about their roles and responsibilities.
2. Make sure to integrate major ideas they produce.
3. Plan and implement student programs that reflect coordinated involvement and not fragmentation.

With building administrators:
1. Inform them in as brief and practical manner as possible.
2. Don't carry tales from a school/district to others.
3. Don't be a spy, or judge, even if asked.
4. Request regular feedback as to your own effectiveness.

With attorneys/hearing officers:
1. State your credentials, certifications, training, and experiences relative to the case.
2. State the nature and extent of knowledge about the student.
3. Discuss assessments, curricula, and modifications used, and their reliability, validity, and appropriateness.
4. Explain all terms, using no acronyms or jargon.
5. Remain calm, honest, and cooperative.

With legislators:
1. Be brief, accurate, and substantiating in all material delivered.
2. Thank legislators for their past interest and help.
3. State situations realistically without unreasonable demands.
4. Consider the whole picture, as the legislator must, and not just your own primary interest.

With the public:
1. Be perceptive about issues of culture, diversity, conflicting interests.
2. Demonstrate reasonable expectations while upholding standards and delivering challenges.
3. Express your dedication to students and commitment to excellent schools.

more. The "Shhhhh!" of the librarian has been replaced with the hum and clicks of computers, the queries and responses of information-seekers and technical assistants, the sliding of printed materials into organizers, and the buzz of small groups sharing information or problem-solving. Many times corners and tables of libraries and media centers are set up for instructing students with special needs using modified curriculum materials and strategies.

In order to use this rich educational resource most efficiently, consultants and collaborators should be familiar with basic units, including:

Educational Resources Information Center (ERIC), a U.S. federal information system of 16 clearinghouses throughout the country

Education Index, an index of titles and citations arranged by topic headings and author headings

Reader's Guide to Periodical Literature, titles and citations covering a wide variety of topics

CompuServe, Dialog, and similar on-line databases

Educational journals and reviews (See Vockell and Asher (1995) for a table of the fifteen most frequently cited journals by *Encyclopedia of Educational Research.*)

Interlibrary loans, another useful source of information for the needs of consulting teachers working with wide ranges of student learning and behavioral needs

Paraeducators/Paraprofessionals/Paras

The role of paras in the inclusionary classroom was introduced in Chapter 9. French and Pickett (1997) provide insight into the history of employing paraprofessionals and the numbers that now assist in U.S. schools. They cite the post-war shortage of teachers in the 1950s, federal legislation such as Title 1 and Head Start in the 1960s and 1970s, and later, P.L. 94-142 and IDEA, as catalysts for the surge in employment of paras. They distinguish paraeducators as paraprofessionals who work alongside school professionals. In this book we use the term *para* to refer to an individual sometimes called paraprofessional, paraeducator, teacher assistant, or teacher aide. Of the 500,000 paras who worked in schools in 1995, some 250,000 were employed in special education programs.

French and Pickett offer several reasons for schools' increased reliance on paras, including large caseloads of special education teachers, need for more individualized attention to students at risk from economic disadvantage or other circumstances, and the cultural and linguistic fit of many paras who live in the school's community. They raise serious questions about the preparation of paras, noting that only one state—Kansas—mandates training for its paraeducators. A few other states have long-standing credentialing policies or funds for some mass training. French and Pickett also note the overlap between special education teacher and para, with fuzzy responsibilities and role lines blurred. They target lack of training to supervise paras as a problem, and they stress the need for research on circumstances and issues affecting training, roles, supervision, community impact, and recruitment of paraeducators.

Salzberg and Morgan (1995) concur that teachers are not prepared to supervise paras. Only a few teacher-education institutions include this topic in their programs. One area of particular importance that they target in regard to para and teacher relationships and success of the supervisory relationship is personality variables. Interpersonal differences may become problems when there are large discrepancies in age, culture, socio-economic group, or ethnic background. Salzberg and Morgan propose that few teachers entered teaching expecting to direct other adults, and very few were prepared to do so.

In spite of these shortcomings in addressing the roles and responsibilities of paras, there are benefits. They can be links to the community, they cost the schools relatively little, and they are willing to work with students who have special needs. They tend to view these students in different and positive ways and to contribute information that helps teachers and consultants provide appropriate learning experiences for their students. Much more effort should be made toward preparing teachers to collaborate with and supervise them, recruiting exemplary paras in spite of the appallingly low salaries, preparing them well, and then delineating roles and responsibilities so that there will be mutual understanding among educators.

Supervising Paras.   The para–supervisor relationship can be likened to a couple on the ballroom dance floor. The two gracefully move together to the rhythm of the music, one partner leading and the other following. Both partners use the same basic dance steps, but the unique timing of special moves are guided by the leading partner who makes certain they do not bump other dancers or wander off the dance floor. The co-teacher relationship, on the other hand, can be likened to a musical duet. Each follows the same score, but with different, preplanned parts. They must keep in rhythm and harmony to create a pleasant experience.

The para–supervisor relationship becomes less obvious when a para is employed to work with a team. Perhaps it can be likened to an orchestra where the para plays an important role in a performance that is directed by a conductor. The team will need to determine who is to assume supervisory responsibilities. The best selection will likely be a person who:

- Holds ultimate responsibility for the outcomes.
- Is in the best position to direct performance.
- Can provide training for the assigned duties.
- Can observe and document para performance.

Supervision requires unique skills and behaviors. A supervisor must plan, schedule, and evaluate another person's actions. The supervisor is responsible for the para's actions, and the para is accountable to the supervisor. No matter how much education or training a person has before taking the position as para (most bringing very little formal training, according to French & Pickett, 1997), a supervisor should provide on-the-job training. For example, co-teachers may develop a teaching plan that includes the para for part of the implementation. For the plan to be successful, the supervisor or co-teacher must train the para to implement the appropriate parts.

Special education teachers may be assigned as many as five or six paras whom they must supervise. French (1997) lists seven functions associated with para supervision, which include:

1. Planning (see Chapter 9 for discussion of this topic)
2. Managing schedules (prioritizing tasks, preparing schedules)
3. Delegating responsibilities (assigning tasks, directing tasks, monitoring performance)
4. Orienting (introducing people, policies, procedures, job descriptions)

5. On-the-job training (teaching, coaching new skills, giving feedback)
6. Evaluating (track performance, summative evaluation of job performance)
7. Managing work environment (maintaining communication, managing conflicts, solving problems)

The more individuals with whom the para works, the more complex the supervision processes. When paras are in the general classroom most of the school day, it is critical for the classroom teacher to be involved in the supervision. In some instances the classroom teacher may take major responsibility for supervising the para. If communication processes among all parties are open, this arrangement can work well. Sometimes, however, confusion occurs.

Managing Schedules.   We have discussed elsewhere the challenges of arranging consultant and co-teaching schedules. Those challenges are magnified when several paras are part of the scheduling demands. Since schedules are likely to change, it is helpful for everyone to have a schedule each week that indicates who does what, and when, and where. The schedule should be available to all special-service staff and the building secretary.

One inclusive school prepared master schedules for all support staff, including special teachers and paras. In order to meet the diverse needs of classroom teachers, they devised another schedule for volunteer paras. Every Friday morning teachers completed a request-for-support form indicating what type of support they needed the following week, often during an activity period when several students would need help. These requests were noted on a master schedule and paras were assigned accordingly. This system was particularly helpful to volunteer paras. They usually could check the schedule and go to assignments without further directions.

Finding Time.   The challenge of finding time to plan and discuss student needs mirrors those issues discussed elsewhere for collaborating teachers when paras work in inclusive

---

APPLICATION **10.1**

Supervising the Para

Consider the example of Sue and Jaime. Sue is one of three paras assigned to Jaime, a teacher of students with behavior disorders. Sue is an experienced para and has clear notions of what she should do in the inclusive classroom. Jaime told Sue just to be in the classroom to intervene whenever a particular student gets off task or refuses to do work. She is not to help the student with the work, but just take steps to keep him "under control." Sue doesn't think that is a good way to use her time. She wants to help this student or others who might be having difficulty with the assignment. She and the regular classroom teacher think a para should help clarify confusing information and outline class lectures on the chalkboard as she did in the previous school where she was assigned. Is it appropriate for Jaime to require certain behavior of Sue even when she isn't comfortable with it? Does the classroom teacher have a voice here? How might this conflict be resolved?

schools. Teachers and paras in self-contained special classes may have common breaks, but that is not likely when paras are working in a different classroom, as is often the case with inclusive schools. In an ideal situation at least 20 minutes a day is set aside for para–supervisor planning.

Role Clarification.   Para roles are more clearly defined in self-contained classrooms, but in inclusive schools much confusion can exist. Communication and problem-solving processes described in Chapters 5 and 6 are needed to work out such conflicts. Problems may be avoided or attenuated if the supervisor clearly writes out role or job descriptions at the beginning of the school year. These written descriptions can always be changed by mutual agreement, but are a necessary part of supervision.

Monitoring Para Performance.   Most supervisors are uncomfortable with the task of monitoring para performance and providing corrective feedback when needed. This task may not be as discomforting as first appears.

   1. *Tell paras exactly what you expect.* Preparing job descriptions will get you off to a good start. Say, "When you help co-teach science, don't try to answer questions. Show the student how to find answers in the textbook or other resource materials," rather than, "Would you please help students in the science class during study time?"

   2. *Commend appropriate behavior.* Everyone likes to have his or her good performance acknowledged. Therefore, it would seem that supervisors can never praise paras too much. But they can. Only commend appropriate performance and make it clearly linked in time with the para action, such as "Good job helping Kim with that assignment." Identify the particular accomplishment, as in "Nice work showing Kim how to find vocabulary words in the index."

   3. *Ignore some behavior.* Sometimes it is best just to ignore a minor but inappropriate action. A powerful management tool is to "catch someone being good," or notice and support those who are doing what is expected. Compliment paras when they perform as directed.

School Administrator Role in Collaboration

The role and responsibilities of the building principal are just short of overwhelming. So many school issues compete for their time and energy that consultants need to make special efforts to accommodate administrator schedules when they ask for their participation in consultation and collaboration.

   Administrators can assist staff immeasurably by freeing up teacher time, staggering schedules, and arranging for substitutes so that consultation and collaboration among school personnel can take place. They can work with consultants to clarify their roles and ensure that they obtain parity among the school staff. One of their most significant contributions is to encourage interaction and staff development among school personnel. When in-service and staff-development sessions are arranged, promoted, and *attended* by building principals, the multiplier ripple effects are profound. It is vital that all related-services and support personnel are included in in-service and staff-development sessions so they are aware of special needs and programs being implemented to serve those needs.

Labels and categories for school personnel are relatively unimportant within a collaborative climate. The service provided for a child's need determines the role. Thousand et al. (1986) emphasize that schools have many natural, untapped pools of skills and interest across a wide range of unassigned areas. When teachers can form teams and move among roles, positive ripple effects occur. Examples are increased adult-to-pupil ratio in a learning program and ability of the school to provide more personalized instruction (Nevin, Thousand, & Paolucci-Whitcomb, 1990).

In order to facilitate appropriate support services for students, consultants can do several things:

- Become knowledgeable about the roles and responsibilities of support personnel.
- Strive for IEPs and informal learning plans that include all facets of the student's learning and involve all roles that will help the student succeed.
- Within the bounds of necessary confidentiality and ethical school practices, ask support personnel for their viewpoints and opinions about helping students with special needs.
- Inform them about the consultation role, schedule, and responsibilities.
- Monitor the student's performance across all kinds of school, home, and community learning in a variety of situations.
- Provide time in the teachers' schedules for co-planning and co-teaching.
- Show ongoing support for inclusionary practices.
- Include support-services personnel in staff-development activities, encouraging their involvement and collaboration.
- Have specific in-services for them to provide awareness and encourage collaboration.

Lugg and Boyd (1993) caution against "contrived collegiality" that is administratively regulated and compulsory. They contend such an environment erodes trust and communication, even that which may already be in effect. Therefore, they recommend restructuring schools into schools-within-schools, where teachers and students are organized into teams that work and play together for sustained periods of time—perhaps over several years—so that strong interpersonal relationships can flourish.

Along these lines of schools-within-schools, Murphy (1995) proposes the whole-faculty study group concept as a way of implementing school-improvement initiatives. Teachers can be organized into small study groups of four to six individuals who meet weekly for about an hour to have collegial interchange that focuses on whole-school improvement and how to help students learn more.

Staff developers LaBonte, Leighty, Mills, and True (1995) set up study groups of teachers, creating collaborative time for them to improve programs and share new practices, and link whole-school improvement with increased student achievement. One focus-team format consisted of having the principal and four or more teachers from each participating school attend a week-long institute and develop a plan for leading their schools in implementation of whole-faculty study groups. These educators believe that whole-faculty study groups are promising vehicles for school improvement that increases both student and teacher learning. They assert that staff developers must create interagency collaboration in order to bring about changes that increase student achievement. (Professional development will be the focus of Chapter 11.)

Consultants as Coordinators for Interagency Collaboration

A vast array of social service agencies exists for serving students with special needs; however, their services often overlap and many are large, unwieldy bureaucracies with a maze of bewildering requirements (Guthrie & Guthrie, 1991; Hodgkinson, 1989). The situation calls for extensive collaboration among agencies for productive integration of services. Educators may be the most feasible linkage in cooperation and coordination among organizations and agencies that serve children with special needs. As budget constraints restrict the continuation or growth of many educational and social programs, special education consultants can play pivotal roles in the future for serving children with special needs. They are in good positions to become effective, cost-efficient links between education and other social agencies.

It will be a challenge for educators to form new paradigms that decompartmentalize services for students with special needs. Guthrie and Guthrie (1991) state that service providers must step outside the boundaries of their job descriptions on occasion to do what needs to be done for students. They suggest going to community centers, schools, and homes, devoting more time than usual to families and outside resources. These functions are compatible with the processes and content familiar to those in school-consultation roles. Guthrie and Guthrie warn against the "all-talk, no action" posture, excessive jargon, and failure to follow up. These points are readily recognizable to school consultants, who have developed skill in avoiding such pitfalls.

"If you think interpersonal and interagency consultation is challenging, wait until you try interagency collaboration!" says one experienced educational consultant. Turf issues, lack of clarity on fiscal responsibilities, and shared personnel, facilities, and equipment agreements are among the barriers to successful interagency collaboration. On the other hand, many educators have had experience with interagency collaboration while working with Interagency Coordinating Councils, as established under Part H of P.L. 99-457 (the Handicapped Infant and Toddler Program), and with Community Transition Councils, as established under P.L. 101-476. Others have valuable experience working with other human service agencies in developing programs such as "One-Stop Shopping" and "Wrap-around" programs. These experiences in collaboration, difficult though they may have been, will serve participants well as they assume new roles in interagency collaboration.

As a process, collaboration is a means to an end rather than an end in itself. The desired end is to engender more effective educational outcomes for students with special needs. Schools are not alone in their responsibility for removing barriers that keep students from succeeding in the adult world. Personnel in mental health, employment and training, child development, recreation, health, and welfare services, as well as education, have a vital interest in promoting school success for all children. (See Figure 10.4.)

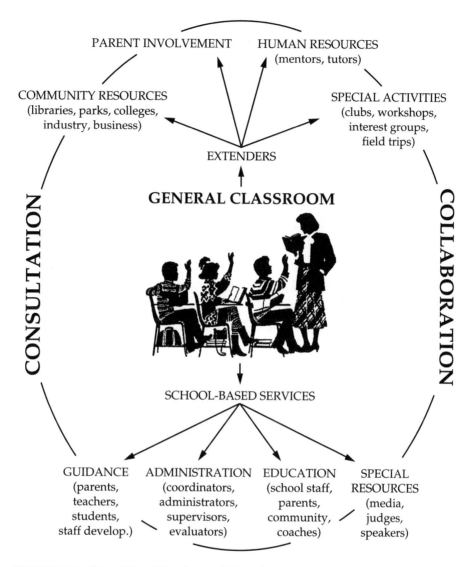

FIGURE 10.4   School-Based Services and Extenders

Coordination of Related Services

Many of the families of children with special needs face a multitude of problems and require services beyond the realm of education. Too often these services are fragmented without a coherent, binding strategy to meet basic family goals (Bruner, 1991). The Education and Human Services Consortium (Melaville & Blank, 1991) proposes that education, health, and human service agencies join each other as co-equals in orchestrating the delivery of services

APPLICATION **10.2**

Important Roles for Student Development

Use the technique of brainstorming, as an individual, with a small group, or as a large-group activity, to think of ways the following roles are vital for fullest development of student potential. Add to the list of roles if other viable ones emerge.

Special Education Facilitators

General Classroom Teachers

Building Administrators

School Psychologists

Educational Policy-makers

Advocates for Schools

Educational Psychologists

University Faculty for Teacher Education

Pediatricians

Entrepreneurs and Innovators in the Public
    Sector

Educational/Social/Psychological Researchers

Staff Developers/Curriculum Coordinators

Diversity Specialists

Media Specialists/Librarians

Textbook/Curriculum Materials Publishers and
    Authors

Mentors/Talent Coaches

Special Education Program Evaluators

Families/Parents/Siblings/Extended Family

Senior Citizens/Statesmen and Stateswomen/
    Notables

to children and families. System-level collaboration is based on the reality that no one agency can provide all necessary services for children with disabilities and their families. Collaborative strategies can:

- Help provide better services to families who are part of several human service systems.
- Keep children and families from falling through the cracks by ensuring that they receive needed services.
- Reduce environmental risks to children.

When systems collaborate, they reduce service duplication, reduce the total cost of services, ensure fewer gaps in services, minimize conflict, and clarify responsibility.

Interagency collaboration includes these elements (Bruner, 1991):

1. Jointly developing and agreeing to a set of common goals and directions.
2. Sharing responsibility for obtaining the goals.
3. Working together to achieve the goals, using the expertise of each collaborator.

There are some common elements of interagency collaboration which contribute to the effectiveness and efficiency of efforts:

Collaborative attitude. Recognize the need for collaboration and take the time to develop positive relationships among the team. Joint ownership will reduce conflict and problems.

Written guidelines. Formulate a written statement of philosophy that stands as the measure of all policies and actions. Delineate roles, responsibilities, and agreements for shared resources.

Team leadership. Leadership roles should be assigned, but they can be shared. Coordination and technical assistance are important roles.

Staff development. Cross-agency training can foster positive relationships and promote the development of the skills and processes of collaboration.

Collective input and supportive environment (Weber, 1994). Clarity of purpose comes from sharing obstacles individuals and agencies face and solutions they envision. Sharing relevant experiences and insights reduces barriers from cultural differences and promotes understanding and empathy.

Identifying and implementing collaborative strategies and evaluating their impact are particularly challenging. The ultimate goal is the future success of students with special needs by eliminating or reducing difficulties that place them at risk—infant mortality, delinquency, youth unemployment, child abuse and neglect, drug involvement, suicide, mental illness, and poverty. Interagency collaboration is not a "quick fix." It is time-consuming and process-intensive. It takes commitment and flexibility to discover new roles and relationships. These new roles and responsibilities utilize collaborative skills that require wide knowledge and much practice.

Sources for Assistance

Every community, large or small, urban or rural, accessible or isolated, wealthy or poor, has agencies and potential resources that can contribute meaningfully to learning programs for the special needs of children and adolescents. The consulting teacher will find it helpful to develop a directory of referral agencies, with addresses and phone numbers, to have available for consultations and staffings. As one example, a consulting teacher in a mid-size town in the Midwest prepared a referral directory containing more than one hundred sources of assistance. Some were national sources which could be called with a hot-line or an 800 number, such as the Missing Children's Network. Others were state-level agencies, including the Resource Center for the Handicapped. Still others were county agencies,

---

APPLICATION 10.3

Assessing Strengths of the Team

Organize into small groups of three to five persons. Discuss the strengths that this group as a team could provide toward a collaborative effort of planning interventions for a student with disability or giftedness in the inclusionary classroom. A second phase of this activity could involve using a case-study approach to demonstrate those strengths in preparing an IEP or a classroom modification for the student described in the case study.

such as the County Family Planning Clinic. But within this average town, many sources were available "just down the street," including a crisis center and a community theater.

Another special education teacher in a large town with a land-grant university found more than 200 agencies, from Alcoholics Anonymous and ACLD (Association for Adults and Children with Learning Disabilities) through Living with Cancer Group and MADD (Mothers Against Drunk Driving), to World Friendship Organization and Young Mom's Group. Resourceful consultants will involve personnel regularly from a variety of agencies to collaborate in planning and implementing student programs that provide support coordinated to students' special needs.

Generating Proposals for External Funding

One of the most welcomed resources that school personnel can contribute is a funded grant proposal. Grant money is available from a wide variety of sources, including federal funds, state funds, private donations, foundations, local business, fund-raising activities, and corporations (Zimet, 1993). These sources provide funds with programs and projects in mind that fit their philosophies and goals. They set their own procedures, which must be followed explicitly by entrants if they wish to be in the running for receiving the grant.

Several benefits can be gained from submitting a collaborative grant proposal. The first is the collaboration experienced by the team, whether or not the grant proposal is funded. Few significant proposals are developed in these times that do not include a number of colleagues interacting to conceptualize and develop the plan and to carry out the project after it is funded. Some people have major roles and others serve in minor ways, but all can profit in tangible and intangible ways. Another benefit is the collection of resources and support needed to meet the goals of the grant. As resources are targeted, and letters of support are generated, more people become involved as supporters and advocates of school programs.

When a grant proposal is funded, then the benefits soar. Money and resources become available for carrying out projects that were only dreams or wishes before funding. This has an energizing, morale-boosting effect that can reverberate throughout a school system. The amounts of money do not need to be sizable for these positive outcomes to be realized. Some of the most invigorating projects have resulted from relatively small grant funds. The projects with the highest payoffs are those that generate ripple effects well beyond the grant funding.

School consultants and collaborators, particularly those who have significant staff-development responsibilities, are in ideal positions to seek grant funds. Even larger districts that employ grant-writers can use the participation of these personnel productively. School districts should designate individuals to be trained in grant-seeking techniques, for there are some important procedures that are vital to success of the endeavor.

Successful proposals emanate from an identified need. A good match must be found between that need and the philosophy and goals of an appropriate funding source. The proposal must be prepared correctly and submitted on time. Proposals that are not funded should not be cast aside, but critiqued thoroughly for possible revision and resubmission.

Proposal development begins with an idea and has two phases: (1) planning; and (2) preparation. The most productive strategy usually is to spend about 80 percent of time and energy on planning the project, and the remaining 20 percent on writing the proposal. Those who switch these priorities often end up with weak projects that are hard to direct even if funded.

Funding Sources

Two general sources of funding are available—public agencies and private foundations. Most companies give some money away as part of their tax structure, and the grant-developer's challenge is convincing companies to give part of it to them (Zimet, 1993). Experts in grant production advise that requirements for proposals are somewhat different between public and private sources, so they must be studied carefully.

Preparing the Proposal

Grant-writing is a combination of technical writing and creative writing (Zimet, 1993). Three mistakes must be avoided at all costs: Failing to read instructions diligently; disregarding specific topic areas and funding source matches; and ignoring deadlines. Because proposal preparation is hard work, astute grant-writers follow basic steps to avoid major pitfalls. They:

1. *Identify a need.* What is the problem that stems from that need? Is it potentially fundable? For example, high-priority topics for successful grant proposals in the mid-1990s included: gangs, violence, drugs, world-class standards, teachers for providing education to meet those standards, math and science education, teen pregnancy, inclusion, integrated curriculum, diversity, and computer literacy for both young people and adults.

2. *Explore the research base* for the identified need. Watch for trends and for connections that link trends and fields.

3. *Get together a team* of productive people. Note the points in Chapter 3 about having a variety of skills and learning styles on the team. Having multiple perspectives and a wide range of competencies will vastly improve the proposal. Teams are particularly helpful for collecting the demographic data that will be required for properly executed proposal preparation.

4. *Identify possible funding sources.* Funding sources are listed in the *Federal Register,* phone 1-202-260-9950. However, for some enthusiastic grant-seekers, this source often is too little and/or it appears too late to give a proposal the attention it needs. So other sources should be consulted, including:

Federal Grants and Contracts Weekly; 1-800-221-0425
Foundation Grants Index; 1-800-424-9836
Foundation Reporter Corporate Giving Directory; 1-800-877-8238
Education Funding Research Council; 1-800-876-0226

These sources and others are available at many libraries. With telecommunications software and a modem, some sources can be obtained online. The Internet includes sources such as the Department of Education at http://www.ed.gov *or* at http://www.fdncenter.org. Each site has links to other sites and additional, more specific information.

5. *Obtain the guidelines* for the selected funding source(s). A guidelines packet is called "Request for Proposal," or RFP. From this point on, each step of the process has an admonition—*Read the guidelines!* At this stage read to be sure there is a good fit between your idea and the funding source. Look for the ability of that source to meet your budget request, for directions on how to apply, for criteria to be used in evaluating the proposal, and most of all, for the *application deadline.* A proposal, even a superior one, submitted late is no proposal at all. The second way to guarantee that the proposal will not be considered is failure to stay within the guidelines.

6. The next step is to *design the project.* As stressed earlier, this phase should take up the major time and energy directed toward the project. Again, read the guidelines thoroughly and often. Typical parts of a proposal are: Description of who will manage the project; personnel involved in implementing and maintaining the project; description of project activities; evaluation plan for assessing the project's effectiveness; dissemination of project results; budget and justification; continuation of the project beyond funding dates; letters of support; and of course, the ubiquitous forms that must be filled out accurately and completely. These parts are weighted in varying percentages to determine the proposals ranking among all submitted proposals, and those weight values are listed in the guidelines. Subcategories under description of the project include expected outcomes that tie back to the problem, objectives that relate to each of the activities, plan of operation, time line, data-collection procedures, and activities.

7. *The budget must be adequate* for the project, but not "padded." All items should be tied to the activities of the project and the key personnel costs involved. If set too low, it would signal poor planning that could undermine the project. Budgets provide for indirect costs (overhead), any cost sharing or subcontracting for services, and primarily, direct costs of the proposed project—salaries and fringe benefits, equipment, supplies and materials, travel (which is getting quite restrictive with many funding agencies), consultant fees, computer expenses, printing and duplicating, postage and telecommunication, along with other direct costs specific to the focus of the project.

8. *Interagency collaborative support* is a very desirable component of most grant projects, and a requirement of some agencies for submitted proposals.

9. *Establish contact with the funding agency* and put to good use any suggestions their program officers have for proposal development.

10. The most singularly important step is to *meet the deadline.* If it is not met, the proposal is eliminated and the time, energy, and costs expended in producing it are wasted.

When proposals are received by the funding agency, they are scanned for ten or twelve key elements, with the first four or five receiving the most attention (Shanteau, 1997):

1. *Identity.* Are the persons submitting well known to the agency?
2. *Topic.* Is it an appropriate topic for the program?
3. *Funding level.* Is the requested amount within the guidelines?
4. *Duration.* Is it within acceptable time limits?
5. *Plan.* What is the approach?
6. *Procedure.* What procedures will be used?
7. *References.* Who is cited, and in what related fields?
8. *Identity of the developer.* What is the background?
9. *Budget.* Do the categories and amounts make sense?
10. *Consultants.* Who are they, and do they add to the team?
11. *Format.* Does the proposal meet requirements?
12. *Double check.* Is anything missing?

If a proposal is not funded, the developer(s) should ask to receive the reviews. Reading reviewer comments is a form of professional development and can help make the next attempt more productive. If the review marks were good, but not quite good enough for the proposal to be selected, the proposal might be revised or modified and resubmitted.

Proposals are funded because of:

The benefits they promise to a targeted population
The uniqueness of the proposal if it is educationally sound
A strong case for local need
Strong collaborative efforts
Local efforts to help with funding
The potential to benefit both local and state or regional efforts
Strong evaluative components
The potential for longevity and positive ripple effects
Justifiable and reasonable budget requests (Stephens, 1994)

Ingredients for pursuing external funding successfully are: An innovative idea, a team of qualified individuals, a close fit with the funding source, and a well-written, persuasive, potentially contributive proposal.

Collaborative school consultants can contribute to their school systems by learning about grant-writing and developing their skills in this area. A grant-writing workshop for the school district is an excellent professional-development activity. (Professional development will be the focus of Chapter 11.) Not only are large-scale grants a boon to service for students, mini-grants to individual teachers or schools for innovative programs are invigorating for staff and students alike.

Collaboration and team effort for serving students' learning and behavioral needs can begin in any worthwhile agency. It takes the effort of all to nurture children and youth in today's complex world. Each element reflects contributions the agency can make to help students realize their potential, as suggested earlier by Figure 10.4. These personnel become powerful partners for education as they create positive ripple effects in homes, neighborhoods, social services, businesses, community organizations, and most of all, schools.

APPLICATION **10.4**

Trying Out the Proposal Plan

As the proposal is being developed, try explaining your plan in 3 minutes to some impartial, objective colleagues or, better yet, to individuals outside the profession whose perspectives you value. If they do not understand it and become enthused by it, your plan probably needs more work or a different focus.

Tips for Using Related-Services and Support Personnel

1. Don't try to do it all by yourself.
2. Develop rapport with librarians. Give advance notice of upcoming topics and try not to make too many spur-of-the-moment requests. Make friends with custodians and refrain from making excessive demands on their time and energy.
3. Keep public remarks about colleagues on a positive, professional level. If you must vent, try using a journal at home. Reviewing it now and then may show you the way to improve the situation.
4. Remember special things about the faculty in each school, and start a card file with comments that will be useful in personalizing the interactions. If you find a news article pertaining in a positive way to a colleague or a student, clip it out and send it along with a congratulatory note.
5. Send a note weekly to teachers of inclusionary classrooms.
6. Advertise successes, both yours and those of classroom teachers. Sometimes teachers are amazed that a student or a situation has shown *any* progress at all.
7. Do not expect the same levels of involvement and commitment from everyone.
8. Write a proposal that results in resources for sharing among schools.
9. Do not try to "go it alone," but look to colleagues for support and counsel.
10. Remember Ralph Waldo Emerson's words, "It is one of the most beautiful compensations of this life that no man can sincerely try to help another without helping himself."

CHAPTER REVIEW

1. Related-services personnel and support personnel represent a wide variety of fields, both in education and beyond. They can contribute to learning programs for students with special needs by collaborating as a team with general and special education teachers to address special needs (disabilities and/or high abilities), interests, talents, transition to school or to work, and achievement (low or high).

2. Paras serve within the inclusive, collaborative school in many helpful ways. Many have little or no formal training, and most earn very low salaries. They often reside in the

school's community and therefore relate well to students culturally and linguistically. Unfortunately, teachers often have little training in supervising the responsibilities and work of paras. There are a number of key elements in supervising and monitoring paras.

3. School administrators have a key role in promoting consultation and collaboration among school personnel. They must provide time, interest, and incentive for teachers to meet, co-plan, implement, and follow through on shared decisions for student learning programs.

4. Successful schools of the future will engage in interagency collaboration, with collaborators working together to achieve goals for serving all students' needs effectively. Bringing about needed school change requires greater emphasis on collaboration and teamwork. School consultation will be an important tool for coordinating health, social, and educational services to help all students, particularly those with special needs.

5. School personnel should seek out external funding to enhance school environments and learning programs for special needs. Such money, even if in small amounts, can be a strong motivational force in carrying out a learning project. Goals of the proposed project should match those of the funding source, and proposal-writers must adhere to the guidelines stringently. The deadline for submitting the proposal must be met.

TO DO AND THINK ABOUT

1. How many support services, related services, and ancillary personnel categories can you list, and how many ways can you find for individuals in these categories to become educational partners with teachers, students, and parents?

2. Develop a plan for ways in which at least three related-services and support personnel could be involved in consultation and collaboration to provide a team effort toward serving students with special needs.

3. Compile a reference list of referral agencies, support groups, and community resources in your area that could be helpful in meeting special needs of students. Preface the list with a brief description of the community where the school is located. Then compare your list with a colleague's list that represents a different type of geographic area.

4. Interview classroom teachers in a variety of subject areas to find out how they would like to collaborate with special education and other support personnel for students' needs. For example, a history teacher may wish for the reading specialist to help with students who have poor reading comprehension; a civics teacher might want a behavioral disorders teacher to explain or model techniques for managing conduct disorders in the classroom; a math teacher might like to have the counselor speak to the class on the importance of math in many career fields, and interesting career opportunities that emanate from a study of mathematics; library and media staff might help journalism students find good subjects for stories.

5. Find out more about several related-services roles that you are not familiar with—for example, the occupational therapist, the audiologist, the social worker, or the school psychologist. What are their responsibilities? What preparation did their roles require? What does a typical day entail for each of them? Interview them and ask their views about consultation and collaboration.

6. With a group of colleagues who have diverse styles and preferences, identify a school need and have a brainstorming session to draft a proposal for funding.

FOR FURTHER READING

Brewer, E. W., Achilles, C. M., & Fuhriman, J. R. (1993). *Finding funding: Grant writing and project management from start to finish.* Thousand Oaks, CA: Corwin Press, Inc.

Carlson, M. (1995). *Winning grants step by step: Support centers of America's complete workbook for planning, developing, writing successful proposals.* San Francisco, CA: Jossey-Bass.

Coley, S. M., & Sheinberg, C. A. (1990). *Proposal writing.* Newbury Park, CA: Sage.

French, N. K., & Pickett, A. L. (1997). Paraprofessionals in special education: Issues for teacher educators. *Teacher Education and Special Education, 20*(1), 61–73.

Ries, J. B., & Leukefeld, C. G. (1995). *Applying for research funding: Getting started and getting funded.* Newbury Park, CA: Sage.

Salzberg, C. L., & Morgan, J. (1995). Preparing teachers to work with paraeducators. *Teacher Education and Special Education, 18*(1), 49–55.

Wienke, W. D. (1996). Book reviews: Current resources for grant writers. *Teacher Education and Special Education, 19*(3), 272–276. This article reviews the Brewer et al., Carlson, Coley et al., and Ries et al. books on grant proposal writing listed above.

11 Professional Development for Collaboration

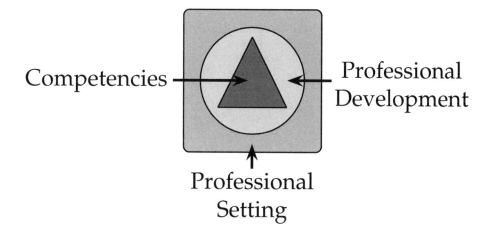

Competencies ← ▲ → Professional Development

↑ Professional Setting

Educators have not been prepared adequately for delivering team-oriented kinds of service (Friend & Cook, 1990; White & Pryzwansky, 1982), and preservice students in teacher-education programs do not receive sufficient training and modeling in collaboration. Nor have many experienced teachers developed the skills needed to carry out collaborative roles effectively. If collaboration is to be an integral part of inclusion, general and special educators must be trained in such techniques (Bassett, Jackson, Ferrell, Luckner, Hagerty, Bunsen, & MacIsaac, 1996).

Professional development is a prime factor in the success of school consultation, collaboration, and co-teaching. When carefully planned, well delivered, and constructively evaluated, it catalyzes these interactive processes. School personnel now in the profession, and teacher-education students preparing to become teachers, need in-service and staff development (ISD) to build the scaffolding that will support their consultation, collaboration, and co-teaching efforts.

Focusing Questions

1. What are the roles, responsibilities, and opportunities for school personnel in regard to professional development?
2. How do in-service and staff development differ?
3. What characteristics and needs of adult learners are important for planning professional development?
4. How should needs for professional development in collaborative consultation be assessed?
5. What target groups and formats should be considered by staff developers in designing and implementing in-service and staff development?
6. What methods and techniques will facilitate productive in-service and staff development?
7. How should professional development be evaluated?

Key Terms

follow-through   job maintenance   personal growth
follow-up   mentor   professional development
incentives   needs assessment   staff development
in-service   needs sensing

Purposes of Professional Development

Staff development serves at least one or more of five overarching purposes (Dettmer & Landrum, 1997):

- *Job maintenance.* Completion of in-service or staff development programs may be required for certification renewal or endorsement for assigned roles.
- *Professional development.* When school reforms such as inclusion and outcomes-based education are initiated, school personnel need information and skills to help them deal with the changes.
- *Role modification.* School reform and restructuring can result in changed roles for a variety of school personnel.
- *Personal growth.* As life-long learners, educators seek more knowledge and new skills that will help them facilitate students' learning.
- *Inspiration.* Educators can be energized by uplifting professional experiences.

The ideal staff development includes goals that address all of these purposes (Dettmer & Landrum, 1997) in personalizing the experience for each participant (see Figure 11.1).

Scenario 11

—(adapted from Dettmer, 1990)

Several teachers at a middle school are conversing in the teachers' workroom on Friday afternoon.

SOCIAL STUDIES TEACHER: What a week! I feel like I've attended to everything this week but students and curriculum. Maybe things will slow down a bit next week.

MATH TEACHER: Guess you didn't look at your office memo yet, hmmm? There's a reminder about the staff development sessions next Tuesday and Thursday mornings before school. Something about working with consultants.

SOCIAL STUDIES TEACHER: Consultants? You mean those experts from more than fifty miles away that breeze in with their briefcases and stacks of transparencies?

MATH TEACHER: I believe this group involves our own special education staff. We're supposed to find out about school consultation service and collaborating with staff who will be consulting teachers.

ART TEACHER: Oh, great. How does that involve me? I had my required course in special education. What I *really* need is a bigger room and more supplies.

SOCIAL STUDIES TEACHER: And if we're supposed to collaborate with these people, where will we find the time?

PHYSICAL EDUCATION TEACHER: Uh-huh. It will be hard enough just carving out the time to go to the *meeting* about it.

MATH TEACHER: Now you know you'll just *love* sitting in that stuffy room trying to stay awake when you'd rather be in your classroom getting set for the day.

SOCIAL STUDIES TEACHER: Well, let me put it this way. If they're not through by 8:20 sharp, I'm leaving!

Roles, Responsibilities, and Opportunities for Professional Development

Educators are caught up in demands for school reform and restructuring efforts that emphasize consultation, collaboration, and teamwork as goals. However, they receive little preparation for the new roles. Teacher education programs may eventually incorporate consultation training into preservice and degree programs, but it will be too late for those who are just completing teacher requirements (novice teachers) and those already on the job (experienced or veteran teachers).

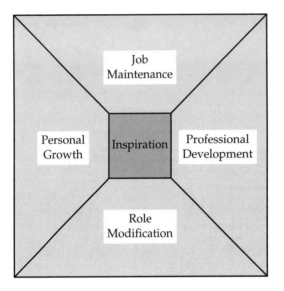

FIGURE 11.1   Purposes of Professional Development

Typical novice teachers, or "rookies," enter the profession having little experience but much enthusiasm. Classroom management was a big concern for this group even before inclusion brought special pressures. They ask questions such as "How can I get everything done? Will I be able to control the class? How can I provide for each child's needs? Will my colleagues respect me? Will my students like me?" Short on experience, they tend to be up to date on current educational research and teaching technology. They often are insecure in pinpointing special needs and prescribing strategies for those needs within the heterogeneous classroom. Furthermore, they have little or no preparation in professional interaction. However, a few undergraduate programs and some student teaching materials (see Rosenberg, L. O'Shea, & D. J. O'Shea, 1998) have begun to include this vital facet of teacher education.

Experienced or veteran teachers are more able to recognize student variability and identify strategies that serve a wide range of needs. They have followed the progress of students through one or several years and know more or less what to expect. Their patterns of teaching and classroom organization may accommodate some facets of student achievement range, and keep the learning environment organized, but they need practical information on contemporary issues such as inclusion, transition, cultural diversity, and accountability. They may be unsure of new philosophies such as class-within-a-class, co-teaching, curriculum compacting, or peer tutoring that seem intrusive and disruptive to procedures they have developed through several years of experience. However, when the boat of education is in swift and changing waters, educators must row forward diligently even to stay where we are, much less make any desired progress. We must be continuous learners within our profession. (See Figure 11.2).

FIGURE 11.2   Differentiated Needs for Staff Development

Educator Level	Current Status	Needs
Preservice	Up-to-date information Enthusiasm Energy	Reality check Confidence Practice with "normal"
Novice	Energy Enthusiasm Motivation	Management skill Self-esteem Incentive to take risks
Veteran	Experience Refined techniques Tried-and-true strategies	New approaches Morale-booster Leadership opportunity
Support Staff	Varied roles Skills for needs Incentive for success	Awareness of whole picture Coordination of efforts Satisfaction
Parents	Knowledge of student Keen interest Advocacy effort	Information on education Support Broad view
Community	Multifaceted knowledge Perspectives on work Multiple skills	Awareness of issues Opportunity to contribute services Ways to support schools

Educational leader Shanker (1993) noted the irony of having car manufacturers set up production teams and train them to build cars *together,* while people in education assume that school staff members will step right into a team concept of doing things with little or no help. He contends, "If it takes 600 courses and 92 hours a year per employee to make a better automobile, it will take that and more to make better schools. And if we're not willing to commit ourselves to this kind of effort, we are not going to get what we want" (Shanker, 1993, p. 3). In more and more schools, professional development is being organized on a total school or district basis and tailored for specific groups of personnel who are engaged in institutional change processes (Reynolds & Birch, 1988). Consultants and consulting teachers should assume an active role in providing leadership for professional development of all school personnel. Their roles are ideal for orchestrating awareness experiences and training activities in a variety of content and process areas, including skills for collaboration and teamwork.

Unfortunately, attitudes toward professional development delivered by in-service and staff development (ISD) are not generally positive. They range from indifference to resentment to disdain. Criticisms cited by Davis (1995) and others in regard to in-service and staff development call attention to the lack of

- Clear purpose
- Relevance

- Meaningful objectives grounded in participant needs
- Integration into the total school program
- Structure and organization
- Emphasis on quality, not quantity
- Practicality and long-term applicability
- Flexibility and choices
- Interest and intrigue
- Attention to adult learner characteristics
- Support from administrators
- Most of all, follow-up activities with continuous evaluation of long-term benefits

Specific problems that contribute to ineffectiveness of staff development in general, and in-services in particular, are

1. Too few teacher preparation programs that put strong emphasis on conducting and participating in ISD
2. Few education texts that feature a post-degree professional development section
3. Too little attention in journals and other professional resources on techniques and processes that ensure high quality ISD
4. Too little networking by educators with other professional organizations interested in education
5. Adherence to old ways of delivering ISD—"dog and pony show" presentations, "inspirational" speakers
6. Lack of time

In order to provide the most constructive staff development experiences possible, planners and presenters need to address several points:

- What are the characteristics of school personnel as adult learners?
- What are the needs of school personnel in serving students with learning and behavior problems?
- What kind of material is most helpful for them?
- How might the material be presented effectively and efficiently?
- How can follow-up and support be provided after the in-service and staff development experiences?

Characteristics of the Adult Learner

First and foremost, participants in ISD must be approached as the adult learners and professionals they are. Participants in in-service and staff development demonstrate several basic characteristics as adult learners. They have (Knowles, 1978)

1. A desire and need to be self-directed in their learning.
2. A wide experience base upon which to draw.

3. A time perspective for learning that is oriented to the here and now.
4. A problem-centered focus on learning.

In his more recent research, Knowles indicates that the most definitive of these four characteristics for educators is the wide experience base they bring to the ISD (Feuer and Geber, 1988). Those who provide ISD for school personnel must recognize that the recipients will be self-directed, experienced, and interested primarily in material they can use at the present for real problems. They desire ownership in the ISD process, and they will resist aspects of staff development that are perceived as attacks on their competence. They can and should serve as resources for their colleagues during professional development activities. And although some fun and reward are refreshing and necessary, adult learners respond best to intrinsic motivations rather than extrinsic motivations.

Staff developers can use knowledge of adult learner characteristics to work more productively with staff development participants. The first step is to acknowledge that each person's perception of the environment reflects and is filtered through his or her own stage of development (Oja, 1980). Because of learning style preferences and variations in ways people process information, as discussed in Chapter 3, presenters of staff development activities must attend to different types of participants. These include (Garmston and Wellman, 1992):

- Those looking for facts, data, and references.
- Those wanting to relate the topic to themselves through interactions with colleagues.
- Those wanting to reason and explore.
- Those who would like to adapt, modify, or create new ideas and procedures.

With these adult learner characteristics in mind, staff developers will need to:

Arrange for participant comfort.
Provide participants with options and choices.
Manage participants' time well.
Deliver practical, focused help.
Follow up on the effectiveness of the experience.

Adult learners value in-service and staff development activities in which they work toward realistic, job-related, useful goals. They need to see results for their efforts with follow-through and feedback experiences, and most of all, with having success in using the activities within their school context.

Guskey (1985) stresses that ISD for busy school personnel must illustrate clearly ways in which new practices can improve student performance, and how these practices can be implemented without too much disruption or extra work. This is particularly important for ISD that focuses on consultation and collaboration, because this kind of professional activity often involves more time and effort initially. In Guskey's model of teacher change, staff development should be designed for the purpose of modifying classroom teaching practices. This causes change in student learning outcomes, which then results in altered teacher beliefs and attitudes. It is a promising concept for promoting collaboration to help students with special needs.

Differentiating In-service from Staff Development

In-service and staff development are two necessary but distinctly different structures for professional growth (Dettmer & Landrum, 1997). In-service is ordinarily a single event or a series of short sessions on a topic of educational interest or school need. School personnel attend in-services on such topics as assertive discipline, critical thinking skills, cooperative learning, drug awareness, student motivation, and a host of other content and process areas. They participate in in-service days as orientation for the new school year, or as refresher sessions during the school term. These one-shot sessions, on a topic of general appeal, are most often provided by an expert, who might be a state official, university professor, professional consultant, corporate leader, or educator from another district. In-service goals generally are directed toward awareness and information.

Staff development, on the other hand, is a process of long-term commitment to professional growth across a broad range of school goals. It should involve all school personnel and usually includes local leadership in place of, or at least in addition to, service by outside consultants. Goals are directed toward involvement, commitment, and renewal. School personnel determine their own needs, develop steps to address those needs, and evaluate their professional growth.

Under ideal circumstances in-service is one useful component of a long-range, ongoing staff development program to provide professional development that serves the needs of teachers, administrators, and support personnel in the school system. Professional development is a fundamental part of the general plan for improving education for all students.

Planning In-service and Staff Development

Many professional growth activities can and should take place among practicing teachers right at the school site, particularly activities designed to improve teacher ability in meeting needs of students at risk. However, the experiences will need to have specific personnel roles assigned to the task of preparing the activity and coordinating it (Howey, Bents, & Corrigan, 1981). "Staff development will never have its intended impact as long as it is grafted onto schools in the form of discrete, unconnected projects" (Joyce, 1990, p. 21). Those who conduct staff development should be selected carefully. They have a much more important role in teacher readiness than has been accorded to them (Joyce, 1990; Dettmer, 1986). Staff development planners and presenters need expertise in content, process, and understanding of the school context.

The consultant role is ideal for coordinating useful in-service and staff development activities. Special education personnel often inherit these responsibilities either as a part of a plan or by default. There are disadvantages as well as advantages in being a "prophet in your own land" for conducting professional development activities, but one of the biggest advantages is knowledge of the school context.

Determining Professional Development Needs

The consultant or consulting teacher who provides staff development will want to assess the needs of other school personnel for the ISD. What do they know about a topic at this point? What do they want to learn? How can they be involved in planning, conducting, and evaluating the staff development for their individual needs? This information should be solicited through needs assessment instruments. Before conducting needs assessment, however, the staff developer should engage in *needs-sensing* activities. In data gathering, it is important to move beyond the surface data to get at what is *really* wanted (Henkelman, 1991). School personnel may assess their needs as wanting classroom strategies for behavior management or for grouping high-ability learners in productive but nonelitist ways. However, the staff developer may sense a need for addressing their concerns about inclusion and accountability for student performance. What do participants *need* to *want* to know? This radar-reading of what the participants-to-be need to know is a subtle but vital precursor to assessing needs. After all, if educators knew what they wanted or needed in every case, they probably would be doing it.

Needs Sensing.   Needs-sensing information allows planners to design formal needs assessment procedures that will reflect the true needs of all involved. For example, if a needs assessment questionnaire asks, "Which of the five topics do you want to know more about?" and the list includes discipline, motivation, computer literacy, alternative grouping structures, and mainstreaming, the ranked results will be somewhat predictable in a typical district. Alternative grouping structures probably would rank low, with discipline and motivation high.

Prior to the needs assessment activity, an interviewer or investigator might ask teachers if they would like to explore possibilities for structuring their classrooms to promote better discipline and stimulate self-regulated learning. If the answer is affirmative, staff development on modified grouping structures could be offered as an area of interest that facilitates discipline as well as student motivation. As another example of needs sensing, teachers could be asked if they wish to explore ways in which children can work together, learn from each other, and share in the results of the learning. If the answer is yes, staff development on cooperative learning could be implemented. For a third example, it would

---

A P P L I C A T I O N **11.1**

Conducting Needs Sensing

Conduct a needs-sensing study by interviewing school personnel to obtain information on these concerns:

1. What do we need to know about to help students in our schools feel good about themselves?
2. How important are test formats, designs, and reporting procedures in helping students learn to the best of their ability?
3. How can we determine which reinforcers work best at what ages and developmental levels and interests?
4. Are we using ancillary and support personnel to the greatest advantage for our students?
5. Does our current material develop critical thinking, or do we need more effort in this area?
6. Do we have the resources for adapting materials to the needs of low-achieving students?
7. In what ways can we build on students' strengths to remediate weaknesses?

be less helpful to assess needs with the question, "Do you want to know more about advanced placement possibilities at your high school?" than to sense where needs lie by asking first, "How might we extend learning of very able students beyond courses that cover grade-level material they have already mastered?"

Needs sensing is a very important precursor to needs assessment. It can be carried out best through

- Classroom observations
- Visits to successful programs, followed by a comparative analysis
- Dialogues and interviews with students, parents, support personnel, and others in the community
- Task force investigations
- Buzz group outcomes

Staff developers should develop instruments that allow target groups to feel able and willing to contribute information.

Needs Assessment.   After needs sensing has been conducted, needs assessment instruments and procedures can be developed from the data. Most school personnel have had experience with completing needs assessments. Formats for needs assessments include:

- Checklists
- Questionnaires and surveys
- Open-ended surveys of areas of concern
- Interviews
- Brainstorm session records

Needs assessment might ask personnel to check topics of need, or to describe their concerns, which can be developed into a staff development activity.

Presenting In-service and Staff Development

Garmston (1988) says that presenting an in-service session or a staff development activity is like giving presents. He suggests the "present" should be something participants (presentees) want or can utilize, personalized to individual taste as much as possible, attractively wrapped, and a bit suspenseful. The presenter should

- Know audience needs and interests
- Conduct the ISD in an interesting, efficient, pleasant manner
- Package the ISD material attractively
- Provide an element of surprise and intrigue
- Deliver follow-up help, support, and additional information

APPLICATION **11.2**

Conducting Needs Assessment

As a needs assessment procedure, ask teachers to check the topics that interest them most, rating them from 5 = greatest need, 4 = strong need, 3 = helpful, 2 = perhaps, and 1 = not needed:

_____ How to create an orderly, positive learning atmosphere

_____ How to develop critical thinking skills

_____ Alternative assessment procedures—including portfolios

_____ Techniques of behavior management

_____ Selecting and using resources beyond the basal texts

_____ Working smarter, not harder, using consulting teachers and resource personnel more effectively

_____ How to modify classroom assignments and/or tests

_____ Ways of dealing with the attention deficit and hyperactivity disorders

It is important to leave space on the instrument for open-ended responses, and to encourage them. After the needs assessments have been returned, summarize the information and use it to plan ISD activities that will be meaningful for participants and relevant to the needs they specified.

Target Groups for In-service and Staff Development

Target groups for school-related in-service and staff development include a wide variety of roles, including classroom teachers; administrators; parents of students; librarians and media specialists; food-service, custodial, and secretarial staff; school board members; special education personnel; paraprofessionals, social workers, and health workers; mentors, talent instructors, and youth directors; pediatricians and dentists; legislators, community leaders, policymakers, and university personnel for teacher education.

Staff development is one of the most productive vehicles for celebrating human diversity. Figure 11.3 provides process, content, and context examples for using staff development to explore ways of using adult differences constructively in consultation, collaboration, and teamwork (Dettmer & Landrum, 1997).

In more and more schools, professional development is being organized on a total school or district basis and tailored for specific groups of personnel who are engaged in institutional change processes (Reynolds & Birch, 1988).

FIGURE 11.3   A Staff Development Focus on Using Adult Differences Constructively in the School Context

Process:

1. Arrange the staff development agenda to have "something for everyone."
2. Allow sufficient time for all to receive and to give input.
3. Structure the environment to facilitate interaction while accommodating individual preferences in style and format.
4. Present information in multimodal format.
5. Pace the interaction so all points are covered, and no input is overlooked.
6. Model support, encouragement, and an appreciation for each person's style or contribution.
7. Strive to have each person receive the kind of outcome he or she values.

Content:

8. Encourage selection and use of curricular materials that recognize diversity and promote constructive use of differences for a better, more interesting world.
9. Host staff development on the topic of adult differences that affect communication and collaboration in the work setting.

Context:

10. Make available books, articles, films, and other materials that celebrate differences. (See "For Further Reading" section as a start.)
11. Display bulletin boards that feature the positive aspects of individual differences among adults in professional settings.
12. Model interest and enjoyment toward the interests, attitudes, and orientations of professional colleagues.

—(adapted from Dettmer & Landrum, 1997)

APPLICATION **11.3**

Planning Professional Development for Related-Services and Support Personnel

Related-services and support personnel were discussed in Chapter 10 as important partners in programs for students with learning and behavior problems. Think of at least two reasons for including each of several pertinent target groups discussed in that chapter as participants in awareness and information sessions about an educational topic. For example, pediatricians and dentists may wish to learn more about characteristics of exceptional children in order to diagnose problems that are brought to their attention. They also may need to know about referral systems in the schools and the possibilities for arrangements such as sheltered workshops for educable mentally handicapped individuals.

Formal and Informal In-service and Staff Development

Just as there are formal and informal approaches to consultation, as discussed in Chapter 2, there are formal and informal approaches to ISD. Formal ISD can be conducted through scheduled sessions, conferences, programs, press releases, presentations, modules, courses, brochures, retreats, and other planned activities. Informal ISD occurs through conversations, observations, reports about one topic that include another aspect of education, memos, references to media productions, software programs, and reading material. One very informal, convenient, and particularly effective in-service technique is to display information, explanations of procedures, invitations to collaborate, and morale boosters on bulletin boards located in places school personnel frequent. The possibilities for both formal and informal ISD activities are limited only by the imagination of the personnel who provide them. Some special education consultants prepare bulletin boards of information about pertinent topics. Others provide staff members with newsletters or columns within existing newsletters. Some request 10 minutes in which to talk to the teachers at faculty meetings.

One enterprising group of teachers organized a series of sessions called "THT—Teachers Helping Teachers," in which they took turns delivering short sessions on topics in which they had expertise. Soon the idea caught on among other teachers. A teacher who had a school-related skill to share was given administrator support to prepare and present a half-day session to teachers in another school within the district. Other teachers followed suit at various times throughout the school year.

A popular practice with some gifted program consultants is to provide calendars of enrichment activities for classroom teachers. As these are used, they become vehicles for carrying out goals of the gifted program, such as creative thinking, independent study, research, and small-group investigations.

A productive in-service could be a brief session to explain the consultant role and what the consultant will be doing. Such endeavors often increase interest in consultation and collaboration dramatically. Consultants also might prepare information sheets of "Questions Frequently Asked About..." and suggest answers for the questions. A bagged treat or a package of peanuts could be stapled on as a friendly, caring gesture.

Learning is often a spontaneous event, occurring as a synergy of learner interest and need, teacher insight, and a supportive environment. This is the ideal "teachable moment." It is not stretching the comparison too much to suggest that there is an ideal "professional development moment." When consultants work with one key teacher and their colleagues observe the results, that is informal staff development. As they ask what they can do to help teachers, then discuss their needs, and finally deliver on their promises to the best of their ability and the resources of their area, they are cultivating professional development among school personnel. Perceptive consultants who seek ways of meeting students' special needs will find that in-service and staff development are appropriate tools. They need not expect all ISD experiences to be formal and planned. Both formal staff development and the informal, or "teachable moment for teachers" approaches, are needed (see Figure 11.4).

The Teachers' Workroom as a Staff-Development Forum

Very little has been written about the teachers' workroom, sometimes known as "the lounge" even though not much lounging goes on there. This lack of attention to the place

FIGURE 11.4 Formal and Informal In-service and Staff Development

Plan	Typically structured Example: Workshop	Usually casual Example: Newsletter column
Method	Designed with care Example: Speaker/discussion	Somewhat spontaneous Example: Hall chat
Evaluation	Data collection Example: Checklist	Reflection Example: Journal note

is surprising, because most teachers drop in at some time or other. Of course, some go quite frequently, and others hardly ever do. Visits usually fall within one of three purposes—physical, social, or personal. There may be the physical benefit of refreshment, a quick "nap," or a restroom break. A few minutes of socialization with adults, squeezed between intensive hours with children and adolescents, is important to some. Personal benefits include attending to professional tasks such as grading papers or reading materials, or getting one's thoughts and plans together before the next barrage of youthful energy bursts into the classroom.

Often teachers just want an opportunity to interact with their professional colleagues and share reflections about teaching practices and student needs. Occasionally this is problematic because the discourse can become quite negative and cynical. When this kind of talk affects one's morale negatively, then going there becomes iatrogenic and should probably be avoided. Nevertheless, the teachers' workroom has long been recognized as a useful hub of interaction, particularly by special education teachers. They have the opportunity to develop rapport with general education colleagues and learn more about their classrooms and students.

It is important that consulting teachers spend enough time in the teachers' workroom ("Don't the special ed people want to be a part of our faculty?"), but not too much ("Don't those special ed people have anything to do?"). Of course, care must be taken to keep professional conversation general in nature. Confidentiality and ethical treatment of information are necessary behaviors for all teachers, and special education teachers in particular. But in this room that is provided for relaxation, reflection, and refreshment, a collaborative spirit can be nurtured and then carried out the door to classrooms and offices beyond.

Suggestions for improving the workroom/lounge in general, and for making it more conducive to collegial interaction, in particular, include (Dettmer, 1989):

- Having a suggestion box in which staff could put ideas for time-savers, student pleasers, or budget easers.
- Having salad luncheon potluck once a month, perhaps on payday. (Set out different salads every half hour or so, if there are many people.) Simpson (1990) describes a "Tuesday Luncheon" concept that has been in effect for many years and supports teachers' efforts to reflect on their instruction.
- Holding a Friday afternoon snack time to encourage teachers to recap the week and think ahead to the next.

- Posting a "Brag Board" on which commendations could be displayed involving anyone and everyone connected with the school, from students to bus drivers to parents of students.
- Providing an "Orientation to Special Education" folder on an accessible table, changing its contents often.

More research is needed on the problems and possibilities of this important facet of school life. However, the consultant will find many opportunities in the workroom for developing rapport with consultees and initiating constructive interactions. This school place must be used wisely and judiciously.

Format for In-service and Staff Development

There is no single pattern for in-service and staff development format that will be appropriate for every school context. However, the following outline is one that can be adapted to a variety of schools and staff needs.

1. Engage in needs sensing.
2. Conduct needs assessment.
3. Select the topic to be featured.
4. Determine the audience to be targeted.
5. Choose a catchy, upbeat title for the activity.
6. Determine presenters who will contribute.
7. Decide on incentives, promotion, and publicity.
8. Outline the presentation.
9. List the equipment and room arrangement needed.
10. Plan carefully the content to be covered.
11. Prepare handouts and visual materials.
12. Rehearse the presentation.
13. Determine an evaluation procedure for the activity.
14. Plan for the follow-up activity.

APPLICATION 11.4
Designing a Teachers' Workroom

In your thoughts, or on sketch paper, create a "dream workroom" that would serve school personnel in their physical, social, and personal needs. What would it look like? What would it sound like? How might a consultant nurture the collaborative spirit there? What would it take to construct and appoint such a room? Could some of your suggestions be carried out right away, with little cost or disruption?

Time for In-service and Staff Development

Time is the enemy when planning in-service and staff development activities. There is not enough of it readily available at student-free times when teachers can concentrate and reflect. Before-school hours and after-school hours might seem workable because participants are coming to school anyway or are required to stay after school for a specific length of time. But teachers find it hard to focus on their own learning at an early hour, when their thoughts are centered on beginning the school day efficiently. By day's end, energy and emotions may be lagging and other responsibilities beckon. Saturday sessions are no more popular and encroach on the family and community life so necessary for sustaining teacher vitality and support.

The arrangement preferred by most teachers is released time. This means that their responsibilities with students will be assumed by others. Loucks-Horsley et al. (1987) recommend providing released time for ISD participants by using substitute teachers, a substitute cadre that conducts planned enrichment activities, roving substitute teachers, or partnerships where one teacher teaches two classes to free up the second teacher.

The substitute cadre eliminates the necessity for detailed lesson planning by the teacher, because the enrichment activities are planned and provided by the cadre. Roving substitutes allow released teachers to have short periods of time for observing, coaching, gathering research data, or assisting in another classroom. Loucks-Horsley et al. (1987) counsel that the time issue is a "red herring," because the problem often lies in the constructive use of time, not its availability.

Released time to attend professional development activities away from the school district must be supported strongly by school administrators. Permission to attend may be granted more readily if you are slated to make a presentation. If that is not possible, you might volunteer to facilitate or chair a session, or to work a few hours in some capacity at the conference. Administrators may respond favorably to a plan for attending and bringing back information in the form of a written report or a summarized presentation to be shared with colleagues. If none of these possibilities is viable, professional or personal leave days will have to be used.

Incentives for Participation in ISD

Incentives for attendance and enthusiastic participation at in-service and staff development sessions need to feature interest, humor, and intrigue. They should include both extrinsic and intrinsic reinforcement for adult learners. Intrinsic incentives for long-range staff development are, of course, personal and professional growth, benefits for students, and advancement in the profession. But there are good reasons for providing pleasurable, extrinsic rewards as well. For example, a drawing could be held in which the lucky winner receives a free class period during which the principal substitutes. Teacher aide time could be provided. Participants could be treated to a gala affair upon "graduation" from a program. They might be transported to this gala affair in a limousine provided by local businesses (Robert, 1973). Recognition for their participation could be publicized in local papers and professional magazines. Released time from playground or lunch duty for specified periods could be provided. The best parking spot in the lot (perhaps the superintendent's!) could be awarded, for a week or so, as a door prize. A starter list of incentives is provided in Figure 11.5.

FIGURE 11.5   Incentives for Participating in ISD

Released time	Sabbatical for long-term ISD
Progress on professional plan	A plush site for the session
Door prize	A commendation on yearly evaluation
Free food	Faculty performance
Choice parking lot spaces	Lots of useful handouts
Have a famous person there	Grab bags
Have a theme party	Recognition for attending
Retreat at a resort	Attendance by administrators
Publicity in local paper	Child care during the ISD
Make-and-take products	Reduced teaching load
Free photocopying of materials	Badges and buttons
Many options and choices	Free teacher supplies
Hair stylist demonstrations	Drawing for weekend at fancy resort
Demonstration of materials	Controversial topic
Endorsement by community leaders	Ticket giveaway (dinner, a banquet, theater, or
Free material from merchants	sports event)
Share-fair	Progressive format—moving from place to place
Funny fashion show	for parts of the session
Assurance of follow-up support	Lively entertainment
Bring-one-idea, take-home-many	Released time from playground or lunch duty for
Paid college credit	specified period
Stipend	

Prospective participants should receive information about the ISD through school newsletters, memos, bulletin boards, and public announcements. Publicity spots that are run on radio and TV provide the added benefit of calling the attention of the community to professional development efforts by the school district. They are a natural prelude for follow-up work to build awareness and support among the public for school improvement issues.

Techniques for Conducting ISD

Consultants who deliver in-service and staff development on their own professional turf may face some difficulty in being accepted as "prophets in their own land" (Smith-Westberry & Job, 1986). They will want to scrutinize their own capabilities and deficits first. Practice sessions can help presenters gain confidence and skill. Smith-Westberry and Job recommend videotaping the practice sessions, discomforting though that may be, and critiquing the taped sessions carefully to correct deficiencies.

Presenter and Participant Responsibilities

Presenters have a responsibility to know their participants well. They should be experienced and confident with the content they are presenting. After assessing participant needs, they should develop the format and content carefully, rehearse for the presentation, plan the closing segment even more carefully, arrange for feedback and evaluation, and form ideas for follow-up to the presentation.

Participants, as presentees, have the responsibility to participate whole-heartedly in the ISD, collaborate and cooperate with the activities and evaluation, and commit themselves to the follow-up activities. One of the most helpful contributions on their part is to defer any negative attitudes toward in-service and staff development and anticipate good experiences from the ISD to come.

Delivery of ISD Content

The ISD may follow one of two basic formats—lecture format, or interactive style (Smith-Westberry & Job, 1986). Lectures should include real-life examples and practical approaches. For lectures, the room arrangement might be configured as semicircles, a theater-in-the-round, or chairs in small semicircles to allow for periodic subgrouping. Stiff formats of straight rows generally should be avoided. For interactive sessions, chairs can be placed in a circle or around individual tables in octagon form. Larger tables might be arranged in a diamond shape. A "maple leaf" format of chairs allows for subgrouping (Knowles, 1970).

Presenters should have with them all supplies that they anticipate needing, such as:

Chalk, eraser, pointer

Overhead transparency markers, extra bulb, extension cord, blank transparencies, three-prong adapter

Pens, pencils, writing paper, pad for sign-up requests

Masking tape, thumbtacks, scissors, strong tape for securing cords, clip-on light to read notes in the dark

Other emergency items (tissues, hose, cup for water, stick-on notes, mints or cough drops, string, screwdriver and pliers)

A good way to begin an ISD is by using an ice-breaker, particularly if participants do not know one another. However, the ice-breaker must not encroach upon presentation time. Early arrivers could begin the brief activity, and time could be called when the hour to begin is at hand. Well-known icebreakers include introduction triads in which one interviews another and then reports, with two more sequences that get each involved in all three roles; a birthday line-up (particularly effective if no talking is allowed); checklists activities on which to get others' autographs (such as "Who loves chocolate?" and "Who plays a musical instrument?"); or matching up puzzle pieces. The boundary-breaking activity might be to share, in small groups, reasons and goals for being there.

It is vital for the presentation to *begin on time.* Also, presenters will want to "begin with a bang." The opening remarks in a presentation should be snappy and to the point. They should "hook" the participants into being interested. Now would be the time to stress that the session was developed from data on needs assessments that participants completed. Presenters should state the goal(s), the procedures to be followed, a *brief* overview of the issue(s) to be addressed, and the range of probable avenues the ISD will take, while remaining somewhat flexible for any circumstances that arise.

ISD content should be presented through more than one sensory channel, just as effective teachers present a variety for their learners. Handouts, visuals, brief tape-recorded messages, and frequent changes in presenter position and style will be as appreciated by adult learners as they are welcomed by students in the classroom. A new activity should occur approximately every fifteen to twenty minutes (Britton, 1989). And, of course, presenters do need to be prepared for inevitable contingencies and emergencies— burned-out bulbs, too few handouts, loud noises, a rude question, or a tornado alert! Presenters can use small-group activities intermittently to encourage involvement and sustain interest. Huddle groups of six people conferring for six minutes, circle response groups in which each person speaks in turn around the small circle, and buzz groups of dyads or triads work well.

Some presenters dread speaking to groups. Would-be presenters may be inexperienced or feel terrified to stand before groups, particularly before their peers. It is a good idea to practice the presentation before the event. A script of remarks can be typed (triple spaced for easy reading) and rehearsed in front of the mirror or a kindly compatriot. Holding private practice sessions before a mirror will allow you to critique gestures and body language. It may help to watch other performers, or to practice with dramatic readings.

Engaging in relaxation exercises before the event has helped some nervous speakers to be at ease. During the presentation the speaker might locate supporters in the audience and key in on them for assurance. If a tense time arises, a cartoon or joke might be brought out to ease the tension, but this must be used with care. The humorous piece must be inoffensive and related to the topic. That is a tall order. At any rate, presenters will find it comforting to remember that most audiences are more interested in the usefulness of the content than in the skills of the presenters; therefore, the key is to provide useful, timely information.

Many of the techniques for high-quality ISD activities are good teaching techniques as well. For example, the presenter should avoid comments such as "We're behind schedule, so I will have to hurry," or "I'm sorry we had to leave so much out," or "Too bad we must do this on such a busy day."

Garmston (1990) stresses that presenters can make or break the success of the session in its last few minutes. Final impressions should encourage participants to sort and store the material. The last comments should stimulate inquiry and support commitment and collegiality. Closing activities need to be planned carefully and calculated precisely. Perhaps the most important criterion of all is to *end on time.*

Visuals for the Presentation.   Many presenters use visuals—transparencies, films, videotapes, charts, and posters. The visuals should be simple, clear, and visible. They must not be cluttered with infinite detail, but represent the "bottom line" about the topic. The audience will attend more to color graphics than to black-and-white. An effective transparency presents one main idea per sheet, with a maximum of seven words per line and seven lines per visual, and does not contain technical language or jargon. A rule of thumb for the display of figures and graphs is to present only information that the audience could sketch freehand with accurate representation of the main idea. The type on transparencies must be BIG! It should be tested for legibility from the back of the room by a person who has never seen it before.

Presenters should not read from the transparency material, but wait until the audience has time to peruse it. When noting information, speakers should point to the transparency, not to the screen. Expeditious use of the on/off switch allows the presenter to control the audience's attention. It is best to leave room lights on unless the visual is a film. After a point is made, turning off the machine and standing away from it directs attention back to the presenter. Clip-on microphones allow presenter mobility. Imaginative use and variation of space, location, volume, and graphics will enliven the presentation and focus participant attention.

A dramatic effect can be achieved with the use of two overhead machines and screens. The main point might be presented on one screen while subpoints or illustrations are flashed on the other. As a variation, two presenters could collaborate, one at each machine, to dialogue about the material. This technique needs to be rehearsed before it is used.

Handouts for the Presentation.   Presentees appreciate good handouts. Handouts are more widely read and better remembered when they are in color. They should be practical, usable, and attractive. There should not be too many nor too few. Unless the handout is needed as a component of participation involvement, it should be distributed at the close of the session. If handed out during the session, an orderly procedure must be preplanned, so that distribution does not consume valuable session time and make the audience restless.

Participants tend to become annoyed when there are not enough handouts to go around. Even with the best planning, this does happen occasionally. Presenters should have a sign-up paper available for those who were short-changed; and must follow through right away by sending the material. It is best not to distribute handouts before the session begins. In order to minimize requests and avoid having to refuse, presenters will want to keep printed material out of sight until it is needed.

Follow-Up Activities

Follow-up to in-service and staff development is the breeze that fans any fires of change that were sparked by the activity (Dettmer, 1990). Educators sometimes avoid trying new concepts and techniques because they are uncomfortable with them or uncertain about the outcomes. It is easy to revert to business as usual, once the ISD activity is over. So follow-up to ISD is vital, just as it is with the consultation process. Follow-up should be a long-term practice of support for the innovation, and as such, might more appropriately be described as *follow-through* (Dettmer, 1990). The possibilities include peer coaching, discussion groups, visits to sites where the innovation is occurring, newsletters, and interviews. Data gathered during follow-up and follow-through can be used to plan future in-services and staff development projects. (See Figure 11.6.)

FIGURE 11.6   Follow-Up Information for Staff Development

Please take a few minutes to respond to these questions about the recent staff development __(date)__ on the topic of __(topic)__ . In doing so you will be helping staff developers and presenters plan effective staff development experiences for you and your colleagues.

1. Have you implemented any idea or strategy that was presented during the staff development? If so, please describe it briefly and rate the success level:

   _____

   _____

   _____

   ____ 1 = not effective   ____ 2 = somewhat effective   ____ 3 = very effective

2. Is there something more you would like to learn about this topic? If so, please describe your need.

   _____

   _____

   _____

3. If you did not use the staff development information, please explain your reluctance to do so.

   _____

   _____

   _____

4. This item is *very* important. Did the information or enthusiasm you received have positive ripple effects that you could identify and describe? If so, please do, and also rate the extent to which this happened.

   _____

   _____

   _____

   ____ 1 = a little   ____ 2 = somewhat   ____ 3 = to a great extent   ____ 4 = profoundly

One caution must be noted regarding ISD outcomes. When educators are introduced to new concepts and challenged to try new approaches, some discomfort is inevitable. Learning new skills involves greater effort than continuing to use old ones (Joyce & Showers, 1983). The adage that training may make you worse before it makes you better is an important point to consider. This accents the need for follow-through efforts and perseverance on the part of the consultant.

Evaluation of the In-service and Staff Development

The tool used most often for in-service and staff development evaluation is a questionnaire participants complete immediately following the activity. The evaluation should include both objective responses and an invitation for open-ended responses. A Likert scale of five to seven values is preferable to a Yes-or-No format. The evaluation data should be used to design more meaningful activities as well as to improve presentation skills. (See Figure 11.7 for an example of an ISD evaluation tool, and consult Chapter 8 for additional information on evaluation.)

Presenters may want to complete a self-evaluation and evaluate the participants as well. By doing so, consultants ascertain participant preparedness and responsiveness to the topic. This provides information that can help them and their host schools plan further consultation and collaboration directed to participant needs. (See Figure 11.8.)

Benefits of In-service and Staff Development

In-service and staff development for consultation, collaboration, and special needs of students have the potential to create positive ripple effects that have no bounds. They encourage

- Increased respect for individual differences, creative approaches, and educational excellence

FIGURE 11.7   In-service/Staff Development Evaluation

In-service/Staff Development Evaluation

Date _____

Name (optional) _____Teaching Area and Level (s) _____

Site of the In-service/Staff Development _____Topic _____

Rate the following with a value from 1 through 5:

1 = None   2 = A little   3 = Somewhat   4 = Considerably   5 = Much

1. The event increased my understanding of the topic. _____
2. The goals and objectives of the event addressed needs I had identified. _____
3. The content was well developed and organized. _____
4. The material was presented effectively. _____
5. The environment was satisfactory. _____
6. I gained ideas to use in my own situation. _____
7. I will use at least one idea from this event. _____
8. Strengths of the event: _____
9. Ways the event could be improved: _____
10. I would like to know more about: _____

FIGURE 11.8   Presenter's Self-Assessment of Staff Development

Rate the following items, using a scale of:

   1 = inadequate, 2 = fair, 3 = satisfactory, 4 = good, 5 = excellent

_____   1. I was well-prepared.

_____   2. I was organized.

_____   3. My material was on target with their needs.

_____   4. I established rapport and got off to a good start.

_____   5. Participants seemed interested.

_____   6. Participants wanted to know even more about the topic(s).

_____   7. I had an accurate perspective of the audience.

_____   8. I got participants involved.

_____   9. I had the right kind and amount of handouts.

_____   10. My presentation materials were high quality.

_____   11. I did my very best in this activity.

_____   12. I have plans for follow-through with the participants.

_____   13. I learned from the experience, too.

_____   14. This is my overall rating of the staff development.

- Teacher proficiency in innovative curriculum and teacher strategies
- Staff and parent involvement and satisfaction with the educational system
- Collegiality and collaboration among all school personnel as well as community and parents

In order to attain these positive outcomes, in-service and staff development must be planned, conducted, and evaluated thoroughly.

Tips for Professional Development

1. If an opportunity arises, suggest certain activities to teachers who might want them. Don't force. Sometimes, although not often, the distribution of material to teachers backfires because they resent the inference that they need it. So let them decide. Instead of stuffing teachers' mailboxes with things they may not want, lay out new books or activities on tables in the teachers' workroom with a sign that invites browsing.

2. Have an in-service on parent-teacher conferences for students with special needs. Ask teachers to submit "stumper" problems. Then use them to determine how to react and deal with those situations. Have lots of ideas to distribute.

3. Do your very best to get administrators to *attend* and *participate* in the ISD activities.

4. About two months after the ISD, send a checklist of outcomes that were sought from the activity, and solicit feedback on progress toward those outcomes.

5. In the teachers' workroom, have treats and note cards with the directions, "Take a treat and take a sheet," meaning to take a sheet that has tips concerning student needs. A variation is "Take a treat and leave a sheet" in which the sheet is a needs assessment or evaluation you wish to collect (Dettmer & Landrum, 1997).

6. Travel with others to workshops and conferences. The trip provides opportunities for conversation and rapport building.

7. Hand out your school's business cards at conferences, writing your name, educational area, and shared interest on them. This opens up possibilities for future interaction and collaboration.

8. After attending a convention, conference, or other helpful meeting, or after reading an informative piece, write a short note describing it and put a copy in teachers' boxes, spreading the news on things learned.

9. Organize a system so you will know all teachers have been reached through informal or formal ISD.

10. Develop calendars and time lines of program activities to post in teacher areas or to distribute among school personnel. Do not overlook secretaries, for whom such information is particularly important.

11. Prepare teaching videotapes that demonstrate activities appropriate for students with special needs.

12. Bring in the expertise of other school personnel to assist with consultations, especially for specific content areas.

13. Make a personal pledge to read at least one article a week from a professional journal.

14. Join a dynamic professional organization and become actively involved in it.

15. Conduct workshops on topics teachers request. If a topic is outside your line of expertise, find someone who can present it.

16. After each informal or formal ISD, check back to see how the ideas were used, and if there were difficulties, to avoid them next time.

17. Learn a new technique and infect others with your enthusiasm for using it. Don't just drop off learning centers and activities you have prepared. Ask teachers if you can help get them started.

18. Become acquainted with people in businesses and organizations who are field-testing products, materials, and processes.

19. Observe programs in other schools and share observations with key people in your own school context.

20. Remember that knowing how to consult does not guarantee you the opportunity to do it! Create the opportunity.

CHAPTER REVIEW

1. Consultants and consulting teachers have ideal roles for planning and implementing inservice and staff development. Through their involvement with professional development

activities, they can share content and help build processes that facilitate learning by students with special needs. They also will have the opportunity to develop consultation and collaboration networks in their local school context.

2. In-service is one specialized component within long-range, ongoing staff development programs involving all school personnel.

3. Adult learners have a need to be self-directed in their learning. A group of adult learners represents a wide experience base on which consultants can draw and build. Adult learners want learning that is oriented to the present and that helps them deal with problems they are now facing.

4. Professional and staff development must be designed to address assessed needs of the participants. Before needs assessment is conducted, needs sensing should be undertaken. Teachers may not always know, or verbalize, what they need to know about helping students with special needs.

5. In-service and staff development for facilitating learning by students with special needs should be presented to a wide range of target groups—teachers, administrators, support personnel, policymakers, teacher educators, and others who are involved with learning programs and materials. Finding time, arranging incentives and publicity, and developing the format are important points in planning ISD.

6. Successful ISD activities are created by effective delivery styles, appropriate visuals, helpful handouts, careful evaluation, and commitment to follow-up after the ISD.

7. Formative and summative evaluation of professional development will provide accountability for resources expended and will help staff developers continue to plan and improve these services for school personnel needs.

TO DO AND THINK ABOUT

1. Propose several ways a consulting teacher might serve the special needs of students through in-service and staff development activities.

2. Reflect on concerns a classroom teacher might express through needs sensing and needs assessment in regard to learning and behavior needs of students in the classroom.

3. Suppose that an in-service session on alternative grouping techniques is scheduled for an elementary school, with attendance by all building teachers required. The one-hour session is scheduled for Thursday after school, in the kindergarten room. A methods instructor from a nearby university will lecture to the group. Later this evening there is a high-school play performance, and the next day is the end of term before the grading period. How do the in-service topic, time, location, and format violate the principles of good adult learning experiences?

4. Design a teachers' workroom bulletin board that could be considered an informal in-service concerning a disability or an example of students at risk.

5. In a brainstorm session, think up a list of "Things I Don't Want to Happen" with regard to in-service and staff development activities. After having fun with this, it may be a good idea to countermand these "ISD Horrors" with a list of preventives.

6. In a teacher's guide for a particular subject, locate instances where collaboration and use of a consultant are referred to, or better still, encouraged.

7. How might in-service and staff development activities promoted by the special education consulting teachers activate positive ripple effects throughout the school for all students?

8. Talk about the following quotations as they might relate to in-service and staff development, and think up others as further examples:

   "It is easier to produce ten volumes of philosophical writing than to put one principle into practice." (unknown)

   "Our goal is not to think alike, but to think together." (anonymous)

   "We're all in this boat together. If you don't care to help row, at least don't drill holes in the bottom of the boat." (some wise, unnamed person)

9. Have a personal scavenger hunt, or go with a small group of your classmates or colleagues, to discover new resources for student and adult learning. Find people, places, and things that can enhance special abilities and serve special needs. As you do this, and have the need to explain what you are doing to those you encounter in your sleuthing, engage them in conversation about education and advocate for collaborative enterprises to help students succeed in school.

10. Develop a file of humor and satire about consultation that would be helpful in developing rapport with colleagues. As a start, consider this one which has been around for awhile.

    "The consultant is one who drives over from the central office and borrows your watch to tell you what time it is."

    How can humor and satire be used to the consultant's advantage in interactions with consultees? If you have a humorous bent, or the creative urge, make up a joke, cartoon, or comic strip about consulting or collaboration that could be used to defuse resistance and build rapport toward school consultation.

FOR FURTHER READING

Caldwell, S. D. (Ed.). (1989). *Staff development:Handbook of effective practices*. Oxford, OH: National Staff Development Council.

Dettmer, P., & Landrum, M. (1997). *Staff development: The key to effective gifted programs*. Waco, TX: Prufrock.

Journal for Staff Development. Manhattan, KS: Kansas State University. All issues.

Joyce, B. (Ed.). (1990). *Changing school culture through staff development*. Alexandria, VA: Association for Supervision and Curriculum Development.

Joyce, B., & Showers, B. (1988). *Student achievement through staff development*. New York: Longman.

Morsink, C. V., Thomas, C. C., & Correa, V. I. (1991). *Interactive teaming: Consultation and collaboration in special programs*. Columbus, OH: Merrill. Chapter 8, on empowering team members through staff development.

CHAPTER

12 Summing Up and Looking Ahead

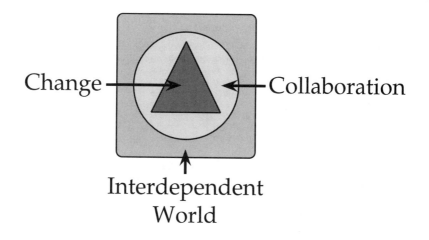

Change ← → Collaboration

Interdependent
World

Never before in history have so many elements of people's lives changed so quickly. No one knows for certain where these changes will lead, but trends help futurists forecast what the world will be like in the twenty-first century. Their insights help educators predict the changes needed in schools to meet the demands of the future.

One thing is becoming increasingly clear. Students who are at risk now because of special learning and behavior difficulties will be placed in even greater jeopardy by ever-accelerating demands upon them to keep pace and measure up in the work world. Schools cannot be the sole institutional provider of all services children need and still meet their substantial academic responsibilities. Interrelationships must be developed with other public and private sector agencies. Collaborative school consultation and teamwork among all professional and parent educators are vital in enabling all students to be successful learners, happy individuals, and productive members of society.

Focusing Questions

1. What changes are predicted in society, and how do these predictions relate to the future of students with special needs?

2. What roles will educators play in serving the needs of students and families in the future?
3. What benefits can result from successful consultation, collaboration, and co-teaching in schools?
4. What obstacles lie in the path toward realizing these benefits?
5. Why are new metaphors needed for education?
6. What are the complex challenges that will be faced by consultative and collaborative personnel in schools of the future?

Key Terms

advocacy	futurist	reification
change agent	metaphor	Zeitgeist
demographic data	positive ripple effects	

Global Trends and Social Concerns Affecting Education

Global trends and social concerns are mandating changes in school and home education. Populations are shifting and becoming more diverse. Complex social issues and health concerns affect people of all ages, and critical shortages of skilled, competent workers exist in a variety of business and service areas. The structures of family and home have undergone tremendous pressures which affect all members deeply, especially children. Resolutions of these concerns are vital in order to help children and youth respond to the challenge of the next century. We must be mindful that children and youth are about one-third of our population, but they are 100 percent of the future.

Scenario 12

Another school day is over. The events of the past week are history. What happens beyond this moment is the future. As teachers in Scenario 11 of the previous chapter conclude their discussion about the upcoming staff-development sessions and head for their rooms to pick up school work they will take home for the weekend, their glances might happen to fall upon a poster that hangs beside the door:

"The Future Is Now!"
Below the poster in smaller type is an often-quoted maxim—"If we do what we have been doing, we will continue to get what we have been getting." And below that in firm, bold letters, is the question, "Can we do better?" It is a good question to ponder over the weekend...

As the twentieth century settles into the history books and the twenty-first century arrives full force, futurists focus on several themes:

Societal changes
Economic trends
Family structure changes
Demographic trends
Educational reforms

Trends, and changes they will bring relevant to these themes, will have major impact on all aspects of society, and particularly on individuals who are now children and adolescents in our schools.

Societal Changes

The next two decades should bring as much change in the world as the past two hundred years produced altogether. Change is a dominant factor in the structure of the modern world (Benjamin, 1989). Many trends point to interdependency and the need for cooperation, collaboration, and teamwork in making decisions. Knowledge is mushrooming at a pace that no one individual can master, and technology connects individuals, schools, businesses, and governments around the world. In this "global village" of interdependent societies, a decision on one side of the globe dramatically affects people on the other side. Each society must learn to cooperate, collaborate, and communicate with all others.

In the future, information-gathering and decision-making resources and responsibilities will be redistributed. In a continual cycle of learning, unlearning, and relearning, workers will master new technologies, adapt to new organizational forms, and generate new ideas. Technology for facilitating team decision-making will replace old hierarchical and bureaucratic structures. "Five-year-olds today experience more information in one year than their grandparents did in a lifetime" (Gayle, 1990, p. 12). It will be impossible for any one person to know everything needed for making good decisions. So collaboration and consultation will be essential.

Greater ties are being forged between academic and vocational content in education. *Goals 2000* outlined educational components of school-based training, paid and unpaid work, mentoring, and community activities. This necessitates new partnerships between educators and employers. In the eight goals put forth by the American School Counselor Association in its publication *School Counseling 2000: Children Are Our Future,* Goal III states that students will demonstrate competency over challenging subject matter and every school in America will ensure that all students learn to use their minds well (Wallace, 1997). This goal is intended to prepare them for responsible citizenship, further learning, and productive employment.

Collaboration is crucial to the employability of school graduates. If a student is having difficulty in today's learning environment, what will be the prognosis for that student's survival in tomorrow's world? What will it take for students with special learning needs to be successful lifelong learners? How can students with behavior disorders be constructive, productive members in increasingly complex social environments? In what ways can the potential of those with special gifts and talents be developed? Because of their experience in transition programming and in such employability-related skill areas as social skills and self-management, special education and general education teachers will be called on to provide leadership in school-to-work transitional programs. Without consultation, collaboration, and teamwork, transition programming will be incomplete.

Economic Trends

During the past decade, poverty levels have increased dramatically. The 1980s and 1990s saw a rise of the working poor. Demographers predict that by the year 2020 one in four Americans under the age of 18 will live in poverty (Woolfolk, 1995). Families in poverty face many environmental stressors as well as institutional bias from many of the systems that serve them. Large numbers of students, especially low-income students of color, fail in school and score poorly on national tests. Beyond that, some students succeed in school and score well on tests, but then turn out not fully prepared to cope successfully with demands of life and work.

Family Structure Changes

Families must be proactive partners in the transition process from present to future. However, the structures and circumstances of families are changing rapidly (Edelman, 1987). A magazine picture of the typical American family today is much different from a similar magazine cover appearing in 1950 or earlier. The picture of mom, dad, two children, and a dog named Spot has become fragmented into a bewildering array of family arrangements. Radical changes have taken place in family life and household economics (Skolnick, 1991), and these changes dramatically affect the learning and behavior of students in school.

Demographic Trends

Educators must respond to changes in the cultural nature of American society by recognizing and respecting cultural factors such as language, race, ethnicity, customs, family structures, adult lifestyles, and community dynamics among culturally diverse groups. Care must be taken not to ignore within-group diversity as well. Examples of such factors are income, education, national origin, social history, levels of assimilation and acculturation, and the rural-urban continuum. While these distinctions may appear minor, they can be quite significant when providing services, advocating on behalf of a student and family, and promoting systematic changes (Mason, 1994). For students with special needs, and their families and communities, educators must ask not only, "What do I need to learn about this person culturally to help her or him?" but also "What is the impact of race, family structure, gender, and ethnicity on the problems this person is having?"

A Visionary Scope: Educational Reforms

A consensus is growing among educators and policy-makers that in schools of the future there will be considerable role change, including increased collaboration and consultation (Jenkins, Pious, & Jewell, 1990) and enhanced collegial relationships (West, 1990). New ways of thinking are happening, whether we are immediately aware of it and ready for it or not. This requires a whole new way of viewing the world (Crowell, 1989, p. 60). There is a shift away from the Newtonian ideas of simplicity, hierarchy, mechanics, assembly, and objectivity that has nourished current views of the world. New views are more integrative, holistic, collective, cooperative, and organizational. Such changes are occurring in scientific thinking, but they have implications for education as well (Crowell, 1989; Meyen & Skrtic, 1988). Now is the time for visionary scope—looking inward to analyze in microscopic detail, scanning in all directions with the periscopic breadth and depth, appreciating the beauty and usefulness of diversity such as we find in the kaleidoscope, and looking beyond toward lofty goals and a promising future with long-range telescopic vision. (See Figure 12.1.)

Schaps (1990) asserts that the public is seeing the necessity of changing the overall *system* for education, while realizing that the efforts will not work if they focus *only* on improved teaching processes, *or* content of the curriculum, *or* goals and policies of schools. Instead, process, content, and policy are strongly tied to one another, so that change in any one necessitates change in all three. "Many concepts in special education are proving increasingly unworkable. Nowhere is this more evident than in our attempts to reify the 'conditions' we decided were evidenced by individuals who failed in school" (Ysseldyke, 1986, p. 22). Reification (converting an abstraction into a concrete thing) of categories, labels, delivery systems based on test scores, and the like, too often has diverted the attention of educators away from improving instruction.

As stressed in earlier chapters, a growing number of special education leaders contend that students at risk of school failure in conventional settings are not disabled, deficient students. The problem lies in the misfit between their abilities and the demands made upon

FIGURE 12.1   Education: A Visionary Scope

—Valeria Converse

them in an inflexible school situation. With school consultation and collaboration as an integral part of the educational program, there is hope for creating the flexibility students need and enhancing the repertoire of teaching practices that can enable them to succeed. The best teachers have always been those who expand, change, modify, and compact the requirements so that the important material is taught, but in a way and to the extent that serves each student's individual, special needs and talents.

Conoley (1989) emphasizes that teachers will need to take some responsibility for achieving the quality of outcomes they desire. However, they must also feel that the extra effort they give to committee work, problem identification, or problem-solving teams is not just added onto their load of responsibilities. They need to perceive this effort as having a positive effect on their daily professional lives.

In their book widely used in special education courses, Hallahan and Kauffman (1991) include several descriptions of collaboration efforts between a classroom teacher and a special education teacher. For example, when an itinerant teacher for the visually impaired and a third-grade teacher work together to adapt material and team up to provide services, there are three beneficiaries of their efforts—consultant, consultee, and client. Even the roles are somewhat interchangeable, depending upon who provides the direct service to whom. When the teacher of emotionally disturbed students and a fifth-grade teacher collaborate on procedures and reinforcements for a seriously disturbed student, all three roles again benefit, with an added positive ripple effect of the student's improved behavior for other school personnel and students in the school.

Crowell (1989) stresses that we need to appreciate where we are and how we got here. As Martin Luther King put it, reading history made him feel eternally "in the red." The challenge of new ways of thinking about schools and education is not a call to abandon our cherished values and history that have provided meaning and given us direction. Instead, it is a challenge to participate in creating a new vision of the human role and educating students to achieve their potential. The time to begin fulfilling the new vision is now. As the ancient proverb tells us, "A journey of a thousand miles begins with a single step."

Benefits of Collaborative School Consultation

School environments that promote collaborative consultation tend to involve all school personnel in the teaching and learning processes. Information is shared and knowledge levels about student characteristics and needs, and strategies for meeting those needs, are broadened. Importantly, many of the strategies are helpful with other students who have similar but less severe needs. A number of specific benefits of school consultation and collaboration can be anticipated.

First, there is much-needed support and assistance for students in the inclusive classroom. Consulting special education teachers help classroom teachers develop repertoires of materials and instructional strategies. Many find this more efficient than racing from one student to another in a resource room as all work on individual assignments. As one learning disabilities teacher succinctly put it, "In my resource room, by the time I get to the last student, I find that the first student is stuck and has made no progress. So I frantically run through the whole cycle again. Tennis shoes are a must for my job!" They also find

APPLICATION **12.1**
Matching Predictions to Roles

Consider the following predictions some educators are making about schools in the next century. How do these changes match your ideas? What will be the role of consultation, collaboration, and teamwork in education from "birth to death" if these predictions come to pass?

> Full inclusion for many special education students who are currently served in pull-out programs will continue well into the next century (Wiederholt, 1989).

> Vocational education will become more prominent in secondary schools (Gayle, 1990).

> More emphasis will be given to early childhood education as a preventive measure and, if this is successful, remedial programs will be decreased (Benjamin, 1989).

> More collaboration will be called for among the preschool teachers, school psychologists, parents, health service providers, and other personnel within and outside the school.

> The Back-to-Basics movement will become Forward-to-Emerging Basics, which will include the use of telecommunications technology in problem-solving and other advanced technical skills (Gayle, 1990).

> There will be a new collaborative role for teachers and students in which students accept an active senior partnership role in the learning enterprise (Benjamin, 1989).

> Professions are products of the Zeitgeist, or the general intellectual and ethical climate and needs of a particular time in history (McGaghie, 1991). So evaluations of schools and school personnel will be interpreted in a broader framework and expanded roles.

> "Education will be respected as a valuable and prestigious profession by the 21st century" (Gayle, 1990, p. 13).

ways of helping classroom teachers to be confident and successful with special needs students. At times they can assume an instructional role in the classroom, which frees the classroom teacher to study student progress, set up arrangements for special projects, or work intensively with a small group of students. When general classroom and special education teachers collaborate, each has ownership and involvement in serving special needs.

Collaborative efforts to serve students in heterogeneous settings help minimize stigmatizing effects of labels such as "handicapped," "exceptional," or "disabled." It also can reduce referrals to remedial programs. In an early study to determine effects of consultation upon teacher referral patterns over a 7-year period, Ritter (1978) notes that the provision of consultation service resulted in decreasing referrals on the part of teachers over time. More recently, in a study of special education in an inclusionary middle school, Knowles (1997) found that collaboration and teamwork decreased special education education referrals and grade retention of students. Fewer referrals for special education services means reduced expenditures for costly and time-consuming psychological assessments and special education interventions. Educators can focus more time and energy on teaching and facilitating, and less on testing and measuring. In addition, a ripple effect extends services to students by encouraging modifications and alternatives for their special needs.

When introduced to the concept of school consultation, some special education personnel are concerned that after a time they will work themselves out of a job. They fear their positions will be abolished if teachers become fully capable of serving the needs of mildly disabled, gifted, and underachieving students in the classroom. However, this possibility is extremely remote. Research since 1980 demonstrates that when consultation service is increased, there is more demand for the benefits generated by the service (Friend, 1988). A successful consultation process becomes a supportive tool that teachers increasingly value and use. As inclusive school systems become more prevalent, collaborative consultation will become even more critical for school program success. Consultation services contribute to the total school program as a bridge between the parallel systems of special education and general education (Greenburg, 1987) and are an effective way of alleviating confusion over goals and relationships of general and special education (Will, 1984).

Administrators can benefit from eased loads of pressure and planning when classroom teachers are efficient in working with a wide range of student needs. Principals find it stimulating to visit and observe in classrooms as team participants, collaborating on ways of helping every student succeed in the school and reinforcing teacher successes with all their students. For many administrators, this is a welcome change from the typical classroom visitations they make for purposes of teacher evaluation.

Another important and frequently overlooked benefit is the maintenance of continuity in learning programs as students progress through their school experiences. This, too, is a savings in time, energy, and resources of the educational staff, and often the parents as well.

A collaborative consultation approach is a natural system for nurturing harmonious staff interactions. Teachers who have become isolated or autonomous in their styles and outlook often discover that working with other adults for common goals is quite stimulating. Sharing ideas can add to creativity, open-endedness, and flexibility in developing educational programs for students with special needs. In addition, more emphasis and coordination can be given to cross-school and long-range planning, with an increased use of outside resources for student needs.

Collaborative consultants are catalysts for professional development. They can identify areas in which faculty need awareness and information sessions, and coordinate workshops to help all school personnel learn specific educational techniques (McKenzie, Egner, Knight, Perelman, Schneider, & Garvin, 1970). Just as removal of the catalyst stops a chemical process, so can the absence of consulting teachers curtail individualization of curriculum and differentiation of strategies for special needs (Bietau, 1994).

Parents or guardians of the exceptional student often become extremely frustrated with labeling, fragmented curriculum, and isolation from peers endured by their children. So they respond enthusiastically when they learn that several educators are functioning as a team for the student. Their attitudes toward school improve, and they are more likely to become more involved in planning and carrying through with the interventions (Idol, 1988), more eager to share their ideas, and helpful in monitoring their child's learning. They are particularly supportive when consulting services allow students in special education programs to remain in their neighborhood schools.

School consultants and collaborators provide increased opportunities for communication, multiple sources of information, broadened perspectives on teaching strategies for special needs, expanded availability of resources, diminished isolation in the classroom, and more involvement with service agencies beyond the school. Positive ripple effects occur when teacher skills are enhanced in preventing learning problems that might otherwise escalate into more serious needs (Idol, 1986; Heron & Kimball, 1988). Students with borderline special needs that are addressed successfully in classrooms represent single case outcomes that can be replicated with an entire class or throughout a school.

Positive Ripple Effects

Positive ripple effects, or multiplier effects as they have also been referred to from time to time in this book, provide compelling arguments for consultation, collaboration, and teaming. They create benefits beyond the immediate situation involving one student and that student's teachers. For example, by collaborating school personnel are modeling this powerful social tool for their students, who are quite likely to experience collaborative climates in their future workplaces.

Direct services for consultees are one level of positive effects (see Figure 12.2). At this level the consultation and collaboration are most likely to have been initiated for one

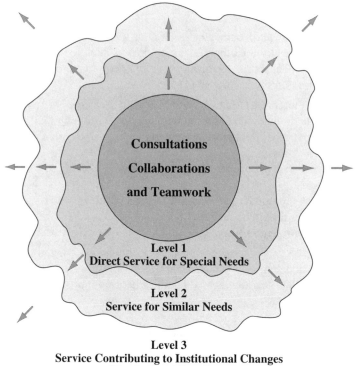

Consultations

Collaborations

and Teamwork

Level 1
Direct Service for Special Needs

Level 2
Service for Similar Needs

Level 3
Service Contributing to Institutional Changes
and Professional Development

FIGURE 12.2   Positive Ripple Effects of Collaborative School Consultation

client's need. (Note that a client can be an entity such as a student group, school, family, or community, as well as a single student.) But consultation benefits often extend beyond level 1 of immediate need. At level 2, consultees use information and points of view generated during the collaboration to be more effective in similar but unrelated cases. Both consultant and consultee repertoires of knowledge and skills are enhanced so that they can function more effectively in the future (Brown et al., 1979). When consultation outcomes extend beyond single consultant/consultee situations of levels 1 and 2, the entire school system can be positively affected by level 3 outcomes. Organizational change and increased family involvement are potential results of level 3 outcomes.

Level 1 effects result from the following types of school situations:

The consultant engages in problem-solving with a high-school teacher to determine ways of helping a severely learning-disabled student master minimum competencies required for graduation.

The audiologist helps the classroom teacher arrange the classroom environment to enable a hearing-impaired student to function comfortably in the regular classroom setting.

Level 2 effects include these examples:

The classroom teacher becomes more familiar with the concept of hyperactivity in children, subsequently regarding fewer children as attention-deficit disordered with hyperactivity, and adjusting the classroom curriculum to more appropriately address very active children's needs in that classroom setting.

The classroom teacher becomes comfortable with enrichment activities provided for gifted students through collaboration with the gifted program facilitator, and makes enriching activities available to a larger group of very able children in the classroom.

Level 3 effects enable these kinds of outcomes:

The efforts toward collaboration and teamwork result in a staff-development plan called "Teachers Helping Teachers," during which teachers in a school system provide training for interested colleagues in their areas of expertise.

The school district's emphasis on consultation, collaboration, and teamwork pleases parents who find that their children are receiving more integrated, personalized instruction for their learning needs. Families become more active and interested in the school's programs.

Consulting teachers sometimes are concerned that if level 2 and 3 outcomes enable classroom teachers to handle some serious learning needs without their involvement, their positions may be eliminated if funds are reduced. It is important that the consulting role is not regarded as an add-on position to be dispensed with when money and personnel are in short supply, but rather as an indispensable component of each school's present and future context.

Use of specialized intervention techniques for many more students than those identified, categorized, and remediated in special education programs is an expected outcome of collaborative school consultation and co-teaching. All in all, the multiplier effect of these interactive processes is a powerful tool for change agentry in education.

Developing New Metaphors for Education

One catalyst for change can be development of constructive, uplifting metaphors. To think differently about education, schools, and students, one strategy would be to envision schools in a new, metaphorical way. Productive thinking about complex issues can be enhanced by metaphor (Pollio, 1987).

Metaphors are mental maps that permit the connection of different meanings through some shared similarity. They appear often in spoken and written communication. For example, the sentences "Life is a loom," and "The fog swallowed the ship," and "Last June my flower garden was a paint box of colors," are metaphorical. They connect in order to explain. People use metaphors to sort out their perceptions, evaluate, express feelings, and reflect upon the purpose of things, in order to make better sense of their world (Deshler, 1985).

Belth (1977) suggests that as we create or reject particular metaphors, we form problems. The world's problems, therefore, become what we form them to be. So, through metaphors we can imagine the world as we wish it to be and fashion it accordingly. The majority of our creative ideas and our problem-solving solutions are born in analogical and

---

APPLICATION **12.2**
Making School Changes

Consider the following typical school needs, and ways that consultation and the collaborative ethic might assist in making school changes:

Create opportunities to interface special education programs with the general program.

Institute communication networks among school staff, parents, advocacy groups.

Contribute to text selections, curriculum revisions, general school reform.

Identify exemplary, successful teaching practices.

Coordinate use of community resources for students' needs.

Help parents identify ways to contribute to school programs.

Help other educators and parents set realistic goals for students with learning and behavior problems.

Contribute to planning and conducting in-service and staff development.

Conduct formative and summative evaluation to improve school programs

metaphorical thinking. We take ideas from one context and apply them elsewhere to produce new ideas or more interesting presentations. We make connections that transform our thinking to more productive heights. Metaphorical thinking is:

Practical (useful and helpful)
Personal (individualistic)
Pleasurable (unconventional, surprising, or humorous)
Powerful (enlarging and attitudinal)
Pedagogical (teaching, exemplifying)

It must be noted that metaphorical thinking sometimes can be problematic. Just as it is a good tool for explaining ideas and achieving new perspectives on both the unfamiliar and the very familiar, so can the misaligned metaphor limit our thinking when it is simplistic or outdated (von Oech, 1983), because then it becomes stereotypic and imprisoning. Schools and education have generated a variety of metaphors, but some of them now are viewed as uninspiring and somewhat demoralizing. Such metaphors shackle our thinking about teaching and learning.

Dobson, Dobson, and Koetting (1985) assert that the outlook on education has been imprisoned by three ill-advised metaphors:

A military metaphor—characterized by concepts and vocabulary such as target population, strategy, objectives, training, standardized, discipline, schedule, and information systems.

An industrial metaphor—revealed by language such as cost effectiveness, product, feedback, efficiency, quality control, and management.

A disease metaphor—reflected in words and practices such as diagnostic, prescriptive, treatment, remediation, label, impaired, monitor, deviant, and referral.

In another context, Futrell (1989) used the metaphor of business to describe education, with knowledge being the commodity, learning an asset, research an enterprise, and intellectual capacity as the capital. These kinds of metaphors—military, industrial, disease, and business—may illustrate schools as we have known them, but seem to be counterproductive for the future. We need good, new metaphors in education—metaphors that uplift, inspire, and promise positive outcomes. An instructive metaphor is the ripple effect discussed earlier in the chapter, showing the results of casting a single pebble (or professional effort) into school context waters so that the movement carries out and on beyond that point of impact.

A promising metaphor is gardening, with concepts and vocabulary that highlight budding potential, special needs, and anticipated productivity. For example, a gardening/cultivator metaphor might include:

Seeds—students
Climate—learning environment
Soil—curriculum
Gardener—teacher, parent, support personnel
Sunlight—ideas

Rain—materials, resources, opportunity for learning
Shade—incubation, protection
Fertilizer—stimulation, interest, curiosity, fun
Weeds—irrelevancies
Pruning/grafting—deficits, talents
Cultivation—teaching, coaching, facilitating
Predators/disease—learning and behavior problems
Seasons—time, rhythm, and cycle of development
Harvest—achievement, fulfillment—and so on

Positive, nurturant metaphors can be used to highlight the benefits of processes such as collaboration and teamwork and to overcome obstacles by pointing out faulty perspectives and myopic viewpoints. A well-developed metaphor is useful for professional-development visuals, bulletin boards strategically placed in school buildings and administrative offices, memo pads and business cards, and newsletters for parents and communities. Figure 12.3 demonstrates this kind of vehicle which promotes public relations for education as it advocates for schools and students.

Development of powerful new personal or institutional metaphors that feature collaboration and encourage teamwork just might help educators think differently about schools and students, and interest even the most skeptical in trying these complex interactive processes. Stimuli for creating new metaphors can come from many sources:

Thinking about important student outcomes.

Finding ways parents, support personnel, and other community members can be involved in learning.

Engaging in collegial interactions among school educators and parent educators.

Highlighting examples of teacher satisfaction.

FIGURE 12.3   **Navigating with the C's**

APPLICATION **12.3**
Developing a Personal Metaphor

School, and education in general, have been portrayed with metaphorical templates and vocabulary as diverse as industry, disease, military, and business. Contemplate your views on learning, teaching, and school. Then decide on a metaphor that best illustrates your personal perspective about education. In words, illustrations, song, pantomime, dance, or other medium of your choice, depict the theme and content of your metaphor for education. You may want to precede this activity with a warm-up exercise to explore the power of metaphorical thinking. For example, you might generate free-association responses to open-ended phrases such as, "Life is a _____." (Zoo? Journey? Pressure cooker? Bank? Car lot? Battle? Party?) "School is a _____." (Prison? Twelve-act play? Family? Game?) A second part of this activity could be to continue on from the initial sentence, "If life is a _____ (zoo, for example), then we are/I am _____."

What new vocabulary does your metaphor contribute? How is it more enlightening and stimulating than the ones that have been around awhile? Does your metaphor encourage cultural diversity, respect for individual differences of children *and* adults, and processes of communication and collaboration? Could you use it productively as a logo on your personalized memo pad or business card? The theme of a speech? An example in a newsletter? A poster or bulletin board? A tool for communicating with legislators or school boards? In your everyday conversation about schools and students and professional colleagues?

Carrying out school reform.

Acknowledging today's students as society's future.

Developing a Plan Infusing Consultation, Collaboration, and Teamwork

Individual differences abound when adults set about the task of developing personal plans for attaining professional goals. School reform, and the student success it is intended to generate, depend upon both individual and organization development (Sparks, 1992). Sparks reminds us that "Continuous improvement is truly an inside-out process in which we first seek to change ourselves before expecting the same of others" (Sparks, 1992, p. 2).

APPLICATION **12.4**
Sharing Personal Metaphors for Education

Participants take turns sharing personal metaphors of education that they created in Application 12.3. These can be assembled into a collage to illustrate the benefits of individual thinking and celebrate the richness of diverse professional perspectives.

In order to develop content and processes for consultation services, and initiate collaboration and teamwork in the school context, educators will want to construct their own personal plans for fulfilling these roles. Brief excerpts from several complete plans by school personnel representing a variety of school roles are:

From Amy P., learning disabilities specialist:

At the end of May I was absolutely exhausted from my first year of teaching. I was tired of trying to think of new ideas for lessons. I was also somewhat dissatisfied with myself for not being more organized and on top of things...Now, because of the consulting class, I have so many ideas now for next fall, that I can't wait to get started.... I had always considered myself a collaborator in my schools, but not so much a consultant. I realize now that many of my attempts such as providing information to others, helping others with students, and discussing ideas with them were common characteristics of the consultant. I also realize now that I have not always been a good consultant. I must stop thinking "I do not fit in," and start thinking, "How can I make myself accepted?" Therefore my priority goal is to change my attitude and discover new ways to be accepted. I have started working toward this goal by asking if I may be on the action team for Outcome 7 of our Professional Development and School Improvement Plan, focusing on inclusion, Class-Within-a-Class, and collaboration. I have many other goals for next year, including writing up a memo to staff explaining my "new" role, and sharing with colleagues the ideas I have learned. I will be teaching an in-service on collaboration, and intend to expand it from the one school I had intended, to several schools...I now feel I have a basis for presenting my ideas on collaboration and consultation to others. Consulting and collaborating are essential in today's schools.

From Martin S., soon to become a special education teacher for learning disabilities after several years in general high school classes:

I'm planning to begin as a listener, not coming in with an agenda...I intend to implement an hour of focused reflection on my job performance every weekend...I will put forth more effort in building my resource bank...Reality has reared its head and I have learned from many hard knocks about working with colleagues and not doing my own thing. In the most practical sense, teamwork works better than a group of solos...Teaming requires appreciation of others and a good sense of one's own role as a team member.... I really believe that being a team player is a state of mind much more than it is a checklist of skills. I can sincerely say that I am eager to be a team member by using my gifts within a larger context than my own classroom and enhancing what others have to offer.

From Priscilla D., speech pathologist:

I have plans for implementing the consultation model during the upcoming school year. I have begun discussing the consultative type of intervention with staff members. Originally I had pinpointed specific teachers with whom I definitely planned to consult, and specific students whom I had recommended would receive the consulting services. At this point, I have begun thinking about altering this approach. It might be better to proceed as planned with teachers with whom I have support already, and act more cautiously with other teachers. Perhaps my most supportive colleagues can help influence some of the more resistant teachers. I plan to set aside specific times each week to use as consulting contact times. These appointment times will become part of my schedule...

From Doris J., high-school facilitator for gifted program:

In my consultation role this year I hope to be more thorough in follow-up, feedback, and evaluation. Many times last year I did not have time (take time) to follow up. If I didn't hear any more from the teacher, I assumed the problem was resolved. I realize now this may not have been the case. A memo in the future might expedite communication.

From Amy Mc., interrelated resource teacher:

I need to put myself into the school consulting role to see how it "fits." I want to involve people from the very start so they feel a sense of ownership. I plan to have bulletin boards in the teachers' lounge that promote collaboration and illustrate the roles more concretely. I also plan to use the newsletter format I have designed to inform parents and staff about the consultation process. I have already made contact with individual teachers to get a feel for who is more receptive to the idea of consultation. I will prepare a presentation for parents, and culminating all of this will be in-service sessions with teachers.

From John B., school psychologist:

As a school psychologist, I am in the consultant role far more than I am a giver of direct service to children. I plan to adapt myself more to the consultant role. The adage, "Plan your work and work your plan" shall be for me. I intend to make myself go to the places I feel least welcome and break new ground...I will record my schedule beforehand as well as during the year so I can know my progress and limitations.... My communication with administrators is important for bringing about change. I will continue to communicate honestly and regularly with them, and ask for suggestions more often. Also, I intend to communicate what I know about the process to parents and teachers. I am not the answer or the expert. I am working toward being a more effective facilitator and consultant.

From Kim Y., interrelated elementary teacher:

There has been some difficulty in getting to know staff and feeling like I am an integral part of the staff. A major obstacle is that my classroom is located in the junior high building. I have found this extremely inconvenient. No one ever walks by my room, nor do I walk by anyone else's room to get to mine. Some of the staff view me as "that teacher over there that some send kids to occasionally." To overcome this, I will try to make myself visible and available before and after school. I will be taking on some collaborative teaching with the sixth-grade teacher in teaching study skills. I also have asked my principal to include me in lunch and recess duties. He was happy I asked, and that I told him my feelings about being included.

From Jan H., consulting teacher for learning disabilities:

In order to free up time for classroom observation and teacher consultation, I plan to spend some of the time that I work with students in seeing them in small groups. This will allow me to do some neat things with students, like role playing and games, and will free some time that I can use to be visible in the regular classroom. I plan on developing more organizational skills. I realize that in the long run being more organized saves time and improves the quality of what one is doing. This probably will be the most difficult for me, since it runs contrary to my personality type, but I feel strongly enough about it that I plan on attempting it.

Challenges for Consultation, Collaboration, and Teamwork in the Future

As educational consultants struggle to establish themselves in school classrooms and buildings, they often find that they are sometimes trail-blazers and usually pioneers in modeling consultation, collaboration, and teamwork. They must serve as consultants and advocates of children with learning and behavior needs when the nature of their needs is changing quickly. They will be collaborating with professionals in fields focusing on problems as varied and alarming as alcohol and other drug abuse, neonatal health, sexually transmitted diseases, disintegration of the family, psychological disorders, poverty, child abuse, English-as-second-language concerns, geographic isolation, environmental hazards, and a host of unresolved or not-yet-recognized needs.

Establishing new collaborative roles is stressful and time-consuming (Newmann, 1991). No simple solution exists for the complex issues and concerns of the future. Now is the time to develop skills of consultation, collaboration, and teamwork on behalf of students with special needs and the society in which they live, because collaboration is the future. It is essential to school reform and restructuring, interagency cooperation, responses to changing student needs, and future global, economic, and technological productivity. As consultants facilitate collaboration and teamwork within the school context to serve special needs each school day, they provide a basis and a framework for continued collaboration throughout the global village. This framework provides help and hope for our students of today who will be the citizens of tomorrow.

APPLICATION **12.5**

A Personal Plan

Develop your personal plan for using concepts of school consultation, collaboration, and co-teaching within the school context and the role responsibilities you anticipate for the future. Make a copy of the plan and mail it to yourself, or ask a course instructor or valued colleague to mail it to you at a designated time in the future, to remind you of the commitment you made when you focused on these issues, set goals, and reflected on actions to achieve those goals.

Tips for Looking Ahead

1. Give talks at community clubs and service organizations about schools, student needs, and consultation, collaboration, and co-teaching.
2. Develop a networking system for support and delivery of positive "strokes" to school personnel and families.
3. Inform teachers of legislative and litigative activity.
4. Host sessions at conferences for policy-makers and administrators.
5. Have an open house and extend invitations to school board members.
6. Follow up the open house with thank-you notes to visitors for their interest and attendance.
7. During the summer send postcards to teachers saying, "I'm looking forward to working with you this year."
8. Don't appear *too* dedicated, in other words, so much so that your involvement is intimidating to others who are still unsure and a bit reluctant.
9. Be an advocate by serving as officer and committee member of organizations whose goals support your consultation goals and role.
10. Never give up!

CHAPTER REVIEW

1. World trends and societal changes in economics, family structure, and demographics will affect students with special needs and their educators in a number of significant ways.

2. Demographers predict that schools of the future will house large numbers of students who are failing and performing poorly on national tests, as well as students who perform better on tests but are not prepared adequately for the demands of the workplace. There will be increasingly large populations of students who have profound learning and behavioral problems brought on by social problems, medical problems, and economic hardships.

3. Benefits of collaborative school consultation include increased assistance for students; minimized labeling and stigmatizing; service to the spirit of inclusion; a more seamless curriculum; parent satisfaction with increased help for their children; enhanced skills through shared teaching; multiplier effects throughout the school context; increased interest among all teachers in helping all students succeed; and student satisfaction with having increased time and attention from their teachers and resource personnel.

4. Obstacles include lack of time, framework, preparation, and evaluation of collaborative school consultation and co-teaching. Also, staff resistance and differing personological and professional perspectives impinge on effectiveness of the combined efforts. The paucity of research on collaborative school consultation's effects on student achievement further hinders promotion of the concepts.

5. Positive ripple effects create benefits well beyond the immediate learning and teaching situations that are the foci of consultation, collaboration, and team efforts.

6. New metaphors are needed for education. Metaphors help define problems and clarify thinking. Visions for the future of learning and teaching that focus upon traditional metaphors for education such as the military, industrial, business, and disease examples, are myopic and demoralizing.

7. Successful schools of the future will require changes in role functions by educators and active involvement by school personnel, families, and entire communities.

TO DO AND THINK ABOUT

1. Discuss three to five major concerns regarding social, economic, and environmental issues of the future that will have a major impact on school learning and teaching. How can consultation, collaboration, and co-teaching help students with special needs succeed in spite of the pressures put upon them by our complex, changing world?

2. What are the major conditions within school contexts and competencies of school personnel that are needed for successful consultation, collaboration, and co-teaching?

3. Select one or more of the issues and concerns discussed in this chapter. Have a panel of four or five members read more about these issues and reflect upon them. Then conduct a panel forum, directing questions from the whole group to panel members for their comments.

   As a variation, have a round-table discussion in which each participant reads about one issue presented in the chapter, and a moderator asks questions having a common denominator of focus—in this case, school consultation and collaboration—of panel members in turn. (A seating arrangement around tables forming a U-shape, with the moderator moving about inside the U-shape space, works well.)

4. Generate a list of possibilities for inclusion in a newsletter to parents, community leaders, or school personnel that reflects consulting teacher roles and the contributions these roles can make to students, school programs, and communities for the future.

5. Create a list of school-reform research questions for the future that might be explored within the context of strong school consultation programs and competent consulting personnel.

6. Find a forum in which to promote your new metaphor for education.

7. Develop a personal plan for implementing collaborative consultation and teamwork in one's own professional role.

8. Now that you have studied the content, process, and context of collaborative schools that utilize consultation services and promote team efforts, what kind of schools would you build if you could start all over in a place where no schools exist?

9. Create a motivational bumper sticker that will proclaim the importance of school and home educators into the next century and the new millennium.

10. AND LAST: Where do we as educators, family members, and lifelong learners, go from here…?….

FOR FURTHER READING

Professional periodicals including:

Educational Leadership
Exceptional Children
Phi Delta Kappan
Teacher Education and Special Education
Journal of Educational and Psychological Consultation
Journal of Staff Development
Remedial and Special Education
Teaching Exceptional Children

REFERENCES

Adler, S. (1993). *Multicultural communication skills in the classroom.* Boston: Allyn & Bacon.

Adults and Attention Deficit Disorder (1997, September 2). *New York Times/Manhattan Mercury,* B-10.

Alberti, R. E., & Emmons, M. L. (1974). *Your perfect right: A guide to assertive behavior* (2nd ed.). San Luis Obispo, CA: Impact.

Alberto, P. A., & Troutman, A. C. (1990). *Applied behavior analysis* (3rd ed.). Columbus, OH: Merrill Publishing Co.

Allington, R. L., & Broikou, K. A. (1988). Development of shared knowledge: A new role for classroom and specialist teachers. *The Reading Teacher,* April 1988, 806–811.

Ammer, J. (1984). The mechanics of mainstreaming: Consider the regular educators' perspective. *Remedial and Special Education, 5*(6), 15–20.

Anderson, M., & Goldberg, P. (1991). *Cultural competence in screening and assessment: Implications for services to young children with special needs ages birth through five.* Minneapolis, MN: PACER Center.

Arcia, E., Keys, L., Gallagher, J. J., & Herrick, H. (1992). *Potential underutilization of part H services: An empirical study of national demographic factors.* Chapel Hill, NC: Carolina Policy Studies Program.

Aronson, E., (1978). *The jigsaw classroom.* Beverly Hills, CA: Sage Publications.

Association of Teacher Educators. (1991). *Restructuring the education of teachers.* Reston, VA: Commission on the Education of Teachers into the 21st Century.

Babcock, N. L., & Pryzwansky, W. B. (1983). Models of consultation: Preferences of educational professionals at five stages of service. *Journal of School Psychology, 21,* 359–366.

Baca, L. M., & Cervantes, H. T. (1984). *The bilingual education interface.* Columbus, OH: Merrill.

Bailey, G. D. (1981). Self directed staff development. *Educational Considerations, 8*(1), 15–20.

Banks, J. A. (1988). *Multiethnic education and practice* (2nd ed.). Boston: Allyn & Bacon.

Banks, J. A., & Banks, C. A. (1989). *Multicultural education: Issues and perspectives.* Boston: Allyn & Bacon.

Bassett, D. S., Jackson, L., Ferrell, K. A., Luckner, J., Hagerty, P. J., Bunsen, T. D., & MacIsaac, D. (1996). Multiple perspectives on inclusive education: Reflections of a university faculty. *Teacher Education and Special Education, 19*(4), 355–386.

Bauch, J. P. (1989). The transParent school model: New technology for parent involvement. *Educational Leadership, 47*(2), 32–35.

Bauwens, J., & Hourcade, J. J. (1997). Cooperative teaching: Pictures of possibilities. *Intervention in School and Clinic, 33* (2), 81–89.

Beakley, B. (1997). Inclusion: Theory, reality, survival. *The Delta Kappa Gamma Bulletin, 63*(3), 32–26.

Beckhoff, A. G., & Bender, W. N. (1989). Programming for mainstream kindergarten success in preschool: Teachers' perceptions of necessary prerequisite skills. *Journal of Early Intervention, 13*(3), 269–280.

Beebe, S. A., & Masterson, J. T. (1994). *Communicating in small groups: Principles and practices* (4th ed.). New York: Harper Collins.

Belth, M. (1977). *The process of thinking.* New York: David McKay.

Bender, W. N. (1988). The other side of placement decisions: Assessment of the mainstream learning environment. *Remedial and Special Education, 9*(5), 28–33.

Benjamin, S. (1989). An ideascape for education: What futurists recommend. *Educational Leadership, 47*(1), 9–14.

Bennett, C. (1999). *Comprehensive multicultural education: Theory and practice* (4th ed.). Boston: Allyn & Bacon.

Bennett, T., DeLuca, D., & Bruns, D. (1997). Putting inclusion into practice: Perspectives of teachers and parents. *Exceptional Children, 64*(1), 115–131.

Bensky, J. M., Shaw, S. F., Gouse, A. S., Bates, H., Dixon, B. E., & Beane, W. E. (1980). Public Law

94-142 and stress: A problem for educators. *Exceptional Children, 47*(1), 24–29.

Berg, I. K. (1994). *Family-based services: A solution focused approach.* New York: W. W. Norton.

Bergan, J. R. (1977). *Behavioral consultation.* Columbus, OH: Merrill.

Bergan, J. R., & Tombari, M. L. (1976). Consultant skill and efficiency and the implementation and outcome of consultation. *Journal of School Psychology, 14*(1), 3–14.

Bevevino, M. (1988). The 87 percent factor. *Delta Kappa Gamma Bulletin, 54*(3), 9–16.

Bickel, W., & Bickel, D. (1986). Effective schools, classrooms and instruction: Implications for special education. *Exceptional Children, 20*(6), 489–519.

Bietau, L. (1994, December). Personal correspondence.

Blackhurst, A. E. (1997). Perspectives on technology in special education. *Teaching Exceptional Children, 29*(5), 41–48.

Blaylock, B. K. (1983). Teamwork in a simulated production environment. *Research in Psychological Type, 6,* 58–67.

Bocchino, R. (March, 1991). Using mind mapping as a note-taking tool. *The Developer, 1,* 4.

Bogdan, R. C., & Biklen, S. K. (1998). *Qualitative research in education: An introduction to theory and methods* (3rd ed.). Boston: Allyn & Bacon.

Bolton, R. (1986). *People skills: How to assert yourself, listen to others, and resolve conflicts.* New York: Simon and Schuster.

Boone, H. A. (1989). Preparing family specialists in early childhood special education. *Teacher Education and Special Education, 12*(3), 96–102.

Bradley, M. O. (1987). Personal communication.

Brewer, E. W., Achilles, C. M., & Fuhriman, J. R. (1993). *Finding funding: Grant writing and project management from start to finish.* Thousand Oaks, CA: Corwin Press.

Britt, S. (1985). Our high priests of process. *Newsweek,* November 18, p. 30.

Britton, N. (1989, May). Training the trainer in Richardson, Texas. *The Developer, 1,* 3.

Brody, C. (1994). Using co-teaching to promote reflective practice. *Journal of Staff Development, 15*(3), 32–36.

Bronfenbrenner, U. (October, 1973). Tear down the walls. *Scholastic Teacher,* pp. 78–79.

Brown, A. L. (1994). The advancement of learning. *Educational Researcher, 23*(8), 4–12.

Brown, A. & Palincsar, A. (1989). Guided, cooperative learning and individual knowledge acquisition. In L. Resnick (Ed.). *Knowing, learning, and instruction: Essays in honor of Robert Glasser;* pp. 393–451. Hillsdale, NJ: Erlbaum.

Brown, D., Pryzwansky, W. B., & Schulte, A. C. (1991). *Psychological consultation: Introduction to theory and practice.* Boston: Allyn & Bacon.

Brown, D., Wyne, M. D., Blackburn, J. E., & Powell, W. C. (1979). *Consultation: Strategy for improving education.* Boston: Allyn & Bacon.

Brownwood, A. W. (1987). *It takes all types!* San Anselmo, CA: Baytree.

Bruner, C. (1991). *Thinking collaboratively: Ten questions and answers to help policymakers improve children's services.* Washington, DC: Education and Human Service Consortium.

Bruner, J. S. (1960). *The process of education.* Cambridge, MA: Harvard University Press.

Bursuck, W. D., & Lessen, E. (1987). A classroom-based model for assessing students with learning disabilities. *Learning Disabilities Focus, 3*(1), 17–29.

Buscaglia, L. (1986). *Loving each other: The challenges of human relationships.* Westminister, MD: Fawcett.

Buzan, T. (1983). *Use both sides of your brain.* New York: E. P. Dutton.

Cain, E. (1985). Developing an administrative plan for the implementation of micro-computers. *Selected Proceedings of Closing the Gap's 1985 National Conference,* 14–16.

Caldwell, S. D. (Ed.). (1989). *Staff development: Handbook of effective practices.* Oxford, OH: National Staff Development Council.

Calhoun, E. F. (1993, October). *Educational Leadership, 51*(2), 62–65.

Campbell, D. E., & Kain, J. M. (1990). Personality type and mode of information presentation: Preference, accuracy, and efficiency in problem-solving. *Journal for Psychological Type, 20,* 47–51.

Campbell, J. (1990). *The hero with a thousand faces.* New York: Work Publishing.

Canning, C. (1991). What teachers say about reflection. *Educational Leadership, 48*(6), 18–21.

Cantwell, D. P., Baker, L., & Rutter, M. (1979). Families of autistic and dysphasic children: Family life and interaction patterns. *Archives of General Psychiatry, 36,* 682–687.

Caplan, G. (1970). *The theory and practice of mental health consultation.* New York: Basic Books.

Carlson, M. (1995). *Winning grants step by step: Support centers of America's complete workbook for planning, developing, writing successful proposals.* San Francisco, CA: Jossey-Bass.

Carlyn, M. (1977). An assessment of the Myers-Briggs type indicator. *Journal of Personality Assessment, 41*(5), 461–473.

Caro, D. J., & Robbins, P. (1991). Talkwalking—thinking on your feet. *Developer,* November 1991, 3–4.

Carolina Computer Access Center (1991) as cited in Male, M. (1994). *Technology for inclusion: Meeting the special needs of all students* (2nd ed.). Boston: Allyn & Bacon.

Cautela, J. R., Cautela, J., & Esonis, S. (1982). *Forms for behavior analysis with children.* Champaign, IL: Research Press.

Cawelti, G. (1997). Making the most of every minute. *ASCD Education Update, 39*(6), 1, 6, 8.

Cawelti, G., & Adkisson, J. (August, 1986). ASCD study documents changes needed in high school curriculum. *Curriculum Update,* 1–10.

Chambers, A. C. (1997). *Has technology been considered? A guide for IEP teams.* Albuquerque, NM: Council of Administrators of Special Education.

Chandler, L. A. (1980). Consultative services in the schools: A model. *Journal of School Psychology, 18*(4), 399–401.

Chavkin, N. F. (1989). Debunking the myth about minority parents. *Educational Horizons, 67,* 119–123.

Cheney, D., Manning, B., & Upham, D. (1997). Project DESTINY: Engaging families of students with emotional and behavioral disabilities. *Teaching Exceptional Children, 30* (1), 24–29.

Christenson, S. L., & Cleary, M. (1990). Consultation and the parent-educator partnership: A perspective. *Journal of Educational and Psychological Consultation, 1,* 219–241.

Cipani, E. (1985). The three phrases of behavioral consultation: Objectives, intervention, and quality assurance. *Teacher Education and Special Education,* 8, 144–152.

Clark, G. M., & Knowlton, H. E. (1988). A closer look at transition issues for the 1990's: A response to Rusch and Menchetti. *Exceptional Children, 54*(4), 365–367.

Cleveland, C. B. (1981). Coming to grips with memo mania. *Penton/I.P.C., Inc. Regency, 33*–87.

Cochran, M. (1987). The parent empowerment process: Building on family strengths. *Equality and Choice, 4,* 9–22.

Coleman, P. G., Eggleston, K. K., Collins, J. F., Holloway, G. D., & Rider, S. K. (1975). A severely hearing impaired child in the mainstream. *Teaching Exceptional Children, 3,* 6–9.

Coley, S. M., & Sheinberg, C. A. (1990). *Proposal writing.* Newbury Park, CA: Sage.

College Entrance Examination Board (1983). *Advanced placement course description: Computer science.* Princeton, NJ: Author.

Collins, C. (1987). *Time management for teachers: Practical techniques and skills that give you more time to teach.* West Nyack, NY: Parker.

Comer, J. (1989). Children can: An address on school improvement. In R. Webb & F. Parkay (Eds.), *Children can: An address on school improvement by Dr. James Comer with responses from Florida's educational community* (pp. 4–17). Gainesville, FL: University of Florida, College of Education Research and Development Center in collaboration with the Alachua County Mental Health Association.

Conoley, J. (1985). Personal correspondence.

Conoley, J. C. (1987). National Symposium on School Consultation. Austin, TX: University of Texas.

Conoley, J. C. (1989). Professional communication and collaboration among educators. In M. C. Reynolds (Ed.), *Knowledge base for the beginning teacher* (pp. 245–253). Oxford, England: Pergamon Press.

Conoley, J. C. (March, 1985). Personal correspondence.

Conoley, J. C., & Conoley, C. W. (1982). *School consultation: A guide to practice and training.* New York: Pergamon Press.

Conoley, J. C., & Conoley, C. W. (1988). Useful theories in school-based consultation. *Remedial and Special Education, 9*(6), 14–20.

Cook, L., & Friend, M. (1993). *Educational leadership for teacher collaboration in program leadership for serving students with disabilities.* Project supported by the Virginia Department of Education (through the U.S. Department of Education, Project #H10034-93).

Corey, M. S., & Corey, G. (1992). *Groups: Process and practice* (4th ed.). Pacific Grove, CA: Brooks Cole.

Correa, V. I., & Tulbert, B. (1993). Collaboration between school personnel in special education and Hispanic families. *Journal of Educational and Psychological Consultation, 4*(3), 253–265.

Correa, V. I., & Weismantel, J. (1991). Multicultural issues related to families with an exceptional child. In M. J. Fine (Ed.), *Collaboration with parents of exceptional children* (pp. 83–102). Brandon, VT: Clinical Psychology Publishing Co.

Covey, S. R. (1989). *The 7 habits of highly effective people.* New York: Simon and Schuster.

Cramer, S., Erzkus, A., Mayweather, K., Pope, K., Roeder, J., & Tone, T. (1997). Connecting with siblings. *Teaching Exceptional Children, 30* (1), 46–49.

Cross, T. (1988). Services to minority populations: What does it mean to be a culturally competent professional? *Focal Point, 2,* 1–3.

Cross, T. (1996). Developing a knowledge base to support cultural competence. *Prevention Report, 1,* 2–5.

Crowell, S. (1989). A new way of thinking: The challenge of the future. *Educational Leadership, 47*(1), 60–63.

Cuban, L. (1986). Persistent instruction: Another look at constancy in the classroom. *Phi Delta Kappan, 68,*(1), 7–11.

Curtis, M. J., & Zins, J. E. (1981). *The theory and practice of school consultation.* Springfield, IL: Charles C. Thomas.

Curtis, M. J., & Zins, J. E. (1988). Effects of training in consultation and instructor feedback on acquisition of consultation skills. *Journal of School Psychology, 26,* 185–190.

Cushner, K., McClelland, A., & Safford, P. (1992). *Human diversity in education: An integrative approach.* New York: McGraw Hill.

Daggett, W. R. (1989). *The changing nature of work—A challenge to education.* Unpublished speech delivered to the Kansas Legislative and Educational Leaders.

Daniels, H. (1996). The best practice project: Building parent partnerships in Chicago. *Educational Leadership, 53* (7), 38–43.

Davies, D. (1988). Low-income parents and the schools: A research report and plan for action. *Equity and Choice, 4,* 51–59.

Davis, G. A., & Rimm, S. B. (1989). *Education of the gifted and talented.* Englewood Cliffs, NJ: Prentice-Hall.

Davis, W. E. (1983a). Competencies and skills required to be an effective resource teacher. *Journal of Learning Disabilities, 16,* 596–598.

Davis, W. E. (1983b). *The special educator: Strategies for succeeding in today's world.* Austin, TX: PRO-ED.

Davis, W. E. (1985). *The special educator: Meeting the challenge for professional growth.* Austin, TX: PRO-ED.

Davis, W. E. (1989). The regular education initiative debate: Its promises and problems. *Exceptional Children, 55*(5), 440–447.

deBono, E. (1973). *Lateral thinking: Creativity step by step.* New York: Harper & Row.

DeBoer, A. L. (1986). *The art of consulting.* Chicago: Arcturus.

Deno, S. L. (1987). Curriculum-based measurement. *Teaching Exceptional Children, 20*(1), 41–47.

Deshler, D. (1985). Metaphors and values in higher education. *Academe,* November–December, 1985, 22–29.

Deshler, D. D., & Schumaker, J. B. (1986). Learning strategies: An instructional alternative for low-achieving adolescents. *Exceptional Children, 52,* 583–590.

Dettmer, P. (1994). IEPs for gifted secondary students. *The Journal of Secondary Gifted Education, V*(4), 52–59.

Dettmer, P. (1980). The extended classroom: A gold mine for gifted students. *Journal for the Education of the Gifted, 3*(3), 133–142.

Dettmer, P. (1981). The effects of teacher personality type on classroom values and perceptions of gifted students. *Research in Psychological Type, 3,* 48–54.

Dettmer, P. (1982). Preventing burnout in teachers of the gifted. *G/C/T.* 21, 37–41.

Dettmer, P. (1986). Gifted program preservice and staff development: Pragmatics and possibilities. *Gifted Child Quarterly, 30*(3), 99–102.

Dettmer, P. (1989). The consulting teacher in programs for gifted and talented students. *Arkansas Gifted Education Magazine, 3*(2), 4–7.

Dettmer, P. (1989). The teachers' lounge: Professional asset or liability? *The Master Teacher State-of-the-Art Papers, 20*(25), 1–4.

Dettmer, P. (Ed.). (1990). *Staff development for gifted programs: Putting it together and making it work.* Washington, DC: National Association for Gifted Children.

Dettmer, P., & Landrum, M. (1997). *Staff development: The key to effective gifted education programs.* Waco, TX: Prufrock.

Dettmer, P., & Lane, J. (1989). An integrative model for educating very able students in rural school districts. *Educational Considerations, 17*(1), 36–39.

Dickens, V. J., & Jones, C. J. (1990). Regular/special education consultation: A teacher education training strategy for implementation. *Teacher Education and Special Education, 13*(3–4), 235–239.

Dishon, D., & O'Leary, P. W. (1989). Tips for teachers: Time saver options. *Cooperative Learning, 10*(2), 30.

Dishon, D., & O'Leary, P. W. (1990). Social skills and processing. *Cooperative Learning, 10* (2), 35–36.

Dobson, R. L., Dobson, J. E., & Koetting, J. R. (1985). *Looking at, talking about, and living with children: Reflections on the process of schooling.* Lanham, MD: University Press of America.

Dorris, M. (1979). Why I'm not thankful for Thanksgiving. *Midwest Race Desegregation Assistance Center Horizons, 1*(5), 1.

Douglass, M. E., & Douglass, D. N. (1993). *Manage your time, manage your work, manage yourself.* New York: AMACOM.

Dover, W. (1994). *The inclusion facilitator.* Manhattan, KS: Master Teacher.

Dragan, E. F. (1994). Transition planning: What schools need to know. *CEC Today, 1*(7), 1, 14–15.

Dunn, R., & Dunn, K. (1978). *Teaching students through their individual learning styles.* Reston, VA: Reston Publishing.

Dyck, N., & Dettmer, P. (1989). Collaborative consultation: A promising tool for serving gifted learning-disabled students. *Journal of Reading, Writing, and Learning Disabilities, 5*(3), 253–264.

Dyck, N. (1997). *Self-advocacy form.* Lawrence, KS: Curriculum Solutions.

Dyck, N., and Pemberton, J. (1997). *A dozen tools for paras.* Lawrence, KS: Curriculum Solutions.

Dyck, N., Pemberton, J., Woods, K., & Sundbye, N. (1996). *Creating inclusive schools: A new design for all students.* Lawrence, KS: Curriculum Solutions.

Dyck, N., Sundbye, N., & Pemberton, J. (1997). A recipe for efficient co-teaching. *Teaching Exceptional Children, 30*(2), 42–45.

Edelman, M. W. (1987). *Families in peril. An agenda for social change.* Cambridge: Harvard University Press.

Edgar, G. (1990). Is it time to change our view of the world? *Beyond Behavior, 1*(1), 9–13.

Educational leadership. (December 1994/January 1995). *52*(4).

Edyburn, D., & Majsterek, D. (1993). Technology applications for individuals with LD: What can we say today? *LD Forum, 19* (1), 3–5.

Edyburn, D. L. (1994). An equation to consider: The portfolio assessment knowledge base + technology = The Grady Profile, *LD Forum, 19*(4), 35–38.

Eisner, E. W. (1988). The ecology of school improvement. *Educational Leadership, 45*(5), 24–29.

Elkind, D. (1994). *Ties that stress: The new family imbalance.* Cambridge: Harvard University Press.

Epstein, J. L. (1987). Parent involvement: What research says to administrators. *Education and Urban Society, 19,* 119–136.

Epstein, J. L. (1989). Building parent-teacher partnerships in inner-city schools. *Family Resource Coalition Report, 8,* 7.

Epstein, J. L. (1995). School/family/community partnerships: Caring for the children we share. *Phi Delta Kappan, 76* (9), 701–712.

Epstein, J. L., & Becker, J. H. (1982). Teacher practices of parent involvement. *The Elementary School Journal, 83,* 103–113.

Epstein, J. L. (1991). Paths to partnership: What we can learn from federal, state, district, and school initiatives. *Phi Delta Kappan, 75*(5), 344–349.

ERIC Clearinghouse on Handicapped and Gifted Children (1987a). Critical presentation skills. *ERIC Digest 449.* Reston, VA: Council for Exceptional Children.

ERIC Clearinghouse on Handicapped and Gifted Children (1987b). Lesson structure. *ERIC Digest 448.* Reston, VA: Council for Exceptional Children.

Evans, S. (1980). The consultant role of the resource teacher. *Exceptional Children, 46*(5), 402–404.

Exceptional Children (October/November, 1994). Special Issue: Technology-Based Assessment within Special Education.

Fad, K. S. (1990). The fast track to success: Social behavioral skills. *Intervention in School and Clinic, 26*(1), 39–43.

Feuer, D., & Geber, B. (1988). Uh-Oh...second thoughts about adult learning theory. *Training,* December, 1988.

Field, S. L., & Hill, D. S. (1988). Contextual appraisal: A framework for meaningful evaluation of special education programs. *Remedial and Special Education, 9*(4), 22–30.

Finders, M., & Lewis, C. (1994). Why some parents don't come to school. *Educational Leadership, 51* (8), 50–54.

Fisher, R., & Ury, W., and Patton. (1991). *Getting to yes* (2nd ed.). New York: Simon & Schuster.

French, N. K. (1997). Management of paraeducators. In A. L. Pickett & K. Gerlach (Eds.). *Supervising Paraeducators in School Settings.* Austin, TX: PRO-ED.

French, N. K., & Pickett, A. L. (1997). Paraprofessionals in special education: Issues for teacher educators. *Teacher Education and Special Education, 20*(1), 61–73.

Friend, M. (1984). Consultation skills for resource teachers. *Learning Disability Quarterly, 7,* 246–250.

Friend, M. (1988). Putting consultation into context: Historical and contemporary perspectives. *Remedial and special Education, 9*(6), 7–13.

Friend, M., & Bursuck, W. D. (1996). *Including students with special needs: A practical guide for classroom teachers.* Boston: Allyn & Bacon.

Friend, M., & Cook, L. (1990). Collaboration as a predictor for success in school reform. *Journal of Educational and Psychological Consultation, 1*(1), 69–86.

Friend, M., & Bauwens, J. (1988). Managing resistance: An essential consulting skill for learning disabilities teachers. *Journal of Learning Disabilities, 21,* 556–561.

Fuchs, D., & Fuchs, L. S. (1988). Evaluation of the adaptive learning environments model. *Exceptional Children, 55,* 115–127.

Fuchs, D., & Fuchs, L. S. (1994). Inclusive schools movement and the radicalization of special education reform. *Exceptional Children, 60*(4), 294–309.

Fuchs, D., Fuchs, L. S., Dulan, J., Roberts, H., & Fernstrom, P. (1992). Where is the research on consultation effectiveness? *Journal of Educational and Psychological Consultation, 3*(2), 151–174.

Fuchs, L. L., Hamlett, C. L., & Fuchs, D. (1990). *Basic math, basic reading, basic spelling* [computer programs]. Austin, TX: PRO-ED.

Fuchs, L. S. (1987). Program development. *Teaching Exceptional Children, 20*(1), 42–44.

Fuchs, L. S., Fuchs, D., & Hamlett, C. L. (1990). Curriculum-based measurement: A standardized, long-term goal approach to monitoring student progress. *Academic Therapy, 25*(5), 5, 615–632.

Fullan, M., & Miles, M. (June 1992). Getting reform right: What works and what doesn't. *Phi Delta Kappan,* 745–752.

Fuller, R. B. (1975). *Explorations in the geometry of thinking synergetics.* New York: Macmillan.

Futrell, M. (1989). Mission not accomplished: Education reform in retrospect. *Phi Delta Kappan, 71*(1), 9–14.

Gajria, M., Salend, S. J., & Hemrick, M. A. (1994). Teacher acceptability of testing modifications for mainstreamed students. *Learning Disabilities Research & Practice, 9*(4), 236–243.

Gallagher, J. J. (1985). *Teaching the gifted child* (3rd ed.). Boston: Allyn & Bacon.

Gallessich, J. (1973). Organizational factors influencing consultation in schools. *Journal of School Psychology, 11*(1), 57–65.

Gallessich, J. (1974). Training the school psychologist for consultation. *Journal of School Psychology, 12,* 138–149.

Gardner, J. E. (1994). The technological edge. *CEC Today, 1*(8),10.

Garmston, R. (1988, October). Giving gifts. *The Developer,* pp. 3, 6.

Garmston, R. (1990, February). Maintaining momentum, part II: Keeping the train rolling. *The Developer,* pp. 3, 7.

Garmston, R. J., & Wellman, B. M. (1992). *How to make presentations that teach and transform.* Alexandria, VA: Association for Supervision and Curriculum Development.

Gayle, M. (1990). Toward the 21st century. *Adult Learning, 1*(4), 10–14.

Geisert, P. G., & Futrell, M. K. (1995). *Teachers, computers, and curriculum: Microcomputers in the classroom* (2nd ed.). Boston: Allyn & Bacon.

Gerber, M., & Kauffmann, J. (1981). Peer tutoring in academic settings. In P. Strain (Ed.), *Utilization of classroom peers as behavior change agents* (pp. 155–187). New York: Plenum Publishing.

Gersten, R., Darch, C., Davis, G., & George, N. (1991). Apprenticeship and intensive training of consulting teachers: A naturalistic study. *Exceptional Children, 57*(3), 226–236.

Giangreco, M. F. (1993). Using creative problem-solving methods to include students with severe disabilities in general education activities. *Journal of Educational and Psychological Consultation, 4*(2), 113–135.

Giangreco, M. F., Dennis, R., Cloninger, C., Edelman, S., & Schattman R. (1993). "I've counted Jon": Transformational experiences of teachers educating students with disabilities. *Exceptional Children, 59*(4), 359–372.

Giangreco, M. F., Edelman, S. W., Luiselli, T. E., & MacFarland, S. Z. C. (1997). Helping or hovering? Effects of instructional assistant proximity on students with disabilities. *Exceptional Children, 64* (1) 7–18.

Gibb, J. R. (1974). Defensive communication. In R. S. Cathcart & L. A. Samovar (Eds.), *Small group communication: A reader* (2nd ed.), (pp. 327–33). Dubuque, IA: William C. Brown.

Goodlad, J. (1984). *A place called school: Prospects for the future.* New York: McGraw-Hill.

Goodlad, J. (1990). Better teachers for our nation's schools. *Phi Delta Kappan, 72*(3), 185–194.

Gordon, T. (1974). *T.E.T.: Teacher effectiveness training.* New York: Wyden.

Gordon, T. (1977). *Leader effectiveness training, L.E.T.: The no-lose way to release the productive potential in people.* Toronto: Bantam.

Gorman, J. C., & Balter, L. (1997). Culturally sensitive parent education: A critical review of quantitative research. *Review of Educational Research, 67*(3), 339–369.

Graubard, P. S., Rosenberg, H., & Miller, M. B. (1971). Student applications of behavior modification to teachers and environments or ecological approaches to deviancy. In E. A. Ramp & B. L. Hopkins (Eds.), *A new direction for education: Behavior analysis* (pp. 80–101). Lawrence, KS: University of Kansas.

Greenburg, D. E. (1987). *A special educator's perspective on interfacing special and general education: A review for administrators.* Clearinghouse on Handicapped and Gifted Children. Reston, VA: The Council for Exceptional Children.

Greenwood, C. R. (1994). Advances in technology-based assessment within special education. *Exceptional Children, 61*(2), 102–104.

Gregorc, A. F., & Ward, H. B. (1977). A new definition for individual: Implications for learning and teaching. *NASSP Bulletin, 61,* 20–26.

Gresham, F. M., & Kendell, G. K. (1987). School consultation research: Methodological critique and future research directions. *School Psychology Review, 16*(3), 306–316.

Guskey, T. R. (1985). Staff development and teacher change. *Educational Leadership, 42*(7), 57–60.

Guskey, T. R. (1988). Mastery learning and mastery teaching: How they complement each other. *Principal, 68,* 1, 6–8.

Guskey, T. R. (1990). Integrating innovations. *Educational Leadership, 47,* 5, 11–15.

Guthrie, G. P., & Guthrie, L. F. (1991). Streamlining interagency collaboration for youth at risk. *Educational Leadership, 49*(1), 17–22.

Gutkin, T. B. (1986). Consultees' perceptions of variables relating to the outcomes of school-based consultation interactions. *School Psychology Review, 15*(3), 375–82.

Gutkin, T. B., & Curtis, M. L. (1982). School-based consultation theory and techniques. In C. R. Reynolds & T. B. Gutkin (Eds.), *The handbook of school psychology* (pp. 796–828). New York: Wiley.

Haight, S. L. (1984). Special education teacher consultant: Idealism versus realism. *Exceptional Children, 50*(6), 507–515.

Halford, J. M. (1996). How parent liaisons connect families to schools. *Educational Leadership, 53* (7), 34–36.

Hall, C. S., & Lindzey, G. (1978). *Theories of personality* (3rd ed.). New York: Wiley.

Hall, E. T. (1959). *The silent language.* New York: Doubleday.

Hall, E. T. (1981). *The silent language.* Garden City, NY: Anchor Press.

Hall, G. E., & Hord, S. M. (1987). *Change in schools: Facilitating the process.* Albany: State University of New York Press.

Hall, R. V., & Houten, R. V. (1980). *The measurement of behavior.* Austin, TX: PRO-ED.

Hallahan, D. P., & Kauffman, J. M. (1991). *Exceptional children: Introduction to special education.* Englewood Cliffs, NJ: Prentice Hall.

Hallahan, D. P., Kauffman, J. M., Lloyd, J. W., & McKinney, J. D. (Eds.) (1988). The regular education initiative. *Journal of Learning Disabilities, 21*(1), special issue.

Halpern, A. S. (1992). Transition: Old wine in new bottles. *Exceptional Children, 58*(3), 202–211.

Hammer, A. L. (1985). Typing or stereotyping: Unconscious bias in applications of psychological type theory. *Journal of Psychological Type, 10,* 14–18.

Hansen, J. C., Himes, B. S., & Meier, S. (1990). *Consultation: Concepts and practices.* Englewood Cliffs, NJ: Prentice Hall.

Harris, A. J., & Sipay, E. R. (1990). *How to increase reading ability.* White Plains, NY: Longman.

Harris, K. C., & Zetlin, A. G. (1993). Exploring the collaborative ethic in an urban school: A case study. *Journal of Educational and Psychological Consultation, 4*(4), 305–317.

Hay, C. A. (1984). One more time: What do I do all day? *Gifted Child Quarterly, 28*(1), 17–20.

Henkelman, J. (1991, February). Staff developers as consultants. *The Developer.* Oxford, OH: National Staff Development Council.

Henning-Stout, M. (1994). Consultation and connected knowing: What we know is determined by the questions we ask. *Journal of Educational and Psychological Consultation, 5*(1), 5–21.

Heron, T. E., & Harris, K. C. (1982). *The educational consultant: Helping professionals, parents, and mainstreamed students.* Boston: Allyn & Bacon.

Heron, T. E., & Harris, K. C. (1987). *The educational consultant: Helping professionals, parents, and mainstreamed students.* Austin, TX: PRO-ED.

Heron, T. E., & Kimball, W. H. (1988). Gaining perspective with the educational consultation research base: Ecological considerations and further recommendations. *Remedial and Special Education, 9*(6), 21–28, 47.

Hillerman, T. (1990). *Coyote waits.* New York: Harper & Row.

Hodgkinson, H. L. (1985). *All one system: Demographics of education, kindergarten through graduate school.* Washington, DC: American Council on Education.

Hodgkinson, H. L. (1988). The right schools for the right kids. *Educational Leadership, 45*(6), 10–14.

Hodgkinson, H. L. (1989). *The same client: The demographics of education and service delivery systems.* Washington, DC: Institute for Educational Leadership, Center for Demographic Policy.

Hogan, J. R. (1975). The three-way conference: Parent, teacher, child. *The Elementary School Journal, 75*(5), 311–15.

Holmes Group Forum. (1990). Back to school basics, *The Holmes Group Forum, 5* (1), 1, 3.

Hoover-Dempsey, K., & Sandler, H. (1997). Why do parents become involved in their children's education. *Review of Educational Research, 67* (1), 3–42.

Howey, K. R., Bents, R., & Corrigan, D. (Eds.). (1981). *School-focused inservice: Descriptions and discussions.* Reston, VA: Association of Teacher Educators.

Howey, K. R., & Zimpher, N. L. (1991). *Restructuring the education of teachers: Report of the Commission on the Education of Teachers into the 21st Century.* Reston, VA: Association of Teacher Educators.

Hoy, W. K. (1990). Organizational climate and culture: A conceptual analysis of the school work place. *Journal of Educational and Psychological Consultation, 1*(2), 149–168.

Huefner, D. S. (1988). The consulting teacher model: Risks and opportunities. *Exceptional Children, 54*(5), 403–414.

Huff, B., & Telesford, M. C. (1994). Outreach efforts to involve families of color in the Federation of Families for Children's Mental Health. *Focal Point, 10,* 180–184.

Hughes, C. A., & Ruhl, K. L. (1987). The nature and extent of special educators' contacts with students' parents. *Teacher Education and Special Education, 10,* 180–184.

Hughs, J., & Falk, R. (1981). Resistance, reactance, and consultation. *Journal for School Psychology, 19*(2), 139–142.

Hunter, M. (1985). Promising theories die young. *ASCD Update,* May 1985, 1, 3.

Idol, L. (1986). *Collaborative school consultation: Recommendations for state departments of education.* Reston, VA: The Task Force on School Consultation, Teacher Education Division, Council for Exceptional Children.

Idol, L. (1988). A rationale and guidelines for establishing special education consultation programs. *Remedial and Special Education, 9*(6), 48–58.

Idol, L. (1990). The scientific art of classroom consultation. *Journal of Educational and Psychological Consultation, 1*(1), 3–22.

Idol, L., Paolucci-Whitcomb, P., & Nevin, A. (1986). *Collaborative consultation.* Austin, TX: PRO-ED.

Idol, L., & West, J. F. (1987). Consultation in special education (Part II): Training and practices. *Journal of Learning Disabilities, 20,* 474–497.

Idol, L., West, J. F., & Lloyd, S. R. (1988). Organizing and implementing specialized reading programs: A collaborative approach involving classroom, remedial, and special education teachers. *Remedial and Special Education, 9,* 2, 54–61.

Idol-Maestas, L. (1981). A teacher training model: The resource/consulting teacher. *Behavioral Disorders, 6*(2), 108–121.

Idol-Maestas, L. (1983). *Special educator's consultation handbook.* Rockville, MD: Aspen.

Idol-Maestas, L., & Celentano, R. (1986). Teacher consultant services for advanced students. *Roeper Review, 9*(1), 34–36.

Idol-Maestes, L., Lloyd, S., & Lilly, M. S. (1981). Noncategorical approach to direct service and teachers education. *Exceptional Children, 48,* 213–20.

Idol-Maestas, L., & Ritter, S. (1985). A follow-up study of resource/consulting teachers: Factors that facilitate and inhibit teacher consultation. *Teacher Education and Special Education, 8,* 121–131.

Inclusion gains ground. (1995, December). *Education Update, 37*(9). Alexandria, VA: Association for Supervision and Curriculum Development.

Ingoldsby, B. B., & Smith, S. (1995). *Families in multicultural perspective.* New York: The Guilford Press.

Jenkins, J. R., & Jenkins, L. (1985). Peer tutoring in elementary and secondary programs. *Focus on Exceptional Children, 17,* 6, 1–12.

Jenkins, J. R., Pious, C. G., & Jewell, M. (1990). Special education and the regular education initiative: Basic assumptions. *Exceptional Children, 56,* 479–491.

Jersild, A. T. (1955). *When teachers face themselves.* New York: Teachers College Press, Columbia University.

Johnson, D. W., & Johnson, F. P. (1987). *Joining together: Group theory and group skills* (3rd ed.). Englewood Cliffs, NJ: Prentice-Hall.

Johnson, D., & Johnson, R. (1980). The key to effective inservice: Building teacher-teacher collaborations. *The Developer,* pp. 223–236.

Johnson, D. W., & Johnson, R. T. (1987). *Learning together and alone: Cooperative, competitive, & individualistic learning* (2nd ed.). Englewood Cliffs, NJ: Prentice Hall.

Johnson, L. J., Pugach, M. C., & Hammittee, D. J. (1988). Barriers to effective special education consultation. *Remedial and Special Education, 9,*(6), 41–47.

Johnson, S. (1992). *"Yes" or "No": A guide to better decisions.* New York: Harper Collins.

Joint Committee on Teacher Planning for Students with Disabilities (1995). *Planning for academic diversity in America's classrooms: Windows on reality, research, change, and practice.* Lawrence: The University of Kansas Center for Research on Learning.

Joyce, B. (Ed.). (1990). *Changing school culture through staff development.* Alexandria, VA: The Association for Supervision and Curriculum Development.

Joyce, B. R., & Showers, B. (1983). *Power in staff development through research on training.* Alexandria, VA: The Association for Supervision and Curriculum Development.

Jung, C. G. (1923). *Psychological types.* New York: Harcourt Brace.

Jung, C. G. (1954). *The development of personality* (R.F.C. Hull, trans.). New York: Pantheon.

Jusjka, J. (1991). Observations. *Phi Delta Kappan, 72*(6), 468–470.

Katz, N. H., & Lawyer, J. W. (1983). Communication and conflict management skills: Strategies for individual and systems changes. *Nonviolence and Change National Forum, 63,* 31.

Kauffman, J. M. (1994). Places of change: Special education's power and identity in an era of educational reform. *Journal of Learning Disabilities, 27*(10), 610–618.

Kay, P., & Fitzgerald, M. (1997). Parents + teachers + action research = real involvement. *Teaching Exceptional Children, 30* (1), 8–11.

Keefe, J. W., & Ferrell, B. G. (1990). Developing a defensible learning style paradigm. *Educational Leadership, 48*(2), 57–61.

Keirsey, D., & Bates, M. (1978). *Please understand me: Character and temperament types.* Del Mar, CA: Prometheus Nemesis.

Keirsey, D., & Bates, M. (1984). *Please understand me: Character and temperament types.* Del Mar, CA: Gnosology Books Ltd.

Keller, H. R. (1981). Behavioral consultation. In J. C. Conoley (Ed.), *Consultation in the schools* (pp. 59–100). New York: Academic Press.

Kerns, G. M. (1992). Helping professionals understand families. *Teacher Education and Special Education, 15*(1), 49–55.

Keyes, R. (1991). *Timelock: How life got so hectic and what you can do about it.* New York: Academic Press.

Knight, M. T., Meyers, H. W., Paolucci-Whitcomb, P., Hasazi, S. E., & Nevin, A. (1981). A four-year evaluation of consulting teacher service. *Behavioral Disorders, 6,* 92–100.

Knowles, M. (1970). *The modern practice of adult education.* New York: Association Press.

Knowles, M. (1978). *The adult learner: A neglected species.* Houston, TX: Gulf Publishing.

Knowles, W. C. (1997). *An investigation of teachers' perceptions of special education placement and inclusion: A qualitative case study of two middle schools.* Unpublished doctoral dissertation, Kansas State University, Manhattan, KS.

Kolb, D. A. (1976). *Learning-style inventory: Technical manual.* Boston: McBer & Co.

Koren, P., & DeChillo, N. (1995). Empowering families whose children have emotional disorders. *Focal Point, 9* (1), 1, 3–4.

Kozoll, C. E. (1982). *Time management for educators,* Fastback #175. Bloomington, IN: Phi Delta Kappa Educational Foundation.

Kroth, R. L. (1985). *Communication with parents of exceptional children: Improving parent-teacher relationships.* Denver: Love.

Kummerow, J. M., and McAllister, L. W. (1988). Teambuilding with the Myers-Briggs Type Indicator: Case studies. *Journal of Psychological Type, 15,* 25–32.

Kurland, D. J., Sharp, R. M., & Sharp, V. F. (1997). *Introduction to the INTERNET for education.* Belmont, CA: Wadsworth.

LaBonte, K., Leighty, C., Mills, S. J., & True, M. L. (1995). Whole-faculty study groups: Building the capacity for change through interagency collaboration. *Journal of Staff Development, 16*(3), 45–47.

Lakein, A. (1973). *How to get control of your time and your life.* New York: McKay.

Land, M., & Turner, S. (1997). *Tools for schools: Applications software for the classroom* (2nd ed.). Belmont, CA: Wadsworth.

Lanier, J. E. (1982). Teacher education: Needed research and practice for the preparation of teaching professionals. In D. C. Corrigin, D. J. Palmer, & P. A. Alexander (Eds.), *The future of teacher education.* College Station, TX: Dean's Grant Project, College of Education, Texas A & M University.

LaTorre, E. (1995). Appreciation of cultural diversity through awareness of personality types. *Delta Kappa Gamma Bulletin, 61*(2), 13–17.

Lawren, B. (1989). Seating for success. *Psychology Today,* September 1989, 16, 18–19.

Lawrence, G. (1982). *People types and tiger stripes.* Gainesville, FL: Center for Applications of Psychological Type, Inc.

Lawrence, G. (1984). A synthesis of learning style research involving the MBTI. *Journal of Psychological Type, 8,* 2–15.

Lawrence, G. (1988, September). *Type and stereotype: Sorting out the differences.* Speech presented at the 1988 conference of Association for Psychological Type—Southwest, Albuquerque, NM.

Lawrence, G., & DeNovellis, R. (1974). *Correlation of teacher personality variables (Myers-Briggs) and classroom observation data.* Paper presented at American Educational Research Association conference.

Leitch, M. L., & Tangri, S. S. (1988). Barriers to home-school collaboration. *Educational Horizons, 66,* 70–75.

Leviton, A., Mueller, M., & Kauffman, C. (1992). The family-centered consultation model: Practical application for professionals. *Infants and Young Children, 4,* 1–8.

Levy-Shiff, R. (1986). Mother-father-child interactions in families with mentally retarded young child. *American Journal of Mental Deficiency, 91,* 141–142.

Lewis, A. C. (1992). All together now: Building collaboration. *Phi Delta Kappan, 73*(5), 348–349.

Lewis, R. B. (1993). *Special education technology: Classroom applications.* Pacific Grove, CA: Brooks/Cole.

Lieberman, L. (1984). *Preventing special education… for those who don't need it.* Newtonville, MA: GloWorm.

Lieberman, L. (1986). *Special educator's guide….to special education.* Newtonville, MA: GloWorm.

Lightfoot, S. (1981). Toward conflict and resolution. Relationships between families and schools. *Theory into Practice, 20*(2), 97–104.

Lilly, M. S. (1987). Lack of focus on special education in literature on educational reform. *Exceptional Children, 53*(4), 325–326.

Lilly, M. S., & Givens-Ogle, L. B. (1981). Teacher consultation: Present, past, and future. *Behavioral Disorders, 6*(2), 73–77.

Linan-Thompson, S., & Jean, R. (1997). Completing the parent participation puzzle: Accepting diversity. *Teaching Exceptional Children, 30* (2), 46–50.

Lindle, J. C. (1989). What do parents want from principals and educators? *Educational Leadership, 47*(2), 12–14.

Lindsley, O. (1964). Direct measurement and prosthesis of retarded children. *Journal of Education, 147,* 62–81.

Lippitt, G. L. (March, 1983). Can conflict resolution be win win? *The School Administrator,* pp. 20–22.

Lippitt, G., and Lippitt, R. (1978). *The consulting process in action.* San Diego, CA: University Associates.

Lipsky, D. K. (1994). National survey gives insight into inclusive movement. *Inclusive Education Programs, LRP Publications, 1,* 3, 4–7.

Lloyd, J. W., Crowley, E. P., Kohler, F. W., & Strain, P. S. (1988). Redefining the applied research agenda: Cooperative learning, prereferral, teacher consultation, and peer-mediated interventions. *Journal of Learning Disabilities, 21,* 43–52.

Lopez, E. C., Dalal, S. M., & Yoshida, R. K. (1993). An examination of professional cultures: Implications for the collaborative consultation model. *Journal of Educational and Psychological Consultation, 4*(3), 197–213.

Loucks-Horsley, S., Harding, C. K., Arbuckle, M. A., Murray, L. B., Dubea, C., & Williams, M. K. (1987). *Continuing to learn: A guidebook for teacher development.* Andover, MA: The Regional Laboratory for Educational Improvement of the Northeast and Islands.

Lovett, H. (1996). Learning to listen: Positive approaches and people with difficult behavior. Baltimore, MD: Brookes.

Lovitt, T. C. (1995). *Tactics for teaching* (2nd ed.) Englewood Cliffs, NJ: Merrill, Prentice Hall.

Lubetkin, B. (January, 1997). *Master the art of apologizing. The Manager's Intelligence Report.* Chicago: Lawrence Ragan Communications.

Lueder, D. C. (1989). Tennessee parents were invited to participate—and they did. *Educational Leadership, 47*(2), 15–17.

Luft, J. (1984). *Group processes: An introduction to group dynamics* (3rd ed.). Palo Alto, CA: Mayfield.

Lugg, C. A., & Boyd, W. L. (1993). Leadership for collaboration: Reducing risk and fostering resilience. *Phi Delta Kappan, 75*(3), 253–258.

Lynch, E. W., & Hansen, M. J. (1992). *Developing cross-cultural competence: A guide for working with young children and their families.* Baltimore: Paul H. Brooks.

Lynch, E. W., & Stein, R. C. (1990). Parent participation by ethnicity: Comparison of Hispanic, Black, and Anglo families. *Educating exceptional children* (5th ed.). Guilford, CT: Dushkin.

Maag, J. W. (1989). Assessment in social skills training: Methodological and conceptual issues for research and practice. *Remedial and Special Education, 10*(4), 6–17.

MacKenzie, A., & Waldo, K. C. (1981). *About time! A woman's guide to time management.* New York: McGraw Hill.

MacKenzie, R. A. (1975). *The time trap.* New York: McGraw Hill.

Madden, N. A., Slavin, R. E., Karweit, N. L., & Livermon, B. J. (1989). Restructuring the urban elementary school. *Educational Leadership, 46*(5), 14–18.

Maeroff, G. I. (1991). Assessing alternative assessment. *Phi Delta Kappan, 73*(4), 273–281.

Maeroff, G. I. (1993). Building teams to rebuild schools. *Phi Delta Kappan, 74,*(7), 512–519.

Maher, C. A. (1985). *Professional self-management: Techniques for services providers.* Baltimore: Paul H. Brookes.

Majsterek, D., & Wilson, R. (1993). Computer-assisted instruction (CAI): An update on applications for students with learning disabilities. *LD Forum, 19* (1), 19–21.

Making assessments of diverse students meaningful. (1997, October). *CEC Today, 4*(4), 1, 9.

Male, M. (1994). *Technology for Inclusion: Meeting the special needs of all students* (2nd ed.). Boston: Allyn & Bacon.

Margolis, H., & Brannigan, G. G. (1986). Building trust with parents. *Academic Therapy, 22,* 71–74.

Margolis, H., & McGettigan, J. (1988). Managing resistance to instructional modifications in mainstream settings. *Remedial and Special Education, 9,* 15–21.

Martin, R. (1991). *Extraordinary children—ordinary lives.* Champaign, IL: Research Press.

Maslach, C. (1982). *Burnout: The cost of caring.* Englewood Cliffs, NJ: Prentice Hall.

Maslach, C. and Pines, A. (1977). The burnout syndrome in the daycare setting. *Child Care Quarterly, 6,* 100–113.

Mason, J. L. (1994). Developing culturally competent organizations. *Focal Point, 8,* 1–8.

McCarthy, B. (1990). Using the 4MAT system to bring learning styles to schools. *Educational Leadership, 48*(2), 31–37.

McCormick, L., & Kawate, J. (1982). Kindergarten survival skills: New directions for preschool special education. *Education and Training of the Mentally Retarded, 17*(3): 247–252.

McDonald, J. P. (1989). When outsiders try to change schools from the inside. *Phi Delta Kappan, 71*(3), 206–212.

McGaghie, W. C. (1991). Professional competence evaluation. *Educational Researcher, 20*(2), 3–9.

McGlothlin, J. E. (1981). The school consultation committee: An approach to implementing a teacher consultation model. *Behavioral Disorders, 6*(2), 101–107.

McKenzie, H. S., Egner, A. N., Knight, M. F., Perelman, P. F., Schneider, B. M., & Garvin, J. S. (1970). Training consulting teachers to assist elementary teachers in the management and education of handicapped children. *Exceptional Children, 37*, 137–143.

McLaughlin, M. J., & Warren, S. H. (1992). *Issues and options in restructuring schools and special education programs.* College Park, MD: University of Maryland, Center for Policy Options in Special Education.

McLoughlin, J., & Lewis, R. (1990). *Assessing special students* (3rd ed.). Columbus, OH: Merrill.

McLoughlin, J., & Kelly, D. (1982). Issues facing the resource teacher. *Learning Disabilities Quarterly, 5*, 58–64.

McLoughlin, J. A., & Kass, C. (1978). Resource teachers: Their role. *Learning Disability Quarterly, 1*(1), 56–62.

Medway, F. J., & Forman, S. G. (1980). Psychologists' and teachers' reactions to mental health and behavioral school consultation. *Journal of School Psychology, 18*, 338–348.

Melaville, A. I., & Blank, M. J. (1991). *What it takes: Structuring interagency partnerships to connect children and families with comprehensive services.* Washington, DC: Education and Human Resources Consortium.

Mercer, C. D., & Mercer, A. R. (1993). *Teaching students with learning problems* (4th ed.). Columbus, OH: Merrill.

Meyen, E. L., & Skrtic, T. (Eds.). (1988). *Exceptional children and youth: An introduction* (3rd ed.). Denver, CO: Love.

Meyer, S. (May, 1977). Personal communication.

Michaels, K. (1988). Caution: Second-wave reform taking place. *Educational Leadership, 45* (5), 3.

Miller, T. L., & Sabatino, D. (1978). An evaluation of the teacher consultant model as an approach to mainstreaming. *Exceptional Children, 45,* 86–91.

Milne, A. A. (1926). *Winnie-the-Pooh.* New York: E. P. Dutton.

Minner, S., Minner, J., & Lepich, J. (1990). Maintaining pupil performance data: A guide. *Intervention in School and Clinic, 26*(1), 32–37.

Morsink, C. V., Soar, S., Soar, R., & Thomas, R. (1986). Research on teaching: Opening the door to special education classrooms. *Exceptional Children, 53*(1), 32–40.

Morsink, C. V., Thomas, C. C., & Correa, V. I. (1991). *Interactive teaming: Consultation and collaboration in special programs.* Columbus, OH: Merrill.

Munson, S. M. (1987). Regular education teacher modifications for mainstreamed mildly handicapped students. *Journal of Special Education, 20*(4), 489–502.

Murphy, A. T. (1981). *Special children, special parents: Personal issues with handicapped children.* Englewood Cliffs, NJ: Prentice Hall.

Murphy, C. (1995). Whole-faculty study groups: Doing the seemingly undoable. *Journal of Staff Development, 16*(3), 37–44.

Murphy, E. (1987a). *I am a good teacher.* Gainesville, FL: Center for Applications of Psychological Type.

Murphy, E. (1987b). *Questions children may have about type differences.* Gainesville, FL: Center for Applications of Psychological Type.

Murphy, K. D. (1987). *Effective listening: Hearing what people say and making it work for you.* New York: Bantam Books.

Myers, I. B. (1962). *The Myers-Briggs type indicator manual.* Palo Alto, CA: Consulting Psychologists Press.

Myers, I. B. (1974). *Type and teamwork.* Gainesville, FL: Center for Applications of Psychological Type.

Myers, I. B. (October 16, 1975). *Making the most of individual gifts.* Keynote address at the first national conference on the uses of the Myers-Briggs type indicator. Gainesville, FL: University of Florida.

Myers, I. B. (1980a). *Gifts differing.* Palo Alto, CA: Consulting Psychologists Press.

Myers, I. B. (1980b). *Introduction to type.* Palo Alto, CA: Consulting Psychologists Press.

Myers, I. B., & McCaulley, M. H. (1985). *Manual: A guide to the development and use of the Myers-*

Briggs type indicator. Palo Alto, CA: Consulting Psychologists Press.

National Center on Educational Restructuring and Inclusion (1994). Unpublished report.

National Information Center for Children and Youth with Disabilities (1997). The IDEA amendments of 1997. *NICHCY News Digest, 26,* 1–38.

Nazzaro, J. N. (1977). *Exceptional timetables: Historic events affecting the handicapped and gifted.* Reston, VA: The Council for Exceptional Children.

Neel, R. S. (1981). How to put the consultant to work in consulting teaching. *Behavioral Disorders, 6*(2), 78–81.

Nelson, C. M., & Stevens, K. B. (1981). An accountable consultation model for mainstreaming behavioral disordered children. *Behavioral Disorders, 6,* 82–91.

Nevin, A., Thousand, J., & Paolucci-Whitcomb, P. (1990). Collaborative consultation: Empowering public school personnel to provide heterogeneous schooling for all—or, who rang that bell? *Journal of Educational and Psychological Consultation, 1*(1), 41–67.

Nevin, A., Thousand, J., & Paolucci-Whitcomb, P. (1993). Establishing collaborative ethics and practices. *Journal of Educational and Psychological Consultation, 4*(4), 293–304.

Newman, J. E. (1992). *How to stay cool, calm, and collected when the pressure's on: A stress control plan for business people.* New York: American Management Association.

Newmann, F. M. (1991). Linking restructuring to authentic student achievement. *Phi Delta Kappan, 72,* 458–464.

Nichols, R. G., & Stevens, L. A. (1957). *Are you listening?*

Nuckolls, C. W. (1991). Culture and causal thinking: Diagnosis and prediction in a South Indian fishing village. *Ethos, 19*(1),3–51.

Oja, S. N. (1980). Adult development is implicit in staff development. *Journal of Staff Development, 1*(1), 9–15.

Osborn, A. F. (1963). *Applied imagination: Principles and procedures of creative problem-solving.* New York: Charles Scribner.

Osborne, S., & deOnis, A. (1997). Parent involvement in rural schools: Implications for educators. *Rural Educator, 19* (2), 20–25.

Ozturk, M. (1992). Education for cross-cultural communication. *Educational Leadership, 49* (4), 79–81.

Parish, R., & Arends, R. (1983). Why innovation programs are discontinued. *Educational Leadership, 40,* 62–65.

Parnes, S. J. (1992). *Sourcebook for creative problem solving.* Buffalo, NY: Creative Education Foundation.

Paulson, F. L., Paulson, P. R., & Meyer, C. A. (1991). What makes a portfolio a portfolio? *Educational Leadership, 48*(5), 60–63.

Pearce, M. (1996, September). Inclusion: Twelve secrets to making it work in your classroom. *Instructor,* 81–84.

Peterson, N. L., & Cooper, C. S. (1989). Parent education and involvement in early intervention programs for handicapped children: A different perspective on parent needs and parent-professional relationships. In M. J. Fine (Ed.), *The second handbook on parent education* (pp. 197–234). New York: Academic Press.

Pfeiffer, S. (1980). The school-based interprofessional team: Recurring problems and some possible solutions. *Journal of School Psychology, 18*(4), 388–394.

Phillips, V., & McCullough, L. (1990). Consultation-based programming: Instituting the collaborative ethic in schools. *Exceptional Children, 56*(4), 291–304.

Phillips, W. L., Allred, K., Brulle, A. R., & Shank, K. S. (1990). The regular education initiative: The will and skill of regular educators. *Teacher Education and Special Education, 13*(3–4), 182–186.

Pines, A., & Aronson, E. (1988). *Career burnout: Causes and cures.* New York: Macmillan.

Pollio, H. (1987). Practical poetry: Metaphoric thinking in science, art, literature, and nearly everywhere else. *Teaching-Learning Issues,* Fall 1987, 3–17.

Polsgrove, L., & McNeil, M. (1989). The consultation process: Research and practice. *Remedial and Special Education, 10*(1), 6–13, 20.

Popham, W. J. (1988). *Educational evaluation* (2nd ed.). Englewood Cliffs, NJ: Prentice Hall.

Posavac, E. J., & Carey, R. G. (1989). *Program evaluation: Methods and case studies* (3rd ed.). Englewood Cliffs, NJ: Prentice Hall.

Preston, D., Greenwood, C. R., Hughes, V., Yuen, P., Thibadeau, S., Critchlow, W., & Harris, J. (1984).

Minority issues in special education: A principal-mediated inservice program for teachers. *Exceptional Children, 51,* 112–121.

Price, M., and Goodman, L. (1980). Individualized education programs: A cost study. *Exceptional Children, 46*(6), 446–454.

Pryzwansky, W. B. (1974). A reconsideration of the consultation model for delivery of school-based psychological services. *American Journal of Orthopsychiatry, 44,* 579–583.

Pryzwansky, W. B. (1986). Indirect service delivery: Considerations for future research in consultation. *School Psychology Review, 15*(4), 479–488.

Pryzwansky, W. B. (1989). School consultation: Some considerations from a psychology perspective. *Professional School Psychology, 4,* 1–14.

Pryzwansky, W. B., & Noblit, G. W. (1990). Understanding and improving consultation practice: The qualitative case study approach. *Journal of Educational and Psychological Consultation, 27*(1), 293–307.

Pugach, M. C. (1988). The consulting teacher in the context of educational reform. *Educational Children, 55*(3), 273–275.

Pugach, M. C., & Johnson, L. J. (1989a). Prereferral interventions: Progress, problems, and challenges. *Exceptional Children, 56,* 117–126.

Pugach, M. C., & Johnson, L. J. (1989b). The challenge of implementing collaboration between general and special education. *Exceptional Children, 56*(3), 232–235.

Pugach, M. C., & Johnson, L. J. (1990). Fostering the continued democratization of consultation through action research. *Teacher Education and Special Education, 13*(3–4), 240–245.

Pugach, M. C., & Johnson, L. J. (1995). *Collaborative practitioners, collaborative schools.* Denver, CO: Love.

Pugach, M., & Sapon-Shevin, M. (1987). New agendas for special education policy: What the national reports haven't said. *Exceptional Children, 53*(4), 295–299.

Quay, H. C., & Peterson, D. R. (1987). *Manual for the revised behavior problem checklist.* Coral Gable, FL.

Raschke, D., Dedrick, C., & DeVries, A. (1988). Coping with stress: The special educator's perspective. *Teaching Exceptional Children, 21*(1), 10–14.

Raymond, G. I., McIntosh, D. K., & Moore, Y. R. (1986). *Teacher consultation skills* (Report No. EC 182-912). Washington, DC: U.S. Department of Education. (ERIC Document Reproduction Service No. ED 170-915).

Raywid, M. A. (1993). Finding time for collaboration. *Educational Leadership, 51*(1), 30–34.

Recording ideas encourages meeting participation. (1994, April). *School Team Innovator,* 7.

Reinhiller, N. (1996). Co-teaching: New variations on a not-so-new practice. *Teacher Education and Special Education, 19*(1), 34–48.

Reis, J. B., & Leukefeld, C. G. (1995). *Applying for research funding: Getting started and getting funded.* Newbury Park, CA: Sage.

Reis, S. M., & Renzulli, J. S. (1986). The secondary triad model. In J. S. Renzulli (Ed.), *Systems and models for developing programs for the gifted and talented* (pp. 267–305). Mansfield Center, CT: Creative Learning Press.

Renzulli, J. S. (Ed.). (1984). *Technical report of research studies related to the Revolving Door Identification Model.* Bureau of Educational Research, University of Connecticut.

Renzulli, J. S. (Ed.). (1986). *Systems and models for developing programs for the gifted and talented.* Mansfield Center, CT: Creative Learning Press.

Renzulli, J. S., & Reis, S. M. (1985). *The schoolwide enrichment model: A comprehensive plan for educational excellence.* Mansfield Center, CT: Creative Learning Press.

Renzulli, J. S., & Reis, S. M. (1986). The Enrichment Triad/Revolving Door Model: A schoolwide plan for the development of creative productivity. In J. S. Renzulli (Ed.), *Systems and models for developing programs for the gifted and talented* (pp. 216–266). Mansfield Center, CT: Creative Learning Press.

Research and Training Center on Independent Living. (1996). *Guidelines for reporting and writing about people with disabilities* (5th ed.). Lawrence, KS: Author.

Reynaud, G., Pfannenstiel, T., & Hudson, F. (1987). *Park Hill secondary learning disability project: An alternate service delivery model implementation manual.* Kansas City, MO: Park Hill School District.

Reynolds, M. C. (1962). A framework for considering some issues in special education. *Exceptional Children, 28,* 367–370.

Reynolds, M. C. (1989). An historical perspective: The delivery of special education to mildly disabled and at-risk students. *Remedial and Special Education, 10*(5), 7–11.

Reynolds, M. C., & Birch, J. W. (1988). *Adaptive mainstreaming: A primer for teachers and principals.* White Plains, NY: Longman.

Reynolds, M. C., Wang, M. C., & Walberg, H. J. (1987). The necessary restructuring of special and regular education. *Exceptional Children, 53*(5), 391–398.

Rich, D. (1987). *School and families: Issues and actions.* Washington, DC: National Education Association.

Rinke, W. J. (1997). *Winning management: 6 failsafe strategies for building high performance organizations.* New York: Achievement.

Ritter, D. R. (1978). Effects of a school consultation program upon referral patterns of teachers. *Psychology in the Schools, 15*(2), 239–243.

Robert, M. (1973). *Loneliness in the schools (What to do about it).* Niles, IL: Argus Communication.

Robinson, A. (1990). Cooperation of exploitation? The argument against cooperative learning for talented students. *Journal for the Education of the Gifted, 14*(1), 9–27.

Rogers, J. (1993). The inclusion revolution. *The Research Bulletin, Phi Delta Kappa, 11,* 1–6.

Rosenberg, M. S., O'Shea, L., & O'Shea, D. J. (1998). *Student teacher to master teacher: A practical guide for educating students with special needs* (2nd ed.). Columbus, OH: Merrill.

Ross, R. G. (1986). *Communication consulting as persuasion: Issues and implications.* (Report No. CS506-027). Washington, DC: U.S. Department of Education. ERIC Document Reproduction Service No. ED 291-115.

Royster, A., & McLaughlin, T. (1996). Parent partnerships in special education: Purposes, models and barriers. *Journal of Special Education, 20* (2), 24–33.

Rule, S., Fodor-Davis, J., Morgan, R., Salzberg, C. L., & Chen, J. (1990). An inservice training model to encourage collaborative consultation. *Teacher Education and Special Education, 13,* 3–4, 225–227.

Rusch, F. R., Rose, T., & Greenwood, C. R. (1988). *Introduction to behavior analysis in special education.* Englewood Cliffs, NJ: Prentice Hall.

Rusch, F. R., & Menchetti, B. M. (1988). Transition in the 1990s: A reply to Knowlton and Clark. *Exceptional Children, 54*(4), 363–364.

Safran, J. (1991). Communication in collaboration/consultation: Effective practices in schools. *Journal of Educational and Psychological Consultation, 1*(4), 371–386.

Safran, S. P. (1991). The communication process and school-based consultation: What does the research say? *Journal of Educational and Psychological Consultation, 1*(4), 343–370.

Salend, S. J. (1994). *Effective mainstreaming: Creating inclusive classrooms* (2nd ed.). New York: Macmillan.

Salend, S. J., & Salend, S. (1984). Consulting with the regular teacher: Guidelines for special educators. *The Pointer, 25,* 25–28.

Salend, S., & Viglianti, D. (1982). Preparing secondary students for the mainstream. *Teaching Exceptional Children, 14,* 137–140.

Salisbury, G., & Evans, I. M. (1988). Comparison of parental involvement in regular and special education. *Journal of the Association for Persons with Severe Handicaps, 13,* 268–272.

Salisbury, C. L., & Vincent, L. J. (1990). Criterion of the next environment and best practices: Mainstreaming and integration 10 years later. *Topics in Early Childhood Special Education, 10*(2), 78–89.

Salzberg, C. L., & Morgan, J. (1995). Preparing teachers to work with paraeducators. *Teacher Education and Special Education, 18*(1), 49–55.

Sapolsky, R. (1994). *Why zebras don't get ulcers: A guide to stress, stress-related diseases, and coping.* New York: W. H. Freeman.

Schaps, E. (1990). Cooperative learning: The challenge in the 90s. *Cooperative Learning, 10*(4), 5–8.

Schatz, E. (1990). Ability grouping for gifted learners. *Educating Able Learners, 15*(3), 3, 5, 15. Denton, TX: Gifted Students Institute.

Schein, E. H. (1969). *Process consultation: Its role in organization development.* Reading, MA: Addison-Wesley.

Schein, E. H. (1978). The role of the consultant: Context expert or process facilitator? *Personnel and Guidance Journal,* February, 1978.

Schenkat, R. (1988). The promise of restructuring for special education. *Education Week,* November 16, 1988.

Scherer, M. (1996). On our changing family values: A conversation with David Elkind. *Educational Leadership, 53* (7), 4–9.

Schindler, C., & Lapid, G. (1989). *The great turning: Personal peace, global victory.* Santa Fe, NM: Bear and Company.

Schlax, K. (1994). Eight Tips for Effective Integration of Therapists. *Inclusive Education Programs 1*(2), 11.

Schmuck, R. A., and Schmuck, P. A. (1979). *Group process in the classroom* (2nd ed.). Dubuque, IA: Wm. C. Brown.

School Team Innovator (April, 1994).

Schrag, J., & Burnette, J. (1994). Inclusive schools. *Teaching Exceptional Children,* 64–68.

Schuck, J. (1979). The parent-professional partnership: Myth or reality? *Education Unlimited, 1* (4), 26–28.

Schulz, J. B. (1987). *Parent and professional in special education.* Newton, MA: Allyn & Bacon.

Scollon, R. O. (1985). The machine stops: Silence in the metaphor of malfunction. In D. Tannen and M. Saville-Troike (Eds.), *Perspectives in silence.* Norwood, NJ: Ablex.

Scriven, M. (1967). The methodology of evaluation. In R. W. Tyler, R. M. Gagne, & M. Scriven (Eds.), *Perspectives of curriculum evaluation.* Chicago: Rand-McNally.

Scruggs, T. E., & Mastropieri, M. A. (1996). Teacher perceptions of mainstreaming/inclusion, 1958–1995: A research synthesis. *Exceptional Children, 63*(1), 59–74.

Scruggs, T. E., and Richter, L. (1986). Tutoring learning disabled students: A critical review. *Learning Disability Quarterly, 9*(1), 2–14.

Seay, M. (1974). *Community education: A developing concept.* Midland, MI: Pendell.

Seeley, D. S. (1985). *Education through partnership.* Washington, DC: American Enterprise Institute for Public Policy Research.

Selye, H. (1993). History of the stress concept. In L. Goldberger and S. Brevitz (Eds.), *Handbook of stress* (2nd ed.). New York: Free Press.

Shanker, A. (1994). Full inclusion is neither free nor appropriate. *Educational Leadership, 52* (4), 18–21.

Shanker, A. (1993, November). Ninety-two hours. *The Developer.* Oxford, OH: National Staff Development Council.

Shanteau, J. (1997, October). *ISBR Newsletter, 7.* Kansas State University: Institute for Social and Behavioral Research.

Shaw, S. F., Bensky, J. M., and Dixon, B. (1981). *Stress and burnout: A primer for special education and special services personnel.* Reston, VA: Council for Exceptional Children.

Shea, T. M., & Bauer, A. M. (1985). *Parents and teachers of exceptional students.* Boston: Allyn & Bacon.

Shea, T. M., & Bauer, A. M. (1987). *Teaching children and youth with behavioral disorders* (2nd ed.). Englewood Cliffs, NJ: Prentice Hall.

Shepard, L. A. (1987). The new push for excellence: Widening the schism between regular and special education. *Exceptional Children, 53* (4), 327–329.

Sigband, N. B. (1987). The uses of meetings. *Nation's Business,* February 1987, 28R.

Sileo, T., Rude, H., and Luckner, J. (1988). Collaborative consultation: A model for transition planning for handicapped youth. *Education and Training in Mental Retardation, 23*(4), 333–339.

Simpson, G. W. (1990). Keeping it alive: Elements of school culture that sustain innovation. *Educational Leadership, 47*(8), 34–37.

Skolnick, A. (1991). *Embattled paradise: The American family in an age of uncertainty.* New York: Basic Books.

Skrtic, T. (1993). The crisis in special education knowledge: A perspective on perspective. In E. L. Meyen, G. A. Vergason, & R. J. Whelan, (Eds.), *Challenges facing special education.* Denver: Love.

Slavin, R. E. (1986). *Using student team learning* (3rd ed.). Baltimore, MD: Center for Research on Elementary and Middle Schools, The Johns Hopkins University.

Slavin, R. E. (1988). *The School Administrator, 45,* 9–13.

Slesser, R. A., Fine, M. J., & Tracy, D. B. (1990). Teacher reactions to two approaches to school-based psychological consultation. *Journal of Educational and Psychological Consultation, 1*(3), 242–258.

Smith, D. K. (1996). *Taking charge of change: 20 principles for managing people and performance.* Reading, MA: Addison-Wesley Publishing Co.

Smith, S. C. (1987). The collaborative school takes shape. *Educational Leadership, 45*(3), 4–6.

Smith-Westberry, J., & Job, R. L. (1986). How to be a prophet in your own land: Providing gifted program inservice for the local district. *Gifted Child Quarterly, 30*(3), 135–137.

Sontag, J. C., & Schacht, R. (1994). An ethnic comparison of participation and information needs in early intervention. *Exceptional Children, 60,* 422–433.

Sparks, D. (April, 1991). Using "benchmarking" to improve schools. *The Developer.* Oxford, OH: National Staff Development Council.

Sparks, D. (September, 1992). Some basic understandings. *The Developer.* Oxford, OH: National Staff Development Council.

Speece, D. L., & Mandell, C. J. (1980). Resource room support services for regular teachers. *Learning Disability Quarterly, 3,* 49–53.

Staff. "I don't think it's right to type people." *The Type Reporter,* No. 37, pp. 1–4.

Staff. (1989, April). Staff development in the journals. *The Developer,* p. 6.

Staff. "Disability or Gift?" *CEC Today,* September, 1997.

Stainback, S., & Stainback, F. M. (1988). In M. C. Reynolds (Ed.), *Adaptive mainstreaming: A primer for teachers and principals.* White Plains, NY: Longman.

Stainback, S., & Stainback, W. (1985). The merger of special and regular education: Can it be done? A response to Lieberman and Mesinger. *Exceptional Children, 51*(6), 517–521.

Stainback, S., Stainback, W., & Forest, M. (1989). *Educating all students in the mainstream of regular education.* Baltimore, MD: Brookes.

Stainback, W., & Stainback, S. (1984). A rationale for the merger of special and regular education. *Exceptional Children, 51*(2), 102–111.

Staples, L. (1990). Powerful ideas about empowerment. *Administration in Social Work, 14* (2), 29–42.

Starko, A. (1995). *Creativity in the classroom: Schools of curious delight.* White Plains, NY: Longman.

Steele, J. (1982). *The class activities questionnaire.* Mansfield Center, CT: Creative Learning Press.

Stephens, P. (1994), October). Developing a successful grant application. Presented at United School Administrators conference in Emporia, KS.

Stephens, T. M. (1977). *Teaching skills to children with learning and behavioral disorders.* Columbus, OH: Merrill.

Stewart, J. C. (1978). *Counseling parents of exceptional children.* Columbus, OH: Merrill.

Sue, D. W., & Sue, D. (1990). *Counseling the culturally different: Theory and practice* (2nd ed.). New York: John Wiley.

Sugai, G. (Winter, 1986). Recording classroom events: Maintaining a critical incidents log. *Teaching Exceptional Children,* pp. 98–102.

Sundbye, N., & McCoy, L. (1997). *Helping the struggling reader: What to teach and how to teach it.* Lawrence, KS: Curriculum Solutions.

Sundel, S. S. & Sundel, M. (1980). *Be assertive: A practical guide for human service workers.* Beverly Hills, CA: Sage.

Swicegood, P. (1994). Portfolio-based assessment practices. *Intervention in School and Clinic, 30*(1), 6–15.

Tannen, B. (1991). *Gender and discourse.* New York: Oxford University Press.

Tannen, B. (1994). *You just don't understand: Women and men in conversation.* New York: William Morrow.

Teagarden, J. (Spring, 1988). Acres wrap-up from a teacher's perspective. *Take Heart, 4.* Manhattan, KS: Kansas State University.

Tharp, R. (1975). The triadic model of consultation: Current considerations. In C. Parker (Ed.), *Psychological consultation in the schools: Helping teachers meet special needs.* Reston, VA: The Council for Exceptional Children.

Tharp, R. G., & Wetzel, R. J. (1969). *Behavior modification in the natural environment.* New York: Academic Press.

Thompson, L., Lobb, C., Elling, R., Herman, S., Jurkiewicz, T., & Hulleza, C. (1997). Pathways to family empowerment: Effects of family-centered delivery of early intervention services. *Exceptional Children, 64* (1), 99–113.

Thousand, J., Fox, T., Reid, R., Godek, J., Williams, W., & Fox, W. (1986). *The homecoming model: Educating students who present intensive educational challenges within regular education environments.* (Monograph No. 7-1). Burlington, VT: University of Vermont, Center for Developmental Disabilities.

Thurston, L. P. (1987). *Survival skills for women: Facilitator manual.* Manhattan, KS: Survival Skills and Development.

Thurston, L. P. (1989). *Rural special education teachers as consultants: Strategies, practices, and training.* Presented at American Council for Rural Special Education national conference, Ft. Lauderdale, FL.

Thurston, L. P., & Dover, W. (October, 1990). *Rural at-risk students.* Paper presented at the 12th annual Rural and Small Schools Conference, Manhattan, KS.

Thurston, L. P., & Kimsey, I. (1989). Rural special education teachers as consultants: Roles and responsibilities. *Educational Considerations, 17*(1), 40–43.

Thurston, L. P., & Navarrete, L. (1996). A tough row to hoe: Research on education and rural poor families. In *Proceedings of American Council on Rural Special Education (ACRES)*. Baltimore, MD.

Timar, T. (1989). The politics of school restructuring. *Phi Delta Kappan, 71*(4), 265–275.

Tindal, G. (1987). Graphing performance. *Teaching Exceptional Children, 20*(1), 44–46.

Tindal, G., & Taylor-Pendergast, S. J. (1989). A taxonomy for objectively analyzing the consultation process. *Remedial and Special Education, 10*(2), 6–16.

Tindal, G., Shinn, M., Waltz, L., & Germann, G. (1987). Mainstream consultation in secondary settings: The Pine County model. *Journal of Special Education, 21*(3), 94–106.

Toffler, A. (October 15, 1990). Power shift: Knowledge, wealth and violence at the edge of the 21st century. *Newsweek,* pp. 86–92.

Tomlinson, C. (1996). Good teaching for one and all: Does gifted education have an instructional identity? *Journal for the Education of the Gifted, 20*(2), 155–174.

Tomlinson, G. (Ed.). (1984). *School administrator's complete letter book.* Englewood Cliffs, NJ: Prentice-Hall.

Townsend, B. L., Thomas, D. D., Witty, J. P., & Lee, R. S. (1996). Diversity and school restructuring: Creating partnerships in a world of difference. *19*(2), 102–118.

Treat, M., & Dyck, N. (1997). *The TREAT program: Including students with high ability.* Lawrence, KS: Curriculum Solutions.

Truch, S. (1980). *Teacher burnout and what to do about it.* Novato, CA: Academic Therapy.

Truesdell, C. B. (1983). The MBTI: A win-win strategy for work teams. *MBTI News, 5,* 8–9.

Tucker, J. A. (1985). Curriculum-based assessment: An introduction. *Exceptional Children, 52* (3), 199–204.

Tuckman, B. W. (1985). *Evaluating instructional programs* (2nd ed.). Boston: Allyn & Bacon.

Turnbull, A. P., & Turnbull, H. R., III. (1982). *Families, professionals, and exceptionality: A special partnership* (3rd ed.). Upper Saddle River, NJ: Merrill.

Turnbull, A. P., & Turnbull, H. R., III. (1997). *Families, professionals, and exceptionality: A special partnership* (3rd ed.). Upper Saddle River, NJ: Merrill.

Turnbull, H. R., III, Turnbull, A. P., & Wheat, (1992). Assumptions about parental participation: A legislative history. *Exceptional Education Quarterly, 3*(2), 1–8.

Turnbull, III, H. R., & Turnbull, A. P. (1985). *Parents speak out: Then and now* (2nd ed.). Columbus, OH: Merrill.

Turner, R. R. (April, 1987). Here's what teachers say. *Learning 87, 55–57.*

Tyler, V. L. (1979). *Intercultural interacting.* Provo, UT: Brigham Young University, David Kennedy Center for International Studies.

Ury, W. (1991). *Getting past no: Negotiating with difficult people.* New York: Bantam Books.

U.S. Department of Education (1985–1986). *Patterns in special education service delivery and cost.* Washington, DC: Department of Education, Office of Special Education Programs.

Valencia, S. (1990). A portfolio approach to classroom reading assessment: The whys, whats, and hows. *The Reading Teacher,* January 1990, 338–340.

Van Tassel-Baska, J. (1989). Appropriate curriculum for gifted learners. *Educational Leadership, 46*(6), 13–15.

Van Tassel-Baska, J. (1998). *Excellence in educating gifted and talented learners* (3rd ed.). Denver, CO: Love.

Vasa, S. T. (1982). *The special education resource teacher as a consultant: Fact or fantasy?* Paper presented at the Sixth Annual Meeting of the Council for Exceptional Children, Houston. (ERIC Document Reproduction Service No. ED 218 918).

Vaughn, S., Schumm, J. S. & Arguelles, M. E. (1997). The ABCDEs of co-teaching. *Teaching Exceptional Children, 30* (2), 42–45.

Vockell, E. L. & Asher, W. J. (1995). *Educational research* (2nd ed.). Englewood Cliffs, NJ: Prentice Hall.

Voltz, D. L., & Elliott, Jr., R. N. (1990). Resource room teacher roles in promoting interaction with regular educators. *Teacher Education and Special Education, 13*(3–4), 160–166.

Voltz, D. L., Elliott, Jr., R. N., & Cobb, H. B. (1994) Collaborative teacher roles: Special and general educators. *Journal of Learning Disabilities, 27*(8), 527–535.

von Oech, R. (1983). *A whack on the side of the head.* New York: Warner.

Walberg, H. J. (1984, February). Families as partners in educational productivity. *Phi Delta Kappan,* 397–404.

Walker, H. M. (1976). *Walker problem behavior identification checklist manual.* Los Angeles: Western Psychological Services.

Wallace, D. (1997). Career counseling for the twenty-first century: A challenge for all. *The Delta Kappa Gamma Bulletin, 63*(3), 57–60.

Walling, D. R. (1990). *Meeting the needs of transient students,* Fastback #304. Bloomington, IN: Phi Delta Kappa Educational Foundation.

Wanat, C. L. (1997). Conceptualizing parental involvement from parents' perspectives: A case study. *Journal for a Just and Caring Education, 3* (4), 433–458.

Wang, M. C. (1986). *The adaptive learning environments model: Design and effects.* Paper presented at Association for Children with Learning Disabilities Conference.

Wang, M. C. (1987). Toward achieving educational excellence for all students: Program design and student outcomes. *Remedial and Special Education, 8,* 25–34.

Wang, M. C., & Birch, J. W. (1984). Effective special education in regular classes. *Exceptional Children,*. February, 1984, pp. 391–398.

Wang, M. C., & Walberg, H. J. (1988). Four fallacies of segregationism. *Exceptional Children, 55,* 128–137.

Waters, D. B., & Lawrence, E. C. (1993). *Competence, courage, and change: An approach to family therapy.* New York: W. W. Norton.

Weber, L. (1994). Diversity and collaboration. *Center News.* Memphis: Center for Research on Women. University of Memphis, *13,* 2, 10.

Webster's new collegiate dictionary (8th ed.) (1981). Springfield, MA: Merriam-Webster.

Webster's third new international dictionary, unabridged: The great library of the English language. (1976). Springfield, MA: Merriam-Webster.

Wesley, W. G., & Wesley, B. A. (1990). Concept-mapping: A brief introduction. *Teaching Professor, 4*(8), 3–4.

Wesson, C. L. (1987). Increasing efficiency. *Teaching Exceptional Children, 20*(1), 46–47.

West, J. F. (1985). *Regular and special educators' preference for school-based consultation models: A statewide study* (Report No. 101). Austin, TX: The University of Texas, Research and Training Project on School Consultation.

West, J. F. (1990). Educational collaboration in the restructuring of schools. *Journal of Educational and Psychological Consultation, 1,* 23–41.

West, J. F., & Brown, P. A. (1987). State departments of education policies on consultation in special education: The state of the states. *Remedial and Special Education, 8*(3), 45–51.

West, J. F., & Cannon, G. S. (1988). Essential collaborative consultation competencies for regular and special educators. *Journal of Learning Disabilities, 21,* 56–63.

West, J. F., & Idol, L. (1987). School consultation (Part i): An interdisciplinary perspective on theory, models, and research. *Journal of Learning Disabilities, 20*(7), 385–408.

West, J. F., & Idol, L. (1990). Collaborative consultation in the education of mildly handicapped and at-risk students. *Remedial and Special Education, 11*(1), 22–31.

West, J. F., Idol, L., & Cannon, G. (1987). *A curriculum for preservice and inservice preparation of classroom and special education teachers in collaborative consultation.* Austin, TX: The University of Texas at Austin, Research and Training Project on School Consultation.

White, G. W., & Pryzwansky, W. B. (1982). Consultation outcome as a result of in service resource teacher training. *Psychology in Schools, 19,* 495–502.

Wiederholt, J., Hammill, D., & Brown, V. (1983). *The resource teacher.* Austin, TX: PRO-ED.

Wiederholt, L. L. (1989). Restructuring special education services: The past, the present, the future. *Learning Disability Quarterly, 12,* 181–191.

Wienke, W. D. (1996). Book reviews: Current resources for grant writers. *Teacher Education and Special Education, 19*(3), 272–276.

Wikler, L., Wasow, M., & Hatfield, E. (1981). Chronic sorrow revisited: Parent vs. professional depiction of the adjustment of parents of mentally retarded children. *American Journal of Orthopsychiatry, 51,* 63–70.

Wildman, T. M., & Niles, J. A. (1987). Essentials of professional growth. *Educational Leadership, 44*(5), 4–10.

Will, M. (1984). Let us pause and reflect—but not too long. *Exceptional Children, 51,* 11–16.

Will, M. (1986). Educating children with learning problems: A shared responsibility. *Exceptional Children, 52*(5), 411–415.

William T. Grant Foundation Commission on Work, Family, and Citizenship. (1988). *The forgotten half: Pathways to success for America's youth and young families.* Washington, DC: Author.

Witt, J. C. (1990). Collaboration in school-based consultation: Myth in need of data. *Journal of Educational and Psychological Consultation, 1*(4), 367–370.

Witt, J. C., & Elliott, S. N. (1985). Acceptability of classroom intervention strategies. In T. R. Kratochwill (Ed.), *Advances in school psychology* (Vol. 4, pp. 251–288). Hillsdale, NJ: Lawrence Erlbaum.

Witt, J. C., Moe, G., Gutkin, T., & Andrews, L. (1984). The effect of saying the same thing in different ways: The problem of language and jargon in school-based consultation. *Journal of School Psychology, 22,* 361–367.

Wolery, M., Bailey, D., and Sugai, G. (1988). *Effective teaching: Principles and procedures of applied behavior analysis with exceptional students.* Boston: Allyn & Bacon.

Wolf, D. P. (1989). Portfolio assessment: Sampling student work. *Educational Leadership, 46*(7), 35–40.

Wood, J. W., & Meiderhoff, J. W. (1989). Bridging the gap. *Teaching Exceptional Children, 21*(2), 66–68.

Woolfolk, A. E. (1995). *Educational psychology* (6th ed.). Boston: Allyn & Bacon.

Working Forum on Inclusive Schools (1994). *Creating schools for all our students: What 12 schools have to say.* Reston, VA: Council for Exceptional Children.

Ysseldyke, J. E. (1986). The use of assessment information to make decisions about students. In R. J. Morris and B. Blatt (Eds.), *Special education: Research and trends.* New York: Pergamon.

Ysseldyke, J. E., & Christenson, S. I. (1987). Evaluating students' instructional environments. *Remedial and Special Education, 8*(3), 17–24.

Ysseldyke, J., Thurlow, M., Wotruba, J. & Nania, P. (1990). Instructional arrangements: Perceptions from general education. *Teaching Exceptional Children, 22*(4), 4–8.

Zabel, R. H., & Zabel, M. K. (1982). Factors in burnout among teachers of exceptional children. *Exceptional Children, 49*(3), 261–263.

Zigmond, N. (1997). *What does co-teaching look like in elementary and secondary schools?* Washington, DC: Presentation at 19th International Conference on Learning Disabilities.

Zigmond, N., Levin, E., & Laurie, T. E. (1985). Managing the mainstream: An analysis of teacher attitudes and student performance in mainstream high school programs. *Journal of Learning Disabilities, 18* (9), 535–541.

Zimet, E. (1993). Grant-writing techniques for K–12 funding. *T.H.E.: Technological Horizons in Education,* November, 1993, 109–112.

Zirkel, P. A., & Knapp, S. (1993). Related services for students with disabilities: What educational consultants need to know. *Journal of Educational and Psychological Consultation, 4*(2), 137–151.

AUTHOR INDEX

SUBJECT INDEX